NATIONAL SECURITY POLICY

NATIONAL SECURITY POLICY
The Decision-making Process

Edited by

Robert L. Pfaltzgraff, Jr.

Uri Ra'anan

International Security Studies Program
The Fletcher School of Law and Diplomacy
Tufts University
Medford, Massachusetts 02155

ARCHON BOOKS
1984

© 1984 The Fletcher School of Law and Diplomacy of Tufts University
First published in 1984 as an Archon Book,
an imprint of THE SHOE STRING PRESS, INC.,
Hamden, Connecticut 06514

Composition by The Publishing Nexus Incorporated,
Guilford, Connecticut 06437
Printed in the United States of America

The paper in this book meets the guidelines
for permanence and durability of the
Committee on Production Guidelines for Book Longevity
of the Council on Library Resources.

Library of Congress Cataloging in Publication Data
Main entry under title:

National security policy.

Includes bibliographical references and index.
1. National security—Decision making—Addresses,
essays, lectures. 2. Military policy—Decision making—
Addresses, essays, lectures. I. Pfaltzgraff, Robert L.
II. Ra'anan, Uri, 1926–
UA10.5.N295 1984   355'.0335   84-2932
ISBN 0-208-02003-9

Contents

About the Authors and Editors

- Admiral Thomas H. Moorer, USN (Ret.), was Chairman of the Joint Chiefs of Staff during the period 1970–74.
- Professor Peter Nailor is with the Department of History and International Affairs of the Royal Naval College, Greenwich, Great Britain.
- Professor John Erickson is Director, Defense Studies, University of Edinburgh.
- Mrs. Harriet Fast Scott is a consultant on Soviet military and political affairs to several major research organizations, and lectures on these topics at universities and military colleges.
- Professor John P. Roche is Professor of Civilization and Foreign Affairs and Academic Dean at The Fletcher School of Law and Diplomacy.
- Colonel Roy W. Stafford, Jr., USAF, is Chief of the (Chief of Staff's) Staff Group, United States Air Force, Department of Defense.
- Colonel John E. Endicott is Associate Dean of Faculty and Academic Programs, National Defense University, Washington, D.C.
- Mr. Michael Hobkirk is a Visiting Research Fellow at the National Defense University and a retired British civil servant.
- Mr. Christopher M. Lehman is Special Assistant to the President for National Security Affairs.
- Lieutenant General John H. Cushman, USA (Ret.), is a management consultant.
- Senator William S. Cohen is U.S. Senator from Maine.
- Richard C. White, Esq., is a lawyer and former Congressman from Texas.
- Mr. Stanley J. Heginbotham is Chief of the Foreign Affairs and National Security Division, Congressional Research Service, Library of Congress.
- Dr. S. Robert Lichter is Assistant Professor of Political Science at George Washington University and Senior Fellow of the Research Institute on International Change at Columbia University.
- Dr. Stanley Rothman is Mary Huggins Gamble Professor of Government at Smith College.

• Mr. Philip A. Phalon is Senior Vice President, Raytheon Company.

Professor Robert L. Pfaltzgraff, Jr., is Shelby Cullum Davis Professor of International Security Studies at The Fletcher School of Law and Diplomacy and President of the Institute for Foreign Policy Analysis in Cambridge, Massachusetts, and Washington, D.C.

Professor Uri Ra'anan is Professor of International Politics and Chairman of the International Security Studies Program at The Fletcher School of Law and Diplomacy.

Preface

In the last quarter of the twentieth century, it has become obvious that security issues constitute the very core of international relations, as far as small- and medium-strength states are concerned, no less than the superpowers themselves. This factor has been present throughout recorded history, of course, but technology, to mention just one aspect, has made the realization of the centrality of security affairs unavoidable.

In the United States, successive administrations have striven to fashion a coherent national security policy, based upon rational design and consistency of purpose. For the greater part of the present century, each President has been compelled to operate within a decision-making process characterized by increasing complexities, both with respect to the number of bureaucratic units—not to mention the amount of personnel involved—and the seemingly discrete factors that must be considered when dealing with policy choices. Moreover, in our country, this process confronts a structure of government that, on the one hand, confers upon the President the position of Commander in Chief of the armed forces, as well as the function of chief diplomat and final arbiter on national security affairs; at the same time, the President shares constitutional authority with the Congress. Indeed, the Constitution devotes many more lines to congressional competence in matters clearly related to security than it does to the powers of the President in that area.

During the current century, the vast increase in size of the Executive Branch has coincided with the emergence of the United States as the first truly global power. The greater the scope of American interests and capabilities, the larger have become the dimensions of our security decision-making structure.

In the remaining decades of this century, as we attempt to evolve a security policy designed to safeguard our interests in a world fraught with proliferating challenges and dangers, it is essential to devote renewed consideration to the adequacy of existing decisional machinery. It is a reasonable assumption that the quality of the decisions taken will reflect the process by which they are made. It is an urgent task, therefore, to review and comprehend as fully as possible the present decision-making process and to suggest options for enhancing its capacity to produce the essential components of an appropriate security policy that will be compatible with an integrative strategic design.

The International Security Studies Program of The Fletcher School of Law and Diplomacy convened a major conference designed to examine, in systematic fashion, the main problems relating to decision making and the development of national security policy. That conference, held 27–29 April 1983, focused primarily upon the United States, although it drew freely upon lessons suggested from the experience of other security decision-making processes, past and present.

In combining historical and contemporary perspectives, as well as utilizing a comparative analytical approach, the conference offered an opportunity to shed further light upon the needs and difficulties facing this country late in the twentieth century.

As in the case of eleven previous conferences organized by the program, the meeting of 27–29 April provided a very useful, indeed necessary, forum to bring together distinguished participants from the United States and abroad, from the official policy community—Executive and Legislative, civilian and military—and from the private sector, from academic life and from other sectors of the defense and foreign affairs "community."

This has proved to be an appropriate environment for in-depth consideration of vital issues of national and international security that are in the very forefront of concerns of the present and the immediate future, and of "the state of the art," resulting in about a dozen major books and monographs. It proved to be a particularly productive way to address the complex issues of national security decision making. The conference yielded policy options for possible consideration within the decision-making structure.

The book presented here to the interested public at large, as well as to those professionally engaged in this field, not only reflects the proceedings of the Conference, but also contains additional material, as well as revisions of the contributions to the Conference intended to ensure that the work reflects more recent developments. The editors hope that the policy implications contained in the concluding chapter, together with the insights provided by each of the contributors, will improve understanding of the complex problems of the decision-making structure and process.

Robert L. Pfaltzgraff, Jr.
Uri Ra'anan
Medford, Massachusetts

Introduction

Thomas H. Moorer

The decision-making process, as it functions at the national level, is not only the most complex aspect (becoming more complex every day) but perhaps the least understood facet of our federal system. As a matter of fact, I have always wondered why President after President brings in a staff that knows absolutely nothing about this process. I should think that with 226 million inhabitants, there must be a few qualified individuals; perhaps the President should cast his eyes upon such institutions as The Fletcher School of Law and Diplomacy.

To start with the evolution of the structure of decision making in the Executive Branch: Before World War II, the United States was more or less isolated from the rest of the world by the oceans. Moreover, we had Britain, with the sun never setting on her Empire; the Dutch were in Indonesia; French possessions were scattered around the world—altogether, we were not lacking all kinds of reasonably strong allies. When the war was over, however, the United States was essentially alone. It should have been clear, then—although obviously it was not—that three significant developments were occurring by the end of World War II.

(Parenthetically, in terms of coalition decision making, the war was managed by Roosevelt, in cooperation and coordination with Prime Minister Churchill—the infrastructure consisting of the American staff working with its British counterparts in a combined staff, and of Admiral Leahy, in the White House, more or less coordinating the efforts of General Marshall and Admiral King. It was a very informal arrangement.)

These three developments at the end of World War II included the fact (1) that nuclear weapons had brought a new dimension to warfare; (2) that the U.S.S.R. was now embarked upon the establishment of a worldwide presence, if not actual conquests of similar dimensions; and (3) that in view of the loss of strength by our European allies, no matter where an incident occurred in the future (whether it be a military or a political confrontation, an earthquake or a famine), the United States of America was going to be involved. History, so far, has demonstrated that these were the three developments of greatest consequence for the United States.

Faced with the resulting problems, the Congress and the Executive

Branch began by the mid-forties to attempt to formulate a structure that could be appropriately utilized by the President, who, in turn, could coordinate the resulting decisions with the coequal branches, namely, the Senate and the House of Representatives—the Congress; it was hoped that this would enable the United States to reach appropriate solutions of whatever global security problems might arise.

The result was the passage of the National Security Act of 1947, which had several important aspects: In the first place, it created another Cabinet member, the Secretary of Defense, and gave him tremendous powers. It also removed the Secretary of War and the Secretary of the Navy from membership in the President's Cabinet, and established another service, the United States Air Force; moreover, it created the National Security Council and, of course, provided for a National Security Council staff.

Actually, President Eisenhower was the first Chief Executive who really utilized the new structure. As is well known, he was quite skillful in matters of organization, and he shaped the staff to serve the President optimally. The National Security Council staff, in fact, is a tool for the President; every Chief Executive, however, has used it differently. Similarly, in any executive pyramid, in business or whatever, the Chairman of the Board, or the President, as the case may be, will follow his own path with regard to utilization of staff. In my own case, I know from experience that my predecessors as well as my successors took different approaches to this aspect of work.

(Parenthetically, in the course of time, the National Security Council staff, headed by the President's Assistant for National Security Affairs, received increasing public attention, particularly during Kissinger's and Brzezinski's tenure. In Richard Allen's case, the situation changed; he was, in a sense, defeated from the start, since the head of the National Security Council staff cannot survive politically unless he has immediate, direct, and daily access to the President—and Mr. Allen was deprived of this essential access since Mr. Meese was interposed between him and the President.)

In any event, subsequent to the Eisenhower Administration, President Kennedy set up an Executive Committee of the National Security Council, but, after the abortive Bay of Pigs invasion when the system was tested in practice, the President was so shocked that he tended thereafter to look for advice on national security decisions to a kind of "kitchen cabinet," some of whose members did not even hold official positions, but simply were persons close to the President. He felt more comfortable with them then he did with the regular organization utilized by President Eisenhower.

President Johnson essentially used the same format as President Kennedy, but it turned into more regular sessions, called the "Tuesday Lunch." At the time when the Vietnam War was escalating at a rather fast pace, we in the Pentagon began to realize that if a major issue had to be tackled during a crisis occurring on a Wednesday, you had to resign yourself to the fact that you would not obtain a response from the White House until the subsequent "Tuesday Lunch."

After President Johnson, President Nixon, having been Vice-President under Eisenhower, reverted to essentially the same structure that had been established by Ike, whereby, in addition to the National Security Council staff, there were also subordinate groups. For instance, we had the Washington Special Action Group to handle crisis management, and we had the Verification Panel. (Although the name implies that it dealt only with verification of arms control agreements, in fact, it was the group that drafted the policy proposals which formed the basis for the instructions given to the arms control negotiating teams in Geneva, Helsinki, etc.) In addition, we had the Senior Review Group, to which the Interdepartmental Groups, chaired by Assistant Secretaries of State, reported concerning implementation of decisions that had been made.

In the procedure utilized by the Nixon Administration, the National Security Council staff drafted a statement of the problem under discussion, as well as stating the advantages and disadvantages of various possible courses of action. At the meeting of the National Security Council itself, the director of the CIA would prsent the latest intelligence bearing upon that particular problem, and the President's Assistant for National Security Affairs, i.e., Henry Kissinger, would follow with a discussion of the various options. The form of his statement would be impersonal, that is to say, he would not name the supporters and opponents of various alternate courses of action—although, of course, everyone knew very well who these unnamed persons really were. At that point President Nixon would ask each of the members of the Council, starting with the Secretary of State, then the Secretary of Defense, and subsequently myself, what our views were; after the completion of that round, he would leave for the Oval Office. Approximately two hours later, the members would receive a PDM (Presidential Decision Memorandum), often containing not much more than a sentence, stating what the President's final decision was. This, of course, was the cue for us to initiate implementation. However, the latter, which meant translating generalities into operational detail, was far more complex than might be imagined. In my own case, I remember one Presidential decision concerning action in Cambodia that involved the dispatch of some sixty-two messages, drafted by me, just to begin implementation.

It is not my intention, of course, to present a detailed, painstaking analysis of the history and evolution of the decision-making process and structure relating to defense and security. That is the task of the chapters that follow. The purpose of this introduction is to convey to the reader some of the flavor and atmosphere of the work, as experienced by a participant. In this manner, I hope to put a little flesh on the dry bones of diagrams of organization.

I

The Conduct of National Security

Historical and Current Comparisons

1

Britain and the Imperial Staff

Peter Nailor

Introduction

The institutional development of the Imperial General Staff, in the period immediately before the First World War, is the point at which a number of the threads in British Imperial designs became a cohesive pattern, in policy terms. But the growth, both of doctrine and institutions, goes back a long way before 1909, and even the change in nomenclature did not in itself impose cohesion across the board. The use that was made both of the ideas and of the institutions carries on to, and beyond, the Second World War.

Imperial Security

The Imperial concept of security self-evidently depends upon an Imperial spread of interests, and in that sense Britain's perspectives, as well as her problems, widened very greatly in scope during the eighteenth century. By the time of the Elder Pitt, a "Grand Strategy" was not only necessary but was made available, to comprehend the problems and the opportunities of the Seven Years' War. In Europe, in the Americas, and in the Indian Ocean, the government articulated a series of objectives that produced a measure of cohesion at the level of national strategy, even if there were failings in the conception and execution of some of the plans. This weakness in execution was due, in part, to the circumstances of the time, not only because planning across great distances in an era of relatively poor communications was expecting a lot, but also because the military instruments were not of an adequate level of sophistication (particularly in logistics matters) to be able to give life to ambitious plans. This was not the first occasion on which British policy has looked like a "Grand Design"; the perspectives of the Marlborough/Godolphin Ministry during the War of the Spanish Succession were, for their time, as broadly drawn as those of Pitt. But the Seven Years' War was planned and, by and large, fought on a scale that the British hitherto had not reached, or indeed, aimed at.

But largely as a consequence of that war, a new concept of imperial security developed. The particular aspect of Imperial defense that pervades and illuminates the British experience is the cooperation (or lack of it) between the Imperial power and its self-governing possessions. In that sense, British Imperial defense is the story of a relationship that in some respects is more like that of an alliance than of a central and dominant authority imposing and executing a series of objectives: a relationship in which persuasion and example—and indecision—have as much place as economic and political uncertainty or agreed strategic perspectives. By and large, a territory that was administered from London was, in security terms, a British responsibility—though in this, as in so many other ways, India was something of an exception; or, at the very least, sufficiently prominent and distinctive to require a mold of its own. When a territory became self-governing and if not wholly, then at least in part, self-taxing, the security problem that arose was what this new political unit would do and how much it would pay toward its own defense. So it was with the Thirteen Colonies, so it became with the Dominions. It would be wrong to overemphasize the purely budgetary nature of the differences that arose, although they were always important in times when all government expenditures were of modest size and scope; issues about what we now call command and control, and about personnel and training, were important, too. Moreover, in the eighteenth and nineteenth centuries, as now, cost was a symbolic as well as a real issue: "no taxation without representation" meant, in defense terms, to have some say in policy determination as well as in local control, and it soon emerged that the sum of the interests of the particular parts of the Empire was not always the same as the British view of the interests of the whole. There was often tension between the urgency attributed by individual colonies to questions of local defense and the problems, as they were seen from London, of the maintenance of the whole network of political and economic connections.

We should bear in mind as well that, extending well into the nineteenth century, the Imperial idea was based very largely upon economic precept. The mercantilist view of empire depended upon issues like trade and raw materials, and the relationship between the Imperial power and its sources and markets. Here was a fruitful area both for exploitation and complaint; and for a long time the complaints in London were that the British were not making a profit from their Empire and that, as their possessions developed, so the profits that did accrue were unfairly shared. The colonists said that they were required unreasonably to trade, in British bottoms and only to British markets, to the detriment of their own local interests. The British complained that the balance of trade was more often than not against them, that they continued to be left with residual responsibilities—like defense—to which the colonies made little or no contributions and that remained a burden that the British taxpayer had to meet.[1] The nineteenth century saw the fading of the mercantilist system and its replacement by an era of free trade that, in one sense, was no more than an assertion that British dominance of the manufactured goods market and her increased need for cheap raw materials and food had grown so as to require a new mode of trade. It was not a response to the growth of a new Imperial idea: " . . . the empire was not the sum total of British power; whether in mercantilist or free trade times, Britain could hardly afford to rely solely upon her colonial possessions to acquire and maintain a position of dominance."[2] Britain had a global as well as an Imperial position, resting upon the possession of a sufficient military (mainly naval) capability to sustain an orderly framework of interests, which extended beyond the security of her colonies.

The period after the ending of the Napoleonic Wars saw the development of the extensive strategic position Britain had obtained. Britain's position in North America was defined; Britain's unchallenged dominance in India was confirmed, and the gateways to India were secured by the settlement of Singapore. From this point of view, the beginning of British involvement in southern Africa, with the occupation of Cape Colony, was more relevant then to India than to Africa.

The ensuing period saw both a stability that gave a chance for further development and then the gradual emergence of challenges to the British position. It was in North America that the challenges first gave rise to the developing concept of an Imperial relationship; and it was over Canada that the ideas both about the local organization of defense forces and the Imperial exchange of personnel were first articulated in modern form.[3] But it was the position of India that set the tone for policy over much of the period. Because there was no immediate or local threat of significance to British India's borders, they could be defended from afar. Second, the approaches to India, particularly during this period the sea approaches, provided the framework within which the defense system could operate; this was the rim of the wheel within which India was the hub. The iron band that kept the wheel together was the Royal Navy, and it was the contention of the "blue-water school" of naval thinkers (which for a long time dominated Imperial defense thinking in the high Victorian period) that it was command of the sea which provided both the basic security of the empire and the mobility which enabled local garrisons to be kept low and to be succored in time of need.[4] But, equally, it was the source of divergence and division of opinion, as soon as some local threat emerged either to some part of the Empire or to the homeland itself. The Royal Navy enabled Britain to separate and isolate any particular problem; but it also highlighted the dissonant demands that emerged from the local government of the area where any defensive problem precipitated a crisis to which the British would have to respond. And in India itself, where large forces, both British and Indian, were maintained, the question became whether the forces in India were primarily established for Indian security or whether, in fact, they embodied an Imperial reserve. Although the government of India was nominally subordinate to the government in London, it pursued a regional policy within its own sphere that tended to diffuse this distinction. The government in India not only initiated policy but showed on occasion a marked independence of viewpoint and priority.[5] In that sense India was more like the other major Dominions (as they became) and colonies than the quite different administrative structures might have implied. But a distinction remained. For the parts of the Empire that moved to self-government, the main question of Imperial defense was, What would the homeland do for them? The problem that eventually confronted the British government toward the turn of the century was, What would these parts of the Empire do for Britain?

In this sense, the main threat that emerged, and that eventually was the spur to the formalization of Imperial defense connections, was political and economic competition from the new nations in Europe; principally the new France, the new Germany, and to a lesser extent, the new Italy. The growing struggle for influence and power lapped over from Europe into the empty continent of Africa by the 1880s, but from time to time the threat of invasion to Britain itself diverted resources and dominated the periodic debates about defense. (It was preoccupation with the security of the homeland that usually secured more money for defense.) In a rather later time scale, the emergence of Japan as a new nation, and a new vigorous actor in the international system, paralleled the threat that arose in Europe to established British interests. The argument of British writers, and then of the British government, contended that if Britain was threatened, then Canada, Australia, and India were threatened, too, and ought to be sensitive to the need of Britain to concentrate its resources for homeland defense. If a colony were lost, it could be regained by the defeat of the European power's pretensions; if Britain were defeated, all would be lost. The response of the Dominions to this cosmic view of empire varied but in no case was fundamentally unsympathetic: the nature of the response had something more to do with the different social and economic preoccupations of the various countries as they emerged toward independence, or at least relative independence, and to their sensitivity toward what they saw as an attempt to retain a measure of British control of their destiny. The problem was really rather more one of persuading the Dominions that the threat to Britain was real, not a device to undercut their assertions of free will, and by 1910–1911 this was no longer difficult to establish; but from 1880–1910 it was a matter of great political controversy.[6]

The Effects of a Changing Technology

Nevertheless, the most profound controversy was not political but professional, and it was British rather than Imperial in scope.[7] The developments in military technology, from about 1860, and the professionalization of war in the same period produced for Britain a number of fundamental problems of a novel sort. It was now evidently possible to train, equip, sustain, and deploy very large land armies: industrialized nations of a larger size than Britain were now more dangerous competitors for Britain in war as well as in peacetime trade. And with the exception of the United States, they were, in this period, all local European powers. Their ability, as well as their need, to search out new markets and sources of raw materials was bolstered by this military potential; and the effects of steam and steel on navies not only affected operational tactics but operational concepts and strategic priorities. Coal-fired boilers freed navies from dependence on the wind, but enhanced the necessity of local bases. Steel drove up the size of ships as well as of weapons; the lethality of war at sea was enhanced; the balance between quantity and quality needed much more frequent assessment. And new navies proliferated. On the sea as well as on land, the ability of Britain's competitors to use firepower and mobility to contest her positions of control, or dominance, were much improved; and, as her economic domination also came under challenge, the breadth of her interests and her relatively narrow manpower base were highlighted as weaknesses.

It was considerations such as these that eventually determined, at the political and at the military level, too, that Britain should seek diplomatic accommodations to seal off some areas of potential conflict. This process, in turn, established the framework for potential, and then actual, alliances that was crucial in defining both the threats and the promises that would have to be met. Although it was events and policies at these high levels that obviously had profound effects upon the pace and shape of Imperial planning, they were parallel, rather than intrinsic, to the development of the Imperial pattern.

The fundamental issue here was how a modern war would be fought and organized. By the time of the first Colonial Conference in 1887, the British concept that a modern war would involve the Empire had become a relatively well developed axiom; any war in Europe would mean that Britain would have to mobilize its resources on an extra-European scale. There was an element of circularity to the argument, of course, but it embodied the central dilemma of an imperial range of interests. If the fleet had to be concentrated and the remaining garrisons brought home, the Empire would have to man the local ramparts; and if the conflict spread outside Europe, to India or Africa or the Far East, Britain's ability to provide reinforcements obviously would be inhibited. Therefore, whether the war centered on Europe or spread outward, the colonies and the Dominions ought to do rather more for themselves; and if they could be brought to do that, they should accept—in some measure, at least—an Imperial conception and an Imperial load. There should be, to use a familiar modern term, burden sharing; and this was a theme that the British delegates developed in all the Imperial Conferences.

The problem for the Empire's components was that, with the exception of India, they were all relatively small units and, without exception, rather underdeveloped, to use another modern term. They might be able to organize more extensive self-defense forces, but even though their governments expanded, to meet and improve upon the Canadian model of self-government, their administrative infrastructures would still need support.[8] In army terms, the Empire's components would need help with equipment, training, and organization, at least. In naval terms, with the Navy's heavy incubus of engineering support for maintenance and repair, they were even worse off. However, their underlying concern, which emerged as a continuous theme throughout the whole of the period of the development of Imperial consultation, was the question of who would control whatever contributions they would raise. For land forces it was primarily a question of military organization and development: of professional forces and militias. The possibility of raising, or contributing toward, fleet units came much later, in the period just before the First World War; though even here the arguments about either raising a local force or contributing toward an Imperial entity were rehearsed.

The British view was, for a long time, diffuse. There was a commonly held assumption that British *contrôle* (in the French sense of the word) was self-evidently necessary because of the size and sophistication of the British resources and experience; but the British conception of what modern war would entail was, professionally, unclear. In these circumstances there could be no model organization to which the Empire could be asked to conform, or join. There was, even until the First World War itself, no cohesive or common view of strategic objectives or priorities. The Navy and the Army responded in quite different ways and time scales to the professional perspectives of experience and threat, and even in Britain there was no permanent system of central management, or even coordination, of a political sort until the experience of war itself forced such a system upon a government that needed to mobilize and regulate the nation's resources on an unprecedented scale. Beginnings were made after the Boer War, but the Committee for Imperial Defense (CID) was in truth more of a sorting house than a powerhouse.

Managing Modern War

The new professional problems of how to manage modern war posed great difficulties for the British. The emergence of highly specialized and professionally dedicated staff training, for which a number of continental armies stood as models by 1875, was antipathetic to a long social tradition that remained suspicious of the costs and influence of standing armies and that rightly saw the General Staff as a core of thought, influence, and control within the Army. This development also impinged upon the social and structural organizations to which both Army and Navy had become accustomed; and in this sense erroneous deductions about the traditions of the Nelson era were just as effective brakes on progress as correct deductions about the preferences of the Duke of Cambridge, who remained Commander in Chief until 1895. Long periods of peace and a reliance upon the ability to improvise on a small scale reduced any receptivity to radical change; and Gladstonian (and Churchillian) precepts of fiscal rectitude emphasized cost above effectiveness, and inhibited the effects of the innovations that were slowly being made.

It was the emergence of continental threats to British security that loosened these constraints, though it was the experience of the Boer War that sharpened the need to take action. The Boer War demonstrated the necessity as well as the ability of the Dominions to provide contributions to any large or sustained military campaign, and it focused the Navy's need to concentrate its forces in order to be able to deal with a fleet-in-being. The Navy was able, because of the Anglo-Japanese alliance and the Anglo-French entente, to respond to a redisposition of its forces and a technological change of gear; but it did not carry through these changes to a professionalization of its operational or logistic planning. The Army was, because of the Boer War, unable to resist reformist pressures to introduce a comprehensive departmental reorganization that made provision for a staff mechanism and a pattern of staff responsibilities upon continental lines.[9] But, although the way forward was now much clearer, the system—for training, for promotion, and for interchange with the Dominions—was only in an early stage of implementation when Haldane persuaded his Imperial colleagues to confirm their acceptance of the symbol of unity, and the change of name, in 1909. It was an important declaration of intent, but it had not had very much effect within the Army by the time war broke out in 1914.[10] What it did produce was an improvement in the Army's capacity to mobilize its arguments and, eventually, to carry the day at Cabinet level for acceptance of the need to provide for a large Expeditionary Force that would be committed to support the French. How to support and maintain that Force, once it had been dispatched, was not worked out in detail. Good staff work had been done, but it owed more to individuals—like Hankey, Haig, Wilson, Nicholson, and Robertson (and in the Navy, Battenberg, Jellicoe, and Madden)—than to a system that embodied agreed doctrine and provided for planned contingencies on an Imperial scale. And the extent to which the need for a General Staff had been accepted was epitomized, on the one hand, by the virtual migration of the Imperial General Staff to France and, on the other, by the recall of Kitchener and Fisher, as war took hold of policy.

Results of the War

It is not entirely fair to say that the War was a succession of improvisations and expedients: the Fleet was mobilized, the BEF was transported to France according to plan. But the intensity and the length of the war taxed the ingenuity of the empire to extremes; the contributions and the sacrifices of the Dominions and colonies demonstrated the realities of Imperial ties and the commonality of the sense of danger, once war had been joined. Their military forces were built up amazingly quickly, managed surprisingly well, and contributed without stint.[11] But if at the level of military affairs the First World War was a unifying experience, at virtually all other levels it enhanced the awareness of separate destinies. Flanders, Gallipoli, Mesopotamia, East Africa enhanced Canadian, Australian, New Zealand, South African, and

Indian nationalism; Imperial bonds were forged, in blood a well as in staff
procedures, but they did not bring Imperial unity. Rather, they emphasized
the voluntarism of the cooperation that was achieved, at the political as well
as at the military level.[12]

In professional military terms, the Dominions grew up to a level of
maturity that emphasized the trends that the prewar period had already
created, and this achievement persisted in the interwar period. Functionally,
it made good sense to cooperate: to participate in common training at
Camberley and the Imperial Defense College, at Kingston, Ontario, and at
Quetta; to save infrastructure costs, by using British-made equipment; to
confer together. Politically, however, the clock could not be put back; and
however much the choice of alternative partners was in practice limited, it
was now necessary for the Dominions, with growing electorates of their own,
to emphasize that their decision about how, and how far, to cooperate with the
Imperial center was now a matter of choice. It was a right that had been won,
on Vimy Ridge and at Suvla Bay.

So there was rather less talk, in the interwar years, about grand Imperial
ideals in the face of a complex and steadily deteriorating international
situation. But there was rather more done, at less exalted levels and in more
practical ways of common training and standards. Cooperation in staff
training, particularly in the armies and in procurement planning, developed
steadily. Day-to-day inhibitions reasserted themselves because of financial
and economic pressures, epitomized in Britain by the Ten-Year Rule and
enforced by the Great Depression.[13] These did not stop innovations in
organization: the value of orderly staff work was accepted, and carried
through to the highest professional levels with the institution of the British
Chiefs of Staff Committee in 1923, followed by comparable developments
elsewhere.[14] There was even a civilian spin-off, in the form of an organized
Cabinet Secretariat in Britain.

But although in a very real sense the onset of the Second World War was
foreseen, and provided for very much more realistically than the outbreak of
the First World War had been, and although the professional expertise of the
various elements in the Imperial staffs was of a higher level of technical
competence, the inhibitions affecting a unified Imperial set of concepts and
practices remained. India was the only Dominion within which British
personnel, at the professional level, participated extensively, and in which
British priorities and perspectives were always likely to prevail. The other
Dominions had not only their own perspectives but their own national
personae; and cooperation with the British was, at least for those strategic
realities on which great issues of policy depend, a matter of negotiation and
acceptance. The fact that these separate governments shared many of the
same values—and apprehensions—was fundamentally important in the
same way that the shared professional preparation of the Services was
important; and it may have enabled institutional factors to be identified,

arbitrated, and argued in advance. But it was not politically inevitable that decisions or commitments would be automatically tripped to common time scales that would suit the technical parameters of subsidiary organizations. Neither Canada nor South Africa committed itself in 1939 without intense debate; and in the course of the Second World War, strategic divergences and critical differences of perspective came to reflect the global extent, and the regional fortunes, of the struggle, particularly for Australia and New Zealand. The apprehensions of prewar British planners about the ability of the Empire's combined resources to sustain a struggle on three widely separated fronts were fully realized, and led, in the post-1945 period, to the end of the Imperial conception of security based upon a mutuality of interests and a sufficiency of capability.[15]

Conclusions

What, then, can we make of the Imperial Staff? Its inception grew out of a historic concern over burden sharing that was implicit in the utilitarian concept of empire peculiar to Britain. Its articulation began under the twin pressures of Imperial development toward self-government and emergent threats to the political and economic stability of the Pax Britannica. Its growth depended upon the compliance of the Dominions, and the creation of institutions and methods by Britain that would give example, leadership, and life to the idea. Its utility could be demonstrated by war, and could be assessed by its performance in war. The very nature of the concept required supplementation at the highest level, by political consultation; and it needed justification, too, by its ability to demonstrate its sufficiency in the face of all the demands that were put upon it. It was a device, at the technical level, to optimize the resources of the Empire; but it could not solve strategic or military problems for which the resources of the Empire were inadequate. At a professional level, it added to, but did not create, the common knowledge that the military forces of the Empire came to have of one another; it was never truly international. It was one of the elements that enabled the Empire, in two World Wars, to act together impressively; but it never bestrode the political fences that established the individuality of the Imperial family, and it never fulfilled the cohesion and the central role that were implied in its name.

NOTES

1. W. Ross Johnston gives some estimates of costs: "It has been estimated that between 1714 and 1788 the American colonies cost the British Treasury over £40.5 million. Naval, military and other such defense costs took up the bulk of this sum, £32.5 million. Administrative costs ran to £4.5 million, and compensation and relief to loyalists affected by the

American revolution to £3.5 million. The colonists were being provided, at no cost to themselves, with the benefit of British naval and military protection. A British politician claimed in 1767 that the cost of troops in America had risen to almost £400,000 annually. Indeed the cost of America was escalating rapidly, from £70,000 in 1748 to £350,000 in 1764; in the early 1760's the British army in America more than doubled, to 7,500 men" (*Great Britain, Great Empire* [London: University of Queensland Press, 1981], 35). Similarly, "Sir Isaac Coffin complained to the House of Commons in 1822 that Canada cost Britain £500,000 per year while contributing not even 500 pence: the timber trade benefitted Canadians to the extent of £300,000 each year. In similar fashion, the purchase of sugar from the West Indies was a costly item for Britain, for example, averaging out the 1835–41 bills she could have saved £5.5 million annually by buying sugar on the world market at the prevailing price. And this deficit was not compensated for by large exports to those colonies" (p. 36).

    2. Ibid., 37.

    3. See Hew Strachan, "Lord Grey and Imperial Defence," in *Politicians and Defence*, ed. I. Beckett and J. Gooch (Manchester: Manchester University Press, 1981).

    4. See, by way of illustration, John Gooch, "The Army and Empire," chap. 2 in *The Plans of War* (London: Routledge and Kegan Paul, 1974); and Jay Luvaas, chap. 8 (on Spenser Wilkinson) in *The Education of an Army* (London: Cassell, 1965).

    5. See the early chapters of P. Darby, *British Defence Policy East of Suez* (Oxford: Oxford University Press, 1973).

    6. The best short account, particularly in respect of the political and administrative aspects, is given by Professor Norman Gibbs, "The Origins of Imperial Defence" (inaugural lecture delivered at Oxford University, 1955).

    7. See the early chapters of Gooch.

    8. The main period of growth was between the organization of the Canadian Federation in the late 1860s, to the South African Union and the Australian Commonwealth in the 1900–1910 period.

    9. The implementation of the recommendations of the Esher Committee took some years to come to anything like fruition; the grading of staff officers, their relocation in the new War Office, and the preparation of suitable training manuals all took time. It was possible to see quite substantial and speedy improvements in the quality of work at the G.S.O. level; but it inevitably took longer to train more senior officers how to use the mechanism they were creating more effectively. See Gooch, chap. 4. The same could also be said, in a rather later time frame, of naval staff-work.

    10. Gooch, chap. 5, details the development of "The Imperial Design" between 1906–14. He sums up the period in this way: "Thus, as far as colonial and dominion participation in the strategic planning of the General Staff went, there was on the outbreak of the war little to see. Some never sent representatives to London at all; others so hemmed their officers round with rigid instructions that they had little opportunity to exploit their position. In either case, Whitehall was never really interested in using to the full what willingness there was to participate. It is therefore hardly surprising that by the eve of the war the term 'Imperial' in the title of Chief of the Imperial General Staff signified little and served only to 'assuage the Imperialism in Australian sentiment.' The events of the first eighteen months of the war were to show that the Imperial design came in practice to nothing" (p. 160).

    11. Imperial assistance, in manpower support, totaled more than £2m, to support Britain's £4.5m (£826,000 from India, £418,000 from Canada, £420,000 from Australia, £146,000 from South Africa, and £10,000 from New Zealand). Canada, in particular, also furnished considerable material assistance with war production. In the Second World War, Canada, Australia, New Zealand, and South Africa provided a gross total of £1.65m, and India £2.3m; the peak enrollment in Britain, in the early months of 1945, was £5.2m (see Johnston, 104). A more extensive analysis is contained in F. W. Perry, "Manpower and Organizational Problems in the Expansion of the British and other Commonwealth Armies during the two World Wars" (Ph.D. thesis, King's College, London, 1982).

    12. Political consultation had taken place more or less regularly since the late 1870s, but with the exception of the Colonial Conferences and occasional attendances at the CID, consultation was most commonly undertaken by correspondence. In the First World War, the pace quickened, and, in the later stages of the war, Field Marshal Smuts became a member of Lloyd George's War Cabinet. In the Second World War, a rather similar pattern was discernible,

but rather more use was made of personal Commonwealth participation, for example with the appointment of the Hon. R. G. Casey, from Australia, as the resident Minister in the Middle Eastern war zone.

13. The "Ten-Year Rule" was a guideline, which persisted until 1932, that defense planning should be based upon the presumption that no major war should be assumed likely for the ensuing ten-year period: it became a "rolling" assumption.

14. Gibbs points out that this structure acted as a model for the United States as well as the larger Dominion governments.

15. The political environment at the end of the Second War was more cautious and inhibited than in 1919–20. There was much less euphoria about "wars to end wars" and a lower, but more reasoned, expectation from the new United Nations Organization as an international forum, to replace the League of Nations. But what could not be gainsaid was the relative diminution of the power of Britain, its economic and physical debilitation; nor the emergence of the United States as a global power of great strength, with regional dominance in the Pacific. And this set of factors was instrumental in precipitating the ANZUS pact, no less than NATO.

2

The General Staff: Theory and Practice
From the Tsarist to the Soviet Regime

John Erickson

"We have the different branches of the military service well organised. . . . But when we come to the co-ordination and direction of all these means and agencies of warfare, so that all parts of the machine shall work true together, we are weak. Our system makes no adequate provision for the directing brain which every army must have to work successfully."

This argument for a "directing brain," part of a classic exposition in favor of an efficient general staff system penned by Secretary of War Elihu Root in his *Annual Report for the Year 1902*, could only have commended itself heartily to the *Genshtabistyi* of Imperial Russia. Similarly, even now in the atomic age, it would receive the approbation of the Soviet military leadership and might conceivably be deemed (according to some) not entirely irrelevant to current American misgivings about the higher direction of the American military effort. In impressively cogent fashion, Secretary Root emphasized that a more efficient higher military leadership—encouraged and promoted by a general staff system—could not be divorced from the effective organization of a national military effort designed to attain victory. If Secretary Root spoke of a "directing brain," Viscount Haldane, the vigorous reformer within the British military establishment, with deliberate flamboyance advertised the virtues of a General Staff as a "thinking department," though the phraseology was not entirely fortuitous. Both men had been much influenced by reading Spenser Wilkinson's examination of the Prussian General Staff, *The Brain of an Army*, which in spite of its classic properties had to overcome monumental indifference on the part of publishers.[1]

"Directing brain" or "thinking department"—whatever the elaboration on this theme, there was (and is) an immediate parallel in Russian formulations[2] of *mozg armii* ("the brain of an army," once again), *voennyi mozg* (the "military brain") of the entire state, or the General Staff as *generator* (powerhouse, or dynamo). All, however, subsume the notion of intelligent, systematized command, with its concomitant of an efficient staff system and the intellectual capacity to grasp the complexities of modern war. Inevitably, all eyes turned to the Prussian General Staff in the first instance— Spenser Wilkinson's book indeed had the avowed purpose of describing this system "in plain English," while the General Staff duties specified in the 1903 Act of Congress (which set up the War Department General Staff) were culled virtually in their entirety from General Bronsart von Schellendorf's *The Duties of the General Staff*. Yet there was a ready appreciation of the distinction between military methods and militaristic concepts. In brief, each nation developed its own "theory" of the General Staff, suited to its own purposes and adapted in varying degrees to its special military requirements. Theory and practice were increasingly conjoined as those very staffs turned to the examination and elaboration of the selfsame requirements in terms of military policy, as well as "strategical science."[3]

The "General Staff," therefore, may be considered as much a concept as it is an institutional arrangement for achieving more effective and efficient higher military leadership, an organizational device for simultaneously optimizing and disseminating officer expertise,[4] at once a "thinking department" and a "directing brain" in its operational mode. Yet in each and every aspect it is ineluctably an expression, arguably the embodiment, of national "style" in varying patterns of tradition, institutionalization, and innovation. In other words, after what fashion and for what reason do nations institutionalize military expertise? Even more pertinently, what success attends this effort, assuming that realistic criteria of success can be conjured up?

It is this approach that informs the tripartite discussion of the Imperial (Tsarist) Russian and Soviet "theory and practice" of the General Staff, from *General'nyi shtab* to *General'nyi shtab Sovetskikh vooruzhennykh sil*. To overlook tradition would be misleading; to ignore institutionalization would emasculate almost the entire context; and to dismiss innovation would foreclose an investigation of the degree to which the present Soviet regime has produced not only a radically new concept of the "General Staff," but also a unique operational style. Dictates of continuity, comparison, and contrast thus properly suggest three interrelated inquiries: the *Imperial Precedent*, the subsequent *Soviet Model*, and the present *Nuclear Command*.

The Imperial Precedent

REFORMING THE SYSTEM

At the close of the Crimean War, the Russian Army, in which Tsar Nicholas I took inordinate pride, crashed to defeat, a baleful humiliation heaped on Russian arms fighting on Russian soil. The fault, however, could not be laid exclusively at the door of the Army, for a system founded in repression could produce neither efficient soldiers nor proficient officers: military competence was not only in decline but actively discouraged, with the Department of the General Staff pushed from disrepair into actual disrepute. No mere reshuffle of generals could substitute for genuine reform, which was given a certain impetus with the accession of Tsar Alexander II. Modernization of the military system was clearly necessary as Russia smarted under defeat, but this demanded major social reconstruction in which the emancipation of the serfs had a crucial role to play. It was in the wake of that act of emancipation (promulgated on 3 March 1861) that Dmitrii Milyutin took up the post of War Minister, losing no time in submitting his expansive plans for military reform to the Tsar in January 1862.[5]

It was inevitable that Milyutin should draw the General Staff into the framework of his reforms. As War Minister he was already served by seven Main Administrations: the War Ministry might concern itself with military policy in the grand sense, while the military district and local organs assumed the routine running of their own affairs in the new decentralized mode. The problem was now how to fit the General Staff —such as it was— into the new system, when the Crimean War had shown up all the serious shortcomings of a staff system manned largely by "book-learners" who simply parroted (*kak popugai*) their classroom lessons. The General Staff system had already suffered a variety of fates: in 1774 it became the "Department of the General Staff," only to be superseded by the "Suite of His Majesty for Quartermaster Affairs" under the direct control of the Tsar, followed in turn by the creation in 1814 of the Guards General Staff and shortly thereafter by the Main Staff (*Glavnyi Shtab*), an entity that continued to grow but in which troop control—operations—became increasingly separated from matters such as supply, handled by the War Ministry. Worse still, the *Glavnyi Shtab* had no control over officer education, which came under a different body; as for weapons and equipment, here its authority was largely nominal, as it was in the matter of troop training.

The bout of reorganization in 1832 did little to improve matters save for the formal reemergence of the Department of the General Staff and the establishment of the Military Academy to train General Staff officers— committed, however, more to perfecting sterile drill procedures and not, for all of Jonini's pleading, to military-intellectual pursuits. The regulations of 1859 marked some improvement in defining the duties of the General Staff, which was identified as an auxiliary organ, beginning at the level of divisional commander and reaching thence into the upper echelons; it was also identified as an entity committed to the military-scientific work necessary for the preparation and conduct of any future war and, within the War Ministry, as the agency to deal with business requiring "special training" related to higher military education.

Milyutin's reform program inevitably embraced the General Staff, having as its immediate objective the need to bring theory and practice into closer alignment, as well as eliminating the "one-sidedness" of the General Staff. The first step was the creation of the *Main Administration of the General Staff* in 1863, an experimental program designed to run for two years. This new administration (*GUGSh*) also brought the Military Topographical Depot under its control and assumed direction of the General Staff Academy. But Milyutin wanted more, espying that the real need was for more better qualified officers; to this end he sought to strengthen the General Staff by combining the "Quartermaster element" with the Inspectorate and, in 1865, formally fused *GUGSh* with the Inspectorate to form a new organ, the Main Staff (*Glavnyi Shtab*), with seven departments, an Asiatic section, and a legal department. In effect, the Chief of the Main Staff became de facto head of the General Staff, though other duties prevented him from acting in any formal capacity as "Chief of the General Staff."

Although not concerned with military policy, the General Staff in its new guise as a component of the Main Staff exercised "General Staff functions" with respect to military organization, mobilization, training, intelligence, and measures related to the preparations for any future war; in short, coordinating activity. Meanwhile, staff structures and staff functions were generally regulated and defined by the 1868 enactment, *Polozhenie o polevom upravlenii . . .*, which assigned a military topographical section to the Field Staff, as well as one *shtabs-ofitser* to direct specialized intelligence work; the same *Polozhenie* also recognized the Chief of Staff at Army level as the right-hand man of the Commander in Chief, with respect to all matters pertaining to the running of the Army—a scheme that proved to have some serious shortcomings.

The expansion of the various staffs could not but create a demand for qualified officers to fill such posts, a requirement magnified by the need to cope with advancing technology—new infantry weapons, improved artillery complicating the task of the gunner and the engineer, the growing railway networks bringing radical changes in the manner of moving and deploying military forces. While Milyutin did not ignore officer education as a whole, he paid particular attention to the training of staff officers, revitalizing the General Staff Academy and thus paving the way for the eventual ascendancy of the *Genshtabistyi*, whose prestige finally came to surpass that of the Guards.

The fundamental reorganization of education and training for high command, entrusted to the General Staff Academy, and the growing influence of the General Staff went hand in hand, creating a distinctive intellectual and elitist tradition within the Russian officer corps. Hitherto a singular position in the military system had been held by artillery and engineer officers by virtue of their educational attainments and their professional skill, while the prestige of the Guards rested on social exclusiveness. At first sight Milyutin's program to bring fresh life to the Nikolaevskii Academy seemed to be both contradictory and self-defeating in view of the shortage of officers making itself felt after the Crimean War. An earlier scheme to set up one giant "Imperial Military Academy" (handling all higher military education), run by a Council with the Chief of the General Staff at its head, foundered almost at once. Milyutin, however, pressed ahead with plans to reform and diversify the curricula of the several Academies, particularly the Nikolaevskii Academy, which in 1869 formally assumed the title of the Imperial Nikolaevskii Academy of the General Staff.[6]

Educational attainment and qualification slowly but surely established itself as a key to success in the military establishment, though it could never obliterate advantages of birth and social privilege, when from the outset the better-off and better placed could exploit their educational background. However, education in the General Staff Academy began to provide its own special foundation for preference, promotion, and the privilege born of belonging to a caste. By and large it was ability that put a man into the Academy, and once there, he became a member (for life) of an "inner group," bonded by the corporate life of the Academy and the growing influence of the General Staff. Over thirty years, from 1852–1882, the Academy graduated 1,329 officers, of whom 903 went directly to the General Staff, 197 to command of regiments, 66 to brigade commands, 49 to divisional commands, 8 to corps, and 7 to Military Districts. But there was more to it than mere "book learning." General Staff officers (*Genshtabistyi*), never previously distinguished as such within the military administration and the military bureaucracy, now sported their own insignia and set "*General' novo shtaba*" (*GS*) before their rank and name.

The *Genshtabistyi* duly proved their worth during the Russo-Turkish War of 1877–78 when the Academy students (much as in 1941–45) went to war. The Tsar himself pointed to the "excellent service" of the General Staff and the achievements of the General Staff Academy. Here, demonstrably, were some of the best officers of the Imperial Army, both brave and accomplished—and none more so than General Dragomirov, commander of the Fourteenth Infantry Division, a professor at the Academy but a first-class soldier who was duly appointed head of the Academy in October 1878. Henceforth the *Genshtabistyi* competed with the Guards to become the true elite of the army, a process accelerated by the general shortage of officers that meant drawing on manpower beyond the confines of the gentry and reflected the changing social profile of those admitted to the military schools. In the Academy, Guards officers were still listed separately as a mark of their innate distinction, but this was more formality than a real social frontier, since life and work in the Academy assumed more and more the characteristics of a melting pot, with a wide variety of backgrounds, tastes, and associations.

The number of officers with a higher military education increased steadily, with a corresponding growth in the number of *Genshtabistyi*, though an odd asymmetry began to reveal itself as the Russian officer corps expanded, so did it assume an increasingly heterogeneous profile, while the *Genshtabistyi* developed into a "closed caste," exclusivity being encouraged by the rigor of the selection process (for the Academy) and the small numbers involved.[7] The qualifying examinations for the Academy were administered by the Military District staffs, with 1,500 officers entering their names in the first instance, being whittled down to 400 to 500 admitted to the examination, and only 140 to 150 actually passing. From that select group, only 100 officers would graduate as "first-class" students, passing thence to the "supplementary course," from which only about half would proceed to the General Staff.

The Academy ran two courses, or "classes," the junior and the senior, followed by the "supplementary course" (*dopolnitel'nyi kurs*) designed for those selected for General Staff appointments: to gain entry to that high-level course meant obtaining very distinguished marks indeed (ten and above) in the senior examinations, with the remainder graduating "second-class" and proceeding to troop units. Thus, the Academy produced three types of officers: the second-class (*vtoroi razryad*) graduate, the graduate completing a three-year course (including the "supplementary" instruction) but not assigned to the General Staff, and finally, the true elite, those selected for the General Staff proper. However, inclusion within the supplementary course, even without automatic posting to the General Staff, came to count for membership in a specially favored, if not entirely charmed, circle—at least some association with the General Staff and recognition by the *Momenty* (a sardonic reference to General Staff officers on the part of line officers, mocking the distinctive mannerism of the *Genshtabist* of prefacing most of his remarks with "*Moment*" ["Ah, but . . . "], an affectation bringing down immediate scorn).

Where and how was this much-vaunted "brain of the army" to be applied? Real weakness showed itself increasingly at the top, accentuated by the lack of operational experience as a result of more than two decades without major war, thereby obliging the high command to develop its art by peacetime maneuver and to advance its interest by political maneuver directed toward the Tsar and the court. The "brain," however, worked in another direction, putting Russian military theory well to the fore in both national and international terms, thanks in no small part to two senior officers at the head of the Academy, General Dragomirov and General Leyer. In fact, these men between them represented both "brain" and "thinking department." Toward the end of the century, the attention of the "thinking department" shifted increasingly to the higher direction of military operations and the coordination of *theater forces*, the "operational" aspect of strategy. Although he was involved in the drafting of Russia's first mobilization plan in 1880, Leyer was less preoccupied with the problems of strategic concentration and operational deployment. The chief of the *Glavnyi Shtab*, General Obruchev, had already worked on a major study that reviewed those new factors governing possible war plans: "Considerations on our plans for waging war" (*Soobrazheniya o planakh vedeniya voiny*). Russia would be obliged to face a coalition superior in numbers and enjoying more favorable conditions for strategic deployment and operational concentration, but Russia could withstand a protracted war in more effective fashion than her potential enemies; hence Obruchev's strategic plan was designed to gain time. He proposed four main armies (the Niemen Army; the Western Army; the Volhynia Army; and the Main Army to act as a reserve, deployed along the second defense line). In considering this deployment pattern, Obruchev also pointed to the increasing role of the railroads.

These ideas, developed within the *Glavnyi Shtab* in 1880, formed the basis of the war plans drafted in 1887 and in 1890, with the final versions (duly adjusted in 1893 and 1897) lasting until the very end of the century. But strategic deployment was not Obruchev's sole preoccupation: For all the praise heaped on the *Glavnyi Shtab* for its part in the Russo-Turkish War, Obruchev realized that all was not well with the "strategic direction" of Russian forces and that modernization must include the *Glavnyi Shtab*.

The new regulations on wartime field administrations went into effect in 1890, the aim being to reduce the administrative load on the C in C at theater level and also within individual army commands, with higher staffs now acquiring sections responsible for the collection and distribution of intelligence as well as reconnaissance information. "Command and control" of theater forces increasingly became the subject of intense debate and discussion, with "strategical science" taking a very practical turn. Both Dragomirov and Leyer had investigated the nature of "operations," with the former insisting that an operation was essentially an extension of a tactical action, the latter arguing that "operations" must be considered part of the whole strategic scene—the effort to relate tactical action with strategic operations leading eventually to the formulation of "operational art" (*operativnoe isskustvo*), an additional "echelon of activity" linking tactics and strategy.[8]

But more than intellectual debate, serious matters were afoot with attempts to improve not only the *operational control* of Russian field forces but also the processes of planning and preparing for war. Once again it was Obruchev in the van with proposals to reshape the *Glavnyi Shtab*, his first proposals going to War Minister Vannikovskii in 1894. It took three years, however, for the requisite commission to be appointed, whereupon everything ground to a halt as both Obruchev and Vannikovskii resigned their posts at the end of 1897. However, Obruchev did not allow himself to be deflected, and in February 1898 returned to the attack. He suggested the creation of a separate "operational-strategic element," but with the main aim of transforming the *Glavnyi Shtab* into an instrument, or agency, capable of handling "higher strategic matters"—deployment in potential theaters of war, force structure, plans for effective concentration and initial operations, readiness of field administrations in frontier military districts, collecting intelligence of the enemy. . . . The first step must be to accord the *Glavnyi Shtab* its rightful place in the structure of the War Ministry and to recognize the Chief of the *Glavnyi Shtab* as immediate assistant (*pomoshchnik*) to the War Minister, empowered to deputize for him in his absence and in the event of such absence on the part of the Minister to have the right of reporting directly to the Tsar.

Therein lay a subtle move but an explosive issue. The regulations of the 1860s governing the *Glavnyi Shtab* had established the high-level staff as a component of the War Ministry, with the corollary that the Chief of the *Glavnyi Shtab* was subordinate to the War Minister. If Milyutin was pressed after 1870 to adopt the "Prussian style" for raising military manpower by universal conscription, it does not seem that he was urged to adopt the same Prussian mode with respect to the Main Staff—where the Prussian General Staff, at Moltke's behest, slipped the War Minister's leash and exploited direct access to the monarch. That lesson was certainly not lost on the Russians, though Obruchev's proposals for reorganization of the *Glavnyi Shtab* did not go wholly unheeded. The new War Minister, General A. N. Kuropatkin, took up the substance of Obruchev's plans, to which the Tsar acknowledging the approval of the Military Council, consented in March 1900.

Expansive though the reorganization seemed, it was not at all politically reckless, for the new plan specifically precluded the chief of the *Glavnyi Shtab* from enjoying any position or rights greater than those enjoyed by other chiefs of main administrations: the road to a Russian Moltke was duly barred. Meanwhile, financial stringency and the growing crisis in the Far East brought an abrupt halt to immediate reorganization, the most urgent task being to buttress the *Glavnyi Shtab* with two new sections—one for operations, the other for statistics—(intelligence data) assigned to the Quartermaster General under Order No. 232 of July 1900.

Not until 11 April 1903 did the *Glavnyi Shtab* emerge in its new guise, rebuilt around five administrations. In addition, four standing committees were assigned a coordinating role with respect to *General Staff functions*— the committee on organization and training, the mobilization committee, the committee on transportation and stores, and a committee on internal affairs (administration). The Chief of the *Glavnyi Shtab* was the president of the first three, all-important committees—which made the Chief, in effect, the principal coordinator of the high-level staff functions and commitments.[9]

Russian staff organization, both in theory and practice, had come a long way by the turn of the century. Though the *Glavnyi Shtab* still existed as a single staff entity, operational staff functions were now clearly differentiated from intelligence staff functions. Consequently, separate administrations were established under Quartermaster General I and II, though precedent was honored and tradition preserved by identifying both with Quartermaster General duties, and allowing "General Staff functions"—*Sluzhba General 'novo shtaba*—to fall more immediately under Quartermaster General II, an arrangement that was too narrowly constrictive in view of the spread of functions. On the other hand, the utter banishment of provisioning (supply) from operational planning, with provisioning buried, of all places, deep within the nether regions of the Duty General's administration, served only to perpetuate a major weakness, one for which more Russian soldiers would soon have to pay dearly and ignominiously in the Far East.

A BRIEF ASCENDANCY

In both concept and organization, therefore, the Russian General Staff was to be understood as an organ of administration and command, emplaced within the central administration (after 1903 identified at this level specifically with the adminstration of Quartermaster General II). It was to be viewed also as an organ for troop administration and command at levels reaching from the staffs of Military Districts to the administrations of independent brigades. The disasters of the Russo-Japanese War, however, proved to be a brutal mockery of the attempts at modernization, and a confused rationalization: the inefficiency of staffs and the ineptitude of commanders threw the harshest light on the shortcomings of military policy, "strategic direction," and tactical handling. Fears on this score went back some years, even before the end of the century, when General Sluchevskii suggested creating a "Supreme Military Council" (*Verkhovnyi voennyi sovet*) to carry out its duties under the chairmanship of the Tsar himself (or his nominee). In March 1904 Count Bobrikov proposed the setting up of a "Council of State Defense" (*Sovet gosudarstvennoi oborony*) to broaden the discussion of defense matters, going beyond the clique of Imperial intimates and officials.

Deepening gloom and impending catastrophe gave many cause to think furiously. In September 1904 the War Minister, General V. V. Sakharov, was in receipt of two memoranda, addressed to the Tsar. One, from General F. F. Palitsyn, proposed the establishment, after the German model, of an independent staff organ directly subordinated to the Tsar and freed from subordination to the War Minister. The second, from Guards Colonel P. N. Engalychev, with considerable service as Military Attaché in Berlin behind him, proposed splitting off the General Staff as an independent organ, but confining it within the War Ministry. The struggle for the soul of the General Staff, if it can be called that, and the battle over the proposed Council of State Defense fused into a debate that was instantly impassioned, frequently embittered, and generally envenomed. The Tsar had already decided in favor of a Council of State Defense, causing Witte to observe that the net result would be to make Grand Duke Nikolai Nikolayevich, in his capacity as president of the new Council, de facto head both of the War and Naval Ministries.

An independent General Staff administration finally emerged from this welter of intrigue, recrimination, and reappraisal, all against the background of revolutionary turbulence sweeping the country. Nor were the fortunes of the General Staff unconnected with the future of the Council of State

Defense. Grand Duke Nikolai lent his support to Palitsyn, while the protagonists of the Council argued that its work would be much enhanced by the
presence of a specific Chief of the General Staff, a "man of authority,
specifically acquainted with questions of strategic planning." On 21 June
1905 that office, or that post, was officially authorized: "Chief of the General
Staff," directly subordinated to the Tsar and with the right of reporting
directly to him. Four days after this order, No. 424 (*Polozhenie o
nachal'nike General'novo shtaba*) the Main Administration of the General
Staff (*Glavnoe upravlenie General'novo shtaba: GUGSh*) was established,
thus formally splitting the General Staff and the *Glavnyi Shtab*. It was not the
administrative move but the status of the Chief—above all, his direct access
to the Tsar—that ignited wrath: Witte thought nothing would come of the
whole arrangement save to create *dvoevlastie*, a dualism of staffs and
prerogatives. The professional military approved of having a designated chief
of the General Staff but frowned on his release from subordination to the War
Minister. There was, however, a certain political subtlety behind the move:
with the War Minister now responsible to the newly created Duma, but the
Chief of the General Staff empowered to report directly to the Tsar, the Duma
would be familiarized only with the routine business of the War Ministry.

As the new Chief of the General Staff, Lieutenant General Palitsyn took
over his own officially delineated domain, consisting of *GUGSh*, the General
Staff Academy, General Staff officers occupying General Staff "slots"
(General Staff officers not occupying such "slots" came within the "superintendence" of the Chief of the General Staff but were not directly subordinated to him), officers of the Military Topographers Corps, "railway troops
and those technically involved in signals." The Chief of the General Staff
himself was charged with supervising the preparation of war plans; integrating the work of the Military District Staffs, together with General Staff
"military-scientific work" and General Staff service duties; pursuing all
avenues leading to the dissemination of military knowledge; presenting an
annual report to the Tsar on the work of *GUGSh*; as well as including his own
proposals for improving General Staff activity and making ready for war.
However, in such matters as troop training and organizing large-scale maneuvers, he was obliged to coordinate his report to the Tsar with the War
Minister.

Disputes over financing delayed the realization of Palitsyn's plans for
GUGSh, but on 22 April 1906 the establishment was confirmed under Order
No. 252. In effect, *GUGSh* involved removing the Quartermaster General II
Administration (but minus the mobilization division) together with the
Military Communications and Military Topography from the *Glavnyi Shtab*.
Now the Quartermaster General Administration became the executive organ
responsible to the Chief of the General Staff for those matters pertaining to
preparing for war and for regulating General Staff duties and assignments.
GUGSh consisted of three administrations—Quartermaster General, Mili

tary Communications, and Military Topography—each with its own internal organization. Reorganization did not result in rationalization. On the contrary, War Minister Rediger observed that Russian higher military administration was split into seven disparate segments—the War Ministry, the Chief of the General Staff, four Inspectorates (working independently), and the chancellery of the State Defense Council, a state of affairs not destined to last but before its resolution the new *GUGSh* did at least earn some of its salary.

Distinct from the *Glavnyi Shtab*, *GUGSh* was able to handle intrinsic "General Staff business" more expeditiously. One innovation was the establishment of a mixed commission drawn from the Army General Staff and the Naval General Staff (*Morskoi General' nyi Shtab*)[10] to coordinate operations in the Baltic and the Black Sea. A major advance was the planned improvement in the collection of intelligence on foreign armies, which had hitherto been on a rather haphazard basis, though both intelligence and counterintelligence proved to be less effective than many desired.

More followed on measures to improve military capability—abolishing the reserve troops (understrength forces assigned to a wartime role in the army rear) and maintaining only field forces in peacetime, introducing modern weapons, raising peacetime military strength, expanding preparatory fortification/engineering work in theaters of war, extending the railway net in frontier zones, greater use of internal waterways and road transport, a building program for the fleet. As for the latter point, Palitsyn and his colleagues were preaching to the converted, in particular to a Tsar consumed with ambitions for his navy. If the two General Staffs cooperated over coastal defense, the War and Naval Ministries nevertheless fought each other tooth and nail over budgetary allocations, with the navy indulging in strenuous and very effective lobbying, duly assisted by the "Russian Navy League" and the "League for Naval Modernization."

The brawling between the Army and the Navy over funds for their respective services, with the Tsar promoting the idea of a strong navy and finding support from progressive ministers attracted by the prospect of commercial and industrial gain, plus the pettifogging approach of the General Staff to Army reorganization in the wake of the Russo-Japanese War, led to the demise of the Council of State Defense and the humbling of the General Staff. Though the Army closed ranks to fight off the Navy, the fruitless squabbling between the haughty gunners and the simple souls of the infantry not only displayed the ineffectiveness of the General Staff—unable to put its own military house in order—but also demonstrated the depth of the class divisions within the Russian officer corps.[11] The revamped system, which envisaged an enlarged role for an independent General Staff, crumpled all too quickly, thanks in no small degree to these same fissures within the officer corps. The struggle for and over the General Staff was itself a reflection of different and divergent social interests, bringing the "patricians" into collision with the "praetorians."[12] The younger officers pressing the cause of the General Staff did so also in pursuit of their own exclusive interests, denouncing the "old guard" and their methods that had dragged Russia to defeat. Unfortunately, this simply meant replacing one kind of privilege with another, with the "old guard" resisting the pretensions of the *Genshtabistyi* and their claim to primacy within the military.

PLANNING AND POLITICKING

In 1908 the Tsar made a clean sweep of his own, removing Grand Duke Nikolai from the Council of State Defense and ridding himself of Palitsyn as Chief of the General Staff. It was now the turn of the "praetorians," with V. A. Sukhomlinov taking over Palitsyn's position at the General Staff—a first step, followed by his assumption of the post of War Minister in the wake of a clever but grubby intrigue managed against the incumbent Rediger. General Sukhomlinov, himself a graduate of the General Staff Academy in 1874 and until his elevation commander of the Kiev Military District, embarked at once on what Golovin called the "turning back" process, reviving the former tradition of subordinating the General Staff to the War Ministry. At the end of 1909, the Chief of the General Staff lost his right of direct access to the Tsar, one item of the reorganization of the central military apparatus demanded by the Tsar. Mishlaevskii, now Chief of the General Staff, submitted further proposals for the restructuring of *GUGSh*, though the only result was Order No. 496 (1910), which prescribed an organization made up of five departments: *Quartermaster General, Troop Organization and Troop Service, Mobilization, Military Communications,* and *Military Topography*.

There were, it is true, some advantages to this new arrangement. Intelligence[13] now came within the competence of the Quartermaster General, while mobilization was withdrawn from the control of the *Glavnyi Shtab*. *GUGSh*, the Main Administration of the General Staff, was intended to be expressly "the brain" of the War Ministry and the Russian military machine as a whole, with the improvements in the General Staff field/troop administration—*VUGSh*—acting as a "neurological link" with the "brain of the army," with General Staff officers implanted as far down as the independent brigades. For coordination, a new General Staff Committee (*Komitet. Gen. Shtaba*) replaced the former *GUGSh* Mobilization Committee and the Main Committee for Fortresses, empowered to review manning, mobilization, wartime reinforcement, and the problems associated with the introduction of new equipment. The Chief of the General Staff presided over this Committee, whose members comprised the Chief of the *Glavnyi Shtab*(General Mikhnevich), the chiefs of the main administrations, the office of the War Minister, the Quartermaster General, and the chiefs of the Mobilization and Military Communications departments in *GUGSh*. For matters concerning Army-Navy relations, the Chief of the Naval Staff was entitled to be present at the General Staff Committee, though all decisions were subject to the War Minister's own final review.

The power of the War Minister, however, was waxing all the while, and Sukhomlinov fully intended that his should be so. In reducing the power of the General Staff—by the simple expedient of rotating his nominees through the post of Chief of General Staff with whirligig speed—he reduced the possibility of opposition to himself. For his own purposes—not all of which were as fell and devious as his critics have maintained—Sukhomlinov used the levers of the promotion machinery and the power of the purse to achieve his ends. Using the War Ministry and the machinery of routine promotions (though not the High Attestation Committee, which supervised senior ranks), Sukhomlinov built his own constituency in the Army, pushing the infantry forward in the face of opposition from the gunners, cavalrymen, and fortress officers, who not unnaturally came to hate him, as did the Duma, snubbed by him in no uncertain terms.

If the civil war—for such it was—in the Russian Army was not set afoot by Sukhomlinov, at least he did much to inflame and to ignite it. The officer corps split disastrously into the protégés of Sukhomlinov, the *Sukhomlinovtsyi*, and the nominees of the Grand Duke—the humbler, technically minded officers versus the grandees of the cavalry, the artillery, and the snobbery of the General Staff. That swathe cut right through the officer corps and across the chasm of the Imperial/Soviet regimes; for it was the *Sukhomlinovtsyi* who in large part steered the infant Red Army—Red artillery coming under the command of those officers promoted by Sukhomlinov over the sustained protests of the Artillery Department, Red infantry directed by senior officers also advanced by Sukhomlinov, while Imperial cavalrymen and the stiff-necked gunners made for the White camp. While all that was for the future, though one not too distant, the Russian military turned its thoughts increasingly to the implications of a war situation, as crisis followed crisis, the Bosnian crisis demonstrating all too clearly the deterioration of Russia's relations with Germany.

War plans, in which Sukhomlinov had a major hand, provoked yet another explosion, largely due to Sukhomlinov's lese majesty in suggesting scrapping most of Russia's massive fortress system, in spite of the fact that artillery and railways had made the bulk of them obsolete. The fortresses literally devoured guns (and money), leaving the infantry bereft of mobile fire support. The Sukhomlinov-Danilov plan of 1910 struck out boldly for an offensive strategy, designed to prevent the isolation of France in the early days of the war: an attack from the center could lay the Russian Army open to great danger, due to the presence of two "bastions" on the flanks, East Prussia and Galicia. Clearly, the most dangerous force lay in East Prussia, but here was a salient exposed to the south and to the east. The 1910 plan proposed the use of four armies against East Prussia, with the smaller force holding off the Austrians.

None of this went unchallenged, splitting the Russian command even further and leading in the event to a fatal division within the field forces, spread-eagling the Russian Army between its northern and southern fronts: neither the attack on East Prussia nor the offensive against Austria-Hungary in Galicia received adequate forces. This was not merely the failure of planning but the total want of any coherent strategy, a situation compounded—as if it needed any compounding—by administrative chaos and organizational muddle. This is not to say that plans for military reform and reorganization did not proliferate in the period from 1909–1913. In the autumn of 1912, officers of the General Staff, in particular General Belyaev's *Otdel po ustroistvu i sluzhbe voisk (GUGSh)*, started work on an ambitious plan to increase both the strength and the combat capability of the Russian army—work coinciding with the revision of the strategic war plan that envisaged simultaneous offensive operations against both Germany and Austria-Hungary. Although envisaging a long lead time in which to bring these measures to fruition—projected up to 1917—the main aim was to increase the field strength of the Russian armies at the very opening of hostilities in order to provide that degree of numerical superiority for offensive operations in what was presumed would be *a short war* (an erroneous assumption by no means confined to the Russian General Staff). This was the "Great Program" (*Bol'shaya programma*), which, as its name suggested, promised great things.

In March 1913 the Tsar approved the outline of the plan, whereupon Sukhomlinov decided for political reasons to split the whole undertaking into two parts, a "small" and a "large" program, seizing the opportunity provided by the "small" program to attend to the extremely urgent task of expanding Russian artillery, the glaring weakness in Russian military strength. The shortage and shortcomings in field artillery seriously offset Russian superiority in numbers: if a Russian division fielded 16 battalions against 12 in a German division, German firepower offset this advantage, since a German corps possessed 160 guns (with 34 heavy guns) as opposed to only 108 (12 heavy) in a Russian corps, leaving a Russian division deficient by 1½ batteries. Even that famed and fabled superiority, Russian numbers, proved to be something of an illusion, thanks to an obsolete conscription system that was not seriously adjusted by the Law of 1912. The pattern of conscription was designed to maintain peacetime military strength, imposing in its wake a lengthy period of service that failed to feed men back into organized, trained reserves (to which Germany paid assiduous attention). The large percentage of exemptions, almost 50 percent of an annual contingent, also required the lowering of standards of physical fitness, while deferment on educational grounds or reduction of service—with complete exemption for teachers in peacetime—reduced the pool of potential officers.

In conditions of great secrecy, a handful of generals and officers of

GUGSh worked on the final details of the "Great Program," which was reviewed by the Tsar in October 1913 and became law on 24 June 1914. Time, however, had virtually run out, for within a matter of days—on 10 July 1914—*GUGSh* began the activation of wartime mobilization schedules. It wanted but one week for the enactment of general mobilization.

WAR AND REVOLUTION

The organization of the command structure in 1914 was an ill-managed affair and a cumbersome process that produced an unwieldy and ultimately unworkable machine. Though holding the post of War Minister, Sukhomlinov adroitly sidestepped the appointment of supreme commander, ostentatiously deferring to the Tsar—who, in turn, lighted on Grand Duke Nikolai, with Yanushkevich as his chief of staff, thus installing two thoroughly benighted men at the *Stavka*. Under the revised *Polozhenie*, the senior officers of the Main Administration of the General Staff, *GUGSh*, formed the Supreme Commander's General Headquarters (*Stavka Verkhovnovo Glavnokomanduyushchevo*), with the post of chief of staff going to the chief of the General Staff (namely, Yanushkevich). Twenty-four General Staff officers were assigned initially to the *Stavka*, first sited at Baranovichi, 16 of these officers coming from the Department of the Quartermaster General, Major General Yu. N. Danilov, thus forming the operations directorate and representing the real power in the *Stavka*. With Yanushkevich now with the *Stavka* as Chief of Staff, General Belyaev took over the post of Chief of the General Staff, though *GUGSh* remained subordinate to the War Ministry and without direct connection to matters of strategic planning or operational direction. *GUGSh* was concerned primarily with mobilization (which in 1914 proceeded smoothly enough); the manning of field, reserve, and militia units; the movement of troops and military supplies; evacuation; and administrative arrangements for the use of prisoner-of-war labor.

The outbreak of war gave a new and vicious twist to the running battle between Sukhomlinov and the adherents of the Grand Duke, the latter gathering at the *Stavka*—pernicious rivalry involving the manipulation of command appointments by one party of the other, the War Ministry of the *Stavka*. If a "*Stavka* man" succeeded to an appointment, then the War Ministry would contrive to have one of its own men made Chief of Staff, though the balance—if it can be called that—was usually held by the Quartermaster General, Director of Operations, and a *Genshtabist*. Army commanders might quarrel violently with each other and their chiefs of staff, but the QMG would provide a useful conduit for the several parties. These tensions within the senior staffs, however, quickly degenerated into bitter feuding, ruining any effort to implant cogent military direction, while the divisions at the very top and the autonomy of the "fronts"—absolute in their control of supplies and transportation systems—eroded any attempt to implement centralized strategic control.

Wartime casualties bit deeply into the Army and its officer corps, bringing replacements and the trebling of the officer strength toward the close of 1916, but the numbers of *Genshtabistyi* did not increase correspondingly. On the contrary, their numbers declined due to war losses, and while in time-honored fashion the General Staff Academy closed its doors as staff and students marched off to war, the *Genshtabistyi* demanded the reopening of the Academy in 1916 to replenish their ranks from their own kind, through the device of short wartime staff courses. Otherwise, the *Genshtabistyi* closed ranks, which, though somewhat thinned, expanded in yet another direction, thanks to wartime promotion patterns. *Genshtabistyi* increasingly held high command appointments, penetrating the *Stavka*, the field commands, and the staffs of the field formations, together with the General Staff and the War Ministry. Promotion for *Genshtabistyi* was ostentatiously rapid, whereby colonels within the space of two years or so would become generals and brigade commanders advanced to the command of corps, all in marked contrast to the "middle-piece" regular line officers whose promotion came extremely slowly. Junior officers would advance to middle-rank positions, as might be expected, but only *Genshtabistyi* speedily reached high command posts.

The calamitous retreat of 1915, which added calculated horrors to forced evacuation—with Yanushkevich indulging to the full his anti-Semitic passions and adding more misery to desperate refugees through his "scorched earth" policy—killed off the old *Stavka*. Though he had carefully kept his distance from the *Stavka*, Sukhomlinov was also dismissed from his post as War Minister, replaced by General A. A. Polivanov, who could be counted one of the Grand Duke's men. Alekseyev pulled the new *Stavka* into shape, assisted by Pustovoitenko as his Quartermaster General and V. Borisov as his confidant and helpmate in matters of strategy. These men became the core of the *Stavka*, from which Rasputin was expressly excluded. However, the reshuffle brought no great improvement in relations between the *Stavka* and the War Ministry, a state of affairs that degenerated still further when War Minister Polivanov assumed the chairmanship of a new body, the "Special Council for National Defense" (*Osoboe soveschanie po oborone gosudarstv*)—the first of a series of "special councils" designed to improve the coordination of the war effort.

The final crash came in the early spring of 1917, the "February revolution" that toppled the Tsar and swept away the *ancien régime*. The engine of disintegration was driven at growing speed by economic disorder, the uncontrollable strains of the forced march toward modernization, with inflation accelerating the physical and visible collapse of "capitalism": money did not convert automatically into bread, and the towns began to starve, ushering in food riots that surged into revolutionary action. In the last resort it was the Army high command that forced abdication upon the Tsar, action that was the culmination of a protracted (and even devious) process to work change within the Army and within the country.[14] Indeed, the tradition of *Genshtab* dissent went back as far as the "Young Turks" of 1908; the military seemed to stir in 1915 but was bought off with the dismissal of Sukhomlinov, and the alliance of the *Stavka* with the Duma was stillborn, while military connections with the political opposition never acquired real sustance until *after* the removal of the Tsar. In the wake of that fundamental move, the cooperation between the leaders of the Duma and the *Genshtabistyi*—the Army high command, now cleared of its courtly appendages—expanded apace: Alekseyev, Ryzskii, and Gurko found common and congenial ground with Rodzianko, Guchkov, and L'vov in seeking to preserve the Army and in keeping Russia at war.

In 1917 the *Genshtabistyi* discovered where their true loyalty lay—not to the Tsar and a corrupt autocracy, but to "the Army": when autocracy no longer served the interests of the Army, then it had to go. Yet ironically (or predictably), though the *Genshtabistyi* acted to unhinge autocracy in the name of the "unity of the Army," their own unity began to come apart at the seams, forcing them to act politically in the name of an "apolitical Army," the younger General Staff officers in particular refusing to stand aside from the activities of the revolutionary organizations. Whether they liked it or not—and as Lenin recognized with absolute clarity — history had made "the military question now the fundamental *political* question." Nor could the mass of Russian soldiers be disregarded, as "soldiers committees" mushroomed in a surge of "democratization," turning the revolutionary turbulence into channels much distrusted, even detested, by the senior *Genshtabistyi*, conservative officers associated with conservative politicians—both steadily losing ground. Reorganizing the Army, though pursued by older and younger *Genshtabistyi* alike, ended only in splitting the one from the other.

The *Kornilovshchina*, General Kornilov's abortive coup, put paid to the political fortunes of the conservative *Genshtabistyi*, much as it sealed the fate of the conservative politicians. "Revolutionary *Genshtabistyi*" were now in the ascendant, many associated with the socialist parties, some with links to the Bolsheviks (the most prominent being Major General M. D. Bonch-Bruevich, brother of Lenin's friend V. Bonch-Bruevich), though the *Genshtabistyi* as a whole lacked leadership and lacked unity, split as they were between "leftists" and "rightists"—the sole link between them being their common detestation of Kerensky. In failing to support Kerensky, the *Genshtabistyi* were at least passively pro-Bolshevik: as if by some kind of osmosis, it was generally accepted that "the Army" could not fight off the Bolsheviks.

Losing little time, the Bolshevik *Narkomvoen* (the Commissariat for Military Affairs) headed initially by Podvoiskii, closed on the War Ministry and the General Staff in Petrograd. The acting War Minister, General Manikovskii, and the Chief of the General Staff, General Marushevskii, received immediate orders to halt all military operations and to prepare armistice talks with the Germans: both protested and both were put under arrest. At once cowed and confused, the General Staff continued to work, now under its new head, Lieutenant General N. M. Potapov, who had developed earlier contacts of his own with the Bolshevik "Military Organization." As head of the General Staff, Potapov acquired a specially appointed "comrade" (*tovarishch*) who was, in effect, deputy chief of the General Staff, charged specifically with the supervision of the several departments of *GUGSh*.

The subsequent history of the General Staff under Potapov and the *Stavka* under Bonch-Bruevich—where Bonch-Bruevich pronounced himself proudly as the first Soviet Chief of Staff—became inextricably involved in a dual and often conflicting process, dismantling the old Imperial Army and building a new "socialist Army," a Soviet fighting force. Though deeply distrustful of the "old" generals and the *Genshtabistyi* at large, the Bolshevik leadership found itself unable to dispense with their skills, a fact anticipated by many *Genshtabistyi* and exploited in his own way by Potapov, who stressed the "technical" role of the General Staff. Bonch-Bruevich, an ardent champion of a regular Army on the lines of the "old" Army, also pressed the point of this professionalism to Lenin, who was inclined to scoff at this much-vaunted "military work" as mere mumbo jumbo—*kakoe-to-zrechestvo*!

If he was not overawed by the "military mind," Lenin certainly recognized the role of and need for professional competence. The Army he desperately needed in the early weeks of 1918 could not be built without the competence possessed by the *Genshtabistyi*. Political labels and demagogic phrases did not build armies. The *Stavka* and the old General Staff did, in fact, disappear. Rather, they dipped below the political horizon, for on 8 May 1918 the All-Russian Supreme Staff, *Vserossiiskii Glavnyi Shtab* (*Vserosglavshtab*), emerged as a new focus of military organization: of its seven departments, no fewer than four—operations, organization, military topography, and military communications—were hauled straight out of *GUGSh*. The *Genshtabist* was dying, if not actually dead. Now the Red Army proceeded to shout, "Long live the *Genshtabist!*"

Reshaping the System: The Soviet Command Model

By the autumn of 1918, with the Soviet Republic in the grip of a vast and pitiless civil war made more ruinous by foreign intervention, Lenin and his associates had succeeded in organizing a "command machine," increasingly centralized if relatively simple, yet sturdy enough to serve Soviet military-political needs for almost two decades. In terms of military organization, the chaotic and inefficient "detachment" system, if not entirely suppressed, was steadily squelched in favor of a regular Army that, toward the close of 1918, consisted of twelve field armies (plus the Independent Western Army holding the western frontier line), forty-two rifle divisions, and three cavalry divisions. Four fronts (the northern, eastern, Caspian-

Caucasian, and the southern) were fully operational. A central and local military apparatus had been established, together with the military-administrative structure of the country (military districts). The mobilization process had been set in train, "command staff" was found by inducting the "military specialists" (and a start was made on training a "Red command" of "proletarian officers"), Party presence in the Army was secured by the commissars and the growing network of "cells" (*yacheika*, the primary Party unit), supply and the organization of "the rear" was brought under a semblance of rational organization and control.

Staff organization and the training of staff officers also demanded urgent attention. On 11 November 1918 the *RVSR* Field Staff (*Polevoi Shtab*) was created and made responsible for the planning of military operations, as well as having its own competence for the structure, manning, and training of field formations in operational zones. The first chief of the Field Staff was a former *Genshtabist*, Major General F. V. Kostyaev, who had voluntarily entered Soviet ranks in 1918, serving as "assistant" to the *voenruk* of the Petrograd District and thus to other appointments. The heart of the Field Staff was the Operations Administration (*Operativnoe upravlenie*), divided into sections (later Departments)—Operations, Intelligence, Naval Operations, Military-Topographic, and Administrative—all with a strength of thirty-six men (sixteen of them *voenspets*). *Genshtabistyi* were also specially assigned to intelligence duties. Yet another *Genshtabist*, Major General V. I. Mikhailov, ran the Operations Administration (though in the autumn of 1919, illness forced him to relinquish this post). The commissar was P. V. Vasilev, a former naval artificer and a man of some ability who was assigned to the Academy in 1919, but who, through eagerness to start upon this course, neglected his health and died suddenly. He was succeeded by M. R. Galaktionov, another able commissar who for all his lack of formal military education succeeded later in making quite a reputation with his military writings.

The main focus of the work of the Operations Administration was maintaining contact with the fronts and marking up the operational maps. Each front (or army) was assigned its own "chief" as liaison officer, who monitored operations and marked up the map situation. These officers would report directly to the duty officer/Operations, with a full report prepared for the Chief at noon and presented by the head of the Operations Administration and other section heads. The irascible and somewhat high-handed ex-Colonel Vatsetis, acting as *Glavkom*, and his Chief of Staff, Kostyaev, tended to dispense with advice and recommendations, but nemesis awaited them in the misfortunes attending their handling of operations on the southern front in the early summer of 1919. Kostyaev fell first and was succeeded as Chief of Staff by that versatile fellow M. D. Bonch-Bruevich, who proceeded to "pull rank" on Vatsetis in no uncertain terms—reminding the ex-colonel that he, Bonch-Bruevich, had been a full colonel lecturing in tactics at the

General Staff Academy when Vatsetis was a mere ensign student, and an indifferent one at that. The sparks flew mightily between Vatsetis and Bonch-Bruevich, but in the event, Vatsetis came off worse and was eventually relieved of his command. For a short while, until July 1919, when S. S. Kamenev (another ex-Imperial colonel) took up the post of *Glavkom*, Bonch-Bruevich acted as overall commander, but Kamenev brought in Lebedev as Chief of Staff, and Gusev arrived as the political representative of the *RVSR*. The Field Staff also moved to Moscow at this juncture and installed itself in the premises of the Aleksandrovsk Military School.

The establishment of the Field Staff as an operations directorate and the existence of *Vserosglavshtab* handling manpower, manning, and mobilization marked the Soviet equivalent of the old *GUGSh*, the "Main Administration of the General Staff," at least in terms of functions and competences. At a none-too-distant date these two entities—the Field Staff and *Vserosglavshtab*—were to be combined to form the Red Army Staff, but the days of a "unified staff" had not yet come.[15]

The idea of a "Red General Staff" (*Krasnyi General'nyi Shtab*), an institution that would be linked with its own "Soviet General Staff Academy," had actually been mooted earlier in 1918, but the desperate need for trained staff officers and the demands of the front pushed aside all these elaborate plans. It was all the more ironic, therefore, that the old General Staff Academy had barely escaped destruction earlier in the year (1918), thanks to Lenin's personal intervention. The newly bolshevized Main Administration for Military-Educational Institutions proposed in March 1918 to turn the General Staff Academy into a civilian institute of higher education, a step countermanded by Lenin, who, in turn, set up a special committee, headed by Podvoiskii, to look into the business of turning the General Staff Academy to Soviet use.

Complete reorganization, however, proved to be a daunting and time-consuming task: Order No. 316 of 3 May 1918, issued by the People's Commissariat for Military Affairs, prescribed reform that would transform the old General Staff Academy into the "Soviet General Staff Academy," and duly transferred it to the hinterland well out of harm's way—solicitude gone disastrously wrong, as the Academy found itself in the midst of the Czech Legion's revolt. The Academy withdrew to Kazan, where Vatsetis arrived in August 1918. In his capacity as front commander, he went at once to the Academy in order to appeal for volunteers to serve with his Red Army units. Only five men responded to his call; the remaining professors and students hung back ostentatiously. That sealed the fate of the old Academy. Vatsetis informed the commandant, Angdorskii, that the Academy was disbanded on the spot and could scatter to the winds. In fact, it scattered largely in one direction, for when Kazan fell to the Czech and White troops, the Academy personnel went over to them and moved subsequently to Vladivostok to prepare *Genshtabistyi* for the White armies.[16]

There was nothing for it but to start again, afresh. On 7 October 1918 the Republic *Revvoyensoviet* issued Order No. 47 establishing the Red Army General Staff Academy, which would open its doors no later than 1 November. The Academy would be located in Moscow, with former Imperial Lieutenant General A. K. Klimovich as its commandant. General supervision was vested in the Main Commissar of the Military-Educational Institutions Administration, I. L. Dzevaltovskii, and the immediate work of organizing the Academy was laid upon a special commission presided over by General Klimovich. This "organizational commission" sent out signals to fronts and military districts advising them of the selection of candidates for admission to the Academy, followed by a final telegram on 26 October to MDs and front staffs announcing the selection of candidates on 2 November between 10 A.M. and 5 P.M. In order not to weaken fronts and armies by denuding them of senior personnel, this first induction to the new Academy would be limited to two hundred men.

The intensity of the fighting at the fronts and the expansion of the scale of operations, however, made it imperative to produce more *"Red Genshtabistyi,"* and more speedily. According to Soviet calculations, in 1917 the Imperial Army had more than 1,600 *Genshtabistyi* available to undertake General Staff duties, while, in the spring of 1919, the Red Army could only count on 323 *"Red Genshtabistyi,"* and a mere 131 of these officers were serving with field formations. To speed up the output of trained officers, the so-called "parallel fast course" was introduced in February 1919, designed to last for nine months—but all too soon the *RVSR*, faced with a critical situation in the south, was forced to reduce this to five months. On the day of the graduation of the first student intake, 19 April 1919, Lenin himself attended the passing-out ceremony for "Soviet *Genshtabistyi,"* an occasion for some celebration but stamped with the urgency of the military situation as forty of the graduates left at once for the eastern front—a group including S. N. Voronov, M. M. Ol'shanskii, A. K. Parm, and V. A. Sedyakin, followed in short order by a graduate group dispatched to the southern front and yet another detachment to the same front (a group that included K. A. Meretskov, V. D. Sokolovskii, and I. V. Tyulenev). The western front also received an allotment of *Genshtabistyi*, including Ya. I. Alksnis, A. S. Danilov, and M. A. Sakharov. In July 1919 General Klimovich himself was posted to the eastern front, and the Academy stripped bare of students save for the men being rushed through the "parallel fast courses."[17]

Late in the autumn of 1919, after a savage burst of fighting and yet another dangerous turn of events, victory seemed to be assured when, in November, the Red Army's capture of Omsk destroyed Kolchak, the Soviet counteroffensive deflected Denikin's drive on Moscow from the south, and Trotskii's stirring defense of Petrograd held the city against Yudenich's sudden lunge from the northwest. Already, on 27 July 1919, Trotskii had instructed *Vserosglavshtab* to prepare a demobilization plan for the multi-million-man Red Army, though "the cadres" of the regular army must be preserved for the moment. However, these cadres should be deployed and distributed in such a manner as to facilitate the raising of military units by *Vsevobuch* (the Administration for the University Military Training), then controlled by Podvoiskii—in other words, a militia-type system. The establishment of *Vserosglavshtab* itself was reduced and the Field Staff of the *RVSR* ordered to carry out a review of the field armies, with the Inspector of Infantry (ex-Imperial General Badezhnyi) looking at units.

The *Vserosglavshtav* report, submitted to the *RVSR* on 3 September 1919, quietly omitted mention of a militia and concentrated on the size and shape of a regular Army, which could discharge four basic roles (securing the state frontiers, garrisoning, supporting civil order, and training the civil population for military service) when reduced to one-quarter of its present size (giving a peacetime establishment of 342,500 officers and men). The *RVSR* promptly threw this plan out and set up a broader inquiry, while the Central Committee at the end of November (1919) instructed the *RVSR* to investigate the "introduction of a militia system based on labor conscription." Podvoiskii now seized his opportunity at a *Komsomol* congress to propound his plans for a militia, or rather, the transition from a "standing Red Army" to a "Red Army of a militia type," involving the territorial cadres of *Vsevobuch* strengthened by the "special detachments" of worker detachments (*otryady osobovo naznacheniya*) while the Red Army retained picked "command and communist staff" elements to stay in post while regular units were disbanded.

Vatsetis, lately *Glavkom* (though superseded by another ex-Imperial officer, S. S. Kamenev), now produced his report for the *RVSR* on 18 January 1920. Though charged with devising a scheme to introduce a militia system, Vatsetis came down unequivocally on the side of a regular Army, a deliberate strategic dispersal to the east, and the creation of a "unified state military-technical base" in Siberia. The red Army must retain not fewer than twenty fully manned regular divisions, ten in the first echelon and ten in the second, with full support from artillery, engineer, and aviation units. Cavalry formations must also come within the regular establishment. The military situation of the Soviet Republic demanded nothing less than a regular Army and continuous combat readiness. The current *Glavkom*, S. S. Kamenev, and the field staff under its chief (P. P. Lebedev) lodged their own report a few days later and argued even more authoritatively for a regular Army with a strength fixed as from the beginning of 1920, namely sixty-six rifle and fifteen cavalry divisions. This force would be split into a first-line Army (twenty-one rifle and nine cavalry divisions) to defend the frontiers, while the remainder would be held back and used as cadres for the militia system.[18]

Having thus "saved" the regular Army, Kamenev and Lebedev went on to discuss the "militia Army," which would be raised on the basis of "divisional districts" into which the second-line regular divisions would be moved, and be used to train recruits on an annual basis—the men then passing into the reserve. This system would be supervised by a "Main Administration of the General Staff" or, alternatively, a "Greater General Staff" (*Bol'shoi General'nyi Shtab*) together with the People's Commissar for Military Affairs and the existing *RVSR*—assisted in turn by the Chief of the General Staff, the Chief of *Vserosglavshtab*, and the Chief of Supply. The main Administration of the General Staff could be formed by amalgamating the Field Staff and *Vserosglavshtab*, while at the local level there would be two administrative agencies to supervise both the military commissariats and the new "militia districts."[19]

POSTWAR CONSOLIDATION

Though reduced in strength, the Red Army survived. The new establishment—with fifty-nine rifle divisions, twenty-one cavalry divisions, and twenty-two rifle brigades—became effective as of 29 December 1920, though complete demobilization took almost three years. While demobilization absorbed the energies of several boards and commissions, little time was lost in refashioning the centralized military apparatus. The most important step was the creation of the Red Army Staff (*Shtab RKKA*), a unified body formed by combining the Field Staff (*Polevoi Shtab/RVSR*) with *Vserosglavshtab*: Order No. 336/41 of the *RVSR*, dated 10 February 1921, enacted this unification and appointed P. P. Lebedev, the ex-Imperial major general and Chief of the Field Staff since July 1919, the new Chief of the Red Army Staff. The rationale behind this unification centered on bringing three functions—war plans (operations), Red Army structure (organization), and mobilization—under a single competence.

The new Chief had three "assistant chiefs" subordinated directly to him, as well as the Chief of Military Communications (transport) and the Chief of the Main Administration for Military-Educational Institutions. These administrations, which had formerly formed part of the Field Staff of *Vserosglavshtab*, were now subordinated to the three "assistants" to the Chief of Staff (and later to the first and second assistants in a further redesignation). In line with the decision taken earlier, the responsibility for territorial units was removed from *Vsevobuch* and assigned to the Red Army Staff. The Main Administration of *Vsevobuch* retained its competence in training conscripts and also controlled the inspectorate of those formations organized under the militia scheme. At the same time, the inspectors formerly attached to the Field Staff were subordinated directly to the *Glavkom*, the C in C.

The new arrangement came into force officially on 14 February 1921, and this was followed in a matter of weeks by further consolidations. In April 1921 the old "Registry" (*Registratsionnoe upravlenie*) of the *RVSR* and the Intelligence Section of the Operations Administration were transformed into the Intelligence Administration of the Red Army Staff (*Razvedyvatel'noe upravlenie Shtaba RKKA: RSVR* Order No. 785/141). Other adjustments were made to the main administrations: the former "armored section" (*bronechast'*) of the Main Military Engineering Administration emerged in May 1921 as an independent administration, that of the "Chief of Red Army Armored Units" (*Upravlenie nachalnika bronesil RKKA*), all in recognition of the importance of "armored units" (armored trains and armored car squadrons) and the growing interest in the tank. This new Administration had an establishment of 120 men. The Main artillery Administration (*GAU*) was now united with the Administration of the Chief of Red Army Artillery and subordinated directly to that officer. The Main Military-Goods Traffic Administration (*Glavnoe upravlenie voenno-gruzovo transporta*) was disbanded and its functions distributed among relevant offices and sections in other Main Administrations. Finally, the duties of the inspectorates of infantry and cavalry were handed over to the troop training and troop service sections of the Red Army Staff.

The Red Army Staff organization was confirmed by governmental decree of 25 May 1922, and, for the first time, Soviet staff doctrine was promulgated more or less officially. Directly subordinated to the *Glavkom* in matters expressly stipulated in the regulation, the Red Army Staff was identified as the "executive organ" of the *RVSR* in administering all the armed forces of the Soviet Republic, the organization of national defense, combat training, and force structures, as well as strengthening defense potential. The Staff was organized into administrations and sections. The *administration* comprised Operations, Organization, Mobilization, "Command Staff," Troop Training, Internal Service, Signals, the Corps of Military Topographers, depots for Training Appliances for Units and Military Commissariats, together with the Central Administration for Military Communications and the Main Administration for Military-Educational Institutions. The *sections* included "manuals and reference," statistics on Red Army and Red Fleet losses, the administrative-economic, and the Military-Historical Commission. In addition, the Intelligence Administration was assigned to the Red Army Staff, while the Administration for Armored Units, the General Staff Academy, and the military section of the state archives were similarly subordinated to the Chief of the Red Army Staff.[20]

One of the great and enduring shortcomings of Imperial staff doctrine had been the failure to recognize the need to integrate operational and logistical planning. With the Chief of Military Communications under his direct control, the Chief of the Red Army Staff had the traditional "operations/logistics" relationship in his organization, but much remained to bring the motley array of "supply" organizations and agencies into some semblance of centralized order. To this end, *Chusonabarm* was wound up in August 1921 and *Glavsnabprodarm* in January 1922, with their functions being taken over by a new centralized body, the Chief of Supply (*Glavnyi nachal' nik snabzhenii: GNS* or *Glavnachsnab*). *Glavnachsnab* supervised those agencies connected with the Foreign Trade Commissariat, which made purchases abroad that were related to military needs and which also, together with the supply administration and a technical inspectorate, was the general planning body for coordinating army and naval requirements. The Main Military-Economic Administration (*Glavnoe Voenno-khozyaistvennoe upravlenie: GVKhU*) was also directly subordinated to *Glavnachsnab* and was responsible for supplying the Red Army with clothing, food, and fodder. The Air Force, the Main Engineering Administration, and the Main Artillery Administration combined both operations and supply within their own organizations, maintaining two separate "channels"—in operational matters to the *Glavkom*, in supply questions to *Glavnachsnab*. In Military Districts, supply came under a "district supply chief," who had the authority of "assistant to the commander" in supply matters and was subordinated to the *Revvoyensoviet* of the district or front or else to the formation commander. The district economic administration was also subordinated to the district *Nachsnab*, as were the engineering and artillery administrations for supply purposes.

This arrangement had serious shortcomings. In the first place, *Glavnachsnab* did not have a centralized organization at its disposal that could supervise current supply questions and also, at the same time, build up war stocks or plan for wartime economic mobilization. The combination of operational with supply functions in the "technical arms" (artillery, engineers) had its own deleterious effects and, in general, military bureaucracy flourished apace under this system, which retained too much of the emergency wartime centralization pattern that now forced units to wade through a sea of paper for the smallest trifle.

This flurry of reorganizaton and consolidation was accompanied by yet another process, the fury of argument and disputation over "military doctrine"—yet one more tactic to gain control of the military machine, even if the route was still more devious. Here the *Genshtabistyi*—ex-Imperial and "Red" alike—played energetic and highly political roles. The General Staff Academy had already begun to produce a stream of technical military works, but its main task was the education of senior officers and the preparation of *Genshtabistyi*. This mission was complicated toward the end of the Civil War, when the need to impart some military education to the officer corps as a whole led to the presence of regimental and battalion commanders (40 percent of the student course in 1920–21) and their immediate seniors, divisional commanders and their deputies (25 percent of the course), with staff officers as such making up only 12 percent of the course. Clearly change was required, and, during April–June 1921, the work of the Academy was reviewed by the *RVSR*, resulting in a change of name and the appointment of a new commandant. *RVSR* Order No. 1675 of 5 August 1921 redesignated the General Staff Academy the Military Academy of the Red Army (*Voennaya Akademiya RKKA*) and placed all military academies—Artillery, Military, Engineering, Military-Economic, Military Electrotechnical, and Naval—directly under the C in C (*Glavkom*), simultaneously relieving General Snesarev of his post as commandant of the General Staff Academy and appointing M. N. Tukhachevskii head of the new Military Academy of the Red Army.[21]

"RED COMMANDERS" AND A "RED STAFF"

It is an established convention in Soviet military historiography to describe the years from 1923–24/25 as the period of "military reform" (*voennava reforma*). Though technically accurate in the sense of identifying institutional change and improvement, this is also a euphemism that conceals the bitter internal struggle for control of the Soviet military establishment and a fierce political conflict that finally brought about the removal of Trotskii as Commissar for Military and Naval Affairs and brought Mikhail Frunze to the fore as his successor. The attack on Trotskii took two forms, beginning with a protracted and at times tense debate on "military doctrine" and broadening into an "investigation" of the shortcomings and maladministration within the military establishment as a whole. The debate on military doctrine was a strange mixture of personal feuding, abstract philosophizing, and Party intrigue, in which the dogged Frunze thrust himself against Trotskii to advance the cause of what he termed "unified military doctrine"—*edinaya voennaya doktrina*. The first shots in this "debate" were fired at the Tenth Party Congress in 1921, but it was at the Eleventh Congress (March 1922) that battle was really joined.

There can be no doubt that this was a genuine (and important) debate that makes its effects felt even today. The "Red commanders" argued that a "new" Army—and the Red Army was a uniquely new army—required a distinctive and "unified" military doctrine, one that bonded Marxism with specific military principles and military-operational characteristics drawn from the Red Army's victory in the Civil War. Frunze (in association with Gusev) set out to delineate the elements of a military-political strategy, a "unified doctrine," connected in turn with an analysis of the "historical revolutionary process." In essence, the Frunze-Gusev theses argued that in view of the inevitability of the "bloody battle of class enemies," the energies of the Soviet state must be directed to increasing its military capability and devising particular operational forms. The first principle, therefore, must be *aktivnost* (a combination of energy, action and initiative): from *aktivnost* there followed *the primacy of the offensive* and the implementation of a *maneuver strategy*, "maneuver operations on a large scale" that would enable the Red Army to use the geographical space at its disposal as well as compensating for its present technical shortcomings. The Red cavalry would provide means for rapid movement and deep maneuver—and at some future date the Red cavalry would become "armored cavalry." As for military organization, Frunze placed little faith in the militia and argued that any transition to a militia system could only be gradual and based on *Vsevobuch*: a regular Red Army was needed to defend the state and meet the demands of the world situation.

Never at a loss for an answer, Trotskii speedily poured his considerable resources of scorn and invective on these propositions, branding much of them as "pseudo-military doctrinairism." He abruptly dismissed out of hand the notion that there was a "special" proletarian way of waging war—during the Civil War the Soviet Republic simply employed those means and methods that lay at hand. As for its class context and connection, the Red Army was the "military embodiment" of the dictatorship of the proletariat, but military doctrine could not be expressly related to the class character of the state. Nor was it possible to discern in the offensive and maneuver any unique aspect of a proletarian military doctrine, for these formed part of the military doctrines of other states and other political conditions. Trotskii did not argue with the idea of "revolutionary war" in the context of the world revolution of the working class. He could not accept Frunze's contention, however, that the Civil War had been a "revolutionary war" in the sense of vindicating the principles of *aktivnost* and the offensive—quite the contrary, Trotskii insisted, the Civil War was largely a matter of dogged defense and judicious retreat.

These were but sighting shots in what proved to be an increasingly acrimonious and embittered debate, in which Trotskii seemed to score hit after palpable hit—but, in so doing, alienated imself increasingly from the group of "Red commanders" who were steadily edging their way to greater influence in the Red Army and were backed by political patrons with no love for Trotskii. Yet, Trotskii's dialectical brilliance was his own undoing at the Eleventh Congress; his stance also demonstrated that strange and somewhat brittle mixture of pragmatism with ideological commitment, so that he was forced to admit only qualified support for "revolutionary warfare" and to confess, finally, that a proletarian military doctrine could well exist though it might take some time to formulate. In the most unexpected fashion, Trotskii had backed himself onto the ropes. In even stranger fashion, Frunze failed to deliver the dialectical knockout, partly because he trapped himself in a tangle of detail—insisting on the unique place of maneuver—and partly because Lenin himself had warned him of the dangers of premature theorizing, "Communist swaggering." "It seems to me," Lenin advised, "that our military communists are still insufficiently mature to lay claim [*pretendovat'*] to the leadership of all military affairs."[22] That advice Frunze did not disclose publicly until Trotskii had been shunted off the military scene, but he did mute the stridency in his call for a proletarian military doctrine.

Since Engels himself had stipulated that the new proletarian state would have its "special expression" in military affairs and would create its own "special, new military method," Frunze could properly claim that he was on the side of the ideological angels. He chose, however, to ignore Engel's rider that the development of such a "proletarian military doctrine" would demand time—a point Trotskii seized on, suggesting that almost a generation would be needed. Lenin made much of the same point. Yet Frunze's very impetuosity seemed to transform him into the fiery revolutionary, and Trotskii's cold pragmatism cast him in the dubious role of a mere functionary, a strange inversion indeed—though both combined to eschew Tukhachevskii's firebrand plans for all-out international revolutionary war, supervised by an international Red general staff. Important though the Trotskii-Frunze debates were in the process of maneuvering for control of the Red Army, their significance far transcends mere political tactics. For the first (and last) time, the Soviet military-political elite embarked on a fundamental discussion of the nature of war and politics, the whole phenomena of military struggles and the relation of Marxism to military doctrine; here Frunze split his presentations into two parts—the political and the "technical" (the military content)—useful and at times illuminating, but inclined to cause him to confuse principle with detail.

For all of Trotskii's derision of Frunze's jejune views, it is those views that have passed into Soviet military-political traditions and perceptions. For Frunze, "strategy" was subsumed in policy, political strategy. The war he envisaged would be protracted and the struggle he delineated was equally protracted: in line with Imperial Russian military thinking, he placed little faith in the "lightning blow," but this did not preclude *aktivnost* and a speedy turn to the offensive. (By way of retrospective proof, the manner in which Frunze's views have been manipulated is a demonstration of their continuing validity or acceptability—a "strategy" of protracted conflict, *aktivnost* and maneuver in all military-political circumstances and the resort to the offensive. In present terms, Soviet military doctrine does approach the "unified" form suggested by Frunze, namely, the absolute primacy of the offensive, the emphasis on maneuver in tactical doctrine, the insistence on *aktivnost*— even "active defense"—the pursuit of *edinonachalie*, or "unitary, military-political command," the maintenance of a regular standing Army trained with due regard for previous operational experience and equipped with the most up-to-date weaponry.)

It was inevitable, therefore, that when these "military Communists" saw the opportunity to revamp the military system, they seized it avidly. The war scare of 1923 provided just that opening, when in June (1923) the Central Committee ordered an investigation of the Red Army and the Soviet military establishment as a whole. The separate investigation commissions fanned out, gathering mounds of material, all of which pointed to a lack of operational readiness in the Red Army, serious flaws in the "command staff," and either chaos or lethargy in the central apparatus. All this was designed to hurt Trotskii, though there were genuine grounds for seeing disarray and disorganization at almost every turn. Demobilization had wrought its own havoc upon the Red Army, whose strength had finally dropped to 600,000 at the beginning of 1924, though even this massive contraction did not suffice: in the summer of that year (1924), the strength of the Red Army was fixed at 529,856 men and the total strength of the military establishment at 562,000. The sheer economic impossibility of maintaining a larger standing Army also forced the "mixed" solution—regular divisions combined with a territorial militia—upon the military leadership, the first regular divisions (ten in all) reverting to this system in the winter of 1923.[23]

If this could be construed as a form of victory for Trotskii, it proved to be both brief and hollow. The reports of the investigating commission proved to be a devastating indictment of mismanagement and incompetence in military affairs. Trotskii, so it was reported, did nothing in the *Revvoyensoviet*, leaving matters entirely in the hands of his deputy, Sklyanskii, and the Chief of the Red Army Staff, P. P. Lebedev, neither of whom could provide "competent" direction of the Soviet Armed Forces. These central organs would have to be overhauled and restaffed to eliminate "unsuitable" personnel. The *Revvoyensoviet* and the Red Army staff were strongholds of bureaucratism and "paper pushing"; little had been done to move out the *voenspets* in favor of qualified Red commanders—the "dead hand" of the old Imperial officers held full sway, the *Sukhomlinovtsyi* who paralyzed the work of the *RVSR*. This stream of calculated complaint poured out at the February (1924) plenary session of the Central Committee, leading to the wholesale reconstitution of the *Revvoyensoviet SSSR* and the virtual displacement of Trotskii. Frunze became deputy chairman on 11 March 1924 (and chairman in January 1925); Voroshilov—that particular crony of Stalin—joined the *RVS SSSR* and assumed command of the Moscow MD; A. S. Bubnov took over the Political Administration (*PUR*) and joined the new *RVS, together with Budenny, Voroshilov, S. S. Kamenev, G. K. Ordzhonikidze, I. S. Unshlikht, and A. F. Myasnikov. With Voroshilov and Budenny installed on the RVS SSSR*, Stalin could now feel that he had his own men strategically placed in the highest echelon.

On 4 February (1924) the *RVS SSSR* had already taken matters into its own hands and appointed a special commission under Frunze to draft a wide-ranging plan for reform of the military system. Nor was this the end of Frunze's new lease of competence: on 19 April (1924) he was appointed head of the Military Academy, thus affording him the opportunity to put certain of his ideas into immediate practice—an opportunity he did not neglect. Within little more than a month the plans for the reorganization of the central military administration were complete and issued under Frunze's signature as *RVS SSSR* Order No. 446/96 on 28 March 1924. The new arrangement subordinated the following administration and agencies directly to the *RVS SSSR*:

1. *The Red Army Staff (Shtab RKKA)*, responsible for general defense preparations
2. *The Red Army Inspectorate (Inspektorat RKKA)*,[24] responsible for combat training and the inspectorates of the Red Army, the Navy, and the Air Fleet
3. *The Political Administration (Politicheskoe Upravlenie RKKA)*, charged with political and cultural-educational work as well as the "political direction" of the commissar apparatus
4. *The Red Army Administration (Upravlenie RKKA)*, the basic administrative organ supervising day-to-day matters
5. *The Air Fleet Administration*, to direct training and combat readiness, also specialist supply
6. *The Naval Administration*, to direct training and combat readiness, also ensuring specialist supply
7. *The Red Army Chief of Supply (Nachal'nik snabzheniya RKKA)*
8. *The Commission for the Investigation of War*, charged with general study of the defense of the USSR
9. *The Council for Red Army Training (Sovet po podgotovke RKKA)*, responsible for coordinating training
10. *The Military-Medical Administration (Voenno-sanitarnoe upravlenie)*
11. *The Military-Veterinary Administration (Voenno-veterinarnoe upravlenie)*

The distinguishing feature of this reforming process was the winding up of the post of *Glavkom*—a relic of Civil War days—and the differentiation of three functions that had hitherto been concentrated in the Red Army Staff, namely, operations, administration, and troop training. However, the Red Army Staff retained its previous primacy, and to underline this, Frunze himself was appointed Chief of Staff on 1 April 1924, by special *RVS* order (No. 78), running concurrently with his post as Deputy Chairman of the *RVS*. The revised arrangements also brought changes in command appointments: Tukhachevskii became assistant to Frunze and commissar of the Red Army Staff, together with B.M. Shaposhnikov as a second assistant chief; N. N. Petin took over the Red Army Administration (*GU RKKA*); S. S. Kamenev—latterly *Glavkom*—the Inspectorate; N. S. Unshlikht, Supply; E. S. Pantserzhanskii, the Naval administration; S. M. Budenny, the cavalry inspectorate; and I. E. Yakir, the Administration for Military-Educational Institutions. The reorganization was also accompanied by a "cold purge" that reduced the personnel in the central staff and administration by 847 (to a total of 2,885), cut the average age, and also introduced a larger cohort of Party members.[25]

During the work of the investigating commissions, the Red Army Staff had come in for heavy criticism. It was far from fulfilling its role as the "brain of the army" and had shown itself far from competent in handling mobilization plans, as well as being isolated from troop units. Worse still, the Staff stood accused of being too much an agency or instrument for the propagation of Trotskii's ideas. At the end of 1923, some attempt was made to rationalize the work of the Staff by introducing two separate "assistants to the chief," each with his own administration—Administration No. 1 (*Upravlenie 1-go*) was concerned with operational questions and the preparation of war plans, the collection of information on potential enemies, troop training, internal troop duties and troop living conditions, geodesic work and the supply of maps, while Administration No. 2 (*Upravlenie 2-go*) was repsonsible for the organization and deployment of troop units, mobilization and the military registration of human and animal resources, as well as the service conditions of command and administrative staff. The establishment of these two administrations was designed to "unify" the work of the Red Army Staff by concentrating operational, mobilization, and administrative functions in one agency—precisely the arrangement that the Frunze reforms intended to undo, all with the intention of freeing the Red Army Staff from routine tasks and administrative chores. In a celebrated phrase, Frunze emphasized that the Red Army Staff must be not only "the brain of the Red Army" but should become nothing less than "the military brain [*voennyi mozg*] serving our entire Soviet state. . . . "

In its new guise as an "operational organ" largely freed from routine administrative matters, the Red Army Staff was charged with preparing the country against possible attack, working out operational and mobilization plans, planning the structure of the armed forces, and utilizing the experience of the Great War and the Civil War, all to be managed through its several administrations (Operations, Intelligence, Organization, Mobilization, Military Communications, and Military Topography), together with its sections (military engineering, military-historical). The March 1924 reorganization also set up two new committees, one for mobilization (*Mobilizatsionnyi komitet*) and one for military-engineering defense works (*Komitet po inzhenernoi oborone*), that were attached directly to the Red Army Staff. Clearly this emphasis on practical operational planning and the investigation of wartime experience (particularly the Civil War) reflected Frunze's own views, which he proceeded to press with great vigor on the Red Army Military Academy—putting "unified military doctrine" into practice, though without flaunting it as much.

Frunze's address of 1 August 1924 to the *RKKA* Military Academy was, if nothing else, an exposition of his view of the "Red General Staff" and the role of the Red *Genshtabist*. It would be impossible, he emphasized, for the Red General Staff to execute its true mission if it remained wedded only to a "nation-state point of view." Rather, it should be thought of as a "potential nucleus" [*potentsialnoe yadro*], as a potential center for a "wider Red General Staff," able to help the proletariat of those countries unable themselves to subdue their own class enemies, though in all frankness such a Red General Staff did not exist as yet. There were major shortcomings in training and education, shortcomings that Frunze had every intention of correcting, implementing his perception of the "unitary" link between Marxism and military doctrine. After a matter of months (December 1924), in celebration of the sixth anniversary of the Academy, Frunze was more explicit and more pointed in his enunciation of the "guiding principles" for the training of the Soviet high command. The General Staff in the old Imperial system had been a caste, laying claim by birth and educational attainment to the direction of all military matters—a curious "requotation" from what Lenin had said to Frunze about the military Communists "laying claim to leadership in all military affairs"—but Red *Genshtabistyi* were no "caste" (*kastovaya gruppa'*), being essentially a "branch of the Soviet organism." Second, the Academy was a worker-peasant institution (with 72 percent of its students drawn from workers and peasants); third, the Red Army commander must be not merely a technician but also a socially responsible and responsive individual; fourth, though the command staff was not homogeneous, *edinonachalie* must form the basis of command organization; fifth, Marxism must be the guiding principle with regard to military science (*voennaya nauka*); sixth, the USSR stands under threat of capitalist attack; and, finally, the unity of Army and Party confers positive military advantage. That latter proposition was the key point: the Red Army was a "class army," and its training and education, therefore, must be as singular as it structure.

An entire generation of Soviet soldiers, many of them finally attaining very high rank during the "Great Patriotic War" and afterward, was subject to the impact of Frunze's reforms in the military-educational system, changes designed to bring "unified military doctrine" (without actually using that term directly) as much to the fore as possible. From the outset, Frunze made the point that the work of the *RKKA* Military Academy labored under the handicap of not enjoying any real identity of views that could regulate military training and education for high command. In addition to "operational-tactical training," Frunze demanded extensive ideological awareness and close contact with troop life: all this necessitated quite considerable change in the organization and the teaching programs of the Academy. At the end of 1925, Frunze ordered the establishment of three faculties in the Academy—the "basic course," the eastern faculty, and the "improvement courses" for senior commanders. In the "basic course," containing the "basic" faculty with its three courses, (first, second, and third), 330 students were duly enrolled, with 60 to 80 assigned to the other two faculties. To the faculty chairs (*kafedry*), Frunze introduced the most experienced commanders he could find, bringing in Tukhachevskii to the chair of strategy, V. K.

Triandafillov (Deputy Chief of the Red Army Staff) to the chair of operational art, K. B. Kalinovskii to the chair of armored warfare (Kalinovskii simultaneously holding the post of Inspector of Armored Troops and becoming one of the major Soviet theoreticians on tank warfare), and D. M. Karbyshev to the chair of military engineering. At the same time, a single faculty chair was established for foreign language instruction, with 40 percent of the students learning English, 30 percent German, 20 percent French, and 10 percent Polish or Romanian.[26]

If Frunze was not willing to surrender to any traditional view of military doctrine, he intended to ensure that the RKKA Academy was not merely a carbon copy of the old Imperial General Staff Academy. To this end he abolished the basic distinction between "junior" and "senior" courses—the Imperial style—and in the "basic course," with its three components, stipulated that the first course should treat tactics of the various arms as well as general tactics; the second course should provide further instruction on general tactics; and the third should teach military operations of armies and fronts, the problems of preparing military districts for war operations, and the conduct of war. Operational art and strategy were to be the main themes pursued at the Academy in the future, with a number of recondite academic subjects such as "the philosophy of war" eradicated from the curriculum

THE ROLE OF THE RED ARMY STAFF

The premature death of Frunze in 1925 brought Voroshilov, intimate of Stalin and military ignoramus—another adherent of that famous and charmed circle, the First Cavalry Army—to the post of People's Commissar for Military and Naval Affairs. The advent of Voroshilov ushered in another spurt of reform in the central administration, bearing on that unsolved question of the relationship between "command" and "staff" functions. Under Order No. 390 of 12 July 1926, the recasting of the central military administration made the following provisions with respect to the *Red Army Staff*:

1. All functions relating to the defense of the country and the preparation of the army for war would be concentrated in the Red Army Staff, with all organs and administrations (Supply, Navy, and Air Force) being incorporated into the Staff, while by the same token, agencies not directly concerned with defense preparations (such as the Military-Topographical Administration) would be excluded from the Staff organization

2. The Red Army Staff itself would henceforth consist of four administrations (*upravlenie*) and a Scientific Section/Manuals and Regulations (*Nauchno-ustavnyi otdel*)

3. *First Administration*—the Operations Administration—was to deal with questions of a strategic nature, with naval defense, engineering defense, and staff duties

4. *Second Administration*—Organization/Mobilization—handled all

questions relating to organizing and deploying in the event of war, securing military supply, and mobilization planning

5. *Third Administration*—Military Communications—dealt with transport (military traffic)

6. *Fourth Administration*—Intelligence

7. The Scientific Section/Manuals and Regulations was under the direct control of the Chief of Staff with all the competence of a GS section.[27]

In yet another rearrangement of responsibility for training, the training administrations and the Inspectorate of the Red Army, together with troop mobilization, recruiting, and routine military administrative matters, were subordinated to the Main Administration of the Red Army (*Glavnoe upravlenie RKKA*), with seven sections—military educational establishments, military topography (though the Red Army Staff could assign work directly to this section), command staff, troop mobilization and manning, troop service and organization, cavalry remounts, and the Inspectorate (supervising artillery, cavalry, engineering, signals, and chemical warfare training). The *RVS SSSR*, for its part, exercised direct control over the Red Army Supply Administration, the Political Administration (*Politicheskoe upravlenie RKKA*), the Naval Administration, the Air Force Administration, the Military-Medical Administration, and the Military-Veterinary Administration.

This new scheme came into force on 1 September 1926, by which time M. N. Tukhachevskii had taken over as Chief of the Red Army Staff (a tenure that lasted until May 1928), all amidst a period of sustained controversy over the role of the Red Army Staff in peace and in war. At the same time, there was continuous conflict over the respective competence of the Red Army Staff and the Main Administration of the Red Army, for, in spite of the effort to demarcate these bodies, their functions inevitably overlapped, particularly in the question of troop training and readiness. Two views prevailed about the function of the Red Army Staff, with one school representing senior officers who had served with or were actually working in the staff—S. S. Kamenev, M. N. Tukachevskii, and latterly B. M. Shaposhnikov—and setting out a comprehensive version of the competence of the Staff, including its role as the "working organ" of the supreme commander, and thus directly involved in the conduct of military operations in various theaters of war, while a second segment of opinion contested this claim for the hegemony of the Staff.

Not surprisingly, Boris Shaposhnikov, himself an ex-Imperial *Genshtabist* and a volunteer into the Soviet ranks in 1918,[28] set out the case for the "greater General Staff" idea, publishing his influential work *Mozg armii* (or rather, the first volume) in 1927, a study of the Austro-Hungarian General Staff from 1908 to 1916. This was an academic theme, but one that plainly advertised the widest role for the General Staff, which *must* of necessity play a central part not only in the preparation of the country for war, but also in the direction of the entire war effort—in short, the implementation of an "integrated strategy" that aligned military and political objectives, thus fusing national leadership into a military-political entity. Not that Shaposhnikov was propounding a wholly novel idea, for in 1926 ex-Imperial General Svechin's fundamental work *Strategiya* (*Strategy*) had advocated the same "greater General Staff" idea, a Staff tied very closely to the political leadership, to the point of virtual integration.

In May 1928 Shaposhnikov assumed the post of Chief of the Red Army Staff adding one more distinction to his career, but he had to face formidable opposition from those who feared the possible "hegemony" of the Red Army Staff, with Levandovskii in particular, as chief of the Main Administration of the Red Army, leading the opposition. Levandovskii's view was that there was a case for two "staffs," one operational and committed to planning (war planning), the other concerned with administration and day-to-day military matters (the province of the Main Administration). Meanwhile, the pretensions of the Red Army Staff to a special place within the Soviet military system came under direct attack, with open expressions of concern about the possible "dictatorship of the General Staff" and attacks on the "young Academy men" (*Akademiki*)—the graduates of the Frunze Military Academy—who had become "infected with the bacillus of the Great General Staff" (*zarazheny batsilloi Bol'shovo genshtaba*). In April 1929, in response to Shaposhnikov's proposals for yet more centralization within the system, Levandovskii returned the tart reply that there was no place in the conditions of a "proletarian state" for a "Chief of the General Staff" as this was conceived in bourgeois circles, and Shaposhnikov's proposals were unthinkable, as well as being downright dangerous.[29]

Already, in March 1928, the *RVS SSSR* had confirmed the first major regulation on the form of wartime field administration—*Osnovy postroeniya polevovo upravleniya voisk v voennoe vremya*—which invested the *RVS* itself with "general control" of all frontline forces and "the rear," while direct control of military operations, in particular theaters of war, passed to the Commander in Chief of the Soviet armed forces. The chairman of the *RVS* must approve and confirm the general war plan and the separate campaign plans adopted by the C in C, but the C in C, while following the *RVS* directives, would be independent and personally responsible for the direction of the field forces and for the organization of "rear services" in the immediate zone of war operations. It was assumed that, in war, the People's Commissariat for Military and Naval Affairs (*NKVM*) would discharge these functions related to the direction of frontline and rear affairs. No special agency or institution designed to operate specifically with and for the C in C was envisaged in the 1928 regulations for wartime command and control.

A number of administrative adjustments in 1928 more or less brought the period of "military reform" to an end, though this hardly closed down the debate on the place of the Staff within the system. The 1928 regulations confirmed the position of the People's Commissar for Military and Naval Affairs as the "immediate chief" of the Soviet armed forces in peacetime and the "central apparatus" made up of the Red Army Staff, the Main Administration of the Red Army, the Political Administration, the Supply Administration, Naval and Air Force administrations, and the Central Financial Administration. The "Commission for Research into War" was wound up and the Red Army Training Council (*Sovet po podgotovke RKKA*) suffered the same fate—but these bodies were superseded by a new group that corresponded more immediately to the needs of the Red Army now that forced industrialization was beginning to bite with the first of the Five-Year Plans, the "Military-Scientific Research Committee" (*Voenno-nauchnyi issledovatel'skii komitet*), committed to advising the *RVS* on questions of modern military technology and weapons development.

THE BATTLE FOR THE STAFF

The struggle over prestige, prerogatives, and competence of the Red Army Staff occupied a conspicuous place in the attention of the Soviet military and political leadership in the late 1920s. It was a battle fought over principles and personalities, with the rough, tough Civil War commanders objecting to the ideas advanced by the "*Akademiki*" (the Academy graduates) and the adherents of the Staff, an opposition supported by none other than the deputy chairman of the *Revvoyensoviet*, I. S. Unshlikht, who was determined to defend the integrity of the central military administration as a whole against the encroachment of the staff. What one side feared was precisely what the other desired, namely, the concentration in the hands of the Staff of "a leading role in all questions concerning the organization and the operational control of the Red Army." Tukhachevskii had fallen at this fence: he had proposed to the *RVS* that the Red Army Staff should be the supreme centralized instrument, able to plan, organize, recommend, and discharge effective inspectorate functions, and, when his proposal was turned down, he asked that he be relieved of his post as Chief of the Red Army Staff. This was duly arranged, and it was at the behest of Stalin himself that Shaposhnikov took over the Red Army Staff in May 1928 and Tukhachevskii—that fiery thorn in Stalin's flesh—went to command the Leningrad MD.

This particular patronage did not prevent Shaposhnikov from speaking out in favor of a strengthened Red Army Staff—in fact, there is much to suggest that Stalin was inordinately interested in Shaposhnikov's ideas and came to respect "*shkola Shaposhnikova*," for all his mocking reference to it. For all of Shaposhnikov's arid erudition, even his labored pedantry in the cumbersome *Mozg armii*, he single-mindedly worked on the theme of *upravlenie*—in modern parlance, "command and control." Shaposhnikov understood quite clearly that the outcome of a future war would depend to a large degree on the effectiveness of "command and control," as much as on the fighting qualities and heroism of the frontline forces. He also grasped that the general staff would have a key role to play and must begin to exercise its specialized functions in peacetime as well as in war. It was therefore, a victory of some considerable significance when the Red Army Staff acquired control over mobilization. Shaposhnikov argued cogently and successfully that it was absurd for the Red Army Staff to be charged with planning strategic deployment and yet be excluded from any control over mobilization. The battle was well and truly joined with the Main Administration of the Red Army (*GURKKA*), and while Shaposhnikov was mindful of the power of this agency, he argued that the voice of the Red Army Staff should be heard above all others in defense matters. And thus it was in January 1930 that mobilization passed under the control of the Red Army Staff.

Shaposhnikov also put his finger on the enduring weak spot of both the Imperial and the Red Army—staff organization and manning, *shtabnaya rabota*. Though a non-Party man, he deftly singled out Engels in support of his arguments about the importance of staff work and staff organization; his ideological rectitude was unassailable! In his lectures on the major 1929 exercises in the Belorussian MD, Shaposhnikov nevertheless painted an impressive and penetrating picture of a future war—one that to a large degree, and particularly in *its opening phases*, would be a war of maneuver, followed by a phase of immense attrition in weapons and equipment, with the armies of the major contestants having lost their professional component and being forced to rely upon "militia" elements (that is, contingents of conscripts lacking extensive military training); finally, the high rate of attrition in weapons and equipment would mean a mighty burden placed upon "the rear." The emphasis on maneuverability would demand rapid and bold decisions on the part of commanders, not only making decisions but also seeing them put into practice, while it would be essential to grasp the means of controlling new types of forces.

Shaposhnikov's successor as Chief of the Red Army Staff, A. I. Egorov, continued to press for the closest coordination of agencies and institutions at the top, both in peace and in war, in order to fashion an instrument capable of "strategic command and control"—strategicheskoe rukovodstvo. Shaposhnikov took command of the Frunze Academy, where he spared no effort to develop and to inculcate a "theory of staff work" fitted to the newest developments in the Red Army. During this period, the early 1930s, the "theory" of the General Staff was also developed, a theory that saw in the General Staff the "operational organ" of the C in C and the agency that coordinated the work of military institutions engaged in preparing the Soviet armed forces for war. To change the metaphor, from the "brain of the army," the General Staff was to establish itself as the "powerhouse" (*generator*) of the military system, committed to applying "scientifc foresight" in unraveling the nature of any future war, developing the "military-technical" capabilities of the country, and evaluating the military-political implications of war situations.[30]

This theoretical work in the field of command organization/staff functions and operational forms—"operations in depth" (*glubokii boi*)—exercised a profound and durable influence on the development of the Soviet armed forces as a whole. A certain sense of urgency was also imparted by the threatening international scene, as Japan invested Manchuria and Germany turned to Hitler, thus posing a "two-front" threat to the USSR. The Red Army was also fortunate in having a galaxy of talent at its disposal, with Tukhachevskii as Chief of Ordnance (*Nachal'nik vooruzheniya*) playing a key role in forcing the technological pace and in adapting tactical doctrine to fit the new "armament norms." Though the Red Army Staff had not yet gained full control of combat training, the Staff worked closely with the Combat Training Administration under Sedyakin, and Tukhachevskii frequently acted as both coordinator and mediator, in addition to producing his own "school" of tactical thinkers—Uborevich, Yakir, Alksnis (at the Air Force), Isserson (on operations in depth), and Triandafillov. All of them were involved in developing new techniques—high-speed mechanized forces and airborne troops in particular—which were demonstrated to foreign military observers in the major maneuvers held in 1934.

THE RETURN OF THE GENERAL STAFF

Yet another bout of reform and reorganization in 1934 not only advanced the cause of further centralization but also brought the creation of the General Staff, the Red Army General Staff, within sight. On 20 June 1934 the old *Revvoyensoviet SSSR*—a survivor from Civil War days—was abolished and replaced with the People's Commissariat for Defense of the USSR (the precursor of the present Ministry of Defense), headed by the People's Commissar for Defense. The statute governing the powers of the *Narkomat oborony*, issued by the Central Executive Committee (*TsIK*), was designed in the first place to eliminate the dualism inherent in having both the Defense Commission attached to the Council of Commissars (*Komissiya oborony pri SNK SSSR*) and the *Revvoyensoviet SSSR*. The new statute (which remains essentially unchanged to this day) prescribed the tasks of the *Narkomat oborony* as "drafting plans for the development, construction and equipment of the Red Army and Red Fleet, directing the military and political training of Soviet servicemen and those liable for military service in war, the operational employment of the Soviet armed forces in peace and war, defense construction, anti-aircraft defense of the USSR, developing and perfecting armaments and military technology, securing supplies, supervising induction into military service (and recall of reservists), directing the medical and veterinary services and attending to pensions and family allowances for Soviet military personnel. . . . " The 1934 statute also subordinated troop commanders directly to the Defense Commissar, who remained, as before, Klementi Voroshilov.

While this reorganization demonstrated the growing trend toward "one-man command," not least by increasing the powers of the Defense Commissar within the Defense Commissariat, the Red Army Staff also received a boost by acquiring control of combat training—an objective long pursued by Egorov. In 1934 Sedyakin's Combat Training Administration (*UBP*) was brought within the orbit of the Red Army Staff rather than being directly subordinated to the Defense Commissar, a state of affairs that had been introduced in January 1931. At the same time another element of "dualism" was eradicated with the change in the status of the Main Administration of the Red Army (*GURKKA*), which now became the Red Army Administrative-Mobilization Administration, charged with manning, troop organization, and establishment tables, troop mobilization, conditions of service and day-to-day matters. All this, however, redounded to the benefit of the Red Army Staff, which under this revised scheme of things was emerging quite indisputably as the main "coordinating" body at the highest level. In addition, the Staff had a firm grip on both combat training and mobilization (though freed from the routine of administration). The Staff was charged directly with planning deployment and wartime operational roles; the structure and the operational utilization of all ground, naval, and air forces; the organization of "the rear"; and supply of matériel in time of war; as well as preparing potential theaters of military operations (*TVD*s) and securing military communications (road and rail facilities). The Red Army Staff was concerned not only with preparations for war, but also with the actual battlefield employment and direction of Soviet military forces.

The 1934 statute on the *Narkomat oborony* established the basic form of the modern Soviet military system. The final step was taken in September 1935, when the Red Army Staff gave way to the formal creation of that other major institution, the General Staff—*General'nyi shtab RKKA*. Not long afterward (on 11 April 1936), the picture was filled out completely with the restitution to the General Staff of its own Academy, the Red Army General Staff Academy (*Akademiya General'novo shtaba RKKA*). In just a little less than twenty years, the wheel had come full circle, from the demise of the General Staff and the abolition of its academy, to the restoration of both within the Soviet system. The *Genshtabistyi* were back in full force and in fitting style.

For the Soviet command, 1935 could undoubtedly be inscribed as *annus mirabilis*. With the establishment of the Red Army General Staff in September 1935—a belated recognition that a centralized system required a strong staff, one not without some measure of independence—came the announcement on the same day (22 September) of formal ranks for the Red Army, with Marshal of the Soviet Union forming the newest and most senior rank. Not much later, in November 1935, the *TsIK* conferred the appointment of Marshal of the Soviet Union on Budennyi, Voroshilov, Yegorov, Blyukher, and Tukhachevskii, and the rank of Army Commander First Grade (the designation "General" was as yet eschewed) on the commanders of the Moscow, Leningrad, Belorussian, and Ukrainian Military Districts. Yegerov, one of the new Marshals, took over the post of Chief of the Red Army General Staff, charged with supervising general problems of national defense, planning the force structure and the mobilization of the armed forces as well as their training programs.

Trotskii pronounced the transformation of the Red Army in 1935 as nothing short of a revolution in its own right, though this was no compliment but rather a barbed observation on the nature of the Stalinist regime—that the armed forces now represented "the most finished expression" of the degeneration worked under Stalin, for leadership had been replaced by the weight of bureaucratism, with all the dangers of stultification.

Though the proponents of a stronger staff had won the day, this scarcely solved the problem of providing adequately trained personnel for the "higher direction" of military operations and furnishing a "military brain" for the Soviet armed forces. In spite of the expansion of military education in the Red Army, with new academies springing up like mushrooms in the early 1930s, neither "all-arms" training nor military-technical education was preparing officers for higher command. On the contrary, the function of the new academies was to train specialists to man the increasingly diversified arms. None of the academies attended to one of the most pressing problems, the "operational-strategic problems" of a future war, though this issue had been investigated by a number of individual commanders, such as Tukhachevskii, Yegorov, and Triandafillov, and military theorists, such as Lapchinskii, Eideman, Isserson, and Shilovskii. These separate studies and researches were leading to the evolution of the theory of "operations in depth," as well as the elaboration of "combined arms" activity on the battlefield, but nowhere was this studied in detail, in terms of large-scale operations at army and "front" level.[31]

The analysis of the results of the 1936 war games confirmed that education and training for "high command" was essential. There was no uniformity of view in the matter of conducting large-scale operations. Although the Frunze Academy ran courses in its "operational faculty," these were for middle-grade officers and did not comprehend the full scope of conducting operations—"combined arms" operations—with large forces of armor, aviation, and parachute troops, as prescribed in the evolving format of "operations in depth." To this end, Voroshilov in February 1936 summoned an enlarged session of the Military Soviet attached to the Defense Commissariat, where the question of education for higher command was debated at length. While it was agreed that the Frunze Academy was turning out commanders to hold posts at the regiment-division level, what was lacking was an institution to train officers for high command and also to carry through systematic studies of *operational art* and *strategy*. The Central Committee therefore approved the reestablishment of the General Staff Academy to train officers for high command and, under the guidance of the General Staff, to pursue studies of strategy.

PLANNING VERSUS PRECONCEPTIONS

In the summer and early autumn of 1940, the General Staff set about preparing a major report for the Central Committee and drafting a general defense plan: Vasilevskii, Vatutin, and G. K. Malandin worked on these submissions under the supervision of Marshal Shaposhnikov. The defense plan rested on the assumption that the potential enemy and main opponent of the Soviet Union was Nazi Germany, with Italy an associate, though Italian forces would be able to mount only limited operations in the Balkans and thus would not constitute a direct threat to Soviet frontiers. Finland would take Germany's side, Romania was a typical "raw material base" for Germany and patently pro-Fascist, while Hungary would also fight on Germany's side. Marshal Shaposhnikov took the view that any major war would be confined to the *western* frontiers of the USSR, though a Japanese attack could not be excluded entirely and adequate forces must be maintained in the east to guarantee "stability."

Shaposhnikov went on to argue that German operations against the USSR would involve a concentration running *northward* from the mouth of the river San. It followed, therefore, that the Red Army should be deployed in strength from the shores of the Baltic to the Polesian marshes, that is, within sectors comprising the northwestern and western fronts. The "southerly axis" could also be secured by two fronts, but with smaller forces. Once German forces had concentrated, they would require ten to fifteen days to deploy into operational positions on the western frontiers of the Soviet Union. This operational assessment—which was remarkably accurate, virtually mirroring the actual planning then taking place in the German command for war against Russia—was submitted to Stalin, though without any date projected for the outbreak of war itself.

Stalin and the Politburo considered the General Staff assessment in September 1940. Shaposhnikov was not present, for he had already been dismissed as CGS and replaced by Meretskov. Stalin admitted to Shaposhnikov that he had been right over Finland, but the time had come to show the world that the Red Army had learned the lessons of Finland—the high command had to be reshuffled and Shaposhnikov had to go. The removal of Shaposhnikov severely weakened the General Staff and the supervision of the Operations Directorate, where the post-purge officers were only just finding their feet. Meretskov was no substitute (and did not last very long as CGS), but it was with Meretskov that Stalin reviewed the Shaposhnikov plan in September, when Stalin altered the line of the main German thrust from a northerly to a *southwesterly axis*—arguing that the main German force would deploy along this axis, for here was the greatest concentration of Soviet industry, the grainlands, and the sources of raw material. The General Staff consequently received Stalin's personal instruction to redraft the main operational plan not later than 15 December 1940, to work out new movement plans with the Commissariat for Communications, and to brief Military District commands so that they might prepare their own operational plans no later than 1 January 1941.[32]

The revised Soviet plan envisaged a Soviet counterblow after the concentration of the main body of the Red Army. In the first stage of preliminary strategic operations, the covering armies deployed in the frontier regions would conduct active defensive operations supported by aviation and front reserves in order to beat back enemy incursion—all to secure the concentration and deployment of the main Soviet force committed to launching the counterblow. The General Staff plan for the defense of the frontiers specified blocking enemy incursions, stubborn defense using "fortified districts" (*URs*) and field fortifications, air defenses to screen movement by road and rail, persistent reconnaissance to determine enemy strength and deployment, air attacks on enemy concentrations, and defense against both parachute troops and enemy infiltration. In the event of any enemy breakthrough, powerful mechanized forces with antitank and air support would counterattack: all Soviet forces would fight to liquidate enemy penetrations and then carry operations on to *enemy* territory.

The General Staff duly incorporated Stalin's own estimate of the main German thrust—the German command in the opening stages would try to concentrate as speedily as possible on the southwestern axis to strike into the Ukraine and the Donets, thereafter advancing on the Caucasus and isolating the USSR from its sources of food and raw materials. There might well be a further German concentration in the north while attacks from East Prussia and central Poland, aimed at the "Smolensk gate," would develop an attack in the direction of Moscow. Finnish and Romanian troops would also strike with the German armies. In December 1940 a high-level command study conference debated the lessons to be learned from the war in Poland and in France, particularly the characteristics of the "initial phase"—with a form of consensus emerging, to the effect that, in any war involving the Soviet Union, the belligerents would require a specific time in which to concentrate and deploy their forces. The "received wisdom" was that the new German methods of waging war could be effective only in the case of a powerful state attacking one much weaker, whereas in the case of an attack on a powerful state, disposing of equal or even greater "military-economic potential," the aggressor *could not achieve surprise* and *could not bring his main force* to bear immediately.

Fundamental mistakes were made by both parties. The first was Stalin's switch of the defensive axis from the north to the southwest, dictated (according to Zhukov) by his view that Nazi Germany could not wage a protracted war without the vital resources located in southern Russia. The second derived from the failure of the professional military to draw accurate conclusions about German "war doctrine," in its *widest sense*. Both the Defense Commissariat and the General Staff assumed that a Soviet-German war would follow the orthodox pattern, with the main forces engaged only after several days of frontier battles and with the conditions for concentration and deployment more or less the same for both Germany and the Soviet Union. *The failure to comprehend the essentials of German military doctrine in a tactical, operational sense and German "war doctrine" in its widest sense—the "style" of war making—was a prime cause of disaster: the effect was devastating, since such a failure impeded effective operational planning*, whatever Stalin's whims and vagaries. And given this outlook, it was all too easy to "fit" intelligence material into a preconceived picture.[33]

THE GENERAL STAFF AT WAR

While Stalin's manic military purge still bit into the high command— arrests and killings continued through 1940 and even to the eve of the German attack—the debacle in Finland and German success in Finland forced some reorganization of the command machine. In May 1940 Voroshilov was "kicked upstairs" to head the Defense Committee (*Komitet Oborony*) of the *SNK* (Soviet of People's Commissars), while Timoshenko took over the Defense Commissariat, with N. G. Kuznetsov still holding the post of Navy Commissar that he assumed in April 1939. At the beginning of 1941, the roles and duties of the main and central administrations of the defense Commissariat were further defined, with inspectorates for all arms now established and an Inspector General emplaced at the head of this organization. On 8 March 1941 fresh regulations set up a form of command organization and a demarcation of responsibilities: the "direction"—not the command—of Soviet armies would come under the Defense Commissar, this operational direction assisted and implemented by the General Staff, the Commissar's own deputies, and his system of administrations. All *operational matters*, mobilization, and "organizational work" were concentrated in the General Staff, to which end—above all, its operational commitments—the General Staff was reorganized into eight directorates and four divisions: *Operations, Intelligence, Organization, Mobilization, Military Communications (VOSO), Rear Services and Supply, Manning*, and *Military-Topographical*. The four divisions comprised one for general administration, cadres (personnel), "fortified districts" (URs), and military-historical.[34]

The ravages of the purges and the rather frantic expansion in the Soviet military establishment in the winter of 1940–41 created a growing demand for trained officers, a demand the General Staff Academy strained to meet. Over five years, from 1936–1941, more than 430 officers passing through the higher education of the Academy had gone to the armed forces, filling command and staff positions in higher formations; with a further 100 officers undergoing the "finishing courses" for staff positions with divisions, corps, armies, and military districts; plus 70 Air Force officers undergoing training for senior and middle-grade command posts—in all, some 600 officers given a form of higher military education. But for all the growing sophistication of military theory and the recondite works of the General Staff Academy, what higher command training failed to provide was instruction in conducting defensive operations under highly unfavorable conditions when it was the *enemy* who held the initiative on the ground and in the air. It helped but little that in February 1941 the General Staff Academy was linked to the name of Voroshilov—in fact, it was almost a portent of doom, for Voroshilov was nothing but a military nincompoop, utterly bereft of any grasp of the essentials of modern warfare, blissfully unaware of what the Wehrmacht could wreak in the way of devastating havoc.

Nevertheless, the graduates of the Academy in the immediate prewar years formed an exclusive and remarkably competent group of officers, destined to become the "hard core" of a successful command group, both in command and staff positions. Both Vasilevskii and Vatutin were promoted with some speed to the posts of Deputy Chiefs of the General Staff; while G. K. Malandin became head of the Operations Directorate; with A. A. Grechko, A. A. Gryzlov, S. M. Enyukov, G. V. Ivanov, N. A. Lomov, M. N. Sharokhin, and A. M. Shtemenko assigned to Operations. Basistyi went on to head the Naval Staff, while I. A. Pliev and A. I. Radzievskii also achieved their own kind of distinction in command of mobile formations, "cavalry-mechanized" and armored alike.

All this, however, was for the future. The massive German surprise attack that swept over the Soviet Union on 22 June 1941 left the high command, including Stalin, reeling from shock and the Red Army torn to pieces within a matter of hours. Nothing illustrates the trauma more than Voroshilov's lurching about Moscow, demanding to know the location of the "supreme commander's" post, only to be told that there was no such thing. The implications and ramifications of that near catastrophe need no further retailing, being thoroughly investigated in both Soviet and non-Soviet accounts. The first three operational orders issued by Timoshenko proved to be tardy, irrelevant, and hugely uninformed about the real state of affairs. Zhukov was ordered to leave the General Staff—abruptly handed over to Vatutin as First Deputy Chief—and fly to Kiev. The main problem was communication with the newly organized fronts, particularly the western front, where the staffs were completely confused.

The *Stavka* organization was hurriedly set up on 23 June, with Timoshenko as Chairman, plus advisers, including Shaposhnikov. In the General Staff the main task was to realign the Operations Directorate with the main strategic axes, northwestern, western, and southwestern. In brief, the General Staff had little or no control over the situation, lacking as it did information about Soviet forces and German forces. On 30 June the State Defense Committee (*GKO*) was set up under Stalin's chairmanship—the highly centralized command machine to run the Soviet Union in wartime— and in short order the High Command *Stavka* became the Supreme High Command *Stavka*, this on 8 August 1941, with Stalin himself assuming the post of Supreme Commander in Chief.

The attempt to build up a high command echelon in the wake of the German attack was itself a confession of failure: forward defense of the western frontiers was to be secured by three "fronts"—northwestern, west- ern, and southwestern—each responsible for the defense of a strategic sector (Leningrad, Minsk, and Kiev). These three commands became "high com- mands" (*Glavkom*) early in the war, though centralized strategic planning and operational control came under the separate *otdely*—sections—of the Operations Directorate of the General Staff. The system may have appeared sound in peacetime, but war soon showed up its deficiencies: in particular, the coordination of multifront operations proved to be beyond the capacity of the system. Basically, the "high commands" could not *command*, lacking as they did the necessary resources and also adequate staffs; nor could they fall back on reserves, because the theaters simply had not been fitted out before the war with the necessary men and matériel. The continuous breakdown in communications due to German attacks simply ruled out any effective control on the part of the General Staff. There was also the fatal split in authority between the "high commands" and the front commands, with the result that the *Glavkom* never became an effective operational entity in its own right.

One of the most immediate innovations was the abolition of the General Staff Operations Directorate *otdely*, the sections, replaced in turn by opera- tions officers assigned to a single front under a "sector chief." The real problem was to establish an effective operational relationship among the *Stavka*, the General Staff, and the high commands themselves. The General Staff also had on occasions to act not only as a command and control agency but as an information/communications link, setting up its own *operativnyi otdel* (*operod*) to link the front, the armies, and the *Stavka*. Within a very short period, by September 1941, both the *Stavka* and the General Staff came to bypass the *Glavkom*s working directly with the front commands.

Not that the General Staff itself in the early days of the war was immune to upheaval and disarray. Zhukov left to take command of the western front, and Shaposhnikov took his place as Chief of the General Staff: the collapse of the western front command forced Malandin to proceed there as chief of staff, while V. M. Zlobin took over the Operations Directorate. Grechko, who had been attached to the operations Directorate before the war, was reportedly booted out by Zhukov, and Grechko left to take command of a cavalry division. The General Staff also "decentralized" itself with the assignment of operations officers to the various fronts: in Moscow the staff was reorganized into two echelons, one echelon within the city itself, the other outside the city limits. The first echelon became the "operations group."

Staff organization as a whole presented the Soviet command with several severe problems, not the least being the inflexibility and immobilism of the prewar staffs now committed to war; indeed, this was the problem that had plagued the Imperial Army, the provision of efficient *field administrations*. Meanwhile, the General Staff embarked on its own system of bringing General Staff "expertise" to the field formations through the "corps of General Staff officer-representatives," specialists for particular "axes" (*napravleniya*), hence *ofitsery-napravlentsii*: they were also designated as "commander-operations officers." At the end of July 1941 the *GKO* ordered that such a group of General Staff officers should be organized, specifying a strength of some 1,124 officers for dispatch to fronts, armies, and divisions; 22 officers to be attached to the General Staff group as such, 24 for front commands, 150 for armies, and 928 for divisions. The first candidates came from the Frunze Academy in September, followed by 14 students of the Voroshilov Higher Military Academy. (The General Staff Academy was redesignated the Voroshilov Higher Military Academy on Stalin's orders in 1942; it was not until 1958 that the Academy regained its General Staff designation.) By 1 January 1942, the General Staff group had grown to 134 officers and in the spring amounted to 202 officers.

By the middle of 1942, the General Staff had more or less assumed the organizational shape it maintained for the remainder of the war and had settled its operational routines and patterns, functioning as the "working body" of the *Stavka* and subordinate only to Stalin as Supreme Commander. The abolition of the *Glavkom*s brought the *Stavka* and the General Staff into direct contact with the front commands, but this did not solve the problem of the coordination of multifront operations, bringing the system of "*Stavka* representatives" into existence, while the General Staff had its own "officer-representatives" in the field, the larger number serving the fronts and armies. Stalin himself established the routine of General Staff officers in Mocow, specifying a timetable for work and for rest; it was also Stalin who frequently switched senior officers from staff to command positions, holding the view that a good staff officer made a good commander and that the staff must have firsthand experience of the battlefield.

The formal functions of the General Staff consisted of collecting and analyzing operational data, as well as preparing operational proposals for the *Stavka*, preparing operational plans, communicating the directives and orders of the Supreme Commander to the field forces and monitoring their execution, assisting front/fleet commanders in planning operations and monitoring their implementation, assembling strategic reserves and supervising the regrouping associated with them, organizing military information for press and radio, maintaining contact with the Allied (Western) command, and preparing briefs for inter-Allied conferences (as at Tehran and Yalta). It was also the direct responsibility of the General Staff to organize and maintain constant and unbroken communication throughout the entire command echelon, through the *Stavka*/General Staff fronts, fleets, and armies system, as well as supervising manpower replacements for the field armies and altering organizations and establishments in the light of battlefield experience (steps such as bringing back the corps administration in 1942, or introducing artillery breakthrough divisions, the tank armies, and the air armies). The General Staff was also charged with evaluating operational lessons and experience, a duty that included disseminating these lessons to frontline forces, managed after 1942 through special bulletins on tactical matters.

Soviet analysts have closely examined the wartime activity of the General Staff and derived certain basic lessons. The first is the correctness of the principle of allowing the General Staff to discharge its prescribed functions, both with respect to strategic-operational matters but also "organizational" aspects, thus implementing *centralization* (placing recruitment and replacement in 1941 under a separate administration was considered a mistake leading to inefficient overlapping and "parallelism"). The second lesson concerns the utility of *specialization* within the various agencies of the General Staff and the practice of assigning General Staff personnel as "operations officers" to the field formations. The third is the absolute necessity of establishing *work regimes* that ensure the continuous functioning of all elements of the General Staff, above all, guaranteeing the timely collection and presentation of operational data. The last, but by no means the least, lesson is *the orderly management of key General Staff personnel*—a principle seriously violated in June–July 1941, when no fewer than 393 officers were shunted about, followed by another bout of changes in August, involving 449 officers.

The heart of the wartime work of the General Staff involved the planning and preparation of strategic operations engaging groups of fronts, together with supervising the course of these operations. On receipt of a *Stavka* directive, the General Staff was responsible for working out the details of the operational plan, the directives and instructions to front commands and the central administrations, that organized coordination with partisan units, and monitored the course of preparations in military units and field staffs.

Quite recently much attention has been paid to the question of the handling of "information"—data—within the General Staff, specifically the relationship between information/data handling and efficient command and control, an issue first highlighted in the 1935 *Instruction* on the work of field staffs under the section "reports and information." Prewar manuals touched on this question, but wartime requirements demanded major modifications. At the outbreak of war, information was handled by the "operational preparedness section" of the Operations Directorate, but it was not until March 1942 that a separate "Information Section" was established within the Directorate, that section becoming a Directorate in its own right by the end of the war. Obtaining precise and timely information from the front caused the *Stavka* to issue formal instruction to front commanders, obliging them to report to the General Staff daily not later than 2 A.M. and, in cases of extreme urgency, to report personally to the duty deputy chief of the General Staff. Army commanders, in turn, received timetables for reporting to front staffs, the exception being the appearance of fresh enemy units, enemy offensive action, or enemy withdrawal, which were to be reported without delay.

It comes as no great surprise to learn that Soviet military analysts and commanders regard the Soviet General Staff at war as a subject that requires further investigation.[35] The immediate lesson derived from the experience of 1941–45 is that the General Staff must be fitted out *in peacetime*—both in terms of organizing its activity and developing its structure—in order to carry through its wartime tasks: peacetime practice must also involve maintaining effective links with the staffs at military district, fleet, and formation levels, together with other central agencies.

During the Great Patriotic War the Soviet General Staff made some giant strides in its development and competence. The "General Staff view" came to count for a great deal and was even accorded Stalin's respect. Above all, the General Staff was effectively integrated into the "high command system," and wartime experience perforce marked a vital stage in the further evolution of the General Staff, toward becoming not only the "military brain" of the state but also a "command-in-being" entity in the conditions imposed by the advent of nuclear weapons, *thus substantially—even radically—altering the whole concept of a "General Staff."*

Toward a Nuclear Command

In June 1946, amidst the first phase of Stalin's postwar reorganization, the wartime General Staff emerged in its new guise as the "General Staff of the Soviet Armed Forces." This proved to be the first step, albeit of a somewhat indeterminate nature, on the long road toward a radical change in the entire concept of the General Staff as well as the diversification of its role and the elaboration of its position in the entire Soviet "national security apparatus." Nevertheless, this whole process involves something of a paradox, namely, the need to innovate institutionally while taking account of the Soviet aversion to making basic changes in the format of "the system"— hence the revival of long-established designations even though the functions are changed substantially. Indeed, the very term *General'nyi shtab* is a case in point, though a review of the activities of the General Staff over three decades and more tends to confirm the notion that here is still *mozg armii*, a "thinking department" of very high caliber, whatever its additional managerial functions.

The major reorganization of the Soviet high command in February 1946 abolished at one stroke the dualism of the two People's Commissariats

(Defense and the Navy), setting up a unified command, the People's Commissariat for the Armed Forces, speedily transmuted into a Ministry (Ministry of the Armed Forces), which at once took over the air forces (previously under Army and Naval direction) as a new separate arm, equal in status with the Army and the Navy. The supply and administrative directorates of the three Services were also placed under unified control with the creation of the "Rear Services of the Armed Forces." While Stalin himself retained the post of Minister until March 1947, five Deputy Ministers were appointed, the first being the Chief of the General Staff of the Armed Forces (Marshal Vasilevskii, who succeeded General Antonov in March 1946 and held the post of Chief of the General Staff until November 1948), and the other four representing the heads of the three services (Army, Navy, Air Force) and the Rear Services. A sixth was added a little later, the Inspector General. Under this preliminary reshaping of the system, the General Staff was subordinated directly to the Minister for the Armed Forces.

Reorganization also went hand in hand with a purge, the postwar "purge of the heroes," managed in part by Bulganin and Shikin (head of the political apparatus). One of the earliest victims of this vindictiveness was Marshal Zhukov, who in June 1946 was dispatched to command of the Odessa Military District. However, while the settling of wartime scores no doubt contributed to these abrupt and sometimes startling changes, there is reason to argue that the debates over the future shape and organization of the Soviet Army (a postwar designation, replacing the "Red Army") were far from amicable, a process agitated still further by the first major postwar senior commanders' conference on wartime operations. Nor was it possible to ignore the advent of the atomic weapon, signaling—to some—the opening of a new era in weapons and warfare, though Soviet doctrine was not only bound by but actually encased in "Stalinist military doctrine," with its emphasis on the "permanently operating factors." But whatever Stalin's rigor in holding to his own formulation and his disparagement—in public, at least—of the atomic weapon, this did not prevent secret, intensive work on the new weapons, in particular Kurchatov's program to produce a Soviet atomic weapon and the effort to develop a Soviet missile, the "R–1," which was tested in October 1947. Even earlier, in July 1946, the first Soviet "missile unit" had been set up at Nedelin's prompting, based on a Guards "*Katyusha*" unit and manned by handpicked, experienced artillery officers of Nedelin's choosing.

More handpicked officers passed through the first postwar courses of the Voroshilov Academy, with the General Staff maintaining its own special record of those who were successful in passing the basic course: such officers were eligible, if not actually marked out, for higher command (or senior staff appointments), thus winnowing out the mass of wartime officers. Entry to the Voroshilov (or Frunze) Academy was a *sine qua non* of further advancement, with General (later Marshal) M. V. Zakharov in charge of the Voroshilov

Academy in the immediate postwar period. This is to say, therefore, that with the onset of postwar reorganization and reequipping, several hundred senior professional military men were assigned to the purposeful and continuous study of the lessons of the war so recently concluded and the implications of advancing military technology. In 1946, in the Voroshilov Academy, a "scientific-research section" began work under the personal direction of General Zakharov, its functions to direct the curriculum (and the teaching) into "operational research channels," not to mention the further exploration of "operational art." The General Staff also intervened directly in the instructional process, commissioning major special studies for its own purposes.

In March 1947 Stalin relinquished the post of Minister of the Armed Forces, handing over custody of the military establishment to a political "trusty," Bulganin, a move that implemented Stalin's notion of the place the military should and would occupy in his scheme of things—it was to be essentially a closed organization, manned by professionals but supervised by political functionaries (and cowed by the *NKVD*, in the last resort). Bulganin was that functionary *par excellence*; certainly he could not be counted a soldier. In addition to dispersing senior commanders across the face of the Soviet Union (Zhukov being but one example), Stalin also put the heaviest brake on promotion, with only four colonels general receiving promotion during the latter years of Stalin's rule.

Nor was any real halt brought to the process of reorganization and redistribution, which elevated Marshal Vasilevskii to the post of Minister in April 1949, thus displacing Bulganin. Stalin brought Sokolovskii back from Germany to act as First Deputy Minister, while entrusting the General Staff to the newly promoted Army General S. M. Shtemenko, hitherto deputy to Vasilevskii, a personal promotion but hardly any real augmentation of talent at the top of the General Staff. Meanwhile, Marshal Zhukov had been packed out of sight to the Urals Military District. (Nor did the Main Political Administration escape the ax, for as a consequence of the anti-Zhdanov purges, Shikin was removed from his post as head and replaced by Colonel General F. F. Kuznetsov).

A further step in Stalinist experimentation followed in the spring of 1950 with the splitting of the Armed Forces Ministry into two separate entities, the War Ministry (*Voenno ministerstvo*) and the Naval Ministry (*Voenno-morskoe ministerstvo*), both All-Union institutions, the bifurcation with separate naval representation doubtless designed to speed Stalin's "big ship" navy. Vasilevskii remained as the new "War Minister," with Admiral Yumashev a somewhat short-lived incumbent as the new "Navy Minister," soon to be replaced by Admiral Kuznetsov, who was recalled from semi-disgrace to realize Stalin's passion for "heavy cruisers" (among other things). Admiral Galler, however, was not so fortunate, dying in prison in 1950, presumably because as head of the Krylov Naval Academy for Naval

Construction and Armament, he had failed to conform with Stalin's express requirements in terms of a naval building program. Making sense of Stalin's naval strategy (or outlook on naval affairs) could only tax the best of men, for here was a highly eclectic mix of provision for a "fortress fleet," a fleet-in-being, and seemingly the additive of great power prestige combined with a means of revolutionary expansionism.

The newly founded Naval Ministry also acquired its own "Naval General Staff"—shades of 1906, though more properly a reversion to the institution that had prevailed until 1921;[36] the General Staff of the Soviet Armed Forces now returned to its former status as the "Army General Staff" (General Staff of the Soviet Army), with General Shtemenko confirmed once more as head of this particular staff. Marshal Vasilevskii continued as War Minister, Kuznetsov duly took over as Navy Minister. None of this, however, resolved the question of strategic control and coordination, a function discharged during the war by the *Stavka* and the State Defense Committee (*GKO*), both disbanded shortly after the war. While the obscure and devious modes of Stalin's rule after 1945 make precise analysis difficult, it appears that the institutional arrangement that followed the *Stavka-GKO* mechanism was set up early in 1947 with the creation (or rather, the restitution) of the "Supreme Military Soviet," *Vysshyi voennyi sovet*, first established in 1918[37] as an "organ of strategic command and control" (*rukovodstvo*). Stalin was President of the *VVS*, and its membership was drawn from the Politburo, the Party Central Committee, and senior military commanders. One month after the bifurcation of the ministries for War and the Navy, in March 1950, the Supreme Military Soviet was transferred to the competence of the Council of Ministers of the USSR, of which Stalin was also Chairman, thus assuring Stalin's continued and immediate personal control. At the same time, the "Main Military Soviets" of the Army and of the Navy, set up in 1938 and abruptly wound up on 23 June 1941 with the creation of the *Stavka*, were brought back to the scene in 1950, together with the two separate ministries; by strict definition and formulation, these were "consultative bodies," not to be confused with the Collegium (*Kollegiya*) of the ministries.

The growing excesses of the "cult of personality," as practiced by Stalin, brought not only immobilism into military affairs, forced into an obligatory acceptance of a warped and dogmatic Stalinist "military doctrine," but also the virtual paralysis of the high command. Where there was movement, it proved to be both dangerous and even incompetent, with Shtemenko at the General Staff one of the prime malefactors. The sinister murk of the "Doctors' Plot" still hangs over the last days of Stalin, but the path toward this final burst of Stalinist megalomania may have been connected with a bitter struggle over military plans hatched by Stalin. Whether Stalin was bent on some ultimate, cataclysmic collision with "the imperialist camp," then settling into its new alliances and containment positions, or merely "rounding off" the acquisitions of the recent war is a moot point.

Stalin even may have hoped to beat the Americans to permanent military emplacement in Western Europe, while also bringing the whole "Stalinist camp" into total Stalinist order, not least through the reduction of rebellious Yugoslavia.[38]

The sequence of command changes in 1951–52 gives some general indication of the course of events. In November 1951 Koniev was given command of the Carpathian Military District, a key position for any military thrust directed to the south and into Yugoslavia; not unconnected, however, was the reappearance of Marshal Zhukov in Moscow, his presence reportedly linked to a review of the operational plans prepared by Shtemenko and Koniev. With Zhukov's ferocious demolition of these "plans," Shtemenko's position crumpled at once and senior officers demanded his dismissal, all in the face of Stalin's resistance to such change. But change there was, with Marshal Sokolovskii replacing the hapless Shtemenko (who was subsequently reduced by two ranks from Army General); in the aftermath of this debacle within the Soviet high command, it is arguable that one of the purposes of the "Doctors' Plot" was to exact Stalin's own revenge on those who had so thwarted him, but death prevented the full implementation of this and other designs.

POST-STALIN TRANSITION

It took only one week after Stalin's death for the first changes to be set in motion, with the unification of the two separate ministries into a consolidated Ministry of Defense under Bulganin as Minister, a member of the newly found "collective leadership" and returned in this capacity to a military position. Marshal Vasilevskii and Marshal Zhukov took up posts as First Deputy Ministers, while Admiral Kuznetsov, erstwhile Navy Minister, reverted to C. in C. Soviet Navy. With the abolition of a separate ministry for the Navy, the Naval General Staff, set up in 1950, was wound up and its place taken by the Main Naval Staff, although the General Staff still functioned nominally as "the Soviet Army General Staff." This state of affairs was not remedied until September 1955, when the "General Staff of the Soviet Armed Forces" came back to official existence, with Sokolovskii again confirmed as Chief.

In the summer of 1953, the military lent its aid in beating Beria and his *NKVD* generals to the ground. Marshal Zhukov took over the seat on the Central Committee left vacant by Beria's arrest and execution. For all the drama of these circumstances, what was stirring behind the scenes proved to be of no mean significance, with the first attempt to modify the grosser, petrified forms of "Stalinist military science" initiated by Major General Talenskii in September 1953. The thrust was not to displace the "permanently operating factors," by which Stalin had set such store, but rather to insist that such factors by themselves did not either comprise or comprehend the "laws" of military science. Talenskii duly recognized the general validity of such factors, but proceeded to push *armed conflict* itself, rather than considerations of economic performance or morale, to the very center of his discussion. With this Pandora's box finally prized open, it was possible to look more specifically at war in the context of nuclear weapons, indeed, to take a further step and intimate that a future war could diverge appreciably from the pattern of previous wars.[39]

Convoluted and even confused though this "debate" proved to be, it was no mere exercise in military metaphysics; the importance of this enterprise was recognized in 1953, with the establishment of the *Military-Scientific Directorate* within the General Staff, under Colonel General A. P. Pokrovskii. Not that the ossification of "Stalinist military science" had induced disinterest in weapons development—quite the contrary—but it virtually inhibited recognition of and concentration upon *"the main tasks"* required of a state to attain victory in war. Bringing Soviet military theory speedily up to date, with a readier appreciation of the nature of modern war, was a major prerequisite for ordering (or reordering) priorities, all with proper "calculation of the character and *all the requirements* of modern war." Not surprisingly, the Voroshilov Academy received instructions to adjust its five-year research plan to include nuclear weapons and the planning and conduct of nuclear operations. Shortly afterward a new position in the Academy, that of "Deputy Head/Military Scientific Work," was confirmed, a post held first by Lieutenant General N. A. Lomov, followed (in 1958) by Lieutenant General A. I. Gastilovich.

The immediate ferment in ideas and arguments, however, did not satisfy those who demanded faster progress in developing an effective and cogent doctrine fitted to the age of nuclear and thermonuclear weapons, a process hindered by bureaucratism and the failure of the military academies to become "creative and organizational centers of military and scientific theory," a complaint pressed with some vigor in 1955. Advances in weapons technology were clearly outpacing developments in military science, though a start had been made in 1953 in modifying "Stalinist military science" and introducing Soviet military men to some features of non-Soviet work in military matters. It was, however, all a little fainthearted and not at all to the taste of Marshal Zhukov, with his contribution to the defeat of Malenkov behind him. Few in the military espoused Malenkov's case for switching investment away from heavy industry, nor could they embrace at this stage what appeared to be a form of "mutual deterrence" suggested by Malenkov. On the contrary, the drift of doctrine seemed to indicate the opposite, the need for a more vigorously realistic and *practical* program.

The dam, if it can be called that, broke early in 1955 when, at the instigation of Marshal Zhukov, Marshal of Armored Forces Rotmistrov published a paper about the contemporary role of surprise, slicing through the previous tergiversation about this topic. The attempt to square the circle of permanently operating factors with surprise was pushed aside. Surprise attack could have a major effect on the outcome of any war, hence the need to guard against surprise yet also have the capacity to exploit surprise. Rotmistrov jumped the previous hurdles by arguing that it was not enough merely "to repulse" a surprise attack, but actively to "frustrate" such an attack by "preemptive surprise blows" (the object being to win the strategic initiative, though preemption after this fashion was not to be confused with or construed as preventive war).

It was certainly neither accident nor coincidence that, in 1955, the "Army General Staff" was elevated to the "General Staff of the Soviet Armed Forces." General Antonov had already been recalled to the General Staff in 1954, though in a short while he was seconded to the newly established Warsaw Treaty Organization (WTO), a political structure grafted onto the framework already established within the Tenth Directorate of the Soviet General Staff,[40] responsible for monitoring the bilateral security treaties concluded with East European states after 1945, and also for maintaining a watching brief over East Germany. Henceforth, this Directorate took on a coordinating role for WTO affairs. This was but one step in a changing pattern of Soviet initiatives relating to security, including disarmament proposals aimed at inhibiting the further spread of U.S. bases and the establishment of a Soviet presence in the Middle East, Asia, and Africa, with an eye to forestalling further Western exploitation of these areas for the military encirclement of the Soviet Union.

This "breakout" from containment, with the Soviet Union bent on building its own anti-imperialist coalition, was merely one element of an emerging strategic concept designed to face the contingency of global nuclear war. The task, propelled into a practical program by the Rotmistrov-Zhukov stipulations about a *realistic* military doctrine, meant bringing doctrine, force structures, military organization, and economic potential into a coherent framework—a task that was to occupy almost a decade, though a decisive start was made in the mid-1950s. The result was to marry the canons of orthodox military thinking with extrapolations derived from recognizing the realities of nuclear firepower. The basic premise, however, remained (and remains now) rooted in the "*means and forms of armed conflict*," with priority accorded to destruction of enemy military forces. Destruction of such forces is a direct route to the destruction of the enemy's will to resist, rather than attrition directed at the enemy's capacity to wage war. Here, in nuclear terms, was a reflection of an earlier Soviet debate on a strategy of annihilation (*sokrushenie*) or one of attrition (*izmor*).[41] It is worth noting, however, that the adherents of a strategy of annihilation did not preclude the possibility of a long (or more protracted) war with intensive phases of action.

The "nuclearizing" of classically configured military principles and previous doctrinal strictures began to produce some working concepts, relevant to Soviet war planning and the establishment of "battlefield norms" for *combined-arms* operations—a logical position in view of the denial of any single "absolute weapon" to accomplish the aims of war. Indeed, the fundamental axiom pertaining to the battlefield destruction of enemy forces required "balanced forces," including large ground forces and effective tactical aviation. Weapons of mass destruction demanded, in turn, mass armed forces, whose mass must be subject to increase. Although the surprise factor had greatly complicated the strategic scene, no "single blow" could of itself decide any outcome. On the contrary, the effect of modern weapons was to *expand* the duration and intensity of any war, thus bringing into sharper focus the relationship between "strategy" and economics (not to mention the morale factor). By the same token, *reserves* took on added importance, not least in sustaining the effort implicit in having gained and retained the stategic initiative. Drawing also on earlier doctrinal work and wartime experience, the "single blow" notion was scuttled in favor of the idea of the "concentration of fires" (an idea propounded even before 1941 by Krasilnikov, now prominent in the "nuclear debate"), the need to sustain successive blows of increasing strength in a nuclear/conventional "mix."

Both the military command and the shape of the Soviet armed forces were duly adjusted to these new requirements. Out of a very ready appreciation of the threat posed by the bombers of the Strategic Air Command, the Soviet air defense organization was established as an autonomous branch of the Soviet armed forces, *PVO Strany*, placed under S. S. Biryuzov (promoted to Marshal to succeed the ailing Marshal Govorov. The *PVO* command took control of AA guns, interceptor aircraft, and the first SAMs, distributed among some twenty air defense districts. At Zhukov's own behest the Ground Forces were drastically reorganized, a cut in manpower facilitating the quest for mobility and flexibility for high-speed operations on a battlefield subject to various types of toxicity, an army fitted for "the conduct of atomic warfare." The Ground Forces, now under Koniev as C in C, consisted only of tank and motor-rifle divisions committed to tank armies (in place of the mechanized armies) and combined-arms armies respectively. With the introduction of the first missiles, the armies and divisions would lose their heavier weapons in favor of tactical missiles, while battlefield SAMs would provide both mobility and greater effectiveness.

While the "mass army" concept was retained, it was subject to two significant modifications—increased mobility and wider dispersal, capable of "closing" with the enemy across the entire Eurasian landmass, while distributing itself into the homeland as part of a recovery/rehabilitation plan, though the problem of maintaining military production under conditions of devastating attack produced little in the way of specific analysis. Only Colonel Lagovskii went so far as to stipulate a planning process that set the military requirements for the *first year* of operations.[42].

Yet another unsolved problem was that of the Soviet Navy, still committed under Kuznetsov to a "big ship" program. Like his cruisers, Kuznetsov had to go, and was duly pushed aside in favor of Gorshkov, who was prepared to do Khrushchev's bidding in building a navy for the "nuclear age," concentrating on submarines, missile-armed destroyers, and lighter surface units. Gorshkov proved himself to be an enthusiast for missile technology but also—as time showed—a stubborn proponent of the large surface ship and a "balanced fleet" of his own shaping.

The consequence of this major upheaval in Soviet military-political affairs was to set the Soviet General Staff upon a round of intensive work in the wake of the Twentieth Party Congress (1956), when at the instigation of Khrushchev, senior military and Party men, already intertwined in the Supreme Military Soviet, embarked on plans to implement the new strategy, with nuclear weapons to the fore. The Supreme Military Soviet evidently was chaired by Khrushchev, much as Stalin did in his time, with its membership drawn from members of the Presidium of the CPSU Central Committee, the Minister of Defense, and the commanders of the main arms, though in practice the key decisions affecting the essentials of national security policy would lie with select members of the Politburo (called the Presidium during the Khrushchev era). In this instance, involving a review of the full range of "strategic policy," Brezhnev—specifically charged with responsibilities connected with heavy industry and the supply of new weaponry—supervised the planning as a whole, with Sokolovskii at the General Staff chairing the military commission with Antonov, Zakharov, Moskalenko, Batitskii, and Varenstov among its members. This same "Brezhnev committee" also prepared the economic plan that was a necessary complement to the proposed military buildup.

The General Staff Academy was also mobilized to contribute to this effort. The head of the Academy, Marshal Bagramyan, and his deputy, General Malandin (who succeeded Bagramyan in 1958, when the former was appointed a Deputy Defense Minister and Chief of the Rear Services), pushed the new program—which required fresh investigation of the characteristics of modern war and modern military science, all requiring a review of previous work. Krasilnikov, Milshtein, Pukhovskii, Lomov, and Lagovskii were among the contributors to this major review intended for the General Staff, with the final editorial stamp put upon it by General Malandin and Colonel General Gastilovich. This was followed by another major analysis of offensive and defensive operations (at front level), while Marshal Rotmistrov and his special research group had completed a study of modern operations by November 1957, though it was not until the beginning of 1959 that it passed General Staff review. Side by side with this theoretical-research work, two Military Districts were earmarked for "field trials" of the new doctrine, which involved a fundamental revision of service manuals and training procedures.

By this time Zhukov had departed the scene, whisked off by Khrushchev in the autumn of 1957, all amidst charges of pursuing "a dangerous anti-Party line." Marshal Vasilevskii was also relieved of his postion as Deputy Defense Minister with responsibility for military science.

It is true that Zhukov exerted pressure, a great deal of pressure, to have the Military Soviets subordinate in their entirety to the military commander, with the elimination of the "political member" (a Party member) as such and that appointments to these Soviets be controlled by the Ministry of Defense and not the Central Committee. Additionally, Zhukov was charged with seeking the dissolution of the Supreme Military Soviet (which reportedly changed its designation in 1957 to the "Defense Council"). If anything, this was part and parcel of an attempt to maximize *military* responsibility for the formulation of strategic plans—all at the expense of the Party leadership, above all, of the personal direction of Khrushchev.

If such was the case and Zhukov suspected overweening, arbitrary, unwarranted interference in formulating both strategy and doctrine, then he displayed unwonted prescience. The General Staff and the General Staff Academy had played their part manfully in bringing about a major change in the understanding of the nature of war, though in 1959—with Khrushchev on the verge of establishing a new preeminent command and about to promulgate his own strategic "new look"—a fresh bout of debate set in, renewing the discussion of "the factors of victory in modern war." Behind this, however, lay an increasingly acrimonious dispute between the supporters of modern weapons technology and the proponents of "balance," who saw neither logic nor utility in sacrificing men to missiles. But this was precisely what Khrushchev planned to do with his "new look" unveiled on 14 January 1960: henceforth missiles would form the basis of Soviet military power, and strategy would be configured round missiles as the means of "total firepower," while defense would revolve round the principle of "deterrence."

In so arguing and simultaneously proposing drastic reductions in the Ground Forces (Soviet Army), Khrushchev backed away with gay abandon at what passed for an emergent Soviet strategy. He ruled out any cause for concern over surprise attack now that "rocket atomic weapons" had come to stay and, by the same token, cut the ground from under any notion of a strategy of preemptive strike. Retaliation-proof capability was inconceivable, which was another way of saying that the Soviet emperor had no clothes. On the other hand, Khrushchev trapped himself in a paradox of his own making, that the deterrence he posited was based on a position of strength— the very item he lacked. A missile-based strategy needs missiles, not rhetoric or bluster; thus, Khrushchev was forced into deception (though he could hardly deceive the General Staff) and into "missile maneuvers" designed to persuade the United States above all that nuclear parity did indeed exist, thus inducing the stabilization that informed Khrushchev's view of deterrence. Not much later, in order to give substance to this "parity," Khrushchev initiated his Cuban venture, a shortcut, high-speed, desperately risky dash to establish parity, or at least a plausible substitute for it. It was that same venture that showed the inherent weaknesses of Soviet strategic forces-in-being, the very factor on which Khrushchev pinned his notion of an effective deterrent. The General Staff did not forgive and did not forget.

As early as April 1960, Marshal Sokolovskii, Chief of the General Staff, fell afoul of Khrushchev over the proposed cuts in general purpose forces and resigned, replaced in turn by Marshal M. V. Zakharov, elevated to Marshal's rank in 1959 and currently C in C, Group of Soviet Forces in Germany, previously head of the General Staff Academy and Deputy Chief of the General Staff. The first formal riposte to Khrushchev's "missile strategy" came in November 1960 with Krasilnikov's attack on ideas of "push-button warfare" and overemphasis on the factor of surprise. If this was "a General Staff view," then *the* General Staff view was presented—albeit in classic guise—by Army General V. V. Kurasov, then head of the Military-Scientific Directorate and Deputy Chief of the General Staff for "military-scientific work." Kurasov, liberally lacing his argument with reference to Lenin, insisted on having "*all* means of warfare," without which "even decisive defeat" threatened. Large modern armies and equally modern weapons systems had to be brought into being before the outbreak of war, while the object of Soviet operations must be the destruction, the physical destruction, of enemy forces—to which end Soviet strategy should *not* forswear a preemptive strike. Kurasov did not take kindly to the view that the enemy might be reduced economically, socially, politically; the new technology did not invalidate the principle of actual annihilation of enemy military forces.[43]

The policy discussions and high-level seminars held in 1960–61 failed to produce any unanimity: "certain comrades" refused to consider the "rocket-atomic weapon" decisive in gaining victory and persisted in referring to the experience of the recent war. Marshal Sokolovskii, returned to duty (together with Marshal Koniev, though Zhukov refused any blandishments to do the same), chaired a commission that produced the strategic handbook *Voennaya Strategiya*, a key volume that did recognize the growing importance of strategic missiles but also held steadfastly to the view that final victory required a capability for large-scale ground-based theater operations. Only Colonel General Gastilovich came out unequivocally for a "pure" missile-based strategy.

Contradictions and ambiguities abounded in the first edition of *Voennaya Strategiya*. Large ground forces *might* be superfluous if the enemy had already been reduced by nuclear strikes, yet theater warfare retained its place and "occupation of territory" could not be eliminated from war plans. The distinctiveness of the new weapons received due emphasis, in that they were not simply super artillery pieces operating in support of massed ground forces; however, "modern ground forces" were also accorded a distinctive place, namely, the capacity to defend native territory, occupy strategically important areas, capture enemy bases and installations that had escaped destruction—all significant components of attaining "final victory." On the other hand, serious reservations were registered about the apparent erosion of the distinction between the strategic offensive and the defensive, and a "comprehensive view" of strategy that, with its attention to the "economic and politico-morale sphere," obscured (if not actually obliterated) the "military factor."

Military resistance to Khrushchev's "strategic doctrine" coincided with military resistance to attempts to tighten the Party's grip on the officer corps. Even Marshal Malinovskii mouthed some carefully modulated phrases about this new "strategy," emphasizing at the Twenty-first Party Congress (October 1961) that final victory required "the *combined operations* of all branches of the armed forces." In an odd quirk, the *MPA* itself—a Khrushchevite instrument in putting pressure on the central apparatus of the Defense Ministry, the General Staff, and the military academies as centers of military elitism—disowned the extravagant missile purism espoused by Gastilovich. Meanwhile, the plot thickened, with preparations set in train as early as October 1961 to promote Khrushchev's Cuban adventure, the attempt at a drastic "shortcut" to parity, using the cheaper and available MRBMs and IRBMs to produce "substitute ICBMs," the emplacement in Cuba designed to complicate and degrade U.S. national defenses. In the event of success the strategic disparity facing the Soviet Union would have been erased and Khrushchev's position not only vindicated but magnified.

The growing involvement with missiles for Cuba (probably debated in general terms at the April plenum, 1962) led to the displacement of Moskalenko as C in C, Strategic Missile Forces, and the introduction of Biryuzov as his replacement (though the move was not disclosed until July of 1962). In the wake of the Cuban missile fiasco, Khrushchev found himself doubly trapped. If his "deterrent strategy" based on fictitious strength failed to satisfy the military, his post-Cuban embrace of a minimum deterrent posture born of overt and visible weakness could only incite the military to further dissatisfaction, fearing, as they did, the prospect of the Soviet Union's being confined to permanent strategic inferiority. Not long after the October (1962) missile crisis, Marshal Zakharov, Chief of the General Staff, increasingly disenchanted with Khrushchev's policies, vanished from view and his duties were assigned to his deputy, General V. D. Ivanov, First Deputy Chief of the General Staff since 1959 (having come from the Baku air defense command).

In March 1963 Marshal Zakharov emerged as head of the General Staff Academy, his place at the General Staff being taken by that all-purpose marshal, Biryuzov, who handed over the Strategic Missile Forces to Krylov. This placed Khrushchev's ultraloyal henchman at the General Staff: Yepishev, expoliceman, had already been put in charge of the Political Administration, bent on hectoring and harrying the military, arrangements that assisted Khrushchev in riding out the post-Cuba storms. Yet, an apparent concession to the military, giving license in discussing military doctrine—

shorn of any political aspects—meant little or nothing as Khrushchev reverted to his previous line, this time virtually forcing "peaceful coexistence" down the throat of the Soviet military. In connection with the provisions of the long-term plan for 1966–70, Khrushchev also intimated that Soviet defense was at a "suitable level," thus foreclosing the debate over resources; but all doubt was dispelled in August 1964, when—as "Supreme Commander"—he simply disbanded the central staff of the Ground Forces and abolished their status as an independent arm, subordinating them directly to the General Staff (probably under the supervision of Shtemenko).

THE RESURGENCE OF THE GENERAL STAFF

Within a matter of weeks (October 1964), Khrushchev was stripped of all power and positions. Marshal Zakharov was whisked back with uncommon speed to head the General Staff once more and with scant regard for decencies, began his assault on Khrushchev's wanton interference in military matters, a prelude to a wholesale assault on "harebrained" ideas of military organization, the dangerous construction of "one-variant" war, and distortions in strategic doctrine. The ranks of the military-industrial apparat were speedily reformed and the defense industry agencies rapidly recentralized, while Zakharov and his fellows insisted that professionalism must be the hallmark of any "new look." Modernization, professionalism, and technocratization became the devices under which Zakharov intended to operate, the results of which began to show toward the end of the decade. The military package presented to the new collective leadership, already gearing up for the Twenty-third Party Congress (1966), was neither a simple reversal of Khrushchev's radicalism nor reliance on earlier conservatism: nuclear war was a realistic possibility, necessitating both a revision of the inferior strategic status of the Soviet Union and a serious investment in damage-limitation forces. Though by no means switching to a conventional strategy as such, the Soviet command came to recognize that a theater operation might open with a nonnuclear phase, a Soviet version of "flexible response" (*gibkoe reagirovanie*) that induced considerable restructuring of the Ground Forces and tactical air.

Zakharov's new broom reached quickly enough into the manning and structure of the General Staff. An early move was to post V. D. Ivanov to the General Staff Academy and install Batitskii (commander of the Moscow District Air Defense) in March 1965 as First Deputy Chief/General Staff. This was also the period in which a major survey of the entire Soviet officer corps was begun, leading to a major revision of manpower policies and manpower structures, formally enacted in the 1967 law. One rapidly rising star was that of N. V. Ogarkov, who became commander of the Volga Military District in 1965, moving as a lieutenant general from his key post as Chief of Staff to the Belorussian Military District after serving in the Far East with Malinovskii and Zakharov. When Malinovskii moved to Moscow in

1957, Ogarkov was not long in following and duly entered the General Staff Academy. It seems quite plain that Zakharov was intent on gathering a group of younger, "technocratic" officers about him, deftly moving them into key postions as well as juggling with the Military District commands to test and try out new commanders, soon to be reflected in significant changes in arms commanders.

It was quite a neat balancing act. The average age of MD commanders was lowered by some five years, but the "old guard" was not entirely neglected, with Moskalenko brought back to prominence after his resignation (or removal) in April 1962. In July 1966 Batitskii took over *PVO Strany* as commander, leaving Zakharov without a First Deputy, a post possibly filled on an ad hoc basis by Shtemenko, charged with the supervision of the Ground Forces, which in any event were soon to reemerge as an independent command under a new C in C, I. G. Pavlovskii, then in his late fifties (and another Far Eastern "old hand"). But in many respects 1967 was a decisive year, not only for the General Staff but for Soviet military policies as a whole. The death of Malinovskii forced a further reconstitution of the military leadership, with Ustinov in the running for the post of Defense Minister but reportedly unable to muster the support of Zakharov, who plumped for Grechko, who had in any event been acting as a "caretaker" chief during Malinovskii's declining years.

The type of approach Zakharov had in mind was made plain in public terms with the publication of a brochure in 1967 on "scientific methods" in military affairs—*O nauchnoi podkhode k rukovodstvu voiskami* (Voenizdat, 1967). While he may not have penned every line, the pamphlet clearly expressed Zakharov's own views on the need for professionalism combined with greater "technocratization." Marshal Sokolovskii also lent his aid in stressing the need for military expertise in planning defense matters and also for recognizing that substantial general-purpose forces were still necessary in an age dominated by nuclear weapons. The political leadership, while recognizing the urgency of the military question, turned the issue quite neatly by insisting that the very destructive nature of modern weapons demanded that "they should not escape from political control"; political expertise, particularly in any future war that would be one of grand coalitions, was just as essential in its own way.

Though any military assertiveness was held firmly in check, the problem of command coupled with management could not be avoided, not only the operational aspects of missile warfare but also the management of strategic weapons programs and the defense sector as a whole. Zakharov had already lent his name to the priority that should be accorded to defense requirements, to the application of highly professional expertise in defense planning as a whole, and to the refurbishing of the general-purpose forces. There seemed to be general recognition that some new (or reorganized) supreme military-political organ was needed in present circumstances, plus a similar agency to handle complex military-economic questions and capable of carrying through the necessary coordination. No formal Commander in Chief had as yet made his appearance, though in 1967 Grechko seemed to suggest that First Secretary Brezhnev would be a suitable candidate.

Under these circumstances, and under Zakharov's direction, the General Staff substantially diversified its activities. It constituted a command-in-being entity (operating the key military command center as a centralized institution in Moscow), it reinforced its role as *mozg armii*—the "brain of the army"—and it also took on (even took over) a managerial role with respect to the Soviet military-economic effort (R and D and weapons development.)[44] Such an arrangement not only explains the functions of the main administrations and committees of the General Staff but also Zakharov's innovations, not to mention his singular appointments. The structure of the General Staff retained what might be called a classical configuration—with the CGS at the head, two First Deputies and five Deputy Chiefs, plus the addition of a "Naval Assistant" and ten Directorates (Operations, Intelligence, Mobilization/Organization, Communications/*VOSO*, Topography, Cryptography, ABC warfare, Military Science, Foreign Assistance, Warsaw Pact), but functions were steadily being widely diversified.

Zakharov proceeded to strengthen not only the intelligence competence of the General Staff, but also its part in the weapons development/R and D process. *GRU* (Intelligence) acquired control over satellite monitoring/observation as well as greater operational authority as the crisis with China grew apace, leading to the military crisis of 1969, together with further competence in handling material dealing with foreign armies, while the Scientific-Technical Committee under Alekseyev enlarged its responsibilities to include not only armament but also command and control systems, developments in space, and military psychology.

The Operations Directorate was the heart of the system, divided into sections, each with its own branches: the first section was organized along geographic lines, corresponding to presumed operational areas[45]—Western Europe, the Balkans and the southern theater, the northern, Middle and Near Eastern, Far Eastern—complemented by sections dealing with operational training, naval forces, air forces, general affairs (liaison with other arms and services) including air defense, artillery, armored forces, engineers, and military communications. Mobilization/Organization, together with Operations, enjoys particular pride of place, being connected with the centralized planning of the size, composition, and structure of the Soviet armed forces as a whole, with new forms of organization derived from close and prolonged study of wartime operations to furnish models of "norms and numbers" with specific operations (and opponents) in mind, in given geographic conditions.

The Ground Forces, newly refurbished, took the field—literally—in 1967, showing off their paces in the massive *DNEPR* exercise, which signaled their return to the military scene. A year later, the same forces were on the move in exercises that became operational, culminating in the invasion of Czechoslovakia. The spring of 1968 was also significant for a series of promotions and command changes, drawing new men into the "central apparatus of the Defense Ministry" (which was virtually a synonym for the General Staff), appointments that consolidated Zakharov's own "net" and demonstrated the power of his patronage. Quite the most striking of these appointments was the elevation of Colonel General N. V. Ogarkov to the post of First Deputy Chief of the General Staff—clearly *not* a move designed to reinforce the Operations Directorate, where Povaly was already installed, but one linked with further "technocratization" and the supervision of the military-scientific work (not least in the field of strategic weapons) carried through by the General Staff, closely related to weapons R and D. This appointment assumed even greater significance as the SALT talks began to loom on the horizon, though apparently the first Soviet preference was for Marshal Zakharov himself to represent the Soviet Union in these exchanges.

Events outside the Soviet perimeter also occupied Zakharov's energies and attention. In the wake of the "Six-Day War" in the Middle East in 1967, Zakharov with Lashchenko and Okunev (from *PVO Strany*) tramped Egyptian ground, advising Nasser on the reorganization and reequipping of the Egyptian Army, though agreeing with Nasser's idea of a three-stage recovery—first the defensive, then active deterrence, and, finally, the great counterblow. Crises in the west and east alike—Czechoslovakia and on the Sino-Soviet border—certainly brought added burdens. On the eve of the invasion of Czechoslovakia, on 7 August (1968), General M. I. Kazakov, Chief of Staff to the Warsaw Pact and ex officio a First Deputy Chief of the Soviet General Staff, was replaced by General Shtemenko, whose chief attribute may have been his experience in handling a major Army Group operational staff. The serious clashes with the Chinese led to a much greater reorganization of the command—a short-term stiffening of experienced commanders—and the restructuring of the Soviet defensive system, splitting the Turkestan Military District into two parts with a revival of the Central Asian Military District, together with reorganization of the Mongolian People's Republic Ministry of Defense. But for all the calculated talk about "preemptive strikes" against China, Zakharov's preferred solution seems to have been for a long-term defensive buildup in the Far East and the strong permanent garrisoning, plus the modernization of Soviet Far Eastern forces, including improved combat training.

Toward the close of the 1960s, it was clear that the General Staff under Zakharov had substantially revised the roles and missions of the various arms; in addition, *systems analysts* had been introduced into both the General Staff and the Main Staffs of all arms, thus augmenting the mangerial role of the General Staff. Something akin to a "national security apparatus" was beginning to emerge, though against the background of subtle and subdued criticism that effective coordination was still lacking. On the other hand, Soviet participation in SALT did require such coordination, and it may well be that an "inner group"—not unlike the six-man "inner group" that supervised the Cuban missile affair—operated as a Defense Council, even *the* Defense Council. Through Alekseyev (appointed a Deputy Defense Minister for Armaments in 1970, doubtless charged with speeding missile production before the conclusion of any strategic arms limitation agreement) and Ogarkov, the General Staff played a prominent part in the SALT talks. All four of the Soviet military's full delegates at SALT held General Staff positions, as well as being able to call on the specialists of the General Staff's own Arms Control section, itself associated with the Operations Directorate.

The main lines of national security planning in the widest sense (including deployments, particular weapon developments, and the configuration of global strategy) appear to be set by this "inner group," Politburo members to a man but embodying the truly supreme authority in the Soviet Union— military, political, and economic. Whatever the divergence of views about Zakharov, his later tenure as CGS clearly laid the foundations for the diversification of the role and influence of the General Staff, with "technocratization" tending to reinforce the managerial aspects of the General Staff activity. When he stepped down in September 1971, Marshal Zakharov left his successor, General Kulikov, a complex and expanding organization, at once a command (operational) entity, a "brain" committed to a prodigious effort in developing advanced ideas that were by no means simply military scholasticism—and a coordinating function extending deep into the military-economic field.[46] The appointment of Kulikov as CGS continued the tradition of appointing the Chief from outside the General Staff and from the command of Group of Soviet Forces/Germany (CSFG); the same appointment also marked a form of "rejuvenation," for Kulikov was only forty-nine when he was promoted to Army General and fifty when he took over the General Staff.

While carrying on the "Zakharov tradition"—with its military reservations about détente and arms control, the maintenance of the combined-arms tradition, professionalism associated with greater scientific usage, the growing interest in and commitment to management techniques—Kulikov nevertheless worked within the framework of the "system," established in 1967, a year that should be adjudged of critical and enduring importance in the evolution of Soviet military-political affairs, not least in its attention to *the system*. Investing Grechko with two First Deputy Ministers (Yakubovskii and Sokolov), plus the CGS as a First Deputy Minister of Defense, produced a certain rationalization that established a firm pattern. This bifurcation of posts also established a particular division of labor, with the Defense Minister acting as "chairman of the board"; the CGS responsible for operational matters, organization (force structures), and mobilization (manning); Sokolov becoming the "administrative officer" of the Defense Ministry; the Warsaw Pact commander supervising his own bailiwick (with his

Chief of Staff/Warsaw Pact hooked into the Soviet General Staff); and, *inter alia*, the Chief of the *MPA* holding a watching brief over discipline and military security.

Into this system, or arrangement, Kulikov proceeded to inject his own men, more of the younger generation, though not without making insistent claims for the General Staff as both *the* brain of the army and as *the* command entity with a decisive place in the system. Kulikov proceeded to replace half the Deputy Chiefs, bringing in men of his own age and ilk: at the end of 1971, Colonel General Volkov, a wartime General Staff "representative" (*pre-dstavitel*), was brought in as a Deputy Chief, while the elevation of General Ogarkov to Deputy Defense Minister meant the promotion to First Deputy Chief/General Staff of Colonel General N. M. Kozlov, who had already moved to the General Staff in 1969 from the post of Deputy Chief of Staff (Operations) in GSFG. Once in the General Staff, Kozlov traveled with Grechko on a number of missions abroad (to Poland and Yugoslavia), but his promotion to First Deputy meant his assuming Ogarkov's responsibilities connected with SALT. In 1974 Kozlov was a member of Brezhnev's party for the Vladivostok meeting with President Ford. Like Kozlov, Lieutenant General V. Ya. Abolins was another member of the "Kulikov circle" drawn into the General Staff as a Deputy Chief after serving in GSFG. Abolins was joined shortly thereafter by Colonel General S. F. Akhromeyev, a tank officer, a gold medalist of the General Staff Academy (1967), and a staff officer in the Belorussian Military District. Colonel General I. I. Beletskii was yet another of Kulikov's men, a latecomer to the SALT talks and a Deputy Chief/GS since 1973, though his previous career had included service with Kulikov in the Leningrad Military District. As a weapons specialist and an officer connected with SALT, Beletskii may well have taken over the duties of Alekseyev with the Scientific-Technical Committee in the General Staff (Alekseyev having been promoted to Deputy Defense Minister with special responsibility for weapons development).

Under Kulikov it appears that the "systems approach" received wider attention, particularly command and control and "troop control" (*upravlenie voiskami*). If anything the "Yom Kippur War" (1973) evidently jolted any Soviet complacency about the effectiveness of their tactical C^3, not to mention the responsiveness of the entire system. On the other hand, the "Kulikov circle," built around able and ambitious younger senior commanders, scarcely won popularity contests, and their patron, Kulikov himself, was soon to be displaced. The sudden death of Grechko (and that of Shtemenko), coupled with the increasing infirmity of Yakubovskii, brought Ustinov finally to the post of Defense Minister at the end of April 1976. The military technocrats had finally taken over; in a relatively swift reshuffle of posts, Kulikov, whose cause was scarcely promoted by his abrasive, even erratic, style and his inability to bring about greater integration within the Soviet forces, was appointed Warsaw Pact C in C, and Ogarkov (raised like

Kulikov to the rank of Marshal) was appointed Chief of the Soviet General Staff. The break with appointing the CGS from the command of GSFG was and will probably remain complete. Ogarkov, a military engineer by training, has never held command of a Group of Forces, much less GSFG, and his must be accounted promotion from *within* the General Staff for all practical purposes.

If 1967 was a landmark in Soviet military affairs, 1976 may yet prove to be a watershed, with the restructuring and rethinking conducted under the aegis of the General Staff projecting Soviet policies and force structures as far as and beyond the end of the century, involving both strategic offensive and defensive capability. It is this change that it has been Ogarkov's brief to master—a commission successfully executed, according to a variety of views. The strategic buildup has not abated, though its emphasis now is on greater flexibility and survivability.[47] Improved missile performance can furnish the Soviet command with the possibility of attacking a whole array of hard and soft targets in the United States, while the development of new intercontinental bombers and long-range cruise missiles provide greater versatility. Since Orgarkov makes reference to "strategic nuclear forces"— not the Strategic Missile Forces as such—it might be argued that he has pursued the development of an integrated strategic strike force, a Soviet "triad" of ICBMs, SLBMs, and bombers, with the possibility of adjusting the "mix" as time and technology dictate. At the same time, a strategic command and control system encompassing the Eurasian landmass—and associated sea areas—has been built out of a series of complex "theater force" structures, deployed along the periphery of the main strategic approaches to the Soviet Union, a Soviet version of *tous azimuts*. Basically, the major theaters of war (*TVs*) are divided into "theaters of military operations" (*TVDs*), each at present being fitted out with its own force structures—consisting of the field forces, air strike elements, and air defense assets, the latter a huge new entity formed by combining national air defense systems (*PVO Strany*) with the air defense component of the Ground Forces. By the same token, forming these "theater force packages" has involved a major reorganization of the Soviet Air Force (*VVS*), eliminating the former "air armies" in favor of "air forces" as such, save for the long-range strike forces, which retain numbered air armies (five such armies—24th, 4th, 30th, 36th, and 46th—for the five theater force complexes).

This search for flexibility of necessity requires effective command and control that is at once survivable and sustainable. Under the previous system, the General Staff exercized its *direct* operational control over all Soviet forces *without* intermediate command echelons: a shadow organization of General Staff battle staffs (modeled on the wartime *predstavitelii*, General Staff "representatives" with front and field commands) had been set up, sensible enough when it was considered that "front-type" organizations would be activated in war. However, as Marshal Ogarkov has made plain, the "front" is too constricted an entity to manage the "larger scale of military operations," nothing less than "the *strategic* operation within the theater of combat operations." This leads to several combinations—intercontinental strategic strike forces, regional nuclear forces (and/or conventional forces, themselves supported by a highly survivable theater nuclear capability— witness the SS-20s).[48]

The establishment of at least two major strategic theater commands— the western and the Far Eastern—forms part of the process of implementing centralized strategic control with decentralized battle management, with this "theater command" echelon forming the link between the General Staff and the major field forces. The strategic air strike elements could also come under direct General Staff operational control, much as the General Staff has "manual override" for strategic forces as a whole. This thrust toward integration, which is as yet unfinished, also requires much greater coordination, a reflection of which might be seen in the command changes within the General Staff. One noticeable feature has been the growing rapprochement between the General Staff and the Main Naval Staff, facilitated to some degree by the appointment in 1978 of Admiral Amelko, a highly experienced naval officer and ASW specialist, as a Deputy Chief/General Staff, replacement for the late Admiral of the Fleet S. M. Lobov, previously "Naval Assistant" to the CGS. The change in status of the Soviet naval representative was perhaps more than compensated for by the increased integration at General Staff level, an "all-arms" approach that was also reflected in the General Staff's concern over the protection of the Soviet SSBN force, the "strategic submarine missile system," which the Soviet Navy operates on behalf of the General Staff.

The reorganization and diversification of the senior levels of the General Staff seemed to gather its own momentum in 1978–79, with Ogarkov obviously ringing the changes, some of which may have been induced by the scale of the military involvement in Afghanistan, or anticipation of such involvement. In May 1979 Army General M. M. Kozlov, First Deputy Chief/CGS, was publicly identified as head of the General Staff Academy, successor to General Shavrov (who left the Academy in September 1978). Far from being in disfavor for his remarks over SALT II and thus put out to academic pastures, Kozlov's appointment to the Academy seems to have been a mark of the professional and political esteem in which he was held, the General Staff Academy being no mere "teaching post." Nor would this appointment have been made without the approval of Ustinov and Ogarkov, while Brezhnev himself emphasized the importance of the work. "Technocratization" thus has taken a formidable stride in the direction of the Academy.

It was perhaps no great surprise when General Akhromeyev (now promoted to Marshal) took over from Kozlov as First Deputy Chief/General Staff, but the appointment of General V. I. Varennikov in November 1979 as a second First Deputy Chief/General Staff raised some questions: with

General Gribkov, Chief of Staff/Warsaw Pact, as yet another First Deputy Chief, this furnished three First Deputy Chiefs. Promoted to Army General in February 1978, Varennikov enjoyed an excellent reputation, based on his work in the Leningrad Military District, as commander of Third Shock Army in GSFG, and as a successful commander of the important Carpathian Military District, one utilized for a number of innovations and experiments. The gap left by Ogarkov's own appointment to the General Staff was apparently filled by Colonel General Engineer V. M. Shabanov, an electronics expert and a Deputy Minister for the Soviet Radio Industry, who was appointed a Deputy Defense Minister and could well carry responsibilities previously undertaken by Alekseyev and Ogarkov in the field of strategic weapons research and development.

The Akhromeyev-Varennikov dualism seems to have been connected not only with the restructuring that began to introduce strategic theater commands, but also with a major General Staff/General Staff Academy contribution managed by a handpicked "brain trust" of experienced officers. Included are General Obaturov (recently appointed head of the Frunze Academy and Varennikov's predecessor as commander of the Carpathian Military District); Colonel General V. N. Karpov (Ogarkov's chief of staff in the Volga Military District, chief of staff in the Central Asian Military District in 1969, and assigned to the General Staff Academy, evidently working on Soviet strategic organization under war conditions); and Lieutenant General A. A. Sokolov, a senior staff officer. It is conceivable, moreover, that E. V. Boichuk, appointed an Artillery Marshal in November 1980, is also closely associated with this group and has particular responsibility for nuclear policy, above all, defense and survivability under changing conditions of nuclear threat—indeed, the "doomsday study" that was reportedly completed on Andropov's instruction.

These changes may well prove to be as profound as anything seen since the early postwar period, both in the expansion of offensive capabilities and the requirements for defense of the homeland. In this respect, the Soviet General Staff under Ogarkov has masterminded change, concentrating on the *integration* and coordination of military force configurations for global operations. Those same principles, integration and coordination, have also been developed extensively to build a "nuclear command machine," whose outlines can be perceived as far back as 1967, and where the General Staff has played its part—doggedly, at times—for more efficient higher military leadership. While the General Staff in all its diversity occupies a key role, it does not dispose of decisive authority, either in command or planning. Kulikov's ideas of such supremacy for the General Staff evidently met neither with approval nor success. Such power lies with the Defense Council, the "inner council" in peacetime, and a possible wartime "State Defense Committee," with its special echelon to deal with wartime economic mobilization/production, again on the model of the last war.[49]

This complex machine—for such it is—took time to develop and to perfect, which may have accounted for Brezhnev's unusual coyness in making public his chairmanship of the Defense Council (and his designation as Commander in Chief), while Andropov entertained no such delay. The Defense Council, with its six to eight members, becomes the wartime supreme control group, with the "*Stavka*-type" body formed from the military membership of the Defense Ministry collegium (arms and services commanders) and the General Staff—as in the Great Patriotic War—the "working organ" serving both the supremo and the *Stavka*. It is this arrangement, in both peace and war, that gives a singular stamp to the duties and position of the Soviet CGS, who is ex officio the most important of the Deputy Defense Ministers: he is authorized to deputize for the Defense Minister himself (shades of the 1900s), and his is the second authorizing signature on operational/mobilization orders. The CGS is also the "coordinator" of the submissions of Deputy Defense Ministers for submission to the Minister. In addition to correlating the requirements and decisions of the several Main Staffs in order to establish "the General Staff view"—which is totally binding—the CGS coordinates the work of the multiple agencies of the Defense Ministry, all of which gives him a unique vantage point with respect to information and requirements.[50]

It is possible that the General Staff itself houses the working secretariat of the Defense Council (which in turn draws on the work of a wide range of military secretariats attached to Party and governmental bodies). Though lacking any voting right, the Soviet CGS must perforce be an assiduous participant in Defense Council meetings (where the Defense Minister as a Politburo member sits of right) and must be generally acquainted with the views of those who also act as special consultants to the Council. Additionally, the CGS by tradition and seeming authority conveys the wider view of military interests to Party, state, and administrative bodies, much as Ogarkov some while ago turned to the problem of investment allocation and choice (or rather, no choice), or, most recently, publicized the possible impact of revolutionary new American weapons and technology for command and control that could "qualitatively" change the management of strategic operations, dialogues meant both for internal and external consumption.

"It will do us no good to have an Army, Navy, Air Force, and Marine Corps, of whatever quality, if we have forgotten how to wage war." Thus spoke Lieutenant General Victor H. Krulak, reflecting on shortcomings in American organization for national security, where managerial functions and "amateur civilian opinions" have become preeminent and predominant.[51] There is need for a military organization that can—on the basis of *continuity of experience*—conduct strategic planning and direct military operations. Institutional continuity, experience, and expertise—such are precisely the distinguishing features of the Soviet General Staff, which is certainly not averse to looking to the traditions and contributions of its Imperial predecessor. Above all, in spite of its growing interest in and commitment to managerial functions, the Soviet General Staff does not fail for an instant to recognize that its prime responsibilities are inextricably bound up with "the exigencies of war" and that they must so remain, as indeed they will.

NOTES

1. First published by Macmillan in 1890.
2. It is worth noting that the "Regulations of the Russian General Staff" were translated by the Second (Military Information) Division of the War Department General Staff: translator Wilfred Stevens (1–9 February: source Russian Government Publications, St. Petersburg, Military Printing Office [in the central staff building], 1899).
3. See Lieutenant General von Caemmerer, German Army, *The Development of Strategical Science during the 19th century*, Pall Mall Military Series (London, 1905).
4. See Colonel William L. Hauser, "Leadership for Tomorrow's Army: An American General Staff System?" *Parameters* 8 (September 1978): 2–9.
5. It is impossible not to make immediate reference to three invaluable works: John Shelton Curtiss (on the Department of the General Staff), *The Russian Army under Nicholas I 1825–1855* (Duke University Press, 1965), 101–5; P. A. Zaionchkovskii, *Voennye reformy 1860–1970 godov v. Russii* (Moscow: Izd. Moskovsk. Universiteta, 1952), a work made the more remarkable considering the times in which it was written; also Forrestt A. Miller (on the General Staff), *Dmitrii Miliutin and the Reform Era in Russia* (Vanderbilt University Press, 1968), 82–84. Among other secondary sources, see esp. L. G. Beskrovnyi, *Russkaya armiya i flot v XIX veke* (Moscow: Nauka, 1973).
6. N. P. Glinoetskii, *Ist. ocherk Nikolaevskii akademii General'navo shtaba* (St. Petersburg, 1882) (BM copy). He was also the author of a two-volume history of the General Staff, published 1883–1894.
7. A feature bitterly assailed in yet another remarkable work by P. A. Zaionchkovskii, *Samoderzhavie i russkaya armiya na rubezhe XIX–XX stoletti 1881–1903* (Moscow: "Mysl," 1973), esp. 178. Zaionchkovskii observes that gunners and engineers did not behave arrogantly or try to constitute a special group.
8. For some convenient references and analysis, see G. P. Meshcheryakov, *Russkaya voennaya mysl' v XIX v.* (Moscow: Nauka, 1973), esp. chaps. 3 and 4; Major General N. Pavlenko, "Iz istorii razvitiya teorii strategii," *VIZ*, 1964, no. 10:104–16; also V. D'yakov, "O razvitii russkoi voenno-istoricheskoi mysli v poslednei chetverti XIX veka," *VIZ*, 1959, no. 5:60–72. In view of the recent intensification of Soviet interest in "theater operations," these are of more than passing academic interest. (*VIZ: Voenno-istoricheskii Zhurnal*).
9. For the most succinct and detailed summary of General Staff development, see the series "Iz istorii russkovo general'novo shtaba" by Colonel A. Kavtaradze, beginning *VIZ*, 1971, no. 12:76–79; continuing through *VIZ*, 1972, no. 7; 1974, no. 12; 1976, no. 3 (bringing the catalog of institutional change to 1918); and 1978, no. 6 (on *VUGSh*).
10. The *Glavnyi morskoi shtab* had been established in 1831, the *Morskoi General'nyi shtab* on 24 April 1906.
11. See esp. Dr. Hans-Peter Stein, "Der Offizier des Russischen Heeres in Zeitabschnitt zwischen Reform und Revolution (1861–1905): bd. 13 in *Forschungen zur osteuropäischen Geschichte* (Berlin, 1967), 346–507; also the invaluable study, Dr. John Bushnell, "The Tsarist Officer Corps, 1881–1914: Customs, Duties, Inefficiency," *American Historical Review* 86, no. 4 (October 1981):753–80.

12. The terminology used in Dr. Norman Stone, *The Eastern Front 1914–1917* (London, 1975), 22.

13. *Osoboe deloproizvodstvo*/Special Registry, dealing with intelligence and counterintelligence, under *I Otdel* (*Gen.-kvartirmeister*).

14. Professor Matitiahu Mayzel has produced a unique and invaluable study with *Generals and Revolutionaries, The Russian General Staff During the Revolution . . .* (Osnabrück: Biblio Verlag, 1979). Of quite extraordinary interest and value is M. Frenkin, *Russkaya armiya i Revolyutsiya 1917–1918* (Munich: Logos, 1978), massively supported and substantiated by material from Soviet archives. See also Allan K. Wildman, *The End of the Russian Imperial Army: The Old Army and the Soldiers' Revolt (March–April 1917)* (Princeton University Press, 1980).

15. For early developments, see Mayzel, chap. 6, "October and After," 173–225; also J. Erickson, "The Origins of the Red Army," in *Revolutionary Russia*, ed. R. Pipes (Harvard University Press, 1968), 236–54; also S. M. Klyatskin, parts 2 and 3, *Na zashchite Oktyabrya* (Moscow: Nauka, 1965), 143–421.

16. On the creation of a Soviet Academy, see General V. G. Kulikov, ed., *Akademiya General'nogo shtaba* (Moscow: Voenizdat, 1976), 16–22.

17. On the Academy and the Civil War, ibid., 22–32.

18. See P. I. Yakir, "Iz istorii pevekhoda Krasnoi Armii na mirnoe polozhenie," in *Oktyabr i grazhdanskaya voina v SSSR* (Moscow: Nauka, 1966), 445–64; also J. Erickson, "Some Military and Political Aspects of the 'Militia Army' Controversy, 1919–1920," in *Essays in Honour of E. H. Carr* (Macmillan, 1974), 204–28.

19. Erickson, "Military and Political Aspects," 212.

20. See detailed account, Colonel V. Danilov, "Sozdanie shtaba RKKA (fevral 1921–mart 1924)," *VIZ*, 1977, no. 9:85–89.

21. Kulikov, 35.

22. This remark of Lenin's (disclosed by Frunze himself in March 1925) is frequently expunged in commentaries on Frunze (and was deleted from the 1957 editions of his works, as it has been from the latest 1977 edition); however, see the important and highly informative study by Colonel I. Krotokov, "K istorii stanovleniya Sovetskoi voennoi nauki," in *Vestnik voennoi istorii*, no. 2 (Moscow: Voenzdat, 1971), 49–50.

23. Although a decision had been taken in 1921 to establish 3 militia divisions in Moscow, Petrograd, and the Urals, only 1 militia brigade was actually formed in Petrograd. In January–February 1923, 10 regular divisions were transferred to the new "territorial-militia" basis, each division having 1,607 permanent staff and 10,959 "alternating" (militia) troops. Three categories of territorial-militia divisions were created, and in 1925 the Red Army infantry consisted of 77 divisions (31 cadre, 46 territorial-militia—of which 28 were "Category 1," 16 "Category 2"; the permanent staff of a Category 1 division was 2,400 men). Of the 11 cavalry divisions and 3 brigades, only 1 had gone over to the territorial-militia system.

24. The Red Army Inspectorate (*Inspektorat RKKA*) consisted of two administrations (for military training and military-educational institutions) plus five inspectorates (infantry and military training for conscripts, cavalry, artillery, engineers, and signals troops). In October 1924 the Inspectorate was again placed under the Red Army Staff only to be detached in subsequent changes and finally attached to the Staff. See details in I. B. Berkhin, *Voennaya reforma v SSSR (1924–1925)* (Moscow: Voenizdat, 1958), 150–51.

25. Ibid., 154.

26. General A. I. Radzievski, ed., *Akademiya imeni M. V. Frunze* (Moscow: Voenizdat, 1973), 70–74.

27. Berkhin, 156–57.

28. Shaposhnikov voluntarily entered the Red Army in May 1918, moving at once to staff appointments with the *VVS*, staff duties in the Ukraine, Chief of the Intelligence Section/Field Staff (1919–21), First Assistant to the Chief of the Red Army Staff (1921–22), commander of the Leningrad MD (1925), and Moscow MD (1927), Chief of the Red Army Staff (1928–31), commander of Volga MD (1931), Chief of the Frunze Academy (1932–35); in 1937 Shaposhnikov became Chief of the General Staff of the Red Army and was made a Marshal of the Soviet Union in 1940.

29. For notes on the literature of this debate, see Colonel I. A. Korotkov, *Istoriya sovetskoi voennoi mysli (1917–1941)* (Moscow: Nauka, 1980, 81, also 80–84 (this is a highly

sophisticated and indispensable work, unaccountably ignored by many); on institutional developments, see Colonel V. Danilov, "Ot shtaba RKKA k General'nomu shtaba Raboche-Krestyanskoi Krasnoi Armii (1924–1935 gg)," *VIZ*, 1978, no. 8:101–6, an excellent summary and survey.

30. For a summary of these views and developments, see Korotkov, 131–36; also chap. 6 on "The Theory of Military Economics/the Military Economy," 185f.

31. See the compilations *Voprosy strategii i operativnogo iskusstva v sovetskikh voen-nykh trudakh 1917–1940* (Voenizdat, 1965) and *Voprosy taktiki v sovetskikh voennykh trudakh 1917–1940* (Voenizdat, 1970). See also "Strategicheski kontseptsii vozmozhnoi voiny" in Korotkov, 120–143.

32. For details see A. Vasilevskii, Marshal SU, *Delo vsei zhizni*, 2d ed. (Moscow: Politizdat, 1975), under "Poslednie mirnye mesyatsy."

33. I take this to be the prime conclusion on Soviet war planning for the "initial period" in Army General S. P. Ivanov, ed., *Nachal'nyi period voiny* (Moscow: Voenizdat, 1974): see chap. 3 (67f.) and chap. 8 (197–216) on Soviet preparations and planning.

34. See Colonel V. Danilov, "General'nyi shtab RKKA v predvoennye gody (1936–iyun 1941)," *VIZ*, 1980, no. 3:68–73; also *Sovetskie vooruzhennye sily*, Istoriya stroitel'stva (Collective authorship) (Moscow: Voenizdat, 1978), 233–34.

35. The wartime role of the General Staff is virtually a subject in its own right, hence this brief profile of materials: see esp. Vasilevskii, under "V General'nom shtabe," 515–51, for something of an "inside" view; also the latest version of General S. M. Shtemenko's account, *General'nyi shtab v gody voiny*, Series "Voennye Memuary," 2 vols. (Moscow: Voenizdat, 1981); also I. Peresypkin, Marshal Sigs., "Svyaz General'nogo shtaba," *VIZ*, 1971, no. 4; also N. Saltykov, "Predstaviteli General'nogo shtaba," *VIZ*, 1971, no. 9; V. Golubovich and I. Kulikov, "O korpuse ofitserov-predstaviteli General'nogo shtaba," *VIZ*, 1975, No. 12; I. Kulikov, "Ofitsery-predstaviteli General'nogo shtaba v oboronitel'nom srazhenii pod Kurskom," *VIZ*, 1976, no. 8; S. Bronevskii, "Ob operpunkte General'nogo shtaba na Leningradskom napravlenii (1941)," *VIZ*, 1979, no. 8; A. Evseyev and O. Gurov, "Organizat-siya informatsionnoi raboty v General'nom shtabe, shtabakh frontov i armii," *VIZ*, 1981, no. 3.

36. See *Sovetskaya Voennaya Entsiklopediya*, vol. 5 (Moscow: Voenizdat, 1978), 405, s.v. "Morskoi General'nyi shtab."

37. VVS: see *Dekrety Sovetskoi vlasti*, vol. 1, doc. no. 336, 4 March 1918 (Moscow: Politizdat, 1957), 522–23.

38. See "Memo: Conclusions Regarding a Possible Soviet Decision to Precipitate Global War," *CIA Research Reports* (Univ. Publications of America, microfilm), 12 October 1950.

39. The two indispensable and enduring works covering these developments are Raymond L. Garthoff, *The Soviet Image of Future War* (Washington, D.C.: Public Affairs Press, 1959), and H. S. Dinerstein, *War and the Soviet Union* (Praeger Press, 1959; rev. ed., 1962).

40. Formed by splitting off a section of the *GRU* (Main Intelligence Directorate).

41. See "Strategicheskie kontseptsii vozmozhnoi voiny" in Korotkov, 120f.

42. See Colonel A. Lagovskii, "Vozmozhnye potrebnosti vooruzhennykh sil," in *Strat-egiya i ekonomika* (Moscow: Voenizdat, 1957), 87f.

43. Army General V. Kurasov, "Voprosy sovetskoi voennoi nauki v proizvedeniyakh V. I. Lenina," *VIZ*, 1961, no. 3:3–14.

44. I find it a little hard to accept Professor Shane E. Mahoney's observation in *The Role of the General Staff in Military Management: Persistence and Change* that the General Staff has substituted the instrumentality of military management for its role as "the brain of the army"; on the contrary, the General Staff very cleverly saw that both go hand in hand, though never relaxing its grip on the "cerebral" side.

45. Present Soviet organization appears to envisage three theaters of war (*TVs*), five *TVDs*, five *MTVDs* (maritime *TVDs*), two *OTVDs* (oceanic *TVDs*–Indian Ocean, Pacific): the three *TVs* are Western, Eastern, Intercontinental; the first two "combined-arms" entities, the latter long-range strategic nuclear forces. In our draft of the *Military District Study*, my colleagues and I suggested that Varennikov and Akhromeyev were initially General Staff "directors" of and for the western and Eastern *TVs*.

46. V. G. Kulikov, "Mozg armii," review of Shaposhnikov's memoirs, *Vospominaniya: Voenno-nauchnye trudy*, Pravda, 13 November 1974.

47. On the evolution of the Soviet missile forces, see Robert P. Berman and John C. Baker, "Soviet Strategic Force Development," chap. 3 in *Soviet Strategic Forces: Requirements and Responses* (The Brookings Institution, 1982).

48. Under war conditions, the separate arms–virtually administered as such on behalf of the General Staff–would be displaced by "force packages" organized on combined-arms lines, with objectives, force levels, deployments, operational patterns previously determined by General Staff specialists. My own view is that often the *First Deputy Commander* (e.g., at Military District level) is the key commander, linked with General Staff Operations: I would also argue that the "General Staff presence" can reach even down to *regiment*.

49. On 8 December 1942 the *GKO* (State Defense Committee) set up its own *Operativnoe byuro GKO* to direct key industrial sectors and supply: V. N. Shredov, *KPSS–organizator voennovo proizvodstva v 1941–1942 gg.* (Leningrad University, 1982), 15.

50. For a very detailed study, see Michael Sadykiewicz, "Soviet Military Politics," *Survey* 26 (1982), pt. 1, 180–210.

51. Lieutenant General Victor H. Krulak, USMC (Ret.), *Organization for National Security: A Study* (United States Strategic Institute, 1983).

3

The Soviet Decision-making Process
For National Security Policy

Harriet Fast Scott

In the United States, each year several books and many articles are written on the decision-making process for national security matters. Many of these publications are by persons who have served recently at high levels in government, from the national Security Council to key positions in the United States Congress. An analyst in Washington, seeking to describe the decision-making process for national security affairs, is overwhelmed with source material; his primary task is one of selection and evaluation.

For those who attempt to study the same topic regarding the Soviet Union, the problem is completely different. Current factual data on the Soviet decision-making process for security matters are extremely rare. On occasion, the curtain is lifted slightly to hint at certain procedures or personalities involved, but generally the information given is insufficient even to place it within a meaningful whole picture. Some of the data released by the Soviet leaders, moreover, may be intended to confuse or to conceal, rather than to reveal.

A great deal is written now in the West about the Soviet Council of Defense, which appears to be the major body concerned with Soviet security policy. However, references to this Council in Soviet publications are limited. Its existence was noted in the Soviet press in 1976, and Leonid Brezhnev was identified as its head. Following his death in November 1982, it was not until 9 May 1983 that *Pravda*, the official newspaper of the Communist Party of the Soviet Union, confirmed that Yuri Andropov was his replacement. Brezhnev and Andropov are the only two individuals specifically identified as being on the Council, and we can only speculate as to its full membership.

We find references in the Soviet press to defense industries, but we are not certain of the role of the Defense Industry Department of the Central Committee of the CPSU. On occasion, references can be found to the Military Industrial Committee (*VPK*), headed by the Deputy Chairman of the Council of Ministers, L. V. Smirnov. His exact authority and relationship to the head of the Defense Industry Department of the Central Committee are not known. In 1971, when Leonid Brezhnev stated before the Twenty-fourth Party Congress that "as much as 42 percent of the [Soviet Union] defense industry's output is used for civilian purposes,"[1] no Western analyst knew exactly to which defense industry's output he was referring.

Despite this Soviet obsession with security, research on Soviet decision making for national security policies is possible, and, one hopes, even some reasonable conclusions can be reached. This is due, first, to the Soviet practice of following historical precedent (history beginning with the Bolshevik takeover in 1917). Policy planning, resource allocation, and monitoring and coordination of operations are discussed in Soviet writings today, but, for instance, in the context of events during the "Great Patriotic War," from June 1941 to May 1945. What is presented by Soviet military literature today does not necessarily reflect how the decision-making process for security policy actually was conducted at the time. Rather, it is an idealized account of what happened, with lessons drawn that are considered applicable for the present and the future.

Second, organizational structures do not change as often in the Soviet Union as in the United States. Lenin is deified, and the sources of Soviet wisdom and of justification for contemporary actions are traced to his writings. Organizations and procedures started in Lenin's day may be used to justify organizational structures and the legitimacy of actions today. It was Lenin's foresight, according to Party spokesmen, that provided guidance for the Party leadership, enabling the Soviet state to emerge victoriously in the Great Patriotic War.

A historical approach, therefore, will be used in this analysis. Known Soviet decision-making bodies for national security will be examined from the time they were instituted to the present. Soviet assertions concerning the functions and competence of these organs during the Great Patriotic War, and the declared necessity to maintain similar bodies for the present and future, provide some measure for determining their current significance.

It is recognized that Soviet decision-making methodology can be traced, in part, to practices found in Imperial Russia. This aspect, however, will not be dealt with here. Essentially, the analysis and conclusions reached will be based on research of Soviet sources.

Formation and Role of the Council of Defense

As noted, very little actually is known of the Council of Defense, as it exists in the early 1980s. It is generally agreed among Western analysts, however, that this is the supreme organ in the Soviet Union concerned with national security policy, and has wide decision-making authority. At least one analyst asserts that the primary ruling body in the Soviet Union today is not the Politburo, but the "Supreme Defense Council," as the Council of Defense is erroneously referred to.[2] To understand the probable role and significance of the Council of Defense, it is necessary to examine in detail the role and functions of its predecessors, Lenin's Council of Labor and Defense (*STO*) and Stalin's wartime State Committee of Defense (*GKO*).

The description given to *STO* and *GKO* by Soviet spokesmen since 1965, when Leonid Brezhnev began his "re-Stalinization" campaign may not be historically accurate. This aspect, rather than detracting from the accounts in question, makes them all the more valuable. The idealized descriptions of how these organizations functioned previously suggest that Soviet writers are attempting to indicate how the Council of Defense is supposed to function now, with accuracy not being the main objective.

Establishment of *STO*

On 2 September 1918 the All-Russian Central Executive Committee (*VTsIK*) declared the Soviet state an armed camp, and decreed the establishment of a Council of Defense. This body was instituted formally on 30 November 1918, with Lenin as Chairman.[3] At that time, Lenin was also Chairman of the Council of People's Commissars (*SNK*). Under his direction, the Council of Defense was the supreme organization for running the entire Civil War effort for the Bolsheviks. In 1920, during a lull in the fighting, soldiers were put to work at various needed tasks, and the Council took the name Council of Labor and Defense, generally referred to as *STO*. Lenin continued as its head.[4]

Soviet Top Decision-Making Structure, 1919,
Indicating Centralized Nature of Control

Council of People's
Commissars (*SNK*)
(chaired by Lenin)

|

Council of Labor and Defense (*STO*)
(chaired by Lenin)

|

Revolutionary Military Council of
the USSR (*Revvoyensoviet USSR*)
(chaired by Leon Trotskii)

Membership in *STO* is instructive when comparing it with the membership of GKO during the Great Patriotic War, and the presumed membership of the Council of Defense today. As can be seen below, members were those senior Bolsheviks most concerned with overall responsibilities for the total Civil War effort. These were:

Chairman–Lenin, the senior Communist Party figure and also
Chairman of the *SNK*

Members—The People's Commissars for Military Affairs, Rail-
roads, Agriculture, Foodstuff, Labor, Workers' and
Peasants' Inspections, and also the Chairman of the
Higher Council of the People's Economy[5]
(Two representatives also sat on this body, one from the *VTsSPC*
[Council of Trade Unions], and the other the director of the
Central Statistical Directorate, who had a deliberative vote.)

Under the direction of *STO*, additional bodies were formed, to include
the Commission for Internal Trade, the Concessionaire Committee, and
Gosplan (State Planning Commission).[6] This latter body appears to have
been given responsibilities for resource allocations, under the direction of
STO.

After the end of the Civil War and the death of Lenin, the work of *STO*
continued in much the same manner as before. A 1930 Soviet book, *Organization of the Armed Forces of the USSR*, defined its functions as follows:

For coordinating and combining work of the central apparatus of the Commissar of Military and Naval Affairs (*NKVM*), with
overall state work in the realm of strengthening the defense of the
country and its economic structuring, there is a special all-state
(supradepartmental) organ—the Council of Labor and Defense—
STO USSR.[7]

At this time *STO* was a small organization. Its Chairman continued to
be the Chairman of the Council of People's Commissars (*SNK*) or his deputy,
and eight members designated by the *SNK*. The 1930 book emphasized that
STO had "the role of the supreme military-economic organ of the USSR"
and that throughout the USSR the decrees of *STO* were "unconditionally
obligatory until they are changed by the Central Executive Committee
(*VTsIK*) or the Council of People's Commissars (*SNK*)."[8]

When the work of the *GKO* during the Great Patriotic War and the
possible role of the present Council of Defense are examined later in this
analysis, it may be well to consider some of the more significant directives of
STO, especially those that were made after the end of the Civil War. They
included:

- supplying troops of the western front with foodstuffs (May 1920)
- inducting citizens of non-Russian nationality into the army on an
  equal footing with the other citizens of the RSFSR (May 1920)
- creating the Cheka (January 1921)
- transforming the short command courses into military schools
  (January 1921)
- elaborating programs to develop the aviation industry and to
  construct the Air Fleet (January 1921)

- the program of ship construction for 1926–1932 (1926)
- the program for naval construction for 1933–1938 (June 1933)
- the system of artillery arming of the Red Army for the second
  Five-Year Plan (March 1934)
- the plan to develop the Air Forces for 1935–1937 (April 1935)[9]

Although *STO* issued certain directives in the 1930s, as shown above, in 1932 there was a Defense Commission, headed by V. M. Molotov, *"pri"* (attached) to the Council of People's Commissars (*SNK*), to ensure that the growing industrialization of the Soviet Union met the needs of the defense establishment.[10] *STO* rapidly was becoming a rubber stamp, legalizing decisions already made by the Defense Commission. Membership of both *STO* and the Defense Commission was affected by Stalin's purges, which took the lives of hundreds of thousands of Party members. On 28 April 1937 *STO* was abolished and its functions were transferred to the Economic Council, which was *"pri"* (attached) to the *SNK* USSR.[11] The Defense Commission was transformed into the Committee of Defense (*KO*).

On 27 April 1937, the day before *STO* was disbanded, the Committee of Defense (*KO*) was formed to coordinate all measures connected with strengthening the defense of the country, in light of what the Kremlin saw as "the growing military threat for the USSR." Molotov was designated Chairman, with Stalin, Voroshilov (the Commissar of Defense), and others serving on the same body as members. This new organization "was given practical leadership for carrying out the programs of the CPSU to strengthen the defense of the country and raise its military potential.[12] The official description of the work of the Committee of Defense, as given in the 1970s, appears identical to that of the earlier tasks of *STO*. The *KO* initiated plans to create and accumulate mobilization reserves, including reserves of raw materials, fuel, and foodstuffs. It was also concerned with plans to build fortified regions, border defense, naval bases, and the method of transforming some industries for the production of military goods. In 1937 *KO* ordered the formation of two new Military Districts.[13]

On 31 January 1938 a permanent Military-Industrial Commission (*VPK*) was formed, subordinate to *KO*, with the specific tasks of mobilization and preparation of all industry for the production of armaments. At the same time the People's Commissariats were directed by *KO* to rebuild and enlarge the production of plants and factories for increased production of armaments and military equipment.[14]

In May 1940 Voroshilov became a Deputy Chairman of the *SNK* and Chairman of the Committee of Defense, replacing Molotov. Timoshenko replaced Voroshilov as Commissar of Defense. In May 1941 Stalin became the Chairman of the *SNK*.

These Soviet agencies for national security matters, under Stalin's tutelage, left an impressive record. Following the end of the Civil War in the

1920s, the Red Army had to depend upon foreign imports of tanks and aircraft engines. Many of the industrial leaders and skilled working cadres had been liquidated or had fled the country. Millions died in the thirties as a result of starvation, brought about by Stalin's collectivization of agriculture, or from the purges. Despite this, the production of armaments never ceased, as shown in Table 3.1.

The Soviet military-industrial leadership, however, had concentrated on quantity rather than quality. The use of Soviet equipment in the Spanish Civil War brought out glaring weaknesses. Soviet aircraft and tanks proved to be inferior to the latest German armaments, at that time. By 1938, the Soviet leaders were attempting to modernize their military equipment, a program that was well under way by 1941.

When Hitler did attack, the Soviet decision-making apparatus for national security matters fell apart. All authority for decision making was in Stalin's hands. Failing to heed the warnings of some of his intelligence sources and of Western leaders, Stalin was mentally unprepared for an invasion. He literally collapsed, and it is reported that he left Moscow for his dacha, unable to face the reality of actual events. When Politburo members came to see him, Stalin thought he would be arrested and suffer the same fate he had dealt out to others. Instead, he was asked to return to Moscow and to resume his place of leadership of the Soviet State.

It is instructive to keep in mind how these previous defense organs were developed and functioned from the 1920s until June 1941, when Hitler launched his invasion. The Soviet decision-making process for national

TABLE 3.1
Annual Output of Defense Industry

Item	Yearly Average 1930–1931	Yearly Average 1935–1937	For the Year 1938
Artillery	1,911	5,020	12,687
Rifles	174,000	397,000	1,174,000
Aircraft	860	3,578	5,469
Tanks	740	3,319	2,271

Manpower

	1933	1935	1 Jan. 1938
Men	885,000	930,000	1,513,400

SOURCE: Adapted from M. V. Zakharov, ed., *50 Let Vooruzhennykh Sil SSSR* (50 Years of the Armed Forces of the USSR) (Moscow: Voyenizdat, 1968), 193; and A. N. Lagovskiy, *V. I. Lenin ob Ekonomicheskom Obespechenii Oborony Strany* (V. I. Lenin on the Economic Support of the Country's Defenses) (Moscow: Voyenizdat, 1976)., 141.

TABLE 3.2
Organization of the Central Apparatus in 1939

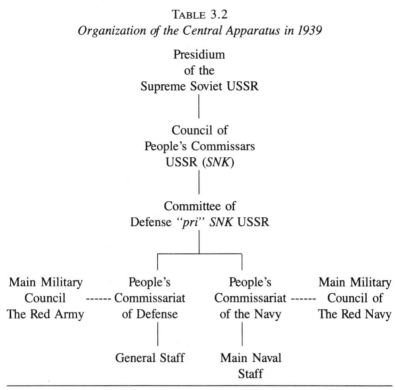

Presidium
of the
Supreme Soviet USSR

Council of
People's Commissars
USSR (*SNK*)

Committee of
Defense *"pri" SNK* USSR

Main Military	People's	People's	Main Military
Council ------	Commissariat	Commissariat ------	Council of
The Red Army	of Defense	of the Navy	The Red Navy

General Staff · Main Naval Staff

SOURCE: Adapted from M. V. Zakharov, ed., *50 Let Vooruzhennykh Sil SSSR* (50 Years of the Armed Forces of the USSR) (Moscow: Voyenizdat, 1968), 237.

security matters, developed in those years, appears to have established the pattern for the Council of Defense and related bodies of today.

The absolute power vested in Stalin poses a problem that still remains unsolved. For a period of two or three days he was incapable of making a decision. Does the Kremlin still place in one person the sole authority to respond to an attack, or to launch an attack, when nuclear weapons are concerned? Or is the much-touted collective leadership in the Soviet Union a reality?

The State Committee of Defense (*GKO*)

Eight days after the German invasion, on 30 June 1941, the Committee of Defense was abolished and the State Committee of Defense (*GKO*) was created. Soviet spokesmen refer to this body as "the extraordinary higher state organ in which complete power was concentrated during the years of the Great Patriotic War."[15] According to official reports, it was formed by the

Presidium of the Supreme Soviet, in coordination with the Central Committee of the Party and the Council of People's Commissars (*SNK*),[16] now known as the Council of Ministers. Stalin was Chairman, with Molotov his Deputy. Other members of the original body were K. Ye. Voroshilov, G. M. Malenkov, and L. P. Beria. Later N. A. Bulganin, N. A. Voznesenskii, L. M. Kaganovich, and A. I. Mokoyan were added.

Each member of *GKO* was assigned specific areas of responsibility, which were similar to the work the individual already was doing. Positions (at that time) are shown below:

- I. V. Stalin, Chairman of *GKO* (30 June 1941), Politburo member (from 1919), Party General Secretary (April 1922), Commissar of Defense (19 July 1941), Commander in Chief of Red Army (8 August 1941), Chairman of *Stavka* of the High Command (10 July 1941), Chairman of *Stavka* of the Supreme High Command (8 August 1941), Chairman of *SNK*

- V. M. Molotov, Deputy Chairman of *GKO*, also Politburo member (1926–1957), First Deputy Chairman of *SNK*, People's Commissar of Foreign Affairs (May 1939), and member of *Stavka VGK*

- G. M. Malenkov, member of *GKO*, Candidate Politburo member, Chairman of Committee for Aircraft Production, Chairman of Committee for Economic Rehabilitation of Liberated Areas

- L. P. Beria, member of *GKO*, head of *NKVD*, Chairman of Committee for Raising Output of Armaments and Munitions, Candidate Politburo member

- K. Ye. Voroshilov, member of *GKO* and *Stavka*, Politburo member, Deputy Chairman of *SNK*, Marshal of the Soviet Union

- N. A. Voznesenskiy, member of *GKO*, Candidate Politburo member, head of Gosplan, Deputy Chairman for Economic Affairs

- L. M. Kaganovich, member of *GKO*, Politburo member, People's Commissar for Railroads

- N. A. Bulganin, member of *GKO*, Deputy Commissar of Defense (1944), General of the Army

- A. I. Mikoyan, member of *GKO*, Politburo member, People's Commissar for Foreign Trade

As shown above, all members except Bulganin also sat in the Politburo. General S. M. Shtemenko, then Deputy Chief of the General Staff for Operations, reported that it was often impossible to determine whether a specific meeting in the Kremlin was one of the Politburo or of *GKO*.[17] This centralization of power ensured that orders and directives of *GKO* were carried out without question.

Even today, *GKO* is the model that Soviet spokesmen assert would be used in the event of a future war. According to Marshal N. V. Ogarkov, writing in 1982, should a future war occur, "a stable system of centralized leadership of the country and the Armed Forces" would be essential. *GKO*, Ogarkov specified, had provided this leadership in the Great Patriotic War, and for the future "there will quite naturally be the need for an even higher concentration of leadership."[18]

Throughout the 1970s, the Soviet press gave considerable attention to the work of *GKO* during the Great Patriotic War. The purpose appeared to be a reevaluation of resource allocation and decision-making directives during that war, and to find lessons that might be applicable to any similar situation in the future.

For example, in May 1971 a conference was held in Moscow to examine the work that was accomplished in the *tyl* (rear areas) during the war. Four major organizations participated: The Institute of Marxism-Leninism of the Central Committee of the CPSU, the All-Union "Znaniye" Society, the Institute of History of the USSR (under the Academy of Sciences), and the Institute of Military History of the Ministry of Defense (also under the Academy of Sciences). In 1974 the findings of the conference were published in a two-volume work, *The Soviet tyl (Rear Areas) in the Great Patriotic War*.

Again, it must be emphasized that this report is an idealized account of how the Soviet decision-making and control structure functioned throughout the interior of the state during that war. Nevertheless, the report is significant both for what it stressed as effective organizations, and what was omitted. It should be noted also that the conference was not a meeting of military personnel, but primarily consisted of individuals either members of, or closely associated with, the Soviet Academy of Sciences and a major ideological institute of the Party.

The study refers to *GKO* as the "highest organ of power, created by decision of the Central Committee CPSU, the Presidium of the Supreme Soviet and the Council of People's Commissars USSR. . . . All citizens and all Party, soviet, Komsomol, and military organs were obliged to fulfill without question the decisions and edicts of *GKO*."[19]

These 1974 books contain an excellent account of the work of the "Operational Bureau of *GKO*," created on 8 December 1942 to ensure the monitoring and coordination of actions associated with resource allocations essential to the war effort. This organization had wide and far-reaching responsibilities for economic matters of many types, and was given "operational control for the fulfillment of military orders." It ensured centralized control of the entire Soviet wartime economy. The Operational Bureau controlled "the daily flow of work of commissariats of defense industry, the Commissariats of Railroads, Ferrous Metallurgy, Non-ferrous Metallurgy, Electrical Production, the Coal Industry, Oil, and Chemical Industries, and also had a plan for the supply of these branches of industry with needed raw materials."[20]

In the spring of 1944, the Operational Bureau was assigned control over additional commissariats (Rubber, Paper and Wood, and Electrical Equipment Industries). The Transport Committee of *GKO*, which had existed for two years, was dissolved and its functions assigned to the Operational Bureau. Later in that same year, *GKO* made the OB responsible for supplying the Red Army and commissariats of defense industry with food and manufactured goods. A commission was established in the OB to ensure that the demands of *GKO* were met. This commission was made up of A. I. Mikoyan, N. A. Voznesenskiy, and A. V. Lyubimov. Voznesenskiy and Mikoyan both were Politburo members, as well as being members of the *GKO*.

Gosplan, which Voznesenskiy also headed, was given increased responsibilities and tasks. *GKO*, with the participation of Gosplan and representatives of the corresponding bodies, decided on military production and the development of the economy as a whole. An idea of this work can be gathered from the report of a meeting "where complex questions of tank construction were decided." The following "representatives" were present at this *GKO* gathering:

- N. A. Voznesenskiy, Candidate Politburo member, *GKO* member, Chairman of Gosplan, member of the Commission of the Operational Bureau, and representative for Gosplan
- D. F. Ustinov, People's Commissar for Armaments
- V. A. Malyshev, Director of Tank Industry
- I. V. Tevosyan, People's Commissar for Ferrous Metallurgy[21]

Voznesenskiy appeared to play a key role and was present at all meetings of *GKO* when economic questions were decided. He was Gosplan's permanent representative to *GKO*.

Sections were formed within Gosplan for armaments, ammunition, shipbuilding, aviation, and tank construction. Gosplan was charged to provide daily summaries on military production and fulfillment of *GKO* priorities. Representatives of Gosplan were located in each of the twenty-five economic regions into which the USSR was divided.

Throughout the war, *GKO* set the military-political tasks for the High Command of the Armed Forces as a whole, and determined the general nature of the use of all Soviet resources. *GKO* representatives regularly visited the fronts. Mini-*GKO*s were formed in many cities in or near the war zone, working to unite the activities of local agencies.

Soviet spokesmen today, in attempting to stress the importance of the Party, state that "*GKO* was a collective agency and all its activities were directed by the Central Committee, primarily the Politburo."[22] In actual fact, as Khrushchev revealed during his de-Stalinization campaign of the late

1950s and early 1960s, the Party had little influence; Stalin exercised virtually absolute control.

In summary, *GKO* carried out the strategic leadership of the Soviet Union during the time of the Great Patriotic War, acting as the supreme decision-making body for all activities related to national security. This included political, economic, diplomatic, and military matters. Specific members of *GKO*, such as Voznesenskiy, who also was a member of the Politburo and head of Gosplan, appear to have had broad authority for resource allocation. The Operational Bureau was created specifically by *GKO* to monitor and coordinate matters related to resource use.

The predecessor of *GKO*, as noted, was Lenin's Council of Defense, later changed to the Council of Labor and Defense (*STO*). At the end of the Civil War, *STO* continued to function and had wide powers for resource allocations associated with security matters. These included allocations for shipbuilding, development of the Air Forces, and military production requirements in the five-year economic plans. Later the Committee of Defense was established, which also was concerned with broad problems of a military-economic nature. The Military-Industrial Commission (*VPK*), formed in 1938, was subordinated to the Committee of Defense. As the record shows, the buildup of Soviet industry for military purposes during the 1930s, when the Soviet Union was not engaged in a major war, was remarkable.

The Present Council of Defense

GKO was abolished officially on 4 September 1945. It was not until 1976 that Soviet spokesmen revealed the existence of the present Council of Defense. It is highly improbable that a similar agency did not exist in the intervening period of over thirty years.

As previously noted, after the Civil War *STO* continued to function, in one form or another, until 1937. A somewhat parallel body, the Commission of Defense, also had existed between 1932 and 1937. In 1937 these two bodies were replaced by a Committee of Defense. Current Soviet writings reveal practically nothing of similar organs functioning between 1945 and 1976 to perform the work of those Soviet organizations that were in place between 1924 and 1941. Surely, however, such organs did exist.

The *Red Star* announcement of the existence of the Council of Defense, published in 1976, did not state that the body had just been created, only that it existed and had done so for an unspecified period of time.[23] L. I. Brezhnev's biography, in the 1981 *Annual* of the *Great Soviet Encyclopedia*, gives 1977 as the date of his beginning the task of Chairman of the Council of Defense, the time when he also became Chairman of the Presidium of the Supreme Soviet.

When apparently conflicting data appear in Soviet publications, it is extremely difficult to determine whether the mistakes are due to carelessness on the part of the writers (unlikely, but possible), or represent a deliberate effort to conceal and to confuse.

The new Soviet Constitution, adopted in 1977, contains this provision:

Article 121. The Presidium of the Supreme Soviet of the USSR shall . . . [paragraph 14] form the Council of Defense of the USSR and confirm its composition; appoint and dismiss the high command of the Armed Forces of the USSR; . . .

In reality, of course, the Council of Defense was established by the Party leadership. In 1977 the new Soviet Constitution made reference to the Council of Defense, just as Brezhnev became Chairman of the Presidium of the Supreme Soviet. Probably this was not a coincidence. A 1981 Soviet text, *Soviet Administrative Law*, states that the "Chairman of the Presidium of the Supreme Soviet *also will be the Chairman of the Council of Defense*" (emphasis added).[24]

Western analysts do not agree on the membership of the Defense Council. Based on an analysis of the membership of similar bodies in the past, such as *STO* and *GKO*, as well as on several years of research on the activities of the Politburo members most closely associated with defense matters, the following, as of 7 November 1982, before the death of Brezhnev, were believed to be members:

- Brezhnev, L. I. General Secretary of CPSU, Chairman of Presidium of Supreme Soviet, Chairman of Council of Defense, Politburo member, MSU
- Andropov, Yu. A., Secretary of CPSU, General of the Army, Politburo member
- Tikhonov, N.A., Chairman of Council of Ministers, Politburo member
- Ustinov, D. F., Minister of Defense, USSR, MSU; Politburo member
- Chernenko, K. U., Secretary of CPSU, Politburo member

Marshal N. V. Ogarkov, Chief of the General Staff, may act as Secretary of the Council of Defense. Other Party and military leaders may be called upon to attend meetings, depending upon the matter discussed. Among these might be:

- Minister of Foreign Affairs A. A. Gromyko
- Chairman of the KGB (since December 1983) V. M. Chebrikov, General Colonel

Since Brezhnev's death, there has been insufficient information concerning Politburo changes to judge who might be on the Council of Defense (as of 1 July 1983). Yuri Andropov was called the Chairman of the the Council of Defense by Defense Minister D. F. Ustinov in his Victory Day article, published in *Pravda* on 9 May 1983. The legal requirement that the Chairman of the Presidium of the Supreme Soviet, USSR, be also Chairman of the Council of Defense was met formally only on 16 June 1983, at the regular session of the Supreme Soviet, when Andropov was officially designated as its head. It should be noted that Brezhnev required thirteen years to achieve the positions of Chairman of both the Presidium of the Supreme Soviet and of the Council of Defense; Andropov attained the same goal in less than eight months.

Assuming that the Council of Defense remains a viable organization, which would appear to be the case, since its new Chairman has been publicly identified, certain tentative conclusions can be drawn. Based on precedent and limited current data, it is believed that Gosplan now functions under direction of this body. As shown previously, Gosplan was formed under *STO*. During the Great Patriotic War it was directly responsible to *GKO*. The present formal subordination of Gosplan, according to Soviet law, is to the Council of Ministers. It plays a prominent role in military-industrial planning.[25]

It is believed also that the *VPK* (Military-Industrial Commission) is directed by the Council of Defense. When created in 1938, this body was subordinate to the Committee of Defense. There is no reason that its control today would be other than in the Council of Defense.

The Soviet conference on the role of the *tyl* during the Great Patriotic War, the report of which was published in 1974, gave glowing accounts of the work of the "operational Bureau," formed by *GKO* in 1942 to control economic operations, and to monitor and coordinate all economic matters related to the total war effort. This Operational Bureau is seldom mentioned in other writings. It is speculated that this organization, in one form or another, exists today within the Council of Defense, still performing its role of monitoring and coordination of matters associated with resource allocation.

The Main Military Council

Members of the Council of Defense, while having vast experience in national security matters, are not military professionals. In time of peace, they look to the Main Military Council (*Glavnyy Voyennyy Sovyet*), sometimes referred to as the *Kollegiya* of the Ministry of Defense, to provide strategic direction and leadership of the Armed Forces. This council is a deliberative (*soveshchatel'nyy*) body attached to the Ministry of Defense and chaired by the Minister of Defense.[26]

Based on historical precedent, which will be discussed later, the Chairman of the Council of Defense also may be a member of the Main Military Council. Other probable members are: the three "First Deputy" Ministers of Defense (the Chief of the General Staff, Commander in Chief Warsaw Pact Forces, and the First Deputy for General Affairs), and Chief of the Main

Political Administration, and eleven "Deputy Ministers of Defense" (Commanders in Chief of the five Services, the Inspector General, Chiefs of the Rear Services and Civil Defense, and Deputy Ministers of Defense for Cadres, Armaments, and Building and Quartering Troops).

Information about the Main Military Council is limited. The first book of an "Officer's Library" series, *V. I. Lenin and the Soviet Armed Forces*, published in 1980, contained the following:

> The most important problems of military policy are discussed collectively at Party Congresses, Plenums of the Central Committee and in the Politburo. There are also organs of collective leadership directly in the Armed Forces such as the *Main Military Council*, military councils of the services of the Armed Forces, military districts, groups abroad and the fleets. Military councils collectively examine and decide all the urgent questions of daily life and activity of the troops.[27] (Emphasis added)

In the above statement the "Main Military Council" is capitalized, indicating that it is a specifically designated body. The *Soviet Military Encyclopedia* clearly states:

> The Main Military Council is a deliberative (*soveshchatel'nyy*) organ attached [*pri*] the Minister of Defense USSR in peacetime.[28]

The designation "*Kollegiya* of the Ministry of Defense" is used somewhat more frequently than "Main Military Council." For example, in 1972 an updated edition of a standard Soviet text, *Fundamentals of Soviet Military Legislation*, contained the following:

> The most important questions of daily life, activity, and building up of the Armed Forces of the USSR are discussed at sessions of *Kollegiya of the Ministry of Defense*, which acts as a deliberative (*soveshchatel'nyy*) organ under the chairmanship of the Minister of Defense USSR, Members of the *Kollegiya* are confirmed by the Council of Ministers, USSR.[29] (Emphasis added)

According to the *Soviet Military Encyclopedia:*

> The *Kollegiya of the Ministry of Defense* is a deliberative (*soveshchatel'nyy*) organ of the ministry which elaborates decisions on problems connected with the building up of the Armed Forces, their combat and mobilization readiness, the state of combat and political training, selection, placing and education of military cadres and on other important questions. Members of the *Kollegiya* are the deputy ministers of defense, the Chief of the Main Political Administration of the Soviet Army and Navy and other leading workers of the Ministry of Defense. The chairman of

the *Kollegiya* is the Minister of Defense. Its members are confirmed by the Council of Ministers, USSR. Decisions of the
Kollegiya are worked out on the basis of the principle of collective
leadership (kollegial'nost') and put into effect, as a rule, by orders
and directives of the Minister of Defense USSR.[30]

Thus, it appears that the Main Military Council and the *Kollegiya* of the
Ministry of Defense are one and the same. The historical precedent for such
an assumption comes from the fact that the Revolutionary Military Council of
the USSR, a predecessor of the present Main Military Council, was the
Kollegiya of the People's Commissariat (as ministries were called in the
1930s) for Military and Naval Affairs. As stated in a 1968 work:

> Direct leadership of the Armed Forces was carried out by the
> People's Commissariat for Military and Naval Affairs and the
> Revolutionary Military Council USSR (*Revvoyensovyet USSR*)
> which operated with the rights of the Kollegiya of the People's
> Commissariat.[31]

Insight into the operation of the Main Military Council of today can best
be gained by an examination of its origin.

The Higher Military Council and the Revvoyensoviet

On 4 March 1918 the Higher Military Council (*Vysshchiy Voyennyy
Sovyet*) was created by decree of the Council of People's Commissars (*SNK*).
Called "the first higher organ of strategic leadership of the Armed Forces of
the Soviet Republic," it was given leadership of all military operations; all
military establishments and persons "without exception" were subordinated
to it. This Higher Military Council was charged with determining basic tasks
for defending the state, organizing the Armed Forces, forming Military
Districts, and implementing the operational-strategic deployment of the Red
Army.[32] L. D. Trotskii served as its chairman.

As Civil War fighting increased, the Red Army military councils in the
field began to call themselves "revolutionary military councils." On 2 September 1918, when the country was declared an "armed camp," the Higher
Military Council was abolished and replaced by the "Revolutionary Military
Council of the Republic" (*Revvoyensoviet of the Republic, RVST*). The
Revvoyensoviet, at the same time, was given the functions and rights of the
Kollegiya of the People's Commissariat on Military Affairs, the members of
which became members of the *Revvoyensoviet*. L. D. Trotskii, who, as
noted above, had chaired the Higher Military Council, was designated as
chairman of the *Revvoyensoviet of the Republic*. At the same time Trotskii
also was the People's Commissar for Military and Naval Affairs. The
Revvoyensoviet was directly subordinate to the Council of Defense.

On 28 August 1923, when the USSR was formed, the *Revvoyensoviet of the Republic* became the *Revvoyensoviet* of the USSR. M. V. Frunze succeeded Trotskii as chairman. In 1925, after Frunze's death, the Chairman's position went to K. Ye. Voroshilov. Soviet spokesmen credit the *Revvoyensoviet* with being influential in building up the Red Army through the military reforms that it instituted, and in developing five-year plans for military equipment and manpower.

The Main Military Council of the 1930s

In attempting to determine who is on the Main Military Council of the 1980s, and what this body does, it is necessary to examine similar bodies of the 1930s. In 1934 the Seventeenth Party Congress abolished *"Kollegiya"* (collective leadership) in all People's Commissariats. The *Revvoyensoviet* was replaced, in 1934, by a Military Council, consisting of 80 members, which acted as a deliberative (*soveshchatel'nyy*) body. After seventy-five of its eighty members were killed in the military purges,[33] it ceased to function, although it was not formally abolished until November 1940.

In 1938 *"kollegial'nost"* (collective leadership) was restored.[34] On 13 March of the same year, a Main Military Council was formed, and in April, a Main Military Council of the Red Navy. These Main Military Councils had as a primary responsibility the determination of new military equipment to be acquired.

A number of Soviet marshals discuss the work of the Main Military Council of the Red Army in their memoirs. One relates that, in April 1940, an enlarged meeting of the Main Military Council took place. Present were members of the Party's Politburo, leaders of the People's Commissariats of Defense, troop commanders, members of military councils and chiefs of staff of military districts, armies, commanders of corps and divisions, and heads of higher military schools. Marshal G. Zhukov stated that:

> Many principal questions in the People's Commissariat of Defense were examined in the Main Military Council of the Red Army. The People's Commissar of Defense was the chairman of the Main Military Council and its members were deputy people's commissars of defense and one of the members of the Politburo [*Tsk VKP* (b)]. Especially important questions were usually decided with J. V. Stalin present and with other members of the Politburo.[35]

With Stalin's attendance at meetings of the Main Military Council in 1940 as a precedent, one may speculate if Andropov would attend a meeting of this organ's successor today.

Stavka of the Supreme High Command

On 23 June 1941, the day after the German invasion, the Main Military Councils of the Red Army and Red Navy were replaced by a single body, the

Stavka of the High Command. Soviet spokesmen today emphasize that, in the event of future war, this body again would be formed and charged with the conduct of military operations. The only information on how such an organ might function is found in writings about the Great Patriotic War.

Initially, *Stavka* was chaired by Marshal S. K. Timoshenko, Commissar of Defense. Stalin and V. M. Molotov, who was First Deputy Chairman of the *SNK* as well as Commissar of Foreign Affairs, were members of *Stavka*. Military members were Marshals S. M. Budennyy and K. Ye. Vorshilov, General G. K. Zhukov, and Admiral N. G. Kuznetsov.[36]

As previously discussed, *GKO*, charged with the total war effort, was chaired by Stalin. *Stavka* was supposed to provide direction and control for all military operations. Timoshenko, however, was ineffective as Chairman. At this time Stalin was gathering up all the reins of power for himself, and, on 10 July 1941, he replaced Timoshenko as *Stavka*'s head. On 8 August Stalin was designated Supreme Commander in Chief of the Armed Forces. Since Stalin, Chairman of *Stavka*, was Supreme Commander in Chief, *Stavka* was redesignated *Stavka* of the Supreme High Command, generally referred to as *Stavka* of the *VGK*.

When Stalin, already controlling the most important elements of Soviet power, took over as head of *Stavka*, the Soviet Union obtained the centralization of control that current Soviet writers emphasize is the ideal structure. A simplified portrayal of Stalin's role follows:

POLITBURO	STALIN
STATE COMMITTEE OF DEFENSE (*GKO*)	STALIN
STAVKA OF THE *VGK*	STALIN

Throughout the war, *Stavka* remained a small body, with membership varying from five to eight. It had permanent advisers, consisting of commanders in chief of the services and other senior officers. To ensure that orders of *Stavka* were being carried out properly, its representatives were sent out to the various fronts. If two or more fronts were combined for an operation, control of such combined forces would be by a headquarters formed by *Stavka* representatives. Representatives of *Stavka* reported directly to Stalin one or more times each day, advising him on specific actions along the various fronts.[37]

An idealized account of how this centralized control worked was given by General of the Army S. M. Shtemenko, writing in the late 1960s:

> It must be stressed that all principal questions of running the country and conducting the war were decided by the Central Committee of the Party—the Politburo, Orgburo and Secretariat, and then carried out through the Presidium of the Supreme Soviet, USSR, the Council of Peoples Commissars and also through GKO and Stavka of the VGK. For operational solution of military

questions, joint consultation of members of the Politburo and GKO, Politburo and Stavka were called and the most important of these were decided jointly by the Politburo, GKO and Stavka.[38]

In this description, Shtemenko first bows to the Communist Party structure, then to the government organization, and finally acknowledges the overwhelming role of the Politburo, *GKO*, and *Stavka*.

Other Soviet spokesmen are specific in stating that *Stavka* would play an equally important role should another major war develop. As explained by Marshall V. D. Sokolovskiy in *Military Strategy*:

> The direct leadership of the Armed Forces during a war will obviously be accomplished, *as before*, by the *Stavka of the Supreme High Command*. The Stavka will be a collegial agency of leadership under the chairmanship of the supreme commander in chief.[39] (Emphasis added)

In 1971 a Soviet military textbook explained the role of *Stavka* as follows:

> ... Each service of the Armed Forces is designated for waging military actions primarily in one definite sphere—on land, at sea, and in the air—and carries out the fulfillment of the tasks under the direction of the commander in chief of these services of the Armed Forces or directly of *Stavka of the Supreme High Command*.[40] (Emphasis added)

There seems to be little question about the future role of *Stavka of the Supreme High Command*, should conditions warrant it being formed. The past and present role of the Main Military Council, however, is less clear.

Postwar Changes

In January 1946, *Stavka* was abolished and a Higher Military Council was formed, attached (*pri*) to the Ministry of the Armed Forces. In 1950 the military structure was divided into two ministries, the Ministry of War and the Ministry of the Navy. At the same time, two corresponding bodies were formed, the Main Military Council of the War Ministry and a Main Military Council of the Naval Ministry. This organization, it will be noted, was similar to the one formed in 1938, at the height of the purges.

In March 1953, within days of Stalin's death, the two councils were recombined into the Main Military Council.[41]

At the same time, the Higher Military Council continued to exist. In 1950 it was removed from the Ministry of the Armed Forces, and attached (*pri*) to the Council of Ministers of the USSR.[42] The continuation of this body provides some clues to the organization that existed between the time

GKO was disbanded in 1945 and the establishment of the present Council of Defense.

Since Stalin was Chairman of the Council of Ministers, he would also appear to have been Chairman of the Higher Military Council. The Council still functioned after Stalin's death. A 1964 Soviet military textbook notes that Zhukov tried to dissolve the Higher Military Council in 1957, but was unsuccessful. The author noted that members and candidate members of the Presidium, as well as military and political leaders of the Army and Navy, also were members of this body.[43]

The famed Soviet intelligence officer, Oleg Penkovskiy, refers to a "Supreme Military Council." Since only a translation is available of what Penkovskiy is supposed to have written, it is believed that the original Russian would have been "Higher Military Council," since other Soviet sources have referred to a similar body. This Council "is directly under the Presidium of the Central Committee CPSU, and is chaired by Khrushchev or in his absence by Kozlov or Mikoyan. There are always a few members of the Presidium of the Central Committee CPSU in attendance at the meetings of the Supreme Military Council. The Minister of Defense and the commanders in chief of the service arms are automatically members of the council. Minister Malinovskiy is in this case just an ordinary member of this council." If Penkovskiy's account is correct, then the "Supreme" Military Council meeting he describes below would have taken place between 1960 and mid-1962:

> In case of disagreements between the Ministry of Defense and civilian ministries on problems of military deliveries or weapon production, breakdown of a plan, shortage of funds, etc., the Supreme Military Council and the Central Committee CPSU decide. Once during Khrushchev's absence Marshal Biryuzov raised the question of additional funds for missile tests in a council meeting. Suslov and Mikoyan, who were present at the meeting, failed to solve the problem. Varentsov said afterward: "They started beating around the bush and kept talking, but never reached a decision. If Stalin were alive, he would have given the word and the whole thing would have been resolved right then and there, but now it's a big mess, just like a kolkhoz meeting. There is no order."[44]

Judging from the few references to the Higher Military Council in Soviet writings, as well as in Penkovskiy's account, the evidence suggests that this body was redesignated the Council of Defense in the 1970s, or possibly even before. There is evidence that earlier in the 1950s, there had been both a Higher Military Council and a Main Military Council, the former attached to the Council of Ministers (as were the Council of Labor and Defense [1920–1937] and the Committee of Defense [1937–1940]). As noted previously, it is highly improbable that an agency similar to the Council of Labor and Defense and the Committee of Defense did not exist in the thirty years between the end of the war and the announcement of the existence of the present-day Council of Defense. It is suggested that the Higher Military Council, just described, is the missing link.

Conclusions

The top Soviet decision-making body for national security matters, regardless of whether or not the Soviet Union is actively engaged in a war, has been a small group within the Politburo. Such a group makes up the Council of Defense at present; the State Committee of Defense during the Great Patriotic War was composed of a similar membership. In time of war, this group is given additional extraordinary powers.

Gosplan has a major role in resource allocations for national defense, and, to a large degree, operates under direction of the Council of Defense. An "operational bureau" of some type probably continues to exist, performing the same function of monitoring and coordination of operations as a similar body did during World War II.

The Main Military Council (or *Kollegiya* of the Ministry of Defense) has a role in policy planning associated with resource allocations for military purposes. Detailed military planning is accomplished by the General Staff; the Main Military Council probably provides general guidelines. In the event of war, this body would be replaced by *Stavka* (headquarters) of the High Command, or *Stavka* of the Supreme High Command, should it be chaired by the Commander in Chief of the Armed Forces, who probably would also be the Party's head, and Chairman of the Council of Defense. This size of this body would be much smaller than that of the present Main Military Council.

There is a popular view in the United States that "institutional interests" dominate decision making in the top elements of the Soviet power structure, much as in the United States. This view appears to be based on mirror-imaging; it is not supported by research of Soviet internal power struggles in the past. Rather, struggles within the Kremlin's ruling bodies seem to be the result of groups or of individuals seeking power for power's sake. They do not seem to fight primarily over guns-or-butter issues, or of heavy industry versus agriculture, for example.

The major strength of the Soviet decision-making process lies in its centralization of power. Once a decision is made, it can be executed swiftly. There is no need for prolonged public debates that often characterize the decision-making process in the United States. On the other hand, this centralization of power could be the Kremlin's greatest weakness. Millions of Soviet citizens may have died needlessly in the first months of Hitler's invasion, due to Stalin's arbitrary rule and decisions (or lack thereof).

Up to the present time, almost all the top Soviet leaders had participated either in the Civil War or in the Great Patriotic War. In one manner or another they have engaged in combat, either in uniform or as partisans. The Kremlin's present position in world affairs is based on its armed forces. Military power has taken the Soviet Union to superpower status. If the past and present are any guide to the future, the Soviet Party-military leadership will continue to give national security matters first priority, both in attention and in allocation of resources.

NOTES

1. Leonid Brezhnev, General Secretary, CPSU, *Twenty-Fourth Congress of the Communist Party of the Soviet Union*, 30 March–4 April 1971 (Moscow: Novosti Press Agency Publishing House, 1971), 47.

2. Michael Sadykiewicz, "Soviet Military Politics," *Survey* 114, no. 1: 179–210. Also John McDonnell in *Soviet Naval Influence* (New York: Praeger Publishers, 1977), 67, 80, 82.

3. N. Vishnyakov and F. Arkhipov, *Ustroystvo Vooruzhennykh Sil SSSR* (Organization of the Armed Forces of the USSR) (Moscow: State Publishing House, 1930), 101.

4. *Sovetskaya Voyennaya Entsiklopediya* (Soviet Military Encyclopedia, hereafter cited as *SVE*), vol. 7 (Moscow: Voyenizdat, 1979), 410.

5. Ibid.

6. Ibid.

7. Vishnyakov and Arkhipov, 101.

8. Ibid.

9. *SVE* 7:410.

10. M. V. Zakharov, ed., *50 Let Vooruzhennykh Sil SSSR* (50 Years of the Armed Forces USSR) (Moscow: Voyenizdat, 1968), 198.

11. *SVE* 7:410.

12. *SVE* 4:266.

13. Ibid.

14. Ibid.

15. *SVE* 2:621.

16. Ibid.

17. S. M. Shtemenko, *General'nyy Shtab v Gody Voyny* (General Staff in the War Years) (Moscow: Voyenizdat, 1968), 117.

18. N. V. Ogarkov, *Vsegda v Gotovnosti k Zashchite Otechestva* (Always in Readiness to Defend the Fatherland) (Moscow: Voyenizdat, 1982), 61.

19. P. N. Pospelov, ed., *Sovetskiy Tyl V Velikoy Otechestvennoy Voyne* (The Soviet Tyl [Rear Areas] in the Great Patriotic War), vol. 1 (Moscow: "Mysl'," 1974), 71.

20. Ibid., 77.

21. Ibid., 72.

22. Ibid., 18.

23. *Krasnaya Zvezda* (Red Star), 7 April 1976.

24. P. T. Vasilenkov, ed., *Sovetskoye Administrativnoye Pravo* (Soviet Administrative Law) (Moscow: Yuridicheskaya Literatura, 1981), 375. The title page of this work notes that it is to be used as a textbook.

25. The death of V. M. Ryabikov, a First Deputy Chairman of Gosplan (1961–74), revealed that he was a General Colonel-Engineer, had served as Ustinov's First Deputy Commissar, later Minister of Armaments (1941–51). He had been awarded an almost unprecedented nine Orders of Lenin for "strengthening the defense capability of the country (*Pravda*, 22 July 1974).

26. *SVE* 2: 566–67.

27. A. S. Zheltov, ed., *V. I. Lenin i Sovetskiye Vooruzhennyye Sily* (V. I. Lenin and the Soviet Armed Forces) (Moscow: Voyenizdat, 1980), 184.

28. *SVE* 2:566–67.

29. A. I. Lepeshkin, ed., *Osnovy Sovetskogo Voyennogo Zakonodatel'stva* (Fundamentals of Soviet Military Legislation) (Moscow: Voyenizdat, 1972), 91.

30. *SVE* 4:235.

31. Zakharov, 198.

32. Ibid., 33–34.

33. John Erickson, *The Soviet High Command* (New York: St. Martin's Press, 1962), 505.

34. Yu. P. Petrov, *Stroitel'stvo Politorganoy, Partiynykh i Komsomol'skikh Organizatsiy Armii i Flota (1918–1968)* (Structure of Political Agencies, Party & Komsomol Organizations of the Army and Navy [1918–68]) (Moscow: Voyenizdat, 1968), 229, 241.

35. G. K. Zhukov, *Vospominaniya i Razmyshleniya* (Reminiscences and Reflections), vol. 1 (Moscow: Novosti Press, 1974), 217.

36. Zakharov, 256.

37. Shtemenko, 125.

38. Shtemenko, vol. 2 (1973), 278.

39. V. D. Sokolovskiy, *Voyennaya Strategiya* (Military Strategy), 3d ed. (Moscow: Voyenizdat, 1968), 361.

40. S. N. Kozlov, *Spravochnik Ofitsera* (Officer's Handbook) (Moscow: Voyenizdat, 1971), 167.

41. *SVE* 2:567.

42. Zakharov, 478n.

43. Yu. P. Petrov, *Partiynoye Stroitel'stvo v Sovetskoy Armii i Flote (1918–1961)* (Party Structure in the Soviet Army and Navy [1918–1961]) (Moscow: Voyenizdat, 1964), 462.

44. Oleg Penkovskiy, *The Penkovskiy Papers* (New York: Doubleday, 1965), 234–35.

4

Contrasting Views of the Role of Strategic (Politico-Military) Doctrine: Soviet and Western Approaches

Uri Ra'anan

Asymmetry is the key to the problem addressed in this chapter. It constitutes the point of departure, not only because of the obvious contrast between the United States and the Soviet Union, with regard to geographic location and resulting force structures, but, even more significantly, because of mutual incompatibilities as far as their respective approaches toward doctrine in general are concerned. We are confronted by the paradox that a leadership which, theoretically, subscribes to an ideology based on economic determinism, demonstrates, on all possible occasions, its belief in the total supremacy of politics over economics—not least with regard to military and strategic issues. Western society, conversely, appears to be tied, hand and foot, to economic considerations, or, to be precise, concerns of resource allocation, which seem to head the agenda, with politico-military concepts relegated to an inferior position—as a derivative, not a cause.

The unity of theory and action is a commonplace of the ideology that provides the analytical precepts and the jargon which assist Soviet leaders in appraising the international situation and in articulating the operational conclusions that are to be drawn. In this context, military doctrine provides the broad parameter within which the Kremlin elaborates the specifics of "military science" and its derivative, "military art."

Soviet leaders do not differentiate sharply between the "military" and "civilian" components of doctrine; altogether their approach is related closely to classical "grand strategy" (described best in German literature). The German "fathers of the Leninist creed," I suspect, were not so much Marx and Engels, as Hegel and Clausewitz. In evidence, one may cite Lenin's personal copy of Clausewitz, scribbled all over the margins, with exclamations of approval and admiration.

Western definitions of military doctrine are far more narrowly circumscribed than "grand strategy." In Soviet thought, moreover, war and peace are not mutually exclusive, they are not antithetical—although Western minds generally assume this to be the case. Perhaps it is not realized how much the Leninist concept of ongoing conflict owes to social Darwinism, as do ideologies of the far right. In that context, "war" and "peace" are no more than hash marks, between which the course of permanent conflict meanders.

Just how broad Soviet definitions of doctrine are, we can gather from the writings left behind by the late Marshal Grechko, who stated:

> The concept of doctrine . . . encompasses teaching, a scientific or philosophical theory, and a system of guiding principles and views. Accordingly, military doctrine is understood to be an officially accepted system of views in a given state and in its Armed Forces, on the nature of war and methods for conducting it, and on preparation of the country and army for war. At the very least, military doctrine answers the following basic questions: What enemy will have to be faced in a possible war? What is the nature of the war in which the state and its armed forces will have to take part? What goals and missions would they face in this war? What armed forces are needed to complete the assigned missions and in what direction must military development be carried out? How are the preparations for war to be implemented? What methods must be used to wage war? . . . All of the basic provisions of military doctrine stem from actually existing conditions, and above all, from domestic and foreign policy, the sociopolitical and economic system, the level of production, the status of means for conducting war, and the geographic position, both of one's own state and that of the probable enemy. . . . The theoretical basis of Soviet military doctrine consists of the following: Marxism/Leninism [incidentally, these are two ideologies that are linked only by a hyphen, since they are really antithetical]; military science; and, to a certain degree, branches of social, natural, and technical sciences related to the preparation of armed struggle, as well as to other forms of struggle—economic, ideological, and diplomatic. Military doctrine, in its turn, has a reverse influence on military-theoretical thought.

(The references to "ideological" or political "struggle" have a bearing, of course, upon the older concept of "psychological warfare," which has faded away from Western awareness.) Regrettably, one looks in vain for contemporary Western documents of similar lucidity, coherence, and all-encompassing thoroughness, even though Grechko's definition owes much to the classics of earlier Western thought.

The basic element in Soviet military doctrine is a rejection of the passive role of a mere reactor, and this itself reflects another aspect, namely that it is imperative to seize and maintain the initiative, in the military and political arenas alike. In turn, this concept is linked very closely to two other components of Soviet doctrine—to be specific, the Russian penchant for the offensive, and for surprise and deception. It should hardly be necessary to spell out the role that these factors can assume in a thermonuclear age.

One should not deduce from these propositions, however, that the Soviet leadership is committed necessarily to short-war scenarios. Soviet literature admittedly stresses that the side which enjoys the initiative, resorts to the offensive, and maximally exploits surprise and deception may be able to achieve a major—and perhaps even a decisive—advantage at the initial stage of a confrontation. This does not mean that, under all circumstances, conflict termination will be achieved rapidly. On the contrary, the Soviet leadership remains convinced of the typically "continental" view that final victory requires seizure and occupation of the enemy's soil. The logical result is that such factors as surge mobilization—economic, technological, and in terms of manpower—continue to be essential components of Soviet military doctrine, which anticipates the possibility that there may be a prolonged interval between the initial surprise, however traumatic might be the blow inflicted on the other side, and war termination. The latter, in the Soviet view, includes not only the eviction of the adversary from the territory of his friends and allies and its occupation by the Red Army, but, eventually, the collapse of his system, and his surrender. Of course, this approach is reminiscent of more conventional warfare scenarios, assumes protracted conflict to be probable and to require all the appropriate preparations, irrespective of the unprecedented and perhaps esoteric dimensions of such a conflagration, which is likely to spill over into outer space as a zone of combat.

In this context, a decisive role is assigned to the "reserves," and this applies particularly to the Strategic Nuclear Forces, which are imbued still with the traditions of the Russian artillery (as John Erickson has pointed out frequently) that dominated their early training; they think and plan in terms of repeated "salvos," in which victory rewards the side that has retained sufficient reserves for a potential last salvo, when the opponent has exhausted his supply. Although there have been major technological changes, and occasional adjustments of Soviet doctrine to these changes—particularly, of course, in the Khrushchev era (as Harriet Scott has pointed out in her works)—certain general principles continue to dominate Soviet thinking:

Lenin agreed fundamentally with Clausewitz that war is an extension of politics, and that, qualitatively, war is not on a different plane from other forms of conflict—political, diplomatic, civil, economic, or social; this view has been reflected in Soviet literature since Lenin's day. In this particular respect, the advent of the thermonuclear age has failed to bring about a basic revision, although there was a brief period, under Malenkov, when it appeared as if such a revision might be imminent. Nor has a tendency been noted to review the tenet that conflict is endemic, that it will continue, from time to time, to take the form of international warfare, and that there are no "compromises"—only the victors and the defeated (who are consigned to "the rubbish bin of history").

In other words, the Soviet Union subscribes to a dynamic—not to a static—view of history. For that matter, Soviet literature continues to posit the belief that ideological struggle is bound to end in the annihilation of one system by the other, not only as a result of a war of words or leaflets, but of physical conflict. It is true that some of the specific components of military doctrine, as opposed to these broader concepts, have undergone modification. In traditional Russian fashion, however, the present Soviet leaders (in this one respect like Stalin before them, although he was a far more cautious operator than they appear to be) still are enamored of sheer size and numbers, quite apart from quality, believing that "more is better."

Because of certain modifications of the late 1960s and the 1970s, short-war scenarios, which had been briefly fashionable, have been revised. It is noteworthy that publications by Soviet military theoreticians and planners stress the need for paralyzing the adversary's C^3I in the opening stage; apparently they do not share the preoccupation of Western analysts with the thought that a functioning C^3I system would be required to enable both sides to negotiate an artificial halt in an escalatory process. Many, on our side, continue to posit this assumption with preciously little support from any Soviet sources that can be found. In the context of war survival and recovery, to which Soviet mobilization scenarios pay very appropriate attention, a particularly important role is assigned to active and passive defense. These, of course, are elements that we seem to have rediscovered only very recently.

As one might expect, Soviet military doctrine does not neglect the possibility that the long shadow of military power could prove sufficiently potent for the purpose of achieving political hegemony, precisely because Soviet war-fighting scenarios seem increasingly credible. Consequently, actual resort to military might, certainly as far as its most devastating strategic manifestations are concerned, may not prove necessary. It is in this sense that one should perhaps interpret the remaining echoes of Khrushchev's contribution to the issue of the inevitability of war (which he questioned); he probably assumed, quite correctly, that if the threat of force will suffice, then the use of force indeed may not be essential. In this context, one should read once more the Soviet classic written by Admiral Gorshkov (both his series of articles and his book), in which he defined the objective (of *Navies in Time of Peace*)[1] as being " . . . to demonstrate to potential enemies the perfection of . . . equipment, to have an effect on their morale, to intimidate with the power of . . . weaponry while still at peace, and to fill potential enemies beforehand with the thought of the hopelessness of their efforts. . . . " Coincidentally, the Soviet Navy has significantly revised the slogan embodying its strategic goals, from an earlier "defense of the motherland" to a subsequent "protection of Soviet state interests," and now to the "enhancement of Soviet prestige and influence." This current articulation of Soviet naval objectives evokes echoes of British Imperial "Gunboat Diplomacy" in the nineteenth century, which may be "no accident."

Such euphoria aside, Soviet literature of recent years is replete with war-fighting assumptions, constrained by very few caveats, apparently as the most realistic point of departure for the tasks that Soviet planners and decision makers have to implement. Western war-avoidance theories, on the other hand, are mentioned usually with contempt, as bourgeois, reactionary, and unrealistic.

Clearly, the Soviet leadership does not feel that it is feasible to eschew war altogether as an instrument of policy. A major doctrinal reason is that Moscow continues to posit a sharp distinction between "just" and "unjust" wars and, in this context goes on to denounce sharply—as Lenin did in 1915—Western pacifists, who oppose all wars, irrespective of their class content. Soviet doctrine maintains flatly that wars waged by "socialist" countries against "imperialists," by their very nature are "just," with regard to the former, and "unjust," as far as the latter are concerned, irrespective of how the conflict originated and who was the initator.

The same concept, of course, applies to "wars to national liberation" and to civil wars between "the bourgeoisie and the proletariat." "Particular attention is paid to such wars, since they are thought likely to involve the "export of counter-revolution by the imperialists," with the concomitant high probability of direct conflict between the Soviet Union and the West. "Export of counter-revolution," in this context, means Western actions in defense of pro-Western regimes. There are some exceptions to the proposition that East-West confrontation is well-nigh inevitable; they refer mainly to "wars between bourgeois states," which may or may not escalate to a nuclear level, and to certain regional conflicts. Amusingly, one particular category of war is not discussed in Soviet literature, although one should not rule it out entirely, and that is armed conflict between "socialist countries" themselves.

This intensely political approach to the question of war explains, at least in part, why distinctions between the "military" and "civilian" aspects of Soviet doctrine are arbitrary and misleading. One is dealing with a highly integrated theory that encompasses both of these aspects, as Grechko's statements demonstrate. It is equally artificial to reduce the analysis of the Soviet decision-making process to some imaginary tug-of-war between civilian "doves" and military "hawks," with the latter "lobbying" for increased "appropriations." The imagination boggles at the thought of the late Marshal Grechko, or Admiral Gorshkov, going to the Supreme Soviet to "lobby." Such paradigms, of course, reflect simply our inordinate propensity for mirror-imaging, and, moreover, at the crudest level. It is correct, admittedly, that military figures in the Soviet Union do write frequently about individual aspects of current military doctrine; there are very few, if any, examples, however, that demonstrate the ability of the man in uniform to shape or to modify overall doctrine. On the contrary, as in other cases linking doctrinal and operational issues, it is the leadership of the Communist Party of the Soviet Union that enjoys an unchallenged monopoly over decision making.

This is not mere theory—the Man on the White Horse, Bonapartism, continues to be a specter haunting the CPSU leaders, and appropriate measures are in force to exorcise this phenomenon. (The last time this was demonstrated, very convincingly, was in 1957, when Marshal Zhukov had to be brought in to rescue Khrushchev from defeat at the hands of the so-called "Anti-Party Group"; it took a mere three months for Khrushchev to "reward" Zhukov by banishing him. This illustrated the aversion of the men in the Kremlin to be beholden to a military figure. Incidentally, one continues to read stories claiming that Andropov owed his position to "Marshal" Ustinov, who, in any case, is a civilian—not a career officer—and that the military forces, therefore constituted Andropov's "base." The source of these "theories" is highly dubious. There is no serious documentation. Of course, it is our privilege if we want to play games with ourselves, but one hopes that such rumor will not be confused with serious study and analysis.)

It is equally misleading to view the defense and international relations literature of the Soviet Union as "purely propagandistic," or, even stranger, intended "for internal consumption only" (whatever that may mean—what could be more important than the domestic power base?), or, for that matter, as "mere deception." There are specifics, to be sure, to which the open literature merely alludes, but which are discussed much more specifically and overtly in the restricted or classified organs that Western analysts have been able to obtain in some instances.

In fact, published literature, in the public domain, presents an accurate reflection of Soviet thinking. If we do not want to read it, that is our problem, not theirs. Very few serious observers would challenge the view that the Kremlin leadership spends an inordinate amount of time and energy discussing, drafting, and vetting doctrinal statements, for general publication, because they serve to guide Soviet "cadres" who are meant to draw operational conclusions. The Soviet leaders have found this to be a convenient form of communication, particularly since the adversary (a) does not see fit to read the literature; (b) when he bothers to read, does not seem to be able to remember the operational implications; and (c) one hopes this does not sound too bitter—those few who do read and remember, appear to have remarkably little influence on policy making in the West. Why, therefore, should the Soviet Union classify material that does not impede the USSR's international relations?

To return to the asymmetry mentioned at the outset—or, perhaps, it would be more accurate to speak of two asymmetries: one refers to the lack of relationship between Soviet reality and the way in which it is perceived by many Westerners, and the other asymmetry relates to our own doctrines (probably, this term is too precise to apply in our case). The Soviet Union, apparently unlike ourselves, develops capabilities to reflect the requirements of doctrine, rather than the other way around. Moreover, there is the additional consideration of resource allocation, which, in the West, seems to take unconditional priority over other concerns.

Analysts of Soviet military affairs have observed a number of cases in which doctrinal revisions anticipated by several years the existence of new capabilities, that became visible only at a subsequent stage. Again, Harriet Scott is eminent among scholars who have duly noted this fact. Soviet doctrine calls, from time to time, for the enhancement or creation of capabilities required in certain areas, and it is articulated, in more specific if somewhat modified form, as soon as Soviet science and technology indicate the feasibility of developing the appropriate hardware.

As for the other problem—mirror-imaging—that seems to be a professional hazard of Western analysis of unfamiliar environments. It is amazing with what ease Western thinkers, and particularly the media, assign to the Soviet scene the concepts, accurate or otherwise, that they apply to their study of bureaucratic and legislative processes in Western capitals. Consequently, terminology like "military-industrial complex," "lobbying for appropriations," "inter-Service rivalries," and so on, abound in Western publications concerning the Soviet Union. Many appear reluctant to ask the appropriate questions, namely: How much resemblance do their descriptions bear to the manner in which Soviet decision-making actually functions? How far are they borne out by material that is relatively plentifully available from the Soviet Union?

Equally surprising, and perhaps even more damaging, is the light-hearted vein in which certain artifacts of Western military thought are ascribed also to Soviet theoreticians—irrespective of whether Soviet literature, the Soviet posture, or Soviet capabilities and operations bear out these assumptions to any meaningful extent. Such gems as "Mutual Assured Destruction," "Mutual War Deterrence," "Defense is Destabilizing in the Strategic Nuclear Arena," and similar jewels of Western invention readily come to mind. Not only does the Soviet Union not subscribe to them, it specifically denies their validity; but, then, it is probably very boring, and very difficult, and very time-consuming to analyze Soviet strategic literature. The Western creators and supporters of these concepts may be motivated by sincere hopes and expectations, but the song "Wishing Will Make It So" is not necessarily applicable to this case.

To repeat, Soviet literature describes these constructs of our imagination, and our resulting terminology, as "bourgeois, reactionary, and unrealistic." As far as the last of these adjectives is concerned, it is not altogether easy to disagree.

NOTES

1. S. G. Gorshkov, *Sea Power of the State* (Moscow: Military Publishing House, 1976), 315 in the English text.

For further details concerning Soviet strategic doctrine and the Soviet sources upon which this chapter has drawn, please see the author's chapter on "Soviet Strategic Doctrine" in Jacquelyn K. Davis, et al., *The Soviet Union and Ballistic Missile Defense*, Special Report (Institute for Foreign Policy Analysis, 1980); as well as the author's testimonoy in *Hearings before the Subcommittee on Strategic and Theater Nuclear Forces of the Committee on Armed Services of the U.S. Senate*, 23 February 1982, pt. 7:4105–4148; also the author's chapter on "Soviet Strategic Doctrine and the Soviet-American Global Contest," in *National Security Policy for the 1980s*, ed. Robert L. Pfaltzgraff, Jr. (Sage Publications, 1981).

II

Alliance Decision Making

5

Grinding Axes: Alliance Politics and Decisions In World War II

John P. Roche

> *There is only one thing worse than fighting with allies, and that is fighting without them.*
>
> Winston Churchill, 1940[1]

> *The President [Roosevelt] said that he supposed Churchill was the best man that England had, even if he was drunk half his time.*
>
> Harold Ickes, 1940[2]

> *How horrible, fantastic, incredible it is that we should be digging trenches and trying on gas-masks here because of a quarrel in a far-away country [Czechoslovakia] between people of whom we know nothing.*
>
> Neville Chamberlain, 1938[3]

> *As a remedy for foreign intrigues [British Foreign Secretary Grey] suggested that foreign statesmen ought to receive their education at an English public school.*
>
> Cited in H. Nicholson, *Portrait of a Diplomatist*[4]

The more reading I have done on the relationships within each of the two alliance systems of World War II—between Germany, Italy, and Japan, on one hand, and the United States, Britain, and the USSR, on the other—the more mythical the concept of concerted, rationally planned behavior on either side becomes. By profession the historian has a bias toward symmetry that is often reflected in assigning far higher levels of rationality to the movers and shakers of the past than were present in fact.

For over thirty years, I have been trying, for example, to find answers to two major strategic questions concerning the origins and conduct of World War II. First, what was the basis of the passionate American love affair with China? Was it not, as George F. Kennan suggested, in our national interest to let our largest economic market in Asia—Japan—play its own hand on the Mainland?[5] What had the Chinese done for us lately except provide plots for Pearl Buck? The issue is discussed later in this chapter.

Second, from the wartime context, why did we persist in thrusting further into Italy, once we had a southern foothold, and air bases in Sicily and Calabria? Instead of engaging in useful work elsewhere, the American Fifth and British Eighth Armies inched their way north against savagely defended positions. To what end? The Dolomites are lovely, but hardly a military objective. A strategic defense, together with tactical attacks, would have forced the Germans to maintain significant force levels, and they would have had the logistical burden of feeding and pacifying the Italians.

To avoid the fallacy of retrospective symmetry, the scholarly order of battle has to be shifted. Instead of viewing wartime efforts at alliance politics with 20/20 hindsight, reaping all the benefits of having read the last chapters of the mystery first, it is essential to project oneself back to the late 1930s and look at events as upcoming. Admittedly, the brush is broad, but it is essential first to capture the mood, the ambience that dominated each of the six powers under consideration. (Already we have sinned: in 1939 France would have been considered a major, seventh player!)

In Berlin, the Nazis were riding high: Hitler's intuition seemed supernal. At every step from the reoccupation of the Rhineland in 1936 through the dismemberment of Czechoslovakia in 1939, the Führer had been warned of disaster by the military. In each instance the Army High Command (OKH) emerged with a reputation for overcaution, if not cowardice.

In the summer of 1939, Hitler sandboxed his macrostrategy: first, neutralize the Soviet Union with a nonaggression pact and plenty of real estate belonging to miscellaneous small powers—a fourth partition of Poland headed the agenda. Then bash the West, avenge Versailles, and negotiate a deal with the British, who seemed to hold appeasement in the same esteem as cricket.

True, in March of 1939, after the Wehrmacht had gobbled up the rump of Czechoslovakia (soon to be followed by Mussolini's Good Friday seizure of Albania), the British and French went into a diplomatic frenzy, issuing "guarantees" to Poland and later to Greece and Romania.[6] But Hitler held the ace of trumps: a Nazi-Soviet Pact would knock these commitments into the proverbial cocked hat. He knew the Western nations were trying to tighten military bonds with Moscow, but they were engaged in an impossible competition: they could not hand Stalin Eastern Europe and the Baltic nations on a platter. Democracies have their drawbacks.

With Hitler chortling in his "Eagle's Aerie" as he plans to admit the Soviet Union as an honorary member to the Anti-Comintern Pact, the view from Moscow has to be considered. Stalin, not without reason, decided after the Munich crisis that the British and French were hardly ideal fighting companions and suspected that "leading circles" in the capitalist world had a private war between Nazi Germany and the Soviet Union on their hidden agenda. So far the only member of the 1936 Anti-Comintern Pact that had given him trouble was Japan: indeed, the first modern tank battles were fought on the Manchurian border in July and August of 1938 between Soviet Siberian units and the Kwantung Army.[7]

Stalin had spent several busy years murdering his cadres—including top Red Army Leaders who were framed by Heydrich's SD—and decided to reverse what he saw as basic capitalist strategy: let the Germans and the British-French stage act 2 of the Leninist drama of mutual imperialist annihilation. Hitler did not want to risk a two-front war; he needed the immense raw material stocks of the USSR, and as a certified *capo di tutti capi* could be counted on to pass out Polish, Latvian, Lithuanian, Estonian, and Romanian real estate without qualm. Also, if Hitler cut a deal with Stalin, the Japanese might get a message. (They did.) So the *mot d'ordre* for 1939 was "wagons in a (bigger) circle."

The first public signal of this abandonment of "collective security" was contained in Stalin's speech to the Eighteenth Party Congress in March 1939, when he announced that the Soviet Union was not going to "pull anyone's chestnuts out of the fire."[8] On 3 May, Maxim Litvinov, the bellwether of collective security, was replaced as Foreign Commissar by Vyacheslav Molotov. Quiet discussions had been under way in Berlin for some time: in 1936–37 Soviet "trade representative" Kandelaki (a member of Stalin's personal secretariat) had raised a proposal for an economic agreement, but Hitler had iced it.[9]

However, in the summer of 1939, the matter was reconsidered, and Hitler, who now had his priorities in order, gave the green light: on 23 August 1939 Foreign Minister Ribbentrop in Moscow signed a Non-Aggression Pact. He felt right at home "as if he were with old Party comrades,"[10] and Stalin did his bit by having a Soviet military band greet him with the "Horst Wessel song." On 1 September, the Wehrmacht invaded Poland; on 17 September, Soviet forces did the same. The split was about even: the Nazis got 72,866 square miles; the Soviet Union, 77,620. Moscow also took the first steps toward the eventual incorporation into the USSR of Latvia, Lithuania, and Estonia, plus, subsequently, the Romanian province of Bessarabia, and fixed its sights on Finland.

In Tokyo 1939 proved to be a hard year for those trying to understand the activities of inscrutable Occidentals. The Japanese were not forewarned of the impending German-Russian love affair and promptly denounced it. However, their most difficult problem was reading the intentions of the United Sates in the Far East. For inexplicable reasons, an American public that snoozed at Hitler's activities in Europe and his vicious anti-Semitism, yawned as Nazi aircraft—the "Condor Legion"—involved in the Spanish Civil War engaged in massive civilian bombing, became very upset at the "rape of Nanking" and other Japanese enterprises in China.

After all, properly understood, Japan was flattering the Americans by imitation: it was establishing a "Monroe Doctrine" for Southeast Asia.[11] But Washington did not seem to appreciate the historical irony. Perhaps the

Japanese attempt to affirm racial equality in the Versailles Treaty had poisoned the atmosphere: a constant Japanese-American issue was the discrimination in the United States against Japanese immigrants, who were ineligible for citizenship.

At the anterior level, I think it is fair to say that the origins of Pearl Harbor arose from a virtually complete Japanese failure to understand the operations of the American government. (It should hastily be added that American racism led to horrendous misperceptions of Japanese capabilities.) The Japanese, who had modeled their modern government on France's, assumed the United States, too, had a highly centralized system in which, if the citizens of San Francisco, for example, segregated Japanese schoolchildren, Washington's *préfet* could step in and reverse the ordinance.

When Wilson's Secretary of State William Jennings Bryan, tried to explain that the (then) rules of the federal system prevented such an invasion of states' rights,[12] the Japanese thought he was not only lying, but insulting their intelligence.

Didn't the United States have a government? The correct answer for all intents and purposes at hand was "No," but this was treated in Tokyo as a bad, racist joke.

The second critical Japanese misperception was a vast exaggeration of the powers of the President. To anticipate, in the interests of specificity, Tokyo assumed that once it made the 1941 decision to go south, FDR could push a button on his desk and the B-17s would sortie from Clark Field against the Japanese transports headed for Malaya, Indochina, and the Dutch East Indies. The Philippines were a dagger pointed at the Japanese line of communication. What Japanese military leaders did not appreciate was that, had they conspicuously avoided the Philippines, their transports would have sailed peacefully south to the background music of Senators and Representatives denouncing British, French, and Dutch "imperialism" and any efforts to "bail them out."

At any rate, back in 1939, Tokyo, facing increased American economic and rhetorical pressures, was working toward a basic strategic decision: whether to accept the demands of the virtually autonomous Kwantung Army in "Manchukuo" for a move into Soviet Far Eastern turf, or to go for the oil, tin, and other resources of Southeast Asia, as advocated by the Navy.[13] Although in September 1940 the Japanese joined the Germans and Italians in a ten-year pact, its ambiguity indicated that Tokyo was thoroughly leery of alliance politics. This was confirmed in April 1941, when Japan's Foreign Minister Yokuse Matsuoka stopped off in Moscow en route home from Berlin and signed a neutrality pact with Stalin; he had not bothered to tell his previous hosts of his plans.[14]

The view from the last among the capitals of the predators can be described briefly: Benito Mussolini's "New Roman Empire" was regarded with traditional skepticism by the history-wise Italian people, but had achieved remarkable status elsewhere. "Il Duce" could draw crowds to his spectacles—his was, of course, a youth movement, and the young are notorious for their delight in vicarious heroism. What is surprising in retrospect is that his standing remained so high both with Hitler and with Chamberlain and Daladier.

By 1939, although Italian trains did not run on time, he had seized Ethiopia and, on Good Friday, launched a quick grab of Albania. His fans kept chanting demands for "Nice, Corsica, and Savoy," but Mussolini's vulpine cunning (he was both courageous and clever, in the British sense of the word) led him not to risk his heavyweight reputation by tackling a heavyweight—until the latter was down. He was not long on planning: we have it on F. W. Deakin's authority that, as late as 1942, "Hitler and Mussolini [had] never discussed . . . a joint, overall politico-military strategy."[15] Rome, in short, was a passive player; no initiative had been taken vis-à-vis Hitler's territorial ambitions since some byplay intended to avoid a German military move against Austria in April of 1937.

Leaving the potential aggressors in their generally euphoric state, the focus has to switch to the Western democracies—Britain, France, and the United States—and the political moods in London, Paris, and Washington must be analyzed. To begin, it is essential to grasp the depth of antiwar sentiment created by the abattoir on the western front in World War I. Although, in population terms, the German butcher's bill was as great as that of the French or British, strong nationalist movements in Germany, eventuating in Hitler's National Socialists, channeled grief into the demand for vengeance.[16]

In Britain and France the message was "never again": nothing could be worse than war. This was shared by the members of the British Commonwealth: the total death toll of Imperial troops from the Somme to Gallipoli to German East Africa and Mesopotamia approximated *one million*! It was designated by some theologians as the "Second Fall of Man."

In the British case, the death toll was distinctive: it was skewed statistically by the absence of a draft until 1916. Thus, as a visit to any Oxbridge college will confirm, those who went out and "bought a farm" in Kitchener's Volunteer Army were heavily drawn from the elite, at least by comparison with the continental nations that had long since established compulsory national service.

Thus, between the wars there was a great leadership gap in Britain—far too many of the guardians turned out by the singular British replication of Plato's elite training machine lay dead in Flanders' Fields. The burden fell primarily on the Conservatives and Liberals since, with the notable exception of Major Clement Attlee, most of the Labour Party's later leaders were essential defense workers, who did not rush to arms in 1914 and were draft-exempt in 1916.

Martin Gilbert's recent *Churchill: The Wilderness Years*[17] (superbly adapted for television) brilliantly limns the political ambience of London in the 1930s.

Both main parties were schizophrenic: the Tories divided between those who, like Churchill, thought "appeasement"—then a positive word—would lead to disaster and war, and the great bulk of the party who believed Hitler could be bought off, that Versailles, which, after all, "had been a bit stiff, y'know," could be revised in a rational way, and perhaps, *mirabile dictu*, Herr Hitler would go off and "bash the Bolshies."

The Labour Party also had its lines of fission: its intellectual leaders were passionately attached to "collective security" and the League of Nations, but adamantly opposed to measures that might make *any* sort of security possible. Anyone interested in the bizarre impact of this antimony on policy proposals should look at the acrobatics engendered by the Spanish Civil War. The Spanish Republic must be saved . . . by all steps short of British belligerence. Instead of writing these endless vapidities, the British left-intelligentsia should simply have sent a wreath.

Then there was a massive exercise in regressive logic, which went roughly as follows: (1) If that saber-rattling mountebank Churchill *should* happen to be right about Hitler, the result would be war; (2) therefore, Churchill can't be right because war is unthinkable; (3) thus, we must look at Herr Hitler's positive side! This convoluted process led George Lansbury, the labour Party's leader (and a simpleton who, in retrospect, makes Michael Foot look like Ernie Bevin) to report in 1938: "I looked deeply into (Hitler's) eyes and was convinced of the man's sincerity when he said he desired peace most of all."[18] (This "good guys syndrome" was shared by Neville Chamberlain, who decided never to "provoke (Mussolini) whose strong sense of humor and attractive smile"[19] convinced the Prime Minister they were soul brothers.)

So both the Conservative Government and the Labor Opposition drifted backward into the 1938–39 crisis. Hard as it is to believe today, the Munich settlement was greeted almost universally as a masterpiece of peacemaking. In the first edition of his *Twenty Years' Crisis*, E. H. Carr, *Times* leader-writer and historian, acclaimed it as the high point of twentieth-century diplomacy.[20] (This passage vanished from the second, 1940, edition!) Lansbury, who had been bounced from the Labour leadership by serious men, knew an epiphany when he saw one: "You have done a most wonderful piece of work," he wrote Chamberlain, "and done it under the guidance and providence of God."[21]

Munich had as its structural consequence the destruction of the whole post-World War I alliance system, or whatever pieces of it were left. The French-British entente was presumably still in place, though the French had never quite forgiven London for the 1935 Naval Treaty with Berlin, and the British had their doubts about French Foreign Minister Laval's 1935 deal with Moscow. If the French could come up with a leader whose name was a palindrome, what might they be up to next?

The fact is that French morale between the wars was dreadful. Half of all Frenchmen between the ages of 20 and 32 in 1914 were *killed*; the body count was 1,385,000 killed in action, 3 million wounded, and another 250,000 missing. Physical damage to industry and agriculture in the war zones was virtually incalculable: 1.5 million head of livestock vanished with the farms where they lived. Politically, France was riven by a powerful right wing, with paramilitary organizations such as the *Croix de Feu* (who hit the jackpot with Pétain in 1940) and the wobbly parties of the Third Republic racked by scandal and internal bickering. Suffice it to say that the same Chamber of Deputies that was elected in Leon Blum's "Front Populaire" victory in 1936, abdicated power to Pétain in 1940.

The myth of the invincible French Army lived on: André Maginot's line of fortifications should keep the "Boches" at bay (as, indeed, it might have done had it been continued to the Channel after Belgium in 1936 repudiated its military alliance with France). But French society was defeatist, cynical, sour, and autistic. The right sympathized with Hitler's campaign against the godless Communists, atheists, freemasons, and Jews.[22]

The left—divided between Communist flunkies of Moscow, who shifted from antimilitarism to superpatriotism after the Seventh Congress of the Comintern in 1935,[23] and the Socialists, who, like their British Labour counterparts, were incapable of supporting both collective security and the military force that would make it possible to, say, save the Spanish Republic[24]—was in a state of paralysis. France in 1939 was not a nation but a nightmare.

In 1918–19 "La Victoire" had opened dreams of a cornucopia in which the aggressors, as defined at Versailles, would rebuild the wrecked French polity. Then—it seems—the Germans had no reparations cornucopia to open. Why? Who got the loot? "Perfidious Albion," which had grabbed the German colonies? The Jews? The munitions makers? The Yankee banks? To summarize a sad psychic syndrome, all elements of French society—for different reasons—agreed, "*On nous a vendu!*" ("We have been sold out!"). This hardly provided support for a vigorous foreign policy as the Nazi menace loomed. France was, in the clinical sense, in Hobbes's "state of nature," i.e., anomic.

Finally, we turn to the giant without a shadow, the United States, which was for all intents and purposes on another planet. If this description has undertones of autobiography, it is no accident: I was born in the shadow of World War I and grew to political awareness in the national mood of disillusionment triggered by that totally un-American occurrence, the Great Depression. The inculcation of disillusion began young: as a child I was raised on the folly of our intervention in World War I, on how we had been tricked by British propaganda and by a coalition of Anglophile capitalists who duped Woodrow Wilson.

Wilsonian internationalism had one of the shortest shelf lives in the history of American political spasms. The nation that seemed to go insane with chauvinism in 1917 was, as the 1920 presidential election indicated, in the midst of a massive withdrawal syndrome. The slogan was the same as that in Britain and France—"Never Again!"—but the meaning was totally different: never again would we get ourselves mixed up in the corrupt, dirty, imperialist tentacles of "Old World" diplomacy. Indicative of this repudiation of Wilson is a 1920 Democratic election poster in my collection. The messge is "Cox and Roosevelt: America First!"

Rather than attempt to summarize this period in diplomatic or foreign policy terms, I suggest a reading of John Dos Passos's *U.S.A.* However, there is one sure index of the extent of American commitment to anything resembling national security: the military budgets and authorized force levels. In 1918 the War and Navy Departments were authorized $6,148,735,000; the following year this rose to $11 billion; by 1921, it dropped to less than $2 billion! Fifteen years later, in 1936, the total was $1,147,469,000, and remained in that range through 1940, when it leaped back roughly to the *1921* level.[25]

What force levels did these sums provide for an alleged "great power"? After World War I, demobilization from a high of roughly 3 million men in 1918, the combined totals for the Army, Navy, and Marines by 1923 settled in for a total of roughly 250,000 until 1935. In 1940, after the outbreak of the war in Europe, we jumped to 458,365, and by Pearl Harbor had reached 1.8 million.[26] And these figures do not reflect the absence of a civilian defense infrastructure designing and producing modern military equipment, i.e., the absence of a draft, which was not set up until September 1940, and then continued for an additional year in October 1941. The enthusiasm with which this was greeted can be inferred from the extension vote in the House of Representatives: 203 to 202.

As far as the "Old World" was concerned, average Americans, who were usually too numbed by the Depression to think cosmic thoughts, profoundly distrusted all hands. After all, we had saved their necks and what had we got in return? Welching on war debts and ungrateful distrust of our intentions, emphasized here by anti-imperialist—particularly anti-British— rhetoric that came from powerful isolationist (then, like "appeasement" in Britain, a "good" word) sources.

This was amply reciprocated in London, where Robert (later Lord) Vansittart of the Foreign Office could write in 1933, "I will only repeat my strengthened conviction that we have been too tender, not to say subservient, with the U.S. for a long time past. . . . It is still necessary [that] we should get on well with this untrustworthy race. We shall never get very far; they will always let us down."[27] This related to Roosevelt's alleged sabotage of the London Economic Conference by deserting the gold standard, though the evidence indicates that FDR was set up for this sinister role by European finance ministers who were themselves in the process of burking the sacrosanct status of gold.[28]

Against this background of profound public disinterest, President Roosevelt and a number of his top advisers began in the late 1930s to realize that the Nazi threat to the fundamental values of Western civilization was real.

They also kept an eye—a malignant eye—on Japanese activities, but only a handful of Americans escaped the solipsism of racism and took the Japanese seriously as a potential enemy. When Bismarck was asked what he would do if the Danes invaded Pomerania, he is reputed to have replied, "Call the police." Americans assumed with less empirical basis that if the "Japs" made trouble, we would mobilize the Boy Scouts.

However, this growing sense of apprehension, which FDR tried with disastrous political results to stimulate with his October 1937 "Quarantine the Aggressors" speech, led the Congress of the United States in the opposite direction, in a vigorous quest for a national belt of chastity that would guarantee absolutely the noninvolvement of the United States in foreign wars. Robert A. Divine has chronicled this initiative in detail;[29] suffice it for our purposes to say that in 1939 the President of the United States found his power to participate in the buildup of the Western democracies crippled by wide-ranging neutrality legislation; public opinion polls, then far less precise than now but useful for macrotrends, indicated a gradual increase in "isolationist sentiment," which, as late as the summer of 1941, hovered around 75 percent.

To understand the nature of coalition politics in World War II, it is essential to engage in this time warp. Our problem is that we know so much more about what they planned than they did. Current flagellation in the American Jewish community, for example, about the failure of American Jewry to rescue the 6 million from the Holocaust rests on two fallacious assumptions: first, that in 1939–42 American Jewish leaders grasped the enormity of Hitler's "Final Solution" (after all, European Jews were equally blind); and second, that if they had, they could have significantly influenced American policy—in 1940 the now-effective "Jewish lobby" was nonexistent, anti-Semitism was part of the American folk culture, and the Jews had roughly the same political clout as the Copts.

Similarly, we tend to assume that because we have read some authoritative documents that appear to lock a position in concrete, the recipients both read and understood their implications. Sir Harold Nicolson put it beautifully when he described Foreign Secretary Sir Edward Grey's attitude toward the "technical" pre-World War I conversations between the British and French admiralties, talks that led to an agreement that in the event of war the Grand Fleet would handle business in the Atlantic, while the French would operate in the Mediterranean. Grey never considered this an "alliance," and the infuriated Germans "did not understand that this perfected type of British parliamentarian did not attribute any but a purely technical and conditional importance to such conversations as soldiers or sailors might hold. These conversations, to his mind, were mere matters of routine which could be reversed with the stroke of a pen. They possessed, to his mind, no more importance than discussions between the London Fire Brigade and the Westminster Water Works."[30]

During World War II, FDR was famous for similar casualness: there is no reason to believe he read the famous "Morgenthau Plan" for the postwar "pastoralization" of Germany before he initialed it. At least, he reversed his imprimatur in record time when Secretary of State Cordell Hull, in a rage, told him what he had done.[31] Later Roosevelt, somewhat shamefacedly, admitted to approving two contrary directives on the occupation of Germany.[32]

The classic case study of FDR in ambiguous action is William M. Franklin's perceptive study of "Zonal Boundaries and Access to Berlin," featuring FDR with a crayon and a *National Geographic* map of Europe.[33] One excerpt gives the flavor: when Roosevelt's revised map of occupation zones reached chief British planner Frederick Morgan, "the General was taken aback. Indeed, by his own account, he thought for a while he was the victim of a practical joke."[34]

Finally, to paraphrase T. S. Eliot, "between the decision and the implementation falls the shadow," in our case, the shadow of the bureaucracy. One of the decisive steps in Tokyo's decision to go to war with the United States was our decision in the summer of 1940 to embargo aviation gasoline shipments to Japan (we were their major supplier). As Jonathan G. Utley puts it in his elegant analysis, "the impact of the embargo depended on the definition of 'aviation gasoline.' The day before the embargo was to be announced . . . specialists met and hurriedly prepared two definitions. Both defined aviation gasoline as 87 or higher octane, while one was broadened to include 'any material from which by commercial distillation there can be separated more than 3% of [87 + octane] gasoline.' This phrase effectively included all crude oil that Japan might import from the United Staes."[35]

State Department "hawks" led by Assistant Secretary Dean Acheson initially succeeded in having the broader definition adopted, but were overruled because of the damage it would do to the domestic oil industry! The bureaucratic effort to strangle Japan economically was by no means over, the next high point being the successful effort to freeze German and Italian funds in June 1941, and Japanese in July. As Utley concludes, given Acheson's superb talents as a bureaucratic infighter, "it was no longer possible to assume that the actions of the nation reflected the will of the policy formulators. As events of July and August 1941 indicate, what Roosevelt and Hull considered a cautious policy became bold action in the hands of those who were supposed to follow orders, but preferred to lead the nation.

The Long Week-End (as Graves and Hodge entitled their perceptive book on Britain between the wars) ended with a bang, in fact, a massive artillery barrage, on 1 September 1939, when Hitler launched the Wehrmacht on Poland. On 3 September, after some dithering, Britain and France declared war to honor their commitment to Poland. This time there were no heroics, but a sense of fatalism; the troops just sat and waited for something to happen. On the other side of the world, the Japanese had, of course, been at war since the invasion of Manchuria in 1931 and were working away on their private agenda.

Stalin moved his forces into Poland and began the takeover of the Baltic states. In November, responding to the request of a bogus Communist front ("The People's Finnish Government"), he invaded Finland to protect Kuusinen's "progressive" regime from suppression by reactionaries and was thrown out of the League of Nations for his non-peace-loving behavior.[36] The Italians went to the opera. President Roosevelt proclaimed neutrality, and the Americans went to the New York World's Fair and the Golden Gate International Exposition in San Francisco. After the initial flurry, and some tears for the brave Poles and Finns, the "sitzkrieg" began in the West and whatever sense of emergency existed in September 1939 vanished.

In this environment, to talk of cooperation among such variegated, not to say bizarre, players is to engage in fantasy. True, there was some military coordination: a key episode in the light of later events was the Polish Army's moving "Enigma" machines, the basis for the whole "Ultra" cryptographic drama, first to France and then to England.[37] But curiously, the big "lesson of Poland" was never appreciated by British and French strategists: the "blitzkrieg," the willingness rapidly to commit armored forces in massive strength with no concern for flank cover, and the substitution of "Stuka" dive bombers for traditional (and slow on the road) artillery support.

By selection of exemplary cases, one may explore the working relationships among the various participants. The Axis constitutes a simple case, since there was no serious effort at any time to coordinate, or even to inform, Germany's allies of Hitler's strategic objectives. For example, in his April 1941 discussions with Japanese Foreign Minister Matsuoka, Hitler never mentioned his plan to invade the Soviet Union.[38] Another instance of a Berlin-Tokyo lapse was that, after the 27 September 1940 Tripartite Pact, Matsuoka gave the German Ambassador to Japan a secret letter, noting that the Pact would in no way interfere with Tokyo's relations with Moscow. The German Ambassador never forwarded this significant document to Berlin![39]

There was some exchange of information and, perhaps, military equipment—allegedly the Germans shipped some upgraded radar equipment to Japan by U-boat, but I am unable to document it. Hitler—fortunately for us—was very impressed by the Japanese Ambassador to Berlin, Baron (General) Oshima, and gave him a great deal of information about the activities of the Nazi military. In the spring of 1944, Oshima was given a tour with interminable briefings on the Wehrmacht order of battle in the West. He meticulously radioed this to Tokyo, and it was equally meticulously decrypted from "Magic" by our code-breakers in time for Overlord.[40]

Earlier, on 29 November 1941, a similar high-grade message was decrypted informing Tokyo that if Japan "became engaged in a war against the United States, Germany would, of course join in the war immediately."[41] So much for the "spasm theory," the view once held by me among others, that Hitler's declaration of war against the United States on 11 December 1941 was a momentary id-discharge, an exercise in psychic vengeance against FDR. Despite Hans Trefousse and Gerhard L. Weinberg's energetic efforts to explain this act of geopolitical madness,[42] in my judgment, the jury is still out. What we do know is that it was set out in an advance scenario. The Japanese had not given Berlin advance notice of Pearl Harbor.

Perhaps the most interesting, and ironic, episode in alliance politics was the zest with which Stalin set to work to carve up the world with his born-again ally. The largely unread details of this scavenging exercise can be found in *Nazi-Soviet Relations—1939–1941, Documents from the Archives of the German Foreign Office*, published by the U.S. Department of State in 1948.[43] Key developments began in the summer and fall of 1940, and, on 13 November, Foreign Commissar V. M. Molotov met with Hitler and Ribbentrop for a love feast: Hitler, to summarize, told Molotov that if Germany and Russia stood "back to back" there would be "no power on earth which could oppose the two countries." Molotov agreed and "stressed the viewpoint of the Soviet leaders, and of Stalin in particular, that it would be possible and expedient to strengthen and activate the relations between the two countries."[44]

(To inject a macabre aside, the Gestapo and the *NKVD* did work out an *entente cordiale* that led to a trade of German Communists in Stalin's Gulag for a group of Soviet spies in Nazi custody. For the details see a participant's chronicle, Margaret Buber-Neumann's *Under Two Dictators*.[45] The widow of a former head of the German Communist Party who was purged, she survived to become a leading authority on comparative concentration camp life. Her considered verdict was that the Nazis were worse because they systematized brutality and dehumanization, while the Russians were simply randomly brutal.)

Molotov and Ribbentrop continued their search for a satisfactory formula, but Hitler—understandably, given his long-term agenda—was cagey about the issues that most concerned Molotov, while Molotov—who had, not accidentally, survived the purges—was cagey on Ribbentrop's desiderata. Unable to agree on such immediate problems as German troops in Finland and Romania, this "odd couple" proceeded to the easier task of dividing the globe. Molotov returned to Moscow to draw up a draft treaty with two secret protocols: "Draft—Secret Protocol No. 1" will suffice as evidence of Stalin's ideal of a jolly alliance. It merits quotation in full:

> Upon the signing today of the Agreement concluded among them, the representatives of Germany, Italy, Japan and the Soviet Union declare as follows:
>
> 1. Germany declares that, apart from the territorial revisions in Europe to be carried out at the conclusion of peace, her territorial aspirations center in the territories of central Africa.

2. Italy declares that, apart from the territorial revisions in Europe to be carried out at the conclusion of peace, her territorial aspirations center in the territories of northern and northeastern Africa.

3. Japan declares that her territorial aspirations center in the area of eastern Asia to the south of the Island Empire of Japan.

4. The Soviet Union declares that its territorial aspirations center south of the national territory of the Soviet Union in the direction of the Indian Ocean.

The Four Powers declare that, reserving the settlement of specific questions, they will mutually respect these territorial aspirations and will not oppose their achievement.[46]

Nothing came of this demarche: on 18 December 1940 Hitler set in motion the most spectacular double cross in history: "Directive No. 21" went out to the Wehrmacht, top secret, announcing, "The German Armed Forces must be prepared to crush Soviet Russia in a quick campaign (Operation Barbarossa). . . . Was it Franz Borkenau who noted wryly that Hitler was the only person Stalin ever trusted? In fact, Stalin, despite all the evidence, including warnings from his own agents, "Lucy" in Switzerland and Sorge in Tokyo, and from Churchill (based on "Ultra" intercepts), denounced all such suggestions of Nazi perfidy as provocations. Indeed, Sir Stafford Cripps, Britain's Ambassador, was *publicly* attacked in the official Soviet press for attempting to sow division among friends a week before the Nazis struck![47] The invasion was a complete strategic and tactical surprise: even Marshal Zhukov's carefully sanitized memoirs begin to smoke in his discussion of this *coup de main*. Khrushchev's equally laundered memoirs state flatly, "Stalin convinced himself that Hitler would keep his word and wouldn't really attack us."[48]

As far as German-Italian relations were concerned, there were no instruments of coordination. Hitler originally had great respect for Mussolini, whom he regarded as a Fascist mentor, but the great debate in the German General Staff was always over whether it would take more Wehrmacht divisions to defend Italy than to fight her. Italian "volunteers" in the Spanish Civil War had performed very poorly, notably at the Ebro River, where a Republican rag, tag, and bobtail force had mauled them.

The *OKH* also remembered Caporetto in World War I and was extremely cautious about any force commitments south of the Brenner Pass. For the time being this was on "hold": Italy did not declare war on France and Britain until 10 June 1940, i.e., after the struggle for France was over. In October 1940 Mussolini did not give the Germans advance information on his plan to invade Greece from Albania.

To summarize, Axis coalition coordination was nonexistent, as fictitious as the great Anti-Communist Pact, which, by the fall of 1941, had become simply a Nazi chorus, in its European manifestation, and a unilateral

Japanese performance in Asia. Even in Europe, that ingrate Francisco Franco refused to move beyond pro-German neutrality, fending off Hitler's efforts to obtain free passage of German troops to the Strait of Gibraltar.

To switch playing fields to the other "team," one is compelled to examine the body-contact sport known as the Anglo-American-Soviet (after Hitler forced a shift in loyalties on Stalin) alliance. There is an enormous body of literature on various efforts to coordinate the wartime operations of the "United Nations," as they were denominated in a masterful exercise of the fallacy of misplaced concreteness. On the military side, there were the Combined [British and American] Chiefs of Staff, once the United States abandoned its traditional allergy to the "Prussian" staff system and allowed the Army Chief of Staff and the Chief of Naval Operations to assume the status of their British peers. (The Joint Chiefs of Staff did not receive formal legislative approval in the United States until 1947.)

However, from the outset of American involvement in the hostilities, there was a distinct difference between the civilian-military relationship in Britain and in the United States. President Franklin D. Roosevelt, encouraged by his Personal Chief of Staff, Admiral William D. Leahy, tended to leave the key decisions on strategy in the hands of his military magnates, General George C. Marshall and Admiral Ernest J. King. True (after the presidential election of 1940), he and Churchill had launched secret staff talks (the American-British Conversations, or ABC) and had come up with a "contingency plan": if the United States were to get into the war, Germany was to be the number one objective and the Japanese problem should be downgraded, indeed, pushed into the future by a defensive policy (ABC–1).[49]

Much to the fury of the State Department, however, FDR in essence decided that foreign policy objectives were to be put on the back burner until the war was won. Secretary of State Cordell Hull, for example, attended only one of the "summit" conferences—at Quebec in August 1943. William Roger Louis, in his *Imperialism at Bay*,[50] a fine if turgid study of American wartime policy toward British colonialsim, put it well when dealing with the Cairo Conference of 1943, where FDR, Churchill, and Chiang Kai-shek settled the future of the Japanese Empire. "So far as the American mission to Cairo was concerned, the Far Eastern authorities of the State Department," said Louis, "could just as well have belonged to a foreign government. Roosevelt took no account of their expert knowledge and, in fact, did not even include a State Department representative in the mission."[51]

The blindsiding of the State Department (for better or worse) by Roosevelt during World War II is worth noting. The ablest Foreign Service officers—e.g., Robert Murphy, George F. Kennan, Charles Bohlen, Edmund A. Gullion, et al.—were seconded to work as "POLADS" with military commanders, or sent on quasi-military missions (Gullion was flown to Helsinki in 1943 in the belly of a Mosquito plane to set up an observation operation). These political advisers were not working for the Secretary of State, no matter what the lines on the chart indicated: they were an integral part of the military machine. One need cite only Robert Murphy's roles in the North African invasion and in Italy,[52] or Kennan's desperate efforts to make sense out of the different instructions sent to the European Advisory Commission in London on the postwar division of Germany.[53]

Since Hull had nothing much to keep him occupied, he encouraged the development of a planning unit in State, which would look to the problems facing us once the war was won. This outfit, headed by Leo Pasvolsky, had a grand time—as Louis has documented—preparing paper mountains premised on great power harmony and the end of imperialism. Roosevelt, without thinking much about it, had a habit of denouncing Western imperialism—he loved to yank the Lion's tail—and suggesting to Churchill, the Dutch, and the French the moral superiority of the United States, which, in 1935, had accorded its former colony, the Philippines, Commonwealth status.

Pasvolsky & Co. took this sentimental anti-imperialism very seriously indeed, and beavered away at trusteeship schemes for all sorts of random real estate, then flying imperialist flags. FDR was most specific in his condemnation of the British in India, the French in Indochina, and the Dutch in the East Indies; but given his track record when he went eyeball to eyeball with Churchill on India, there is no reason to suspect this was more than a rhetorical hobby.[54] Those who say that had Roosevelt lived, things would have gone differently in Indochina, assume a purposefulness that the evidence does not support.

Ironically, it was Cordell Hull's concern to maintain the colonial status quo for the French that led to one of the most bathetic incidents of the War: the little-known battle of St. Pierre and Miquelon, several rocky islands off the coast of Newfoundland, which are the remnants of the French North American Empire. The islands themselves were of little intrinsic value, but on St. Pierre was one of the strongest radio stations in the North Atlantic area, which Nazi submarines could employ as a convenient direction-finder. On Christmas Eve 1941, the Free French, with obvious British and Canadian connivance (Admiral Emile Muselier of the FFF took his squadron out of port on the St. Lawrence, allegedly destined for Halifax) popped in on the islands for a Christmas liberation. The latter development had two high points: first, a plebiscite in which the inhabitants overwhelmingly opted for De Gaulle, and second, the silencing of the radio station.[55]

Hull and Assistant Secretary A. A. Berle went berserk: the Secretary actually invoked the Monroe Doctrine against the slightly startled Free French,[56] who had been laboring under the illusion that they were doing British and American shipping a favor. The extent to which trivia were capable of paralyzing the State Department can be gathered from Berle's diary: "Monday, January 5th. [1942] Yesterday was an almost solid day of

St. Pierre and Miquelon. It is curious to be working over a row kicked up
over two no-account islands, when there is a whole wide world in
peril . . . ."[57] But on 9 January, "St. Pierre and Miquelon are still burning
questions."[58] For all I know, they may still be burning, but what interests me
is that I have no recollection of a Hull complaint when we seized that Vichy-
held tropical paradise, New Caledonia, on our way to the New Hebrides and
Solomons. Of course, the Monroe Doctrine would not have covered the
Southwest Pacific, a point perhaps brought to the Secretary's attention by the
Department's legal counsel.

More seriously, unlike Roosevelt, Churchill took a very (some might
say over-) active hand in strategic determinations. He had three major items
on his agenda after becoming Prime Minister in May 1940: first, defend
Britain from the Nazis, a task requiring American economic and probably
military aid; second, maintain the British Empire in all its glory—he was the
very model of the romantic imperialist; and third, keep a sharp eye out for
Soviet expansionism, always remembering Lenin's devotion to Clausewitz
and the Soviet view that war is simply an extension of politics.

Churchill, despite his American mother and familiarity with the United
States, shared British upper-class prejudices against Vansittart's "untrustworthy race." Recall his reaction to the news that we had successfully tested
the A-bomb: "The idiot child has the matches."[59] In the period before Hitler
declared war on the United States, when Churchill was hoping that Roosevelt
would charge to the rescue of Britain, he waxed quite bitter on occasion at
what he saw as the American President's casualness, if not timidity. His
intimate, Lord Beaverbrook, Minister of Aircraft Production, added another
dimension to the distrust: he was convinced the Americans wanted to gobble
up the British Empire in economic terms, a fear shared by other high
officials.[60]

The root of this controversy was not American meretriciousness, but
Congressional suspicion of Great Britain. True, Secretary of the Treasury
Henry Morgenthau did state in 1946 that, throughout his long tenure, his
main objective had been to "move the financial center of the world from
London and Wall Street to the United States Treasury,"[61] but his concern was
not nationalistic; he wanted to remove vital decision making in areas of
public policy from private hands in London *and* New York. His concern for
free trade did run counter to the British policy of Empire Preference, but
again—as shown by the current debate over restrictions on Japanese and
European Community imports—parochialism in international economics
was never a British monopoly.

No, sinister American capitalist forces conjured up by a wonderful
alliance of right-wing Tories and Communists, were not responsible for the
de facto bankruptcy of the British Empire, allegedly caused by Washington's
policies. Congress, most notably in "Cash and Carry" laws, demanded that
the British liquidate their worldwide assets to buy munitions and other

necessities. Ironically, the motivation for this "In God [only] We Trust" legislation was fundamentally *anticapitalist*, based on the mythology (which I absorbed with the air I breathed in the 1920s and 1930s) that wicked capitalists had lured us into World War I to rescue their investments.[62] We were fond of quoting William Jennings Bryan's aphorism that "money is the greatest contraband of all because it buys all the others."

In any event, there was an inherent contradiction between Churchill's first and second objectives: hocking British assets to fulfill American demands hardly contributed to the maintenance of the British Empire. As Churchill wrote in a mordant December 1940 draft cable to Roosevelt, the United States seemed like "a sheriff collecting the last assets of a helpless debtor. . . . It is not fitting that any nation should put itself wholly in the hands of another, least of all a nation which is fighting under increasingly severe conditions for what is proclaimed to be a cause of general concern."[63] The message was never sent, but the rancor lingered, intensified in 1941 by the sentiment in Britain that "we are doing their fighting for them."

Finally, there were bound to be conflicts between Roosevelt and Churchill over the conduct of the war, once Hitler had forced us into the European conflagration. For one thing, in real terms the United States did not fight one war, but two with virtually no linkage.[64] Without downplaying the patriotism of the Navy, it is fair to say that it considered Europe a sideshow: Admiral Ernest King, C.N.O., and his top brass wanted vengeance for the destruction of Pearl Harbor; they had agreed to the Europe First strategy before the Pacific fleet lay in ruins, but never, thereafter, really accepted it.

This may seem tangential until one includes in the equation that the Navy controlled the allocation of such useful items as landing craft, and an army really cannot be put ashore on the European mainland without LSTs, LSIs, LCMs, and the rest. Once Nimitz and MacArthur broke out in the Pacific and started island-hopping, there was a virtually unlimited demand from the PTO for more landing craft, and on occasion it took a full-court press by the President, Marshall, and any other available players to make King divert landing craft to the ETO. (This had its occasional utility: the lack of LSTs, for example, could be used by Eisenhower to stalemate some of Churchill's loonier schemes for grabbing essentailly useless Mediterranean real estate.)

Brief case studies of two interallied scenarios are worthy of examination at this point: first the Anglo-American dispute on how to reconquer Europe; and second, the Anglo-American-Soviet discussions on the postwar shape of Eastern Europe.

The minute the Wehrmacht invaded the Socialist Motherland, the worldwide Communist movement shifted gears and went into patriotic overdrive. Stalin did his best to cooperate: priests were dug out of Gulag and put back in vestments, government Commissars became "Ministers," "The Internationale" vanished from the airwaves, and, in 1943, out of particular consideration for FDR, the Comintern was abolished. (Boris Ponomarev, who took the sign off the door, still appears to be sitting behind the same desk, in charge of "relations with non-ruling parties."

By early 1942, Moscow had sent out the slogan "A Second Front Now!" and the orchestration that is so familiar to those of us who have watched it over the years ("Free Tom Mooney," "Save the Rosenbergs," "Recognize the NLF," etc.) had begun. As is always the case, most of the participants in the campaign for a Second Front were not Communists, but as Peter Lorre observed in *The Maltese Falcon*, "It's not who pulls the trigger, but who buys the bullet." And Stalinist cadres were (and still are) experts at setting up what the Comintern's organizational genius, Willy Münzenberg,[65] frankly called "transmission belts" to (in Lenin's phrase) "useful idiots ." Hence, from Sydney to London to San Francisco, from Buenos Aires to Delhi to Chicago, "Second Front Now!" committees popped up like mushrooms, none complete without at least one bishop. (Willy's term was "innocents" clubs.)

For reasons that are almost impossible to discern, the American Chiefs of Staff and the President became firm advocates of a cross-Channel invasion in 1942. This put the cat among the pigeons in Whitehall: the Prime Minister, with his "Passchendaele Complex," wanted no repetition of the head-on butchery of World War I and favored a war of maneuver of "peripheral strategy." The British Chiefs of Staff, leaving aside Churchill's cosmic reservations, thought the proposal insane on military grounds alone. There is a rumor that will not die that Churchill and his Chiefs launched the Dieppe Raid in August 1942 (where the forces, mainly Canadian, took 70 percent casualties) to demonstrate to the American cowboys that invading the Continent was not a Sunday picnic excursion.

It is mind-bending that, at that time, men as intelligent as Marshall, King, and Admiral Harold Stark (Leahy was still our Ambassador to Vichy France and did not assume duty as FDR's Personal Chief of Staff until late in 1942) could have considered laying on an invasion with untrained troops, no logistical backup, and an acute shortage of both armor and the craft that would transport it to the far shore. As Omar Bradley put it in his posthumously published autobiography: "A last word on North Africa. A year earlier, Marshall and Ike had been passionately committed to an early direct invasion of France—Roundup. The invasion of North Africa, Torch, had been a British concept reluctantly undertaken by Marshall and Ike."[66] (Sherwood stated this was "one of the very few major military decisions of the war which Roosevelt made entirely on his own and over the protests of his highest ranking advisers.")[67]

"On reflection," Bradley concluded, "I came to the conclusion it was fortunate that the British view prevailed, that the U.S. Army first met the enemy on the periphery, in Africa rather than on the beaches of France. In Africa we learned to crawl, to walk—then run. Had that learning process been launched in France, it would surrely have—as Alan Brooke [Churchill's military "Keeper," later Lord Alanbrooke] argued—resulted in an unthinkable disaster."[68]

In the event, Roundup was scrubbed and Torch was on: on 8 November 1942 the Anglo-American invasion force, commanded by General Dwight Eisenhower, hit the beaches in Morocco and Algeria, at that time the largest amphibious operation in history. It was designed to close the vise on the Afrika Korps, which was in full retreat from El Alamein, but in large part failed to cork the Tunisian bottle.

The argument concerning the reasons fills countless memoirs, but the gist of the American complaint is that "Monty" stopped the Eighth Army after every victory to wash and rest his tanks, while, according to British claims, the American command structure was such a shambles that nobody was really in command.[69] (With his characteristic candor, Bradley gives a good deal of support to the latter view.)[70]

By May of 1943, the Axis was out of North Africa and the big question was "Where next?" To decide this momentous issue, President Roosevelt had met with Churchill and their respective advisers at Casablanca, 17–27 January. (The French, in the St. Pierre and Miquelon tradition, were generating disproportionate attention; suffice it to note that the greatest photograph from Casablanca shows a frozen De Gaulle shaking hands with his rival, General Henri Giraud, as a symbol of French "unity." Marshall wanted the victorious forces shipped to Britain to prepare for a 1943 cross-Channel invasion, Bolero. The British argued for cleaning up the Mediterranean.

By now, senior American officials, both military and civilian (Secretary of War Henry L. Stimson, for example), were reaching the conclusion that the British would stonewall, or end run, a direct invasion commitment until the Greek kalends; consequently, a stream of leaks indicated that Washington was rethinking its "Europe First" strategy and planning to put the big push in the Pacific. Some advocates, notably the Admirals, were sincere; others were using the disinformation gambit to blackmail London into consenting to an invasion of the French Channel coast—taking the short route to Berlin.[71]

Later, Stimson said it was a "bluff," FDR called it a "red herring,"[72] and in the event it did not work: on 18 January 1943 the Combined Chiefs of Staff (CCS) agreed the next target was Sicily, Operation Husky, a victory for the peripheral strategists. Eisenhower was named Supreme Allied Commander. On 23 January the CCS gave fourth priority to "Operations in and from the United Kingdom," involving an American force buildup for Bolero and for raids against the Channel Islands and the Cotentin Peninsula on 1 August 1943.[73] (Note: this was not a flat endorsement of a main force assault in 1943, but it gave FDR political cover in dealing with the "Second Front Now!" enthusiasts.)

The interesting aspect of this conference is its treatment of Sicily *in vacuo*, that is, the capture of Sicily was justified on the ground it would free about 225 ships from the Mediterranean for duty elsewhere, not as a jump-off point for the invasion of Italy. "Hap" Arnold of the USAAF may have had visions of air bases in Calabria and Apulia, and there was some talk of the impact of a successful seizure on internal Italian politics. However, walking to Berlin via the length of Italy and the width of Austria would have been considered a bad joke.

Two other points merit short notice: Roosevelt felt it was essential to reassure Stalin that the Anglo-Americans would not cut a separate deal with the Axis, and persuaded an unenthusiastic Churchill to agree to the doctrine of "Unconditional Surrender." This slogan had a stirring impact on Nazi propaganda, may briefly have moved Stalin to his existential depths, and was, of course, not applied to either Italy or Japan. The second was a formal British commitment to throw their full resources into the defeat of Japan once the war in Europe was won.

Since a cross-Channel invasion in 1943 was obviously out of the question by the time the Anglo-American-Canadian forces cleaned the Germans out of North Africa—the lead time for logistical preparation and the weather window in the stormy North Sea area alone disposed of that notion—the Allies had a problem. Two big armies were now perched in Tunis, Algeria, and in Morocco with no mission. Well, on a clear day you could almost see Sicily, and, although there were those who argued for the Sardinia-Corsica option because these islands menaced the only real "soft underbelly of Europe" so beloved by Churchill (the French coast from Toulon to Sète), the Chiefs decided on operation Husky, a Sicilian invasion. A political dimension of this decision was its potential impact on Italian morale.

As Omar Bradley's autobiography amply documents,[74] the Sicilian operation was a bit of a drunken square dance. The original plan envisaged a fast seizure of Messina, which would have trapped the Nazi troops who had escaped from Tunis to Sicily. It reflected the American maxim: find the enemy, pin the enemy, kill him. However, in the famous men's room discussion in Algiers, Montgomery talked Ike's Chief of Staff, Walter Bedell Smith, out of this simpleminded view of corking the bottle and substituted one of his famous envelopment plans. This had the dubious merit of forcing the Wehrmacht back on Messina, whence they were evacuated to Italy with remarkable efficiency. This and his perceived slow trip from Egypt to Tunis led a number of American generals to the view that "Monty" didn't want to kill Germans; he just wanted to chase them. The "Passchendaele Complex" again?

While Sicily was being conquered—Messina fell on 18 August—Benito Mussolini's regime was ended on 25 July by a military coup lead by Marshal Pietro Badoglio, who opened negotiations for an armistice. On 2 September, Allied forces crossed the Straits of Messina to Italy, and, on the third, an armistice was signed in Algiers. However, the *OKH*, and Hitler in particular, were not sitting on their hands. A contingency plan had long been in the drawer: Operation Alaric, which had German forces moving into northern Italy and taking over control of Italian responsibilities in south-eastern Europe. On 26 July Hitler instructed the *OKH* to launch the coun-teraction, and by the end of the first week in August, roughly seven new German divisions were moving south through Italy to reinforce the ten, mostly veterans of Africa and Sicily, already in place.[75]

What now occurred was a dispute on each side as to the mission of their forces in Italy. The Allied capture of Sicily was viewed by the *OKH* as the preliminary step in invading southern France and Italy, notably the Gulf of Genoa. Once the Allies moved into the "boot" of Italy, the possibility existed of a flank attack on Yugoslavia. The powerful team of Rommel and Kesselring was placed in charge of setting up Wehrmacht strategy. For starters, all Italian military units were bagged and disarmed, including thirty-two divisions in the Balkans. Initially, the Germans following a plan devised by Rommel and Field Marshal Jodl with the Führer on 11 August, con-templated establishing a strategic defensive line running from Pisa to Rimini on the Adriatic.[76]

However, as "Monty," safely in Italy, seemed once again to be washing and polishing his tanks rather than smashing north, Rommel decided against giving the Fifth and Eighth Armies a free ride and rushed reinforcements to the Naples region, where they were in place to greet the American landing at Salerno on 9 September. This was, as the Duke of Wellington observed of Waterloo, a "damned close run thing": German resistance was as ferocious as that of the Japanese at Iwo Jima, and the landing force was badly bloodied.

Then, for reasons that I find inexplicable, as noted earlier, two magnifi-cent armies—the American Fifth and British Eighth—were given the mis-sion of taking Italy yard by yard against dogged fighters, with the unusual defensive advantages provided by Italian terrain. Yet, with the exception of some divisions diverted to Overlord and later Anvil (Normandy and southern France), this was their fate for the remainder of the war. If, alternatively, we had established a line north of Naples and gone on the strategic defensive, with vigorous tactical probes to keep the Germans loose, it probably would have maintained Nazi force levels in the area, while we could have thrown a formidable left hook (like Anvil late in 1944) into, say, Toulon.

The war for Italy, however, became a self-justifying enterprise—with Italian-American opinion in the United States (the "liberation of Rome" had symbolic clout) probably providing political background music.[77] Most interesting is the almost total lack of discussion at the highest levels—the innumerable conferences, which will be assessed briefly—of the rationale of inching up Italy. Why not let the Nazis feed and police the area? To summarize, by the end of 1943, King Victor Emmanuel, Marshal Badoglio, and a desultory collection of Italian politicians were in Brindisi running an Italian government, which, in February 1944, was given de facto jurisdiction over southern Italy, Sicily and Sardinia.[78]

Clearly, it was a creature of the victors, and, ironically, only the Soviet

Union (briefly: until the United States and Britain objected) accorded it de jure status.[79] Palmiro Togliatti, the long-exiled leader of the Italian Communist Party (PCI), arrived from Moscow with this news. It was "no accident." The Soviet position prefigured Togliatti's policy of a PCI-conservative alliance, which, in the postwar period, would lead to the PCI and the Christian Democrats coalescing to include Mussolini's 1929 Concordat with the Papacy in the 1947 Italian Republican Constitution.[80]

Stalin was prepared to hunt where the ducks were, and the flexible Togliatti brazenly sought the Catholic, monarchist vote. Togliatti's action, which reversed the PCI's position on the monarchy and on Badoglio, was an important signal that Stalin was no longer worried about the outcome of the war, but was putting his pieces in place for the postwar era.

The various "summit" meetings that began with the FDR-Churchill meeting off Newfoundland in August 1941 and concluded in the summer of 1945 at Potsdam, have been given scant treatment so far, because they were largely unproductive, except in terms of atmospherics and in getting the principal figures acquainted. Once the United States had thrown its power massively into the war, the British reluctantly found themselves playing second fiddle.

At the August 1943 Quebec Conference, for example, we and the British agreed to pool our efforts at producing an atomic bomb. The British demanded previous consultation before any such weapon was employed. This was accepted, but, in August 1945, simply ignored. At the Quebec Conference in September of 1944, there was much discussion of the future British role in the Pacific war—all of which proved superfluous—and Henry Morgenthau blackmailed Churchill (he used the threat of a cutback in Lend-Lease) into approving his bizarre German "pastoralization" plan, which, in the event, was a horse dead at the post.[81]

The meetings with Stalin at Teheran, Yalta, and Potsdam will be discussed later, but (as is clear to one who has drafted the final communiqués of two "summits" before they began) inter-Allied policy emerged from constant interplay on specifics, not from cosmic declarations. Churchill, at Quebec, to take a case in point, might extract agreement for an amphibious assault on Rangoon by Lord Mountbatten's orphaned forces in the C.B.I. theater, but, unless "Ernie" King provided the LSTs, et al., the show, as the British say, simply "wasn't on." The ships didn't materialize until 1945.

Similarly, Churchill got vague strokes from the Americans on his schemes for driving to Vienna from "the Adriatic armpit," and invading the Balkans; however, by the end of 1943, the European War was an America enterprise, there was going to be an end to such peripheral dispersion of forces, a cross-Channel invasion was laid on for May–June 1944, and General Dwight Eisenhower was named Supreme Commander.

Ike brought his top Mediterranean generals to London to play key roles in Overlord; Bradley hints that Eisenhower may later have regretted bringing

Montgomery, instead of the quiet but extraordinarily talented Sir Harold Alexander, from Italy.[82] However, the top team was Ike, Chief of Staff, "Beetle" Smith, "Monty," commanding British and Commonwealth forces, and "Brad," heading up the American armies.

George Patton, in disgrace for abusing some sick troops, but considered by Hitler and Rommel as the ace of field commanders, was also shipped to England to run the greatest charade in history: Operation Fortitude, the creation of a fake invasion force in northern Britain, targeted on the Pas de Calais sector of the French coast. Patton put on such a spectacular that, even after Rommel received reports that our troops were ashore in Normandy, he kept the bulk of his forces north of the Seine, convinced that Overlord was a feint and Patton was coming. Masterman's "Operation Doublecross," a British disinformation masterpiece, also helped to delude the Germans.

From here on, there was no strategic story; eventual victory, for Ike, was just a matter of catching the Germans, chopping them up, and continuing in the tradition of U. S. Grant until the supply of Germans ran out. There were some tactical brawls, invariably featuring the ineffable Montgomery suggesting that Ike and Bradley were in over their heads and needed a nanny, namely, himself. The final debate arose on whether we should move on until we met the Red Army, despite the fact that our armies had reached the limit of the American and British zones on the E.A.C. map. Ike compromised by moving to the Elbe, but, to Patton's fury, refused to allow him to liberate Prague. In order to avoid plunging into the postwar period, this chapter will refrain from discussing the significance of guaranteed land access routes to Berlin.

Suffice it to say, once the Soviet armies mopped up the other side of the Elbe, Eisenhower pulled back British and American troops from a substantial chunk of what is now the DDR; when challenged on this later, he replied that he was a soldier obeying orders, not a strategic operator.[83] Given the chaos in Washington after FDR's death on 12 April 1945, Harry Truman, a wholly unbriefed President (he was unaware of the Manhattan Project until 13 April!), would hardly have reversed previous instructions and told Ike to hang on to German real estate for future bargaining. Truman's bogey then was *British* imperialism.[84]

Anglo-American relations with the Soviet Union, i.e., Stalin, can be explored in far shorter compass. The fundamental premise is that Stalin was allergic to cooperating with anybody, particularly after the traumatic end of his love affair with Hitler. As was mentioned earlier, the United States and Britain had warned Stalin, on the basis of "Ultra" intercepts, of the upcoming Nazi invasion. However, in the first week of October 1941, Stalin's master spy in Tokyo, Richard Sorge, informed him "there will be war with the U.S. this month or next," and that the Japanese armies were going for Southeast Asia, not Siberia.[85] The information was vital—Stalin withdrew his battle-scarred Siberian divisions from Mongolia to the defense of Moscow—but it could have been useful for Washington also to know. It was not communicated.

Indeed, American officials found Soviet paranoia mind-warping: at a time when the Wehrmacht was closing in on the Caucasian oil fields, for example, we offered to send heavy bombers with American crews. Stalin said he would take the B-24s, but no crews—except trainers, who would soon be redundant.[86] Once "Hap" Arnold got his USAAF based in Foggia, it seemed like a bright idea to shuttle heavies to the Ukraine, dropping their loads on the Ploesti oil field in Romania en route. It was 565 miles from southern Italy to Ploesti, 225 miles from Kiev to the Romanian target (275 from Poltava, where a base was finally established).

General John Deane has recounted his adventures in inaugurating shuttle-bombing; the Soviets balked, stonewalled, and found "technical problems" at every turn. Finally, we were ejected from Poltava, ostensibly for "technical reasons," but actually because Stalin felt we were supporting the Polish Government-in-Exile in London against his stooge Lublin regime.[87] Needless to say, a B-24 that had to fly an eleven-hundred-plus-mile round trip from Italy to northern Romania could hardly carry an optimal bomb-load, but Stalin seemed less interested in the destruction of Hitler's biggest oil supply than in keeping Americans at a distance. (Strangely, the Soviets expended little effort on strategic bombing.)

There was a rerun of this scenario in the fall of 1944, when the Polish Underground Army, the *Armia Krajowa*, responsible to the London government, launched a massive insurrection in Warsaw—with the Soviet forces in box seats on the other side of the Vistula. Those interested in details are referred to the Roosevelt-Churchill correspondence;[88] suffice it to say that, although Moscow radio had helped to incite the revolt, the Soviet forces refused to provide aid; only after interminable cabling back and forth were a few American planes allowed to drop essentials in Warsaw and land in the USSR.[89] If the Nazis wanted to do Stalin a favor by butchering Polish nationalists, he was not prepared to object.

Soviet refusal to cooperate on any level was disconcerting, baffling, and infuriating. Obtaining the names of American POWs liberated by the Soviet advance into Europe and making sure they received decent care became a lunatic numbers game, with Red Army spokesmen varying the figure day to day and putting innumerable "technical difficulties" in the way of bringing members of the United States mission in Moscow into contact with these Americans. There was a flat refusal to exchange technical or intelligence data.[90] For example, when, shortly before Overlord, we asked to send our engineers to examine the German underwater defenses encountered by the Red Army in its amphibious assault on the Crimea, the same "technical difficulties" made it impossible.

The classic example of Soviet fun and games in the area of scientific cooperation was related by R. V. Jones in his splendid *Wizard War*.[91] The V-2 rockets were coming into deployment, and their testing ground at Blizna was captured by the Soviet Army. British scientific intelligence immediately asked for access to the place and a chance to go over the captured material. Jones had Churchill cable Stalin, and on 25 July 1944 "a very civil reply" was received from Stalin. A group was organized and arrived in Cairo, whence it was to proceed to Russia via Teheran. But, on 3 August, a message came from there saying that the Soviet Union would not admit the team without visas. This "technical difficulty" was overcome, and on 1 September the group cabled that it was off to the test range.

On 18 September the British experts reached Blizna and began putting together a rich collection of rocket parts and other scientific goodies. By 27 September, they were on their way back via Teheran, from where they reported, "The Russians have temporarily lost main part of our R(ocket) specimens in transit between Blizna and Moscow, but they have promised to do all in their power to see that they follow us without undue delay." The grand climax, in Jones' words, was that "when the crates which the Russians had forwarded to Teheran were brought back to England under top security and opened by members of the Mission, they were found to be not the items packed at Blizna but parts of old aeroplane engines which the Russians had substituted instead."[92] Dealing with Stalin brought a laugh a day.

There were three first-order strategic issues between the Anglo-Americans and the Soviet Union: the first was putting heavy military pressure on the Germans to ease the Soviet burden, the question discussed earlier in terms of relations between the Western powers themselves. The second was the future of the formerly independent nations of Eastern Europe, with the initial focus on Poland. The Polish specter, then as now, haunted the Kremlin and will be discussed further in connection with Yalta.

Comic relief of sorts was provided by Churchill, who, in October 1944, sat down with Stalin in Moscow to discuss the future of Eastern Europe, notably the Balkans. I'm told on excellent authority both men were in their cups,[93] and, without any American moralists around to summon him to his highest ideals, Churchill, the old *capo* who once urged strangling the Bolshevik baby in its cradle, had an idea. He took a piece of paper and wrote down the names of Romania, Bulgaria, Greece, Yugoslavia, and Hungary— with the Soviet Union to receive 90 percent predominance in the first, 75 percent in the second, 10 percent in the third, and a 50/50 split in the two remaining. It takes one to know one: Stalin looked at Churchill, ticked the document with O.K., and gave it back. Churchill wondered if he should burn this evidence of cynical realpolitik. Stalin was reassuring: "No, you keep it."[94]

This meeting was distinctive, if only in its atavism: Napoleon and Tsar Alexander once again sat on a raft in the river and carved up the map. When Roosevelt was informed of this development by Harriman, and Wilsonian naîfs from the State Department started muttering ominously about the wickedness of "spheres of influence," his only reaction seemed to be, in essence, "boys will be boys."[95] His big concern in October 1944 was not whether the British obtained a 25 percent share of Bulgarian stock, but whether he would be reelected to a fourth term in November.

The third top-grade strategic issue between the Western powers and Stalin—one particularly compelling to the Americans—was Russia's prospective entrance into the war against Japan, once the Nazis were defeated.

The Teheran Conference, the first with the "big three" present, in November 1943 was the high point of American-Soviet camaraderie, with FDR obviously convinced that he could make an honest democratic statesman out of Stalin. (The latter, after all, was comparable to a Chicago mayor with an overactive police force.) This involved Roosevelt in some Churchill-baiting to demonstrate to the impressionable Old Bolshevik that there was no Anglo-American conspircy against him.[96]

Churchill took an extremely sour view of this byplay, though FDR was persuaded that it did the trick: "From that time on our relations were personal and Stalin himself engaged in an occasional witticism. The ice was broken and we talked like men and brothers."[97] I wonder if Roosevelt noted the irony when Stalin, for whom the slogan had originally been coined, questioned the doctrine of "unconditional surrender" on the ground it was a bonus for Goebbels and helped unite the German people?[98]

With regard to Soviet intentions toward Japan, at Teheran Stalin dropped a gnomic comment when pressed on the matter: with the Germans out of the way, he said, "we shall be able by our common front to win"[99] the Japanese war. This generated a great optimism, but was masterfully ambiguous. By late 1944 and early 1945, as Nazi Germany collapsed, the issue moved front and center. The "big three" scheduled a summit at Yalta in the Crimea for February 1945, with two major strategic agenda items, one essentially British: the future of Eastern Europe; and the second, the American need, emphasized by the Chiefs of Staff, to get the Soviet Army into the war against Japan. Roosevelt, on a different level, was desperate to persuade Stalin to become an active supporter of the proposed international organization, the United Nations.

Roosevelt, we now know, was a dying man, but whether this influenced the outcome vis-à-vis Eastern Europe is doubtful. The Soviet Union had its armies on the ground, went through some pseudo-democratic electoral farces, and then established Communist dictatorships. Although Churchill tried manfully for a genuine Polish compromise, Stalin was implacable. Roosevelt and Churchill did not "sell out" Eastern Europe at Yalta; indeed, Stalin cheerfully agreed to free elections, and the Four Freedoms were imbedded in the communiqué. In power terms, the option to accepting the unhappy status quo was to fight the Red Army. Was that realism? Anyone who thinks that the American Armed Forces and their families would have backed fighting the Soviet Union to establish Polish or Hungarian democracy, or, in a different region, to save Chiang Kai-shek from Mao's forces, badly needs psychiatric help.

With regard to the Japanese question, the American Chiefs, stimulated by General MacArthur and Admiral Nimitz, who were running the two great thrusts toward the Japanese home islands, were close to hitting the panic button.[100] Japanese resistance defied rational or irrational explanation. When the time came for the invasion of the home islands, Operation Olympic, it would be essential for the Soviet Union to prevent the powerful Kwantung army in "Manchukuo" from returning home to reinforce the defenses.

In fact, the Kwantung Army had been broken up and dispersed throughout Southeast Asia by 1943, but MacArthur's Intelligence Chief, General Charles Willoughby (who, in 1950, missed half a million Chinese infiltrators into Korea), thought the Kwantung veterans were still in place. The Army was still there, but it was now composed of youngsters, semi-invalids, and men overaged for active duty. No matter: as far as the Chiefs of Staff and the President knew, this powerful force had to be contained.

Stalin was now, for the first time, in a position to dictate his own terms on the conduct of the war to Roosevelt and Churchill. As a payoff for Soviet entry into the war against Japan, the Soviet dictator demanded, in the spirit of "Great Russian Chauvinism," a restoration of all the turf and privileges lost to Japan in 1905. In addition, he wanted Outer Mongolia granted de facto independence (it is now the Mongolian People's Republic). Needless to say, with the exception of the annexation of the southern half of Sakhalin Island and the outer Kuriles, this exercise was at China's expense. FDR and Churchill in effect were "fences," trading stolen goods to Stalin. It did not seem to cause either a sleepless night.

Nor, in passing, did Stalin have any objections to Chiang Kai-shek's being recognized as one of the permanent members of the prospective United Nations Security Council (he had more doubts about France). He never demonstrated any fondness for Mao and the Chinese Communists, whom he seemed to consider a crew of rural bandits: Chiang, on the other hand, had—in Marxist terms—strong "objective" merits: any Chinese regime run by him and the KMT would be weak, and Russia is fond of a weak China.

There was a massive giveaway by the Western powers at Yalta, but the deal at China's expense was far less excusable than the slightly disguised acceptance of Soviet *faits accomplis* in Eastern Europe. Stalin played cat-and-mouse games, obviously enjoying every minute of it: he had the chutzpah to tell Roosevelt in mournful tones that, unless his demands were met, it would be very difficult to explain to the Russian people why they must go to war with Japan![101] For Roosevelt, however, the key was Russian entry, and Stalin agreed that within two or three months after the surrender of Germany, the Soviet Union would declare war on Japan.

Roosevelt left Yalta happy: like Woodrow Wilson, he had decided that the key to future peace was a world organization, but this one would have teeth. While Stalin, who had his own agenda, reacted negatively to the concept of the "Four Policemen" enforcing the peace of the world, he had otherwise been most obliging. Several vital issues—German reparations, for one—had been pushed forward to a later meeting, which FDR assumed would demonstrate sincerity and good will by all hands. Best of all, twenty-five Soviet divisions shortly would be moving east to positions on the Japanese (Manchukuo) border, ready to join in the final demolition of Japanese power. Admittedly, there were faults: as Roosevelt told Berle on his return: "I didn't say it was good, Adolph, I said it was the best I could do."[102] Six weeks later, FDR was dead.

In the interim between Yalta and the Japanese surrender on 10 August, there were two events that demonstrated how rational strategic projections can seem the essence of realism one day, and be antiquated the next. The first was the appalling slaughter at Iwo Jima, and then, Okinawa. The former, a hunk of volcanic rock that was invaluable for Japanese early warning against B-29 sorties from Saipan and Tinian, took a month and *twenty thousand* Marine casualties to reduce.

The butcher's bill at Okinawa, which was taken by three Marine and three Army divisions, with strong Naval support, after almost three months of savage fighting, was close to sixty thousand. Staff planners in Washington and the Pacific began talking about a possible casualty total of over a million in the upcoming invasion of the home islands. The Soviet Union had to prevent the Kwantung Army from getting back to Kyushu and Honshu.

The second development, which, in the event, rendered all these calculations academic, was the successful development of the A-bomb. Everybody today knows that it works, but the best physicists in the business were not certain until 16 July 1945, when Operation Trinity (a curious designation suggested by J. Robert Oppenheimer) was successful: the A-bomb was successfully tested in the New Mexico desert. The news came to President Truman as he was at sea, en route to a summit at Potsdam with Churchill and Stalin.

After much dithering, it was decided to inform Stalin we had a "powerful new weapon," without going into details. Stalin, who doubtless knew about the success of Trinity as soon as Truman, congratulated us and said he hoped it would be used against the Japanese. Several present were surprised by his indifference, but they were unaware of the Soviet espionage network that had penetrated Los Alamos and the top levels of the British bureaucracy. Stalin, who had a black sense of humor, probably got a good laugh out of such innocence.

It was too soon, however, to count on the "ultimate weapon" bringing Japan to its knees without an invasion. There were only two more completed prototypes, and the fact that the first had worked under optimal experimental conditions, nursed by a dedicated battalion of scientists, was no guarantee that one tossed out of a B-29, or dropped by parachute, would go off. However, on 6 August the second operational model detonated over Hiroshima with devastating physical and psychological impact (in fact, it killed fewer persons than the March fire-bombing of Tokyo), and, on 9 August, the sole remaining specimen was parachuted into Nagasaki. The Japanese could take no more, particularly since on 8 August—well timed for the finale—the Soviet Union declared war and invaded "Manchukuo," meeting virtually no resistance from the Kwantung Army, now a *Heimwehr*.

There is evidence to suggest that the peace party in Japan tried to persuade the Soviet Union to arrange for a negotiated peace, but Stalin— knowing about the potential of the A-bomb—blocked any efforts to this end.[103] Until we read Stalin's diaries, or those of Jacob Malik, the Soviet Ambassador to Japan, this must remain in the realm of speculation. In sum, the Soviet Union was on hand for the division of spoils when, on the tenth of August, the Japanese surrendered: a good two days' work.

Thus ended all discussions of wartime strategy. To the extent that there is a lesson to be drawn from the studies of relations among the various Axis powers, on one hand, and among the sundry "United Nations," on the other, it is that, despite elaborate histories of the coordinating genius of the Chiefs of Staff, fundamental decisions were made far more by improvisation than by plan. The invasion of Italy, to return to my hobby horse, seems to have had as its rationale the observation made by Hillary when asked why he wanted to climb Mt. Everest: "Because it's there."

Finally, how can one cope with the personal element, e.g., Hitler's dream that the V-1 and V-1 rockets wouldn't work, which held up German production by two years, or Stalin's conviction that Hitler would not double-cross him? In this connection, I asked General Matthew Ridgway in 1982 why Ike had not scrubbed Operation Market-Garden when "Ultra" revealed there were two S.S. Panzer divisions and Walter Model, a very tough German Field Marshal, parked in Arnhem, where British and American paratroops were scheduled to seize the key bridges. Ridgway, whose Eigh-teenth Airborne Corps was the matrix of the enterprise, meditated and said sadly, "I don't think Ike wanted to hurt Monty's feelings." *Sic transit gloria mundi.*

NOTES

1. Quoted by David Reynolds, *The Creation of the Anglo-American Alliance, 1937–41* (Chapel Hill, N.C., 1981), 283.
    2. Ibid., 114.
    3. Quoted in Francis L. Lowenheim, ed., *Peace or Appeasement* (Boston, 1965), 55.
    4. Quoted by Harold Nicolson, *Portrait of a Diplomatist* (Boston, 1930), 227.
    5. See George F. Kennan, *American Diplomacy* (Chicago, 1951), 72.
    6. For a devastating analysis of Anglo-French activity, see Sir Lewis Namier, *In the Nazi Era* (London, 1952).

7. See John Toland, *The Rising Sun* (New York, 1970), 59. Generally, see Ian Nish, *Japanese Foreign Policy, 1869–1942* (London, 1977), 218ff.

8. This statement led veteran Stalin-analysts in the United States, notably Raphael Abramovich and David J. Dallin, and Boris Nicolaevsky, then in Amsterdam, to predict a Nazi-Soviet Pact. Their English articles appeared in the *New Leader*. Communists and their fellow travelers were incensed at this "fascist" calumny and organized a full-page denunciation that appeared in the *Nation*, 28 August 1939 (p. 228), signed by "more than 400" intellectual luminaries. Only about 50 were listed in the *Nation*, a fact that must have overjoyed those omitted, since the 28 August issue's lead story was the Stalin-Hitler Pact.

9. See Walter Krivitsky, *I Was Stalin's Agent* (London, 1939), 37–39. Nicolaevsky also discussed the Kandelaki connection in the *New Leader*.

10. Quoted in Alan Bullock, *Hitler* (New York, 1961), 474.

11. See Toland, 56; also Gerald K. Haines, "American Myopia and the Japanese Monroe Doctrine," *Prologue* (Summer 1981): 101–14.

12. State laws on the West coast, e.g., forbade "aliens ineligible for citizenship" (Asians) to own land. This and similar restrictions were sustained by the U.S. Supreme Court until 1948. See John P. Roche, *The Quest for the Dream* (New York, 1963), 190–93.

13. Tokyo's enthusiasm for a go at the Soviet Union was tempered by the knowledge that in the 1938 encounters with the Red Army, the Kwantung Army had taken two severe beatings. The brand-new Navy, on the other hand, seemed regionally invincible—if the U.S. Pacific Fleet could be put out of action. The presence of the strengthened Fleet in Hawaii plus some essentially useless military staff talks in Singapore among the British, Australians, Dutch, and Americans in 1941 also pushed the Japanese toward a preemptive strike.

14. Toland, 65–66. Indeed, Matsuoka was convinced Ribbentrop would be delighted! Stalin, on the other hand, thought the project must have Hitler's blessing and was further proof that Germany had no designs on the Soviet Union: kissing Matsuoka, he observed, "There is nothing to fear in Europe now that there is a Japan-Soviet neutrality pact."

15. F. W. Deakin, *The Brutal Friendship* (London, 1962), 16.

16. See William L. Shirer, *The Rise and Fall of the Third Reich* (New York, 1968).

17. (London, 1982).

18. *My Quest for Peace* (London, 1938). His son-in-law and biographer, Raymond Postgate, in his generally deferential work *George Lansbury* (London, 1951), says Lansbury genuinely believed that had he been fluent in German, he could have converted Hitler to "Christianity in its purest sense" (pp. 314–15).

19. Quoted in *London Economist*, 2 June 1979, 126.

20. (London, 1939).

21. Ian Macleod, "In Defense of Chamberlain," in Lowenheim, 172.

22. See Pertinax [pseud.], *The Gravediggers of France* (Garden City, N.Y., 1944); Robert Aron, *Histoire de Vichy* (Paris, 1954); Charles Antoine Micaud, *The French Right and Nazi Germany, 1933–1939: A Study of Public Opinion* (New York, 1943); W. Laqueur and George Morse, eds., *International Fascism, 1920–1945* (New York, 1966), 27–74.

23. See Gérard Walter, *Histoire du Parti Communiste Français* (Paris, 1948), 213ff.

24. See Paul Louis, *Histoire du Movement Syndical en France*, vol. 2 (Paris, 1948), 137–70.

25. Figures taken from U.S. Bureau of the Census, *Historical Statistics of the United States* (Washington, D.C., 1975.

26. Ibid.

27. Quoted in *London Economist*, 7 October 1978, 129.

28. See Frank Freidel, *Franklin D. Roosevelt: Launching the New Deal* (Boston, 1973), 463–65.

29. *The Illusion of Neutrality* (Chicago, 1962).

30. Nicolson, 130.

31. See John Lewis Gaddis, *The United States and the Origins of the Cold War* (New York, 1972), 120.

32. Ibid., 130.

33. *World Politics* 16, no. 1 (October 1963). See also Gaddis, 109–11.

34. Franklin, 12.

35. "Upstairs, Downstairs at Foggy Bottom: Oil Exports and Japan, 1940–41," *Prologue* (Spring 1976): 19.

36. It is odd how this patented Leninist ploy is used time and again with no recognition of its ancestry: the Polish "Soviet Government" Lenin established in 1920 in turn called for Red Army aid against the "reactionary" Warsaw government. Its latest reincarnation is, of course, in Afghanistan.

37. See Ronald Lewin, *Ultra Goes to War*(New York, 1978).

38. The Japanese Ambassador in Berlin, Baron Oshima, did inform Tokyo, but Matsuoka ignored the message. Toland, 78.

39. Reynolds, 139. He has the sequence slightly garbled, with Ambassador Oshima sending Matsuoka the letter, but not notifying Berlin. The secret gloss on Article 3 was Matsuoka's.

40. See Omar N. Bradley and Clay Blair, *A General's Life* (New York, 1983), 237–38. It might be noted that the Germans did give the Japanese some intelligence aid. For example, they provided Japanese attachés in Berlin facilities to go to Italy and inspect the damage done by British carrier plan attacks at the battle of Taranto, where the Italian fleet was virtually destroyed. They also told "their" agent Dusko Papov (a.k.a. "Tricycle" in British intelligence circles, to whom his real loyalty belonged) to visit the U.S. in the summer of 1941 and urgently get to Pearl Harbor and fill out a detailed questionnaire about its defenses. See Ewen Montagu, *Beyond Top Secret Ultra* (New York, 1977), 74–75.

41. Robert Sherwood, *Roosevelt and Hopkins* (New York, 1948), 441.

42. "Germany and Pearl Harbor," in Robert A. Divine, ed., *Causes and Consequences of World War II* (Chicago, 1969), 123–39; Gerhard L. Weinberg, *World in the Balance* (Hanover, N.H., 1981), 53–95.

43. Edited by Raymond J. Sontag and James Stuart Beddies.

44. Ibid., 238.

45. (London, 1949).

46. Sontag and Beddies, 257.

47. Cited in Shirer, 842–44.

48. Nikita Khrushchev, *Khrushchev Remembers* (Boston, 1970), 168. He adds that Stalin was literally out of psychological commission for several weeks.

49. Reynolds, 184.

50. (New York, 1948).

51. Ibid., 275.

52. See *Diplomat Among Warriors*, (New York, 1964).

53. See George F. Kennan, *Memoirs: 1925–1950* (Boston, 1967), 164–87.

54. See Louis, 122–24; James M. Burns, *Roosevelt: The Soldier of Freedom* (New York, 1970), 238–42.

55. For overelaborate discussion of "the infernal business of St. Pierre and Miquelon," see Adolph A. Berle, *Navigating the Rapids, 1918–1971* (New York, 1973), 388–97.

56. Ibid., 393. (The strength of the signal arose from the fact that it was the only Francophone station in local operation and hence covered Quebec.)

57. Ibid., 395.

58. Ibid.

59. Quoted in a speech by Winston S. Churchill, M.P. (grandson of the wartime leader) at Hillsdale College, Michigan, and reprinted in *Imprimis* 11, no. 12 (December 1982): 2.

60. Reynolds, 159.

61. Ibid., 270.

62. The standard fare was Charles and Mary Beard's American history texts, plus such polemical trimmings as Mauritz A. Hallgren's *The Tragic Fallacy* (New York, 1937).

63. Reynolds, 159.

64. This point is emphasized in passing by Russell F. Weigley in his masterful *Eisenhower's Lieutenants* (Bloomington, Ind., 1981). The lessons of the Pacific war, notably "island hopping," were ignored, and the few "Pacific Generals" (Corlett, Collins, and Patch) were not debriefed on, for example, the *lack* of need for great harbors to guarantee logistical support. Had an "over the beach" strategy been employed (with appropriate equipment), far better invasion spots could have been found than the Norman bluffs and bocage. The main argument centers on Bradley's insistence on cleaning out the "Brittany pocket" with great effort and casualties rather than—in the Pacific style—leaving the German units behind to rot in this European New Guinea. Bradley has vigorously defended his policy: see Bradley and Blair, 285 –86.

65. See R. N. Carew-Hunt, "Willi Muenzenberg," in D. Footman, ed., *International Communism* (Oxford, 1960), 72–87. Also Arthur Koestler, *The Invisible Writing* (New York, 1954), 250–59.

66. Bradley and Blair, 159.

67. Sherwood, 615.

68. Bradley and Blair, 159.

69. Patton was the outstanding advocate of the first view. See Ladislas Farago, *Patton* (New York, 1963). Of course, Montgomery took the latter position. See his *Memoirs* (New York, 1958). Sir Basil Liddell Hart, *History of the Second World War* (New York, 1971), took a highly critical approach to "Monty's" tactical needlepoint.

70. See the treatment of command confusion in Torch in Bradley and Blair, 118–76.

71. Generally, see Maurice Matloff, *Strategic Planning for Coalition Warfare* (Washington, D.C., 1953), and Kent R. Greenfield, ed., *Command Decisions* (Washington, D.C., 1960). On the possible shift of American strategy to "Japan First," see Sherwood, 594.

72. Sherwood, 594.

73. Ibid., 690.

74. Bradley and Blair, 160–200.

75. Deakin, 499–516.

76. Ibid., 512.

77. See James E. Miller, "The Politics of Relief: The Roosevelt Administration and the Reconstruction of Italy, 1943–44," in *Prologue* (Fall 1981): 193–208.

78. See Charles F. Delzell, *Mussolini's Enemies* (Princeton, N.J., 1961), 315ff.

79. Ibid., 336.

80. See Aldo Garosci, "The Italian Communist Party" in Mario Einandi, ed., *Communism in Western Europe* (Ithaca, N.Y., 1951), 154–218.

81. See Burns, 520; and Sherwood, 818, for the decision by FDR to deep-six the Plan— which was probably the brainchild of the coven of covert Stalinists, led by Harry Dexter White, who provided Morgenthau with his ego's much-needed valet service.

82. Bradley and Blair, 216.

83. Weigley, 721–26.

84. See Sidney Hook's report of a meeting of several Senators concerned about Soviet intentions held with Truman in early 1945 at which the President dismissed their views and started denouncing the British, "Living with Deep Truths in a Divided World," *Free Inquiry* (Winter 1982/3): 31.

85. F. W. Deakin and G. R. Storry, *The Case of Richard Sorge* (London, 1966), 246. Throughout the war we provided Moscow with advance notice of Wehrmacht plans based on "Ultra" intercepts. (These were disguised as "information from a high-level prisoner" since theoretically Stalin was unaware of the "Ultra" operation. As "Kim Philby" was plugged into the "Ultra" circle by 1943, Stalin must have chuckled over his vodka at these elaborate ruses.)

86. Sherwood, 639–41; John R. Deane, *The Strange Alliance* (Bloomington, Ind., 1946), 231. (The time frames of these offers were different, but Stalin's response was the same: ignore or reject the offer.)

87. Deane, op. cit., pp. 122–124.

88. See Francis L. Lowenheim, Harold D. Langley, and Manfred Jonas, eds., *Roosevelt and Churchill* (New York, 1975), 563–73. For details from ground zero, see J. K. Zawodny, *Nothing But Honor: The Story of the Warsaw Uprising, 1944* (Stanford, 1978).

89. Stalin's strategy of permitting the Nazis to extirpate the Home Army's 1 August uprising is detailed by Zawodny. Finally, on 18 September 1944, American planes were permitted to overfly Warsaw, drop assistance, and land at Poltava (p. 135). Until then, British and American flights had to do a round trip from Britain or southern Italy, with volunteer crews— often Polish RAF personnel. The 18 September flight from Brindisi, for example, consisted of 306 heavies, with 91 Poles, 50 British, 55 South African, and 110 American crewmen. A second run was scheduled for 2 October 1944, but was blocked by the Soviets who said (falsely) the rebellion was over and the fighters evacuated (pp. 120–36).

90. See F. H. Hinsley et al., *British Intelligence in the Second World War*, vols. 1 and 2 (London, 1979, 1981), 2: 58–67.

91. (New York, 1978).

92. Ibid., 441–42.

93. Conversation with W. Averell Harriman, 1967. Harriman was U.S. Ambassador to Moscow and a nonparticipating observer in the Stalin-Churchill fete.

94. Burns, 537.
95. Ibid.
96. Ibid., 412–13.
97. Ibid., 412.
98. Ibid., 409.
99. Ibid., 408.
100. Probably the nadir was reached in late December 1944, when a fog of confusion lay over the Ardennes, the British had literally run out of troops, while the body count in the Pacific seemed utterly disproportionate to the forces involved. For example, the ten thousand Japanese holding the small island of Peleliu in the Palaus inflicted as many casualties as we took at Omaha Beach—and half the defenders were service troops. This was just a curtain-raiser for Iwo Jima and Okinawa. (One by-product of the JCS concern was a medical reevaluation of all U.S. forces, and of the essentiality of service personnel ["the tail"], in quest of more combat troops. Ironically—and fortunately in a selfish sense—I was adjudged "essential" because as a top classification NCO I was the individual responsible for the "hot press" [as they used to call it in the Royal Navy].)
101. Burns, 575.
102. Ibid., 580.
103. Toland, 746–48.

6

Defense Planning in NATO:
A Consensual Decision-making Process

Roy W. Stafford

NATO has an elaborate and well-practiced system for coordinating Allied defense plans, yet the Alliance exerts relatively little influence on national defense programs. Alliance members regularly bemoan the state of NATO defenses and pledge increased efforts to strengthen collective military capabilities, but the results of such efforts have been disappointing. Progress occurs only gradually, and long-recognized deficiencies in NATO forces remain uncorrected.

This chapter addresses the reasons and examines the formal process by which the Alliance attempts to draw Allied plans toward collective defense requirements, as well as considering why NATO frequently resorts to special, out-of-cycle efforts to encourage more substantial improvements in Alliance defenses. It investigates the Long-Term Defense Program (LTDP), adopted by Alliance leaders in 1978, as an example of NATO's resort to ad hoc defense initiatives, and discusses the genesis, process of reaching agreement, and Allied implementation of the LTDP. Where applicable, comparisons are made with the American defense planning process, since the NATO force planning procedures have been influenced significantly by those of the United States.

The NATO force planning process was selected for analysis because NATO's principal function is collective defense, attempts to broaden the Alliance's scope of activities notwithstanding, and because of the author's familiarity with this aspect of NATO's consultative procedures. While there is a broad range of consultation mechanisms in NATO—political, economic, scientific, as well as military—many of these activities are better described as an exchange of views than as decision making. Through the force planning process, NATO makes specific though not binding

The views in this chapter are those of the author and are not intended to reflect positions of the U.S. Government.

decisions—agreement to undertake force improvement actions, commitment of specific forces to the Alliance, acceptance of defense spending targets, and so forth.

Background

In the aftermath of World War II, the Soviet Union emerged as the dominant military power on the Eurasian continent. The Western armies had demobilized, while, in contrast, the Soviet Union maintained more than 4 million men under arms,[1] brutally consolidated its control over Eastern Europe, and threatened to expand its influence into an economically and militarily weakened Western Europe.

NATO was formed in 1949 to protect the countries of Western Europe against such expansion. Its formation reflected a coincidence of interests between the United States and the states in the region. America's involvement in two World Wars during the first half of this century convinced American policy makers that the security and well-being of the United States and of Western Europe were inextricably intertwined. The vital interest of the United States in protecting the countries of Western Europe against Soviet expansion coincided with their determination to preserve their independence. By committing itself, in advance, to the collective defense of a threatened member state, NATO was designed to prevent the piecemeal loss of territory to the Soviet Union and to bind the United States formally to the defense of Western Europe.

Sixteen countries—Belgium, Canada, Denmark, France, Iceland, Italy, Luxembourg, the Netherlands, Norway, Portugal, the United Kingdom, and the United States, joined by Greece and Turkey in 1952, the Federal Republic of Germany in 1955, and Spain in 1982—have agreed to resist collectively an armed attack against any one of them.

By any measure, the Atlantic Alliance has been a success. Its continued vitality after thirty-four years is notable in itself. NATO has survived marked changes in defense strategy, the nuclear balance, and other superpower relationships; open conflict between Allies; the withdrawal of France (and, for a while, Greece) from the integrated military structure; and a dramatically changing international environment. For nearly four decades Western Europe has been free of aggression. Under the framework of security provided by the Atlantic Alliance, its members have enjoyed an unprecedented period of social, economic, and political progress.

Alliance Structure

Before analyzing defense decision making in NATO, one has to understand what the Atlantic Alliance is and what it is not. NATO is not a supernational organization with real clout over its members. NATO does not have mandatory authority. It can advise, exhort, or exercise moral suasion, but it cannot direct its members to implement even those measures that they have previously agreed to undertake. Members regularly agree collectively to increase defense spending, expand their stocks of munitions, increase the readiness of their forces, and so on, yet their implementation record is spotty at best—a host of internal constraints, financial and otherwise, may intervene to prevent governments from carrying out what they (or their predecessors) have agreed to do. The goal of a 3 percent annual real increase in defense budgets agreed upon by NATO Defense Ministers in 1977,[2] and reaffirmed at subsequent ministerial meetings,[3] is a case in point—in each year since the 3 percent goal was adopted, less than half the countries have met that objective.[4] While member states "commit" to NATO specific forces—army brigades, fighter squadrons, destroyers, etc.—these forces remain under national command, with the exception of the new NATO Airborne Early Warning Aircraft (AWACS) and a few air defense units.

NATO is a coalition of the willing.[5] Though a single country can block action, such veto power is exercised infrequently. Unless vital interests are perceived to be at stake over a particular issue, those opposed to a specific measure attach reservations and/or choose not to participate, but do not prohibit those who are in agreement from acting. NATO is a voluntary association of sovereign states only loosely linked together by essentially collegial institutions in which each member has an equal voice—although some members clearly have a larger say than others. NATO's loose structure reflects wisdom as well as weakness. It is doubtful that a less voluntary organization would have survived the various squabbles between Allies over the past three-plus decades. NATO has succeeded as a defensive alliance because dissenting members have not been forced to follow actions they would find unacceptable, and because its members have not undermined its cohesion by divisive arguments over greater authority. A serious weakness is that NATO has not been able to move its members toward a more effective collective defense posture.

Civil (Political) Organization

The North Atlantic Council, made up of representatives of the sixteen member countries, is the highest decision-making authority in the Alliance.[6] It provides a forum for wide political consultation and coordination among Allies, addressing, as a perusal of its communiqués indicates, such issues as arms control, East-West relations, political developments in various areas, environmental concerns, and armaments cooperation.[7] Military policy is discussed in the Defense Planning Committee (DPC), composed of countries participating in the Alliance's integrated defense system—the Council minus France.[8]

The Council and the DPC convene at least twice yearly in ministerial sessions where member states are represented by Foreign and Defense Ministers respectively. These biannual ministerial meetings follow a highly formalized agenda set well in advance. Ministers generally present set-piece speeches, routinely endorse a number of reports, and approve a communiqué largely drafted in advance of the meeting.[9] Ministers, for the most part, ratify agreements previously reached by their permanent representatives at Evere (Brussels). Important and sensitive subjects are usually addressed in bilateral discussions and in executive sessions where attendance is restricted and discussions not encumbered by the formalized ministerial agenda.

For the conduct of business throughout the year, there is a permanent representative of ambassadorial rank for each government, supported by staffs varying in size, from a handful in the case of Iceland and Luxembourg to nearly one hundred for the United States. The Council/DPC in Permanent Session functions as a standing committee of governments or as a continuous diplomatic conference and engages in regular and intense multilateral consultation. As a general rule, the Council/DPC meets weekly, but more frequently in the weeks leading up to the biannual ministerial meetings.[10] The Council/DPC is chaired by the Secretary General,[11] an appointed international officer charged with organizing, subject to Council approval, and directing the International Staff—a tenured body of talented and experienced civil servants specializing in political, economic, scientific, or defense affairs. The International Staff prepares materials for Council/DPC action and is responsible for monitoring the implementation of decisions.

Below the Council/DPC level, NATO depends on a committee structure to address the bulk of day-to-day matters and to prepare major issues for ambassadorial action. In NATO defense planning, for example, the Defense Review Committee—composed of the defense counselors of each participating country plus military representatives—is the principal civil body that addresses Allied defense programs. The Defense Review Committee meets frequently—almost daily in the weeks preceding the DPC ministerial meetings—to examine the force plans and defense budgets of the Allies, to prepare Alliance defense planning guidance, and to review the force improvements proposed by the NATO military authorities. The committee structure is the locus of the "real" day-to-day business of NATO. It provides useful fora for consultation on a wide range of issues. National differences are identified and worked out at the committee level, sparing the Ambassadors involvement in all but the most sensitive and difficult issues.

Not unlike the U.S. Congress, much of the business of NATO takes place outside the formal committee structure. Through bilateral discussions, negotiations on the fringes of committee meetings, social contacts, and working out texts with the International Staff, proponents and opponents attempt to build coalitions. Favors are exchanged, differences settled, and compromises made. In most cases, agreement is struck before Ambassadors or Ministers formally address the issue in question—the formal meeting placing an imprimatur on accords already reached.[12]

Military Structure

The Military Committee, composed of the Chiefs of Staff of each member country, except France,[13] is, in a formal sense, the senior military authority of the Alliance. The Military Committee meets three times a year at Chiefs of Staff level and convenes at least weekly in permanent session at the level of Military Representatives. It is charged with providing military advice to the Council/DPC, recommending measures for the common defense, and giving guidance to the major NATO commanders—the Supreme Allied Commander, Europe (SACEUR); the Supreme Allied Commander, Atlantic (SACLANT); and the Allied Commander in Chief, Channel (CINCHAN). The Military Committee's formal status and responsibilities, however, are misleading. In practice it has little influence on Alliance defense decision making.[14] The Military Committee has found it difficult to provide timely, unfettered military advice to the Council/DPC, and many important military planning and analysis functions have been assumed by supposedly subordinate organizations.

The Military Committee's relative lack of influence in the process by which NATO reaches decisions on defense matters stems from several factors. Although the Military Committee gives "guidance" to the major NATO commanders, it lacks command authority—that authority rests with the three major NATO commanders. Moreover, the makeup of the Committee—national representatives of fifteen sovereign states—and the Committee's decision process—negotiation of a position acceptable to all—do not lead to prompt, concise military advice. With each Military Representative acting under formal instructions form his own military authorities, the output is a compromise among national views—which are themselves often the products of internal negotiations among the various armed services. Thus, the Military Committee suffers from the frequently described debilities of the Joint Chiefs of Staff,[15] multiplied by fifteen. Rather than crisp, hard-hitting military advice, it provides lowest-common-denominator responses. NATO needs a source of independent military advice on Alliance defense needs, rather than the present composite of national military preferences produced by the Military Committee.

The Military Committee is overshadowed by SACEUR.[16] No Chairman of the Military Committee has acquired the status of a SACEUR, of a General Norstad, Goodpaster, or Haig. It is to SACEUR, not the Military Committee, that the Council and Allied governments look for military advice. SACEUR symbolizes the U.S. commitment to the defense of Europe and has the political and organizational clout to develop, negotiate, and put into action NATO defense plans. SACEUR has the authority to deal directly with Allied governments and with the Secretary General, bypassing the Military Committee, and he exercises that right regularly. The usual *modus operandi* for developing NATO military plans and coordinating Allied actions is for SACEUR's staff to work out an agreed position with national defense staffs, a decision that the Military Committee then normally approves.[17]

Finally, the small International Military Staff of the Military Committee is not adequately staffed to accomplish either military planning or analysis.

With frequent turnover of personnel, its staff positions filled on a basis of national quotas, and the problem of language barriers, the International Military Staff has not been an effective body and has had little impact on NATO's decision-making process.[18]

In short, in NATO, as with most organizations, theory and practice do not coincide; formal organizational responsibilities and wiring diagrams tell little about the actual influence of the component parts. As the following discussion of the NATO force planning process will show, defense planning initiatives normally come from outside the formal organization. They rarely "bubble up" from within; ad hoc groups, only loosely connected with established NATO bodies, are created to handle such initiatives; policy steps are worked out between staffs before surfacing for NATO "decision"; and decision sheets and communiqués are prepared well in advance of high-level meetings.

NATO Defense Planning System

The NATO force planning system is an elaborate two-year process with three major stages: establishment of defense planning guidance, setting of force improvement goals, and review of Allied defense programs and of progress in achieving NATO force goals.[19] The defense planning cycle begins with a military evaluation of the threat confronting the Alliance and the NATO military needs, as well as an economic assessment of countries' abilities to support defense efforts. Drawing upon these assessments, the Defense Review Committee prepares a planning guidance document (Ministerial Guidance) to establish the framework for the NATO military authorities in their preparation of force improvement measures (force proposals) and set an overall framework for Alliance defense planning. This guidance document is reviewed and approved by Defense Ministers every other year, at their spring plenary meeting. Although it is much shorter and less specific (as well as less directive), Ministerial Guidance is roughly comparable to the Defense Guidance prepared annually by the U.S. Department of Defense. Ministerial Guidance addresses political, economic, technological, and military factors affecting the development of NATO forces; recommends priorities for force improvements; and sets budget objectives. Significant features of recent Ministerial Guidance documents have included the emphasis on increased rationalization and standardization (in the 1975 Ministerial Guidance) and the goal of a 3 percent annual increase in defense spending, adopted in 1977.

Taking this guidance into account,[20] the NATO commanders, in close coordination with national military authorities, prepare a set of force improvement recommendations, called force proposals, for each country. These force proposals vary in specificity from calling for procurement of a certain number and type of aircraft, tanks, howitzers, etc., to urging a country to study or investigate the possibility of upgrading some aspect of its military forces. The specificity of language generally reflects the extent of a country's acceptance of the force proposal; the prospects of a "study" proposal being turned into actual defense improvement are slim indeed. The force proposals are reviewed by the Military Committee and, then, the Defense Review Committee, for their military, political, and economic acceptability, and their compatibility with Ministerial Guidance. Following this review process, the DPC approves the resulting set of NATO force goals, which members are enjoined to use as the basis of their force programs for the following five years. The normal practice is for the NATO commanders to propose a set of improvements that challenge governments to do significantly more than contained in their forward defense plans, for the International Staff and, usually, the United States representatives to support such a challenge, and for the country concerned to try and pare down the list of force proposals, or to circumscribe with caveats recommendations incompatible with existing national plans so as to justify noncompliance.

The final stage of the NATO force planning process is a critical analysis of Allied plans every autumn. In response to the NATO Defense Planning Questionnaire, members, each July, provide NATO with detailed information on their defense programs and budgetary plans for the next five years.[21] These data are examined by the NATO military authorities and the International Staff, and representatives from each country appear before the Defense Review Committee to explain and defend their government's programs. During these multilateral reviews, countries are subjected to critical questioning on their record in fulfilling NATO force goals, making changes in defense plans (particularly any reductions in forces committed to NATO), and budgetary forecasts—for example, achievement of the goal of 3 percent real increases in defense spending. As in the force proposals review process, the military authorities, International Staff, and U.S. representatives are the principal inquisitors and critics attempting to persuade Allies to do more, while the respondents plead their cases largely on economic grounds. Following these multilateral reviews, the International Staff prepares a report to the Defense Ministers commenting on each country's performance in fulfilling force commitments to NATO and in implementing NATO force goals.

Despite this elaborate and well-practiced force planning process, NATO has relatively little direct influence on the members' defense programs.[22] A number of factors account for this phenomenon. The five-year time frame of the NATO force planning system is not long enough to cover the selection, development, and procurement of major weapons systems, which can take a decade of more from inception to deployment. National defense planning periods are much longer than NATO's, and important programs are well in hand before NATO organs have the opportunity to influence them in a manner more in keeping with Alliance defense needs.

The Alliance's force planning process does not draw Allied actions effectively toward NATO-wide defense needs. The size and configuration of military forces in member countries are based upon a number of domestic and external factors, of which NATO requirements constitute only one, and not necessarily the most influential element. This is particularly true for countries with far-flung defense commitments and a sophisticated and complex defense planning structure, such as the United States and Great Britain. As a general rule, member plans direct NATO plans, and not the other way around. For the most part, NATO force goals simply reflect what individual countries were planning to do in the first place. Attempts by NATO military authorities and civil staffs to persuade countries to take on new programs and to adjust existing laws to meet common defense needs are watered down or eliminated in the lengthy and repetitive approval process concerning force proposals wherein members, to all intents and purposes, have a veto. What emerges each December as the NATO force plans, is, in fact, a sum of country plans only marginally influenced by NATO considerations.

Changing defense programs, when funds have already been committed, contracts signed, interservice bargains struck, and parliamentary backing garnered, is a very low-success venture and one that NATO organs are not eager to tackle. Thus, NATO organs almost never advise a government not to pursue an existing program, however meager that program's contribution to the common defense may be; rather, the country concerned is urged to continue all that it is doing, plus more. The NATO force goals process is additive; trade-offs are not suggested. And, in an inevitably resource-constrained environment, additional, costly measures receive a cool hearing and are rarely carried out.

The NATO planning process itself reinforces this national as opposed to Alliance orientation. Both the NATO force goals, and the annual review of performance, focus almost exclusively on country-by-country actions and touch only tangentially on collective efforts or functionally related programs. The process is ill-equipped to address collective efforts such as standardization, interoperability, logistics support, and other cooperative activities. By focusing on the "trees" of individual country programs, the NATO force planning system risks losing sight of the "forest" of functionally related defense efforts. Common defense requirements are splintered throughout the force goals for each country. Nowhere in the force planning system does one obtain a collective picture of Alliance-wide or even regional requirements and capabilities in anti-armor, air defense, electronic warfare, reinforcement, etc.

Parochial national views dominate the planning and programming of NATO forces. The result is a nationally balanced force structure rather than a coherent and balanced collective Alliance force posture. Countries maintain separate and overlapping force structures, logistics support, training facilities, and research and development activities. The Alliance pays a steep price in terms of duplication of efforts, inefficient use of scarce resources, and, most important, reduced combat capability. The whole of NATO military capability is less than the sum of its parts, as is shown starkly in NATO–Warsaw Pact military comparisons. Over the years, NATO countries have spent about as much on defense as the Warsaw Pact and have comparable manpower under arms, yet NATO fields significantly fewer combat formations and is outnumbered in almost all equipment categories.

The shortcomings in NATO force planning should not be a surprise. They reflect the basic makeup of the Western Alliance, which, as noted previously, is a voluntary grouping of sovereign states that has no fiscal or management authority over national programs. Member states have not relinquished and, short of the outbreak of war, are not likely to give up their control over such important matters as the makeup of their armed forces, how these will be equipped and from what sources, the stationing of nuclear weapons on their soil, and what portion of the state treasury should be devoted to military preparedness. All that NATO can do is cajole and prod, and make Allied governments think twice before taking action that would weaken Alliance defenses. The NATO force planning process is a comfortable shoe. It binds countries only to the degree they have consented to be bound. It enables them to retain independence in structuring defense programs and setting priorities and, at the same time, provides an Alliance imprimatur on what they planned to do in the first place.

Its deficiencies notwithstanding, progress is being made. Over time and incrementally, NATO does influence the members' defense programs. NATO requirements are considered by national defense planners, countries think twice before reducing force commitments, and NATO's many armaments working groups have some impact on long-range weapons development. A particular success story is the coordinated improvement of NATO antiarmor capabilities in the mid-1970s, which predated the emphasis on antiarmor in the Long-Term Defense Program. As would be expected, while the NATO force planning process does not have much influence on American or British defense programs, it plays a considerably larger role in the forward planning of the smaller Allies.

It is also a mark of the extent of Allied cooperation that, through the NATO force planning process, the members systematically exchange detailed information on their military and financial programs on a scale unprecedented among free countries in peace or even in war, and submit their programs to the examination and criticism of their Alliance partners.[23] Through this lengthy and elaborate consultative process, NATO can influence the plans of a country, but only at the margin. The process is not suited to deal with new requirements or substantial change. New defense initiatives traditionally have been proposed and implemented outside the formal NATO planning system. NATO's Long-Term Defense Program, launched in the spring of 1977, is a case in point—it was proposed by the United States, patterned after U.S. programs, broader in scope than NATO's formal force planning process, and developed and approved outside of regular NATO defense planning procedures.

NATO Long-Term Defense Program (LTDP)

The LTDP, proposed by President Carter at the London NATO summit in May of 1977, addressed some of the above-mentioned shortcomings in the regular NATO planning process—in particular, its focus on national programs rather than collective requirements.[24] The LTDP looks much farther into the future, up to fifteen years forward, compared to six years for NATO force goals; organizes requirements and proposed actions in functionally related programs—antiarmor, air defense, electronic warfare, etc.; focuses on a limited number of selected priority programs—about 120 measures contrasted to the 1,000-plus force goals adopted for each two-year cycle; and emphasizes collective action.

The setting was right in the spring of 1977 for the launching of a major new defense effort in NATO. There was a growing recognition among Allied governments that the rapid growth in Warsaw Pact military capabilities demanded concerted action to counter the adverse trends in almost all aspects of the military balance between the two coalitions. Soviet defense spending had been rising steadily at 4 to 5 percent yearly, while that of NATO had stagnated—reflecting the sharp decrease in U.S. defense budgets as the Vietnam War wound down. NATO defense spending actually declined in real terms during the first half of the 1970s.[25] In that same period, the Soviet Union added over 250,000 men to its armed forces while total NATO military manpower dropped by more than a million.[26] The firepower, mobility, and logistical support of Warsaw Pact forces had increased markedly, and Soviet tactical airpower was changing from a short range, day-only, primarily air defense force to a longer range, heavier payload, potent offensive air arm. Overall, there was a notable increase in Moscow's ability to mount an attack on Western Europe with little warning.

NATO communiqués reflected concern about the alarming increase in Warsaw Pact capabilities and the need to strengthen Alliance defenses. In the spring of 1975, the DPC ministerial communiqué reported blandly that Defense Ministers were "briefed on latest developments in the growth of the military power of the Warsaw Pact"; there was no call for action.[27] By December, however, the Ministers "expressed their grave concern" at the changing military balance.[28] And, a year later, Alliance Defense Ministers again voiced their alarm at the Warsaw Pact emphasis on offensive capabilities and called for further measures "to reverse effectively the adverse trends in the NATO–Warsaw Pact conventional military balance."[29]

The corollary shift in the strategic nuclear balance from clear U.S. superiority toward parity with the Soviet Union underlined the importance of shoring up NATO's conventional defenses. Gone was the U.S. nuclear dominance of the 1950s and much of the 1960s that, at least perceptually, had offset Warsaw Pact conventional advantages and served as a rationalization for not correcting longstanding deficiencies in Allied forces.

There was also growing recognition of some of the shortcomings in the NATO force planning system. The Dutch had urged that attention be given to longer-range planning and to specialization of defense tasks among Allies to avoid duplication and conserve resources. British and Canadian representatives had joined the United States in proposing changes to NATO force planning procedures so as to provide clearer determination of priorities and to focus on functionally related force improvement measures. Reflecting these stirrings, the 1975 and 1977 Ministerial Guidance placed much greater emphasis on cooperative defense measures—rationalization of defense tasks among Allies, standardization of equipment and procedures, and cooperation in development and production programs.

Finally, the European Allies welcomed the new Administration's commitment to strengthen the American contribution to the Alliance. Only a few days after the Carter Administration took office, Vice-President Mondale was dispatched to Brussels to reaffirm the American commitment to NATO and to express the Administration's concern over the state of NATO defenses. His central message to the North Atlantic Council was that the United States was prepared to do more to improve Alliance defenses if the Allies likewise would increase their efforts.[30] Despite economic difficulties, the Europeans had done more in the first half of the decade, when U.S. budgets, military manpower, and war stocks in Europe had declined markedly.[31] The European Allies had waited patiently for a renewed emphasis on Europe in an American foreign policy that had fallen victim to Vietnam, the 1973 Middle East War, and Watergate. Though wary about American initiatives that called for greater defense efforts, the Europeans were willing to stretch a little to encourage the Europe-first focus of the new Administration in Washington.

The LTDP was the brainchild of Robert Komer, who had set out a detailed framework for it in a classified RAND study completed in the fall of 1976, and who had prepared background papers on NATO for the Carter Administration.[32] Ambassador Komer sold his ideas to the new Secretary of Defense, Harold Brown, and was given a mandate to put together an action plan to improve the U.S. contribution to NATO and to lay the groundwork for a new Alliance defense initiative patterned after his RAND study. President Carter then proposed this plan to Allied leaders at the London summit meeting—the regular spring ministerial meeting having been raised to summit level so as to give added visibility and impetus to the new U.S. defense initiatives.

Allied leaders agreed to President Carter's proposal,[33] and, a week later, the Defense Ministers set in motion the development of a long-term defense program, "to enable NATO forces to meet the changing defense needs of the 1980s," for ministerial approval the following spring, and subsequent consideration by NATO heads of government at their summit meeting in Washington.[34] The Ministers agreed also to undertake a set of near-term defense improvements in the areas of antiarmor, war reserve munitions, and readiness and reinforcement.[35] The LTDP was launched and was to be endorsed a year later by heads of government, rather than Defense Ministers, to signal its special, priority nature and to place it in a separate, elevated status compared to the routine NATO force planning process. This separate, out-of-cycle procedure was accepted only reluctantly by the Allies.

In NATO a key step in the decision process is the preparation of the postmeeting decision document; since formal votes are rarely taken, decisions are reached by consensus, and the participants frequently carry away varying interpretations of what was agreed. In the case of the LTDP, Ministers had agreed that NATO would prepare a time-phased action program concentrating on a limited number of priority areas outlined in the U.S. proposal, but had not agreed specifically how the program would be developed. Recognizing the criticality of the measure, officers in the U.S. Mission to NATO drafted a decision document that fully incorporated the U.S. proposal and successfully negotiated that draft with a supportive international staff.

The Defense Planning Committee commissioned ten semiautonomous task forces, composed of NATO civil and military officials, to develop coordinated, long-term defense improvement programs in the following areas:[36] readiness; reinforcement; reserve mobilization; maritime posture; air defense; communications, command, and control; electronic warfare; rationalization; logistics; and theater nuclear forces.[37] Purposely separated from the constraint of the regular NATO force planning process, the task forces were able to take a collective approach to Alliance defense needs, relatively unburdened by standard procedures and national instructions. The United States established parallel groups within the Department of Defense to provide inputs to the NATO task forces and made experts available to the latter to assist in program development.[38] Not surprisingly, many of the actions recommended by the NATO task forces reflected U.S. views, and most of the measures proposed for action by the United States corresponded to American plans and programs already underway.

The nine task forces addressing conventional forces were responsible directly to the Executive Working Group chaired by the Deputy Secretary General—an organizational level above the committee that deals with the regular NATO force planning process, the Defense Review Committee. Furthermore, for key meetings on the LTDP, such as the extensive review of the task force reports in the spring of 1978, the United States pressed successfully to have the Executive Working Group meetings reinforced by senior officials from the capitals, the U.S. representative being Ambassador Komer.

The task forces forwarded their reports to the Secretary General in March of 1978. The reports exceeded U.S. expectations, particularly in light of the relatively short time the task force directors had to assemble their teams, gather data, test the water with Allies, and prepare their reports. The task force reports provided in-depth analyses of Alliance defense needs in the nine selected conventional areas and focused on a limited number of priority defense improvement measures. While the task force reports presented some fresh ideas, for the most part they built upon previous studies and plans, and their recommendations reflected frequently proposed improvement actions.[39] The difference was that the recommended measures were pulled together into a coherent, functional framework; called for specific, time-phased actions by Allies and the NATO authorities; and, most important, received high-level attention and visibility.

Most of that attention was aroused by the United States. During the weeks between the completion of task force reports in March and the end of May, the United States pressed the Allies, both in NATO forums and bilaterally in the capitals, to obtain the highest order of agreement to the task force recommendations. The results of this intensive lobbying effort were mixed. In the process of obtaining Allied agreement, many of the measures were watered down. Meeting in Washington during May of 1978, NATO leaders agreed to undertake more than 120 individual defense improvement measures.[40] In the case of many of these, however, commitment to implement the actions required had been circumscribed by caveats. "Agreed" LTDP measures were endorsed "in principle," remanded for study, or deferred, pending further elaboration and refinement. As with all major NATO decisions, Allied leaders accepted a consensus document, with adequate maneuver room built in to preserve national prerogatives and make monitoring of compliance difficult.

As noted earlier, most of the LTDP measures directed at the United States were already contained in American defense plans. According to the LTDP's chief architect, more than 90 percent of the funding for U.S. LTDP measures had been included previously in the Five-Year Defense Program and Extended Planning Annex.[41] Consequently, carrying out the LTDP required far fewer program adjustments for the United States than for most Allies.

NATO has not wanted for studies of Alliance military deficiencies and recommended defense improvements. There had already been two such major efforts earlier in the decade. In 1970 the Defense Planning Committee generated a comprehensive study of Alliance defense needs, known as AD-70, that identified many of the shortcomings addressed later in the LTDP, and Defense Ministers agreed to place high priority on correcting these deficiencies. Five years later, SACEUR's flexibility studies presented over eight hundred recommendations for corrective action.[42] As is so often the case in NATO, however, many of the recommended actions, long recognized as essential to cope with increasing Warsaw Pact capabilities, remained unfulfilled. A key feature of the LTDP, therefore, was the call in the communiqué of the Washington Summit for "vigorous follow-through action."[43]

While the European countries argued that the LTDP should be channeled into existing NATO force planning procedures and no special monitoring arrangements were needed, Washington insisted that a separate, systematic follow-through process was required to ensure that LTDP measures bore fruit and to avoid having the LTDP turn into another NATO "paper exercise." At America's urging, the Defense Planning Committee appointed senior NATO officials to serve as "program monitors" for each of the nine conventional program areas and charged these monitors to keep track of progress in implementing the LTDP, to identify problem areas, and to provide periodic reports evaluating progress in their functional areas of responsibility.[44]

To provide program monitors and NATO authorities with the information necessary to assess LTDP implementation and to identify areas needing greater attention, countries were asked—again at the urging of the United States—to provide detailed information each July on the specific actions they had programmed or planned to take in implementation of LTDP measures.[45] Drawing on these data and the program monitors' appraisals, the International Staff prepared comprehensive reports each fall on the status of LTDP implementation for consideration by the Defense Ministers at their December meetings, as well as preparing a separate report each spring focusing on key problem areas.

In short, an elaborate set of follow-through procedures, distinct from the regular NATO force planning process, was established to monitor LTDP progress. Just as the LTDP was patterned after U.S. proposals, so, too, were the follow-through procedures to which the Allies agreed only reluctantly. The European countries argued that special handling of the LTDP detracted from regular NATO force planning efforts, and the separate reporting requirements placed an unnecessary burden on their relatively small staffs. As a senior British official put it, "Special arrangements cutting across normal patterns can be very helpful . . . ; but, if they are prolonged too far, the law of diminishing returns and increasing dissipation of effort may set in. If there is joint national will and effort . . . the proven and extensive machinery of the Alliance's normal workings can be quite powerful and flexible enough to serve the Alliance's purposes effectively."[46] Other Allies, particularly the Germans, were more blunt in their criticism of U.S. efforts to maintain the distinctive character of the LTDP.[47]

The other members, however grudgingly, went along with American proposals for separate handling of the LTDP follow-up, because they agreed that the recommended defense measures were needed and did not want to take a chance of sidetracking U.S. defense improvements under way. The United States had set in motion a range of actions to enhance its military contribution to NATO, and the Allies were willing to put up with some inconvenience, if that was necessary to keep Washington's efforts on track. Moreover, the United States was persistent in pressing its case both in the capitals and at NATO headquarters. No sooner was the ink dry on the Washington Summit agreements, than U.S. representatives were calling on each Ally to press America's case for effective follow-up and working with the International Staff to ensure that U.S. views were incorporated in the key decision documents. The need for such persistence was demonstrated by the reaction of the defense counselor of a major European country who, when urged by his American counterpart just after the Washington Summit to support vigorous follow-through action, responded: "The LTDP . . . that's over. It was settled in Washington."[48]

In NATO, as in other large organizations, the one who prepares the first draft has considerable influence on the decisions eventually reached. Working closely with the International Staff, the United States was able to influence the key documents in their formative stages. Allies who opposed were thus put in the uncomfortable position of attempting to amend or attach reservations to the draft on the table.

Over time and at European urging, however, the LTDP has been folded into the regular NATO force planning process, while the special handling procedures designed to promote effective implementation and to preserve the distinctive nature of the LTDP have faded away. Almost all applicable LTDP measures have been incorporated into NATO force goals, the separate LTDP section of the NATO Defense Planning Questionnnaire has been dropped, and November of 1982 marked the final separate LTDP report to the Defense Ministers. What began as an ambitious attempt to coordinate Alliance defense efforts and to overhaul NATO defense planning procedures had but a brief period on the stage before going the way of previous NATO initiatives.

Less than five years after Allied leaders had approved a far-reaching, long-term program to shore up Alliance defenses, NATO defense planning had returned to its familiar rut. The shortcomings in regular NATO procedures—national rather than collective focus, inadequate prioritization, lack of long-term planning—remained relatively unaffected by the undertakings launched in London during 1977, which Secretary Brown described as a "watershed in NATO's development."[49] The LTDP fell victim to Allied unwillingness to alter national defense plans in the interest of strengthening collective capabilities, as well as to budgetary constraints, bureaucratic inertia, and the changing of the guard in Washington to a new team with its own foreign policy agenda. Well before the new Administration took office, however, the momentum behind the LTDP had begun to wane, as the Carter Administration's attention shifted from Europe to Southwest Asia, in the aftermath of the Soviet invasion of Afghanistan and the seizure of the American Embassy in Teheran. An out-of-cycle defense initiative like an LTDP that challenges long-accepted procedures requires consistent, forceful U.S. efforts to keep up the momentum. Wahington's attention was distracted, its efforts slackened, and the LTDP withered on the vine.

This is not to say that there were no accomplishments. The LTDP set forth a coherent long-term planning framework that should continue to assist military authorities in the member countries and in NATO with their defense planning. Reflecting the LTDP's emphasis on organizing defense measures into program areas, NATO has agreed to include a functional analysis of national plans in the annual NATO review cycle. The LTDP focused high-level attention on Alliance defense needs and galvanized NATO action on a set of high-priority defense measures. As a result, some progress has been made in strengthening NATO capabilites, particularly in the areas of antiarmor, reinforcement, and logistics. A March 1983 Department of Defense report stated that over 70 percent of LTDP measures were progressing satisfactorily,[50] although other sources paint a far less optimistic picture of LTDP implementation, reporting that progress has been disappointing and a number of planned actions remain unfulfilled.[51] These measures will not be carried out unless the Allies are willing to increase resources devoted to defense. Yet, short of a major crisis, the prospects for increased defense spending are not bright. In 1982 only three countries, apart from the United States, met the 3 percent real growth goal, and nearly half had a real decline in defense spending.[52]

Conclusions About NATO Decision Making

Decisions in the Atlantic Alliance are reached through a process of consultation, of consensus building. Unlike the executive power of a state to direct action, NATO possesses no mandatory authority that can compel its members to act in the common interest. National sovereignty remains the overriding factor, and a single country can, in effect, exercise a veto and frustrate the will of the majority. Thus, consensus building offers the only means available to resolve differences of view and reach agreement on a common course of action. For the most part, divisive issues such as extension of the treaty area, internal affairs of the members, and "French" issues, are avoided. The NATO decision process attempts to accommodate the concerns of all, and the resultant policy frequently turns out to be the lowest common denominator among conflicting positions.

The process is not unlike the consideration of legislation in the American Congress—widely different constituencies and concerns are involved, and representatives usually protect these local interests (which may or may not coincide with the common concerns of the entity at large). The common good often is relegated to second place, favors are exchanged, and compromises struck that satisfy none of the parties fully. Although there are such parallels between NATO and national processes, it is a lot tougher to move sixteen than it is to move one. Change occurs in NATO, policy is made and carried out, but progress is slow and decisions are encumbered with caveats and reservations. What would be relatively easy decisions in a national stucture, such as filling mid-level posts within the organization, become troublesome, time-consuming affairs involving national prestige, even when relatively minor staff positions are being addressed. Fortunately, Alliance members have been able to work out flexible ways to handle most contentious issues. While a single country can block majority action, the "rule of unanimity" is flexibly applied. Rather than vetoing a move, the "opposition" may decline to participate in collective action or attach reservations to its participation; however, generally it does not prevent those in agreement from moving ahead jointly in a "coalition of the willing"—French and Greek selective participation being a case in point.

Defense initiatives in the Alliance rarely originate within the formal structure. They do not "bubble up." Major new efforts—the adoption of the flexible response strategy, the AD-70 program, the emphasis on standardization, the LTDP, and the post-Afghanistan measures—were originated by the United States. For the most part, they were also developed outside the formal NATO force planning process to circumvent the barriers to change that are part of that process. Obtaining Allied agreement to and implementation of such initiatives is not easy; it requires U.S. leadership; a well-planned and well-executed effort to persuade Allies, the Secretary General, key persons in the International Staff, and SACEUR to go along; and, above all, persistence. If Washington pushes hard and consistently, gains the active support of SACEUR and the Secretary General, and at least the acquiescence of key Allies, it can normally gain Allied agreement. In the process of gaining the widest possible agreement, however, reservations will be attached and the impact of the initiative watered down. Such is the nature of reaching agreement among independent, sovereign states whose interests coincide, but rarely, if ever, are identical on a particular issue.

NATO is not well suited to deal with new defense requirements . As is common with large organizations, NATO resists change to long-established ways of doing business. Change occurs, but it takes place gradually—in the view of some observers, glacially. The rather brief flowering of the LTDP demonstrates the strong preference of members for the status quo—the existing, familiar force planning system. From the early days of the LTDP, the Allies have signaled their concern about a special, out-of-cycle program and their opposition to revision of existing planning procedures. They have called for maximum use of existing machinery and urged that LTDP measures be channeled into the regular force planning process as quickly as practicable.

In European eyes, such U.S.-inspired defense initiatives, even though they may promise significant defense improvements and more effective use of scarce resources, carry the risk of reduced local control over individual defense programs. The established NATO force planning process is comfortable; it binds Allies only to the extent that they choose to be bound. It reflects a carefully worked out compromise between the need to coordinate Allied defense efforts and the desires of members to be free to size and shape national forces as they choose. In spite of the major changes that have taken place in the NATO defense environment since the mid-1960s and new demands on Alliance forces, the NATO defense planning system has remained virtually unchanged since it was adopted in 1966. It has weathered several U.S. attempts to restructure it and, barring a major crisis, it will survive more.

European patience outlasts the staying power of the United States. Washington proposes a new Alliance effort, looks for quick results—which are not forthcoming—and then becomes impatient with the deliberate pace of NATO action. Despite Allied endorsement, a new defense program flourishes only briefly and fades away, absorbed into NATO's routine defense planning procedures.

The major shortcomings in NATO defenses are rooted in the very nature of an alliance of sovereign states—the price we pay for the benefits of democratic political processes. An alliance with mandatory authority over national programs could correct major deficiencies in Allied defenses—duplication of efforts, malpositioning of combat units, nonstandard equipment and procedures, etc.—but it would no longer be an alliance of independent, sovereign states.

Improvements are being made in NATO's military capabilities. The Alliance is making major strides, *inter alia*, in antiarmor weapons, equipment interoperability, coordination of air operations, and modernization of theater nuclear forces; NATO's air and maritime forces maintain significant qualitative advantages over those of the Warsaw Pact. However, progress is gradual. Short of a major crisis, a more rapid pace of improvement is unlikely. The unanswered question is whether the halting pace of Alliance defense improvements will continue to be sufficient to maintain a credible NATO deterrence and defense posture in the face of the steady buildup of Warsaw Pact military capabilities.

NOTES

1. In 1945 the armed strength of the Allied Forces in Europe was about 4.6 million. Only one year later, it had dropped to 880,000. *NATO Facts and Figures* (Brussels: NATO Information Service, 1981), 14.

2. Approving Ministerial Guidance for 1977–1982, the Defense Ministers agreed to "aim" for an annual increase in defense budgets "in the region of 3 percent" (in real terms). At

British insistence, and reflecting the slump in Britain's economy and cuts in British defense spending, the 3 percent goal contained the caveat, "economic circumstances will affect what can be achieved." Media coverage, following NATO's adoption of the 3 percent aim, ignored the caveats and, much to the embarrassment of the Labor Government, proclaimed that London had agreed to a 3 percent rise in defense spending. See "Carter Defence Appeal Finds Support," *Times* (London), 18 May 1977, 7; and "NATO States Agree to Spend 3 pc More," ibid., 19 May 1977, 8. For texts of NATO communiqués, see *NATO Final Communiqués*, vol. 2, 1975–1980 (Brussels: NATO Information Service, 1981).

3. At almost every succeeding ministerial meeting, NATO Defense Ministers have reaffirmed the 3 percent goal. *NATO Final Communiqués*. NATO communiqués after 1980 may be found in *NATO Review*, nos. 3 and 6 for each year.

4. Outside of the United States, which has exceeded the goal every year, and France, a nonparticipant, only five allies met the target in 1978, four in 1979, five in 1980 and 1981, and three in 1982. U.S. Department of Defense, *Report on Allied Contributions to the Common Defense*, March 1981, 67; ibid., March 1983, 51.

5. The author is indebted to Charles V. McLaughlin for this term. It appears in E. W. Boyd et al., *NATO Management: Peace to Crisis Transition*, RAND Report R-2576 (Santa Monica, Calif., RAND Corp., February 1980).

6. For a description of NATO organizational structure, see *NATO Facts and Figures*, 89–112.

7. Though defense matters are the purview of the Defense Planning Committee, the Council addresses those aspects of NATO military activities in which France chooses to participate, including armaments production, selected air defense matters, arms control discussions, and the NATO Infrastructure Program.

8. The Defense Planning Committee was established as a separate body, when France withdrew from NATO's integrated military structure in 1966. With the exception of areas such as those noted in the preceding note, where France chooses to participate, the DPC is the supreme authority of the Alliance for defense matters. It provides an effective way to bypass French obstructionism, a lesser problem than in the de Gaulle era, but still a factor. Greece also avoided DPC meetings following the Cyprus conflict of 1974 and did not return to full participation until October 1980. Spain participates in DPC deliberations, but has not yet resolved the extent of Spanish participation and does not commit forces to NATO.

9. Drafting of ministerial communiqués begins several weeks in advance of the ministerial meeting. Drawing on the reports Ministers will address, the International Staff prepares a draft communiqué, which national representatives review and revise in the weeks leading up to the ministerial session. Usually by the time Ministers address the communiqué (the last item on the meeting agenda), virtually the entire text has been agreed and Ministers haggle only over a few phrases.

10. To a large extent NATO Headquarters operates on a "semester" schedule, with the fall and spring "terms" consisting largely of preparing the reports Ministers will address during their end-of-semester meetings.

11. The Secretary General can play a crucial role in Alliance deliberations. By his presentation of the issues in question, structuring of discussion, and use of a quick gavel, he can influence the outcome of sticky issues. Since votes are only rarely taken and decisions reflect the sense or consensus of the meeting, the Secretary General's summing up of discussions is, in effect, the committee decision. Furthermore, it is his staff that prepares the decision documents following Council and DPC meetings. Because of the influence he can exert, before raising issues with their Allies, countries privately seek the Secretary General's counsel and support.

12. For a practitioner's view of the NATO consultation process, see Harlan Cleveland, *NATO: The Transatlantic Bargain* (New York: Harper & Row, 1970).

13. France is represented by a military mission to the Military Committee. Iceland, having no military forces, may be represented by a civilian but rarely attends either Military Committee or DPC sessions.

14. For an opposing view, see Edward L. Rowny, "Decision-Making Process in NATO," (Ph.D. diss., American University, 1977). Rowny, who was Deputy Chairman of the Military Committee from 1971 to 1973, argues that the Military Committee has played a central role in NATO's decision-making process and the relative influence of SACEUR has declined. The author's observation of NATO procedures during the latter half of the 1970s leads him to the

opposite conclusion. General Haig was clearly the dominant military voice in the Alliance, the Military Committee made only minor changes to the proposals of the major NATO commanders, major defense planning initiatives came from outside the formal NATO force planning structure, and the Military Committee played little more than a kibitzing role.

15. See General Edward C. Meyer, "The JCS—How Much Reform Is Needed?" *Armed Forces Journal International (AFJI)*, April 1982, 82–90; General David C. Jones, "Why the Joint Chiefs of Staff Must Change," *AFJI*, March 1982, 62–72. For an excellent collection of views, see House Investigations Subcommittee of the Committee on Armed Services, *Reorganization Proposals for the Joint Chiefs of Staff*, 97th Cong., 2d sess., April–August 1982.

16. SACEUR also plays a substantially larger role in the NATO process than does SACLANT. The forces committed to SACLANT are almost exclusively British and American; SACLANT's headquarters are in Norfolk, Virginia, over three thousand miles from Europe; and SACLANT's area of operations is the "blue water" Atlantic, not Europe or even the Mediterranean. The latter, and with it the U.S. Sixth Fleet, falls under SACEUR.

17. Elliot Vandevanter, *Some Fundamentals of NATO Organization*, RAND Memorandum RM-3559 (Santa Monica, Calif., RAND Corp. 1963), 47.

18. Rowny, 148–50.

19. For a description of the NATO force planning process, see *NATO Facts and Figures*, 146–51.

20. Theory and practice do not quite coincide. The NATO commanders actually begin the preparation of their force proposals nine months or more before the publication of Ministerial Guidance. There is, however, more than adequate time to adjust the force proposals in the year between the adoption of Ministerial Guidance and the approval of NATO force goals.

21. The NATO Defense Planning Questionnaire (DPQ) requests countries to report the action they are taking on each applicable NATO force goal and provide detailed data on, *inter alia*, their major equipment programs, munitions stock levels, status of units/ships/aircraft committed to NATO, personnel strengths, and defense spending plans.

22. Critiques of NATO planning can be found in U.S. General Accounting Office, *NATO's New Defense Programs: Issues for Consideration*, 9 July 1979, 16–19; and House Committee on Government Operations, *The Implementation of the NATO Long-Term Defense Program (LTDP)*, 97th Cong., 1st sess., 14 May 1981, 10–12.

23. *NATO Facts and Figures*, 149.

24. Descriptions of the LTDP can be found in U.S. General Accounting Office, *NATO's New Defense Program*; House Committee on Government Operations, *The Implementation of the NATO Long-Term Defense Progam*; and U.S. Department of Defense, *Rationalization/Standardization within NATO*, report of the Secretary of Defense, January 1981, 16–75.

25. American defense spending declined by nearly 25 percent in constant dollars between fiscal years 1970 and 1975, while our Allies' defense budgets increased by about 10 percent in real terms over the same period. Overall NATO spending declined about 14 percent in real terms. Calculations drawn from *Report on Allied Contributions*, 19.

26. NATO manpower figures are taken from ibid., 27. Soviet manpower figures are drawn from John M. Collins, *U.S./Soviet Military Balance: Statistical Trends, 1970–1981* (Washington, D.C., Congressional Research Service, 15 September 1982).

27. *NATO Final Communiqués*, 23.

28. Ibid., 34.

29. Ibid., 57.

30. "America Sets Conditions for Increased NATO Spending," *Times* (London), 25 January 1977, 1.

31. American equipment and munitions stocks in Europe had been drawn down to supply Israel during the October 1973 war. Senate Subcommittee on Manpower and Personnel of the Committee on Armed Services, *NATO Posture and Initiatives*, 95th Cong. 1st sess. 3 August 1977, 75.

32. Robert W. Komer, et al., *Alliance Defense in the Eighties*, RAND Report R-1980 (Santa Monica, Calif., November 1976). Although the overall report is classified, the large section, which describes Komer's proposal for a revamping of NATO defense planning procedures, is unclassified. See also Robert W. Komer, "The Origins and Objectives," *NATO Review*, June 1978, 9–12.

33. *NATO Final Communiqués*, 66.

34. Ibid., 68. The ground was prepared in the weeks and months preceding the London summit meeting. Ambassador Komer outlined the U.S. proposal to Secretary General Luns and Allied Ambassadors at NATO Headquarters several weeks before the London meeting, and had been carrying on a dialogue with SACEUR on structure of the LTDP for the previous several months. At U.S. initiative, the Ministerial Guidance drafted in the spring of 1977 included a call for the "establishment of a more comprehensive framework for defense planning incorporating a longer term approach." *NATO Final Communiqués*, 73.

35. The short-term measures program was (a) designed to give impetus and visibility to defense improvement actions called for in SACEUR's flexibility studies and (b) reflected the American penchant for seeing quick results. The short-term measures called upon countries to carry out a number of improvement actions by the end of 1978, and a glowing report on progress was presented to Defense Ministers at their December meeting. In fact, the touted improvements in antiarmor weapons, munition stocks, and pre-positioning of equipment mainly reflected actions that countries had set in motion well before the short-term measures program was adopted. There were few new improvements. Short of a major crisis, national defense programs simply cannot be adjusted significantly in that short a time; there were only eighteen months between the "launching" of the short-term measures in May 1977 and their "completion" in December 1978. Production lead times alone often run more than two years.

36. The DPC spread the wealth in assigning task force direction: SACEUR was made responsible for the readiness, air defense and communication, command and control task forces; SACLANT for reinforcements and maritime forces; the Assistant Secretary General for Defense Support for rationalization; the Director of the International Military Staff for reserve mobilization; and a private consultant for logistics. SACEUR was the logical choice for the electronic warfare task force as well, but so as not to leave the third major NATO commander out of the picture, CINCHAN was given this responsibility though his staff had virtually no electronic warfare expertise. The United States provided experienced officers to CINCHAN to assist in the preparation of the task force report. To the surprise of many observers, CINCHAN produced a first-rate effort and, in this writer's view, was the most effective program monitor.

37. Though not included in the U.S.-proposed LTDP program areas, theater nuclear force (TNF) modernization was added at Allies' insistence. TNF modernization was handled by the NATO Nuclear Planning Group separately from the nine conventional program areas and will not be addressed in this chapter. Alliance work on long-range TNF modernization culminated in the December 1979 decision to deploy U.S. ground-launched cruise missiles and Pershing II ballistic missiles in Western Europe, beginning in late 1983. See *NATO Final Communiqués*, 121–23.

38. *NATO Posture and Initiatives*, 67; *Rationalization/Standardization within NATO*, 4th report, January 1978, 2–3.

39. *NATO's New Defense Program*, 16; Komer, "Origins and Objectives," 12.

40. *NATO Final Communiqués*, 94.

41. Robert W. Komer, interview in *Armed Forces Journal*, September 1978, 47.

42. *NATO's New Defense Program*, 17.

43. *NATO Final Communiqués*, 95.

44. *Rationalization/Standardization within NATO*, 5th report, January 1979, 9.

45. A separate, U.S.-developed LTDP section was added to the annual NATO Defense Planning Questionnaire. It called on countries to provide detailed schedule and budget data for each LTDP measure, data that Allies claimed were neither available nor needed. The U.S. position was that NATO needed to establish a baseline against which progress in implementation could be measured. Ibid., 9–10.

46. Michael Quinlin, "The LTDP from a National Perspective," *NATO Review*, June 1978, 16.

47. A number of Allies showed their displeasure with the U.S. demands for detailed statistical data on plans to carry out LTDP measures by providing very skimpy information in their DPQ responses. In NATO committee meetings on the LTDP, German representatives repeatedly voiced their criticism of U.S. "ad hocery," claiming such exercises diverted attention from more fruitful planning efforts—the NATO force goals.

48. Personal notes of author, June 1978.

49. *Rationalization/Standardization within NATO*, 5th report, January 1979, 8.

50. *Report on Allied Contributions*, 54.

51. *Implementation of the Long-Term Defense Program*, 19–41; Simon Lunn, "The Management of Intra-NATO Relations," in *NATO: Agenda for the Next Four Years*, RAND Report R-2836 (Santa Monica, Calif.: RAND Corp., January 1982), 144–61.

52. *Report on Allied Contributions*, 51.

III

U.S. Decision Making on Defense
The Executive Branch

7

The National Security Council:
Formalized Coordination and Policy Planning

John E. Endicott

Background

Since the creation of the NSC in 1947, it has frequently measured up to its original model, the British Committee of Imperial Defense, as a body to ensure coordination of national security matters at the highest level.[1] Of course, the post–WW II national decision makers did not need to go back to that 1904 British committee to recognize the requirement for a coordinative body or a model for it. In fact, the "Committee of Three," consisting of the Secretaries of State, War, and Navy, that had been established during WW II could be considered the U.S. predecessor of the NSC. As a result of the intense debate over "unification" of the armed forces in the immediate postwar period, the NSC, plus the CIA and NSRB, were created.

One of the first and most farsighted studies to recommend the formation of an NSC specifically was the Eberstadt Report. This study was commissioned in June 1945 by the then Secretary of the Navy, James V. Forrestal; the former Chairman of the Army-Navy Munitions Board and Vice Chairman of the War Production Board, Ferdinand Eberstadt, was asked to address: "What form of postwar organization should be established and maintained to enable the military services and other government departments and agencies most effectively to provide for and protect our national security?"[2]

Eberstadt finished this two-hundred-page report in slightly over three months. While it was very specific as to the future of three military departments, "Air, Navy, and War," it proposed the creation of several coordinative and ancillary bodies in general terms only: a National Security Council, a National Security Resources Board, the Central Intelligence Agency, and a military education and training board.[3]

The National Security Council, as proposed by Eberstadt, was to have a membership consisting of the Secretary of State, the Chairman of the NSRB, and the Secretaries of the three military departments. Headed by a Chairman who would coordinate the members' activities, it was described as "a policy forming and advisory body."[4] The chairman was to have "ready access" to the President and power to resolve "differences" that might develop among the various Services.

While the Eberstadt Report is viewed as the precursor of the National Security Act of 1947, its concepts were not universally recognized as "the truth" in 1945. It was, in essence, the Navy Department's opening position

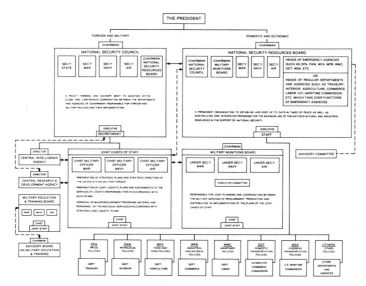

THE EBERSTADT PLAN[5]

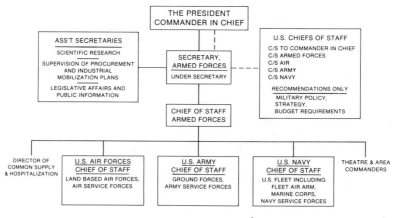

THE COLLINS PLAN[6]

that was placed in opposition to that of the War Department, which "advocated a centralized defense establishment focused on military policy and strategy,"[7] and was presented as the Collins Plan after Lieutenant General J. Lawton Collins, who had reworked to a "more palatable version . . . what the War Department had been advocating since 1942."[8]

By April 1946, the issue of defense reorganization was addressed in Senate Bill 2044. It had gone through nine drafts and among other things, provided for a "Department of Common Defense" (see Table 7.1) with a single Secretary at its head, as well as a "Council of Common Defense, the Central Intelligence Agency, and the National Security Resources Board." While the original Eberstadt Plan had envisaged participation in the "Council" by the Service Secretaries, they were not to be included in this Senate bill, only the Secretary of Common Defense.[9]

As the battle over the shape of the U.S. defense structure continued, the Council of Common Defense became an important means to assuage the Navy Department, since the War Department seemed to be getting its way regarding a single Cabinet-level Secretary for Defense. In this case, each service was guaranteed that it would be represented by its sub-Cabinet-level Secretary on the Council of Common Defense.[10]

By early 1947, President Harry Truman forwarded a draft bill to Congress that created a National Defense Establishment and included NSC, NSRB, and CIA as prime coordinating elements for national security.[11] This bill was considered flawed by some, especially Brigadier General Merritt A. Edson, USMC, who, upon retiring from the Corps, submitted a series of recommendations and criticisms to the Expenditures Committee of the House of Representatives. One of his strongly Marine-serving suggestions was "Purge the NSC of the 'overwhelming military character' proposed in the bill."[12] This last-ditch effort, which was designed more to save the Marines than define the nature of the NSC, all but ended the heated debate and, by 26 July, the National Security Act of 1947 had been passed and sent to the President. The chart below shows the national Security Council as stipulated in the Act. Note the "militaristic" memberships:

According to the Act, the newly created Council was to "advise the President with respect to the integration of domestic, foreign, and military policies relating to the national security so as to enable the military services and other departments and agencies of the government to cooperate more effectively in matters involving the national security,"[13]

It also provided that responsibilities of the Council would include, upon Presidential direction, to:

> a. . . . assess and appraise the objectives, commitments and risks of the United States in relation to our actual and potential military power, in the interest of national security, for the purpose

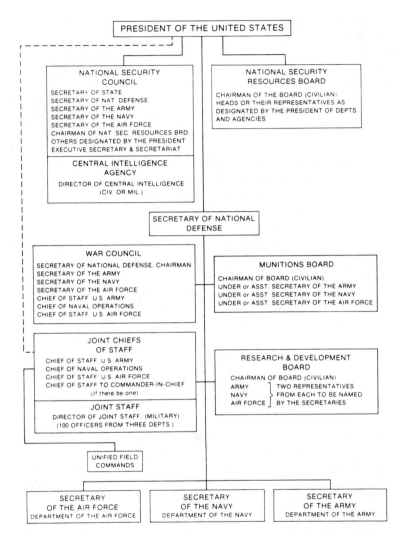

THE NATIONAL SECURITY ACT OF 1947[14]

of making recommendations to the President in connection therewith; and

    b. . . . consider policies on matters of common interest to the
departments and agencies of the government concerned with the
national security, and . . . make recommendations to the President
in connection therewith.[15]

The President was to preside over the meetings, but could be represented by another member of the Council.

While most of the debate had been couched in terms of military "unification," another interesting question was frequently just below the surface. That was the question of Presidential-Congressional relationships. The free world had entered a period of reaction to unbridled executive authority. The British electorate had retired their Prime Minister, Winston Churchill, during the Potsdam Conference, bringing in Clement Attlee. In 1947 the same phenomenon was also at work in the United States. A Republican-controlled Congress was reacting not only to the turbulent war years but the long period of executive predominance that had begun in March 1933. The NSC was being viewed by some as a system that might attempt to ensure some regularized control over a President's foreign policy course. Other questions also surfaced concerning its nature as a "super-cabinet on the Biritsh model."[16] This, of course, Harry Truman opposed since he saw considerable constitutional problems involved in such a model.[17]

In the words of Dillon Anderson, Special Assistant to the President for National Security Affairs during the Administration of President Eisenhower, the coordinative role for U.S. security policy by 1947 had become a requirement that could not be denied. He stated: " . . . no longer could appropriate military policy on the one hand or supportable foreign policy on the other be formulated in isolation one from the other; and by the same token neither military nor foreign policy could be considered adequately without taking into account the best integrated intelligence estimates of the world situation and the availability of U.S. resources to support our objectives and commitments with respect to the rest of the world."[18]

Other observers noted during the initial period that the NSC under a weak President could act to "diminish or diffuse the power of the Chief Executive";[19] under a strong one, however, it would tend to enhance his power by incorporating a mechanism for oversight and implementation of decisions. Both of these possibilities have emerged, as eight Presidents and over thirty-five years have demonstrated the continuing need for the NSC in the American system.

Thirty-Five Years of Experience: Coordination and Planning

After three decades can we say retrospectively that we truly appreciate the role played by the NSC? We may now assert that the success of the NSC, in fact, its role, has been dependent on three major factors: the structural organization of the NSC Staff, the manner in which the corporate body—the NSC staff—has interacted with the rest of the interagency arena; and finally, and most important, the nature of the specific relationship of the President's adviser for national security affairs with the President himself. These aspects are worthy of serious review and continuing research. It is possible, from our current vantage point, to underline and emphasize the personal nature of the power that has flowed from the NSC. The gradual tendency of the Chief Executive to politicize the office has moved in tandem with the particularistic nature of the council. From the viewpoint of career civil servants functioning between departments as brokers, staff personnel policies have evolved so that each new Administration brings with it, or soon creates, a NSC staff that reflects the President's policy inclinations. This point, in itself, reflects the NSC's most important development over time. Rather than being the constraining influence first anticipated by Truman, it has become the single most important foreign policy actor representing presidential aspirations and policy. Unlike the Departments of State and Defense, whose career bureaucracies can have a very real policy life of their own, in the NSC every employee, from statutory members to clerks and typists, is linked by a special bond to an elected President. Thus, over the thirty-five years of the Council's existence, a special recognition has developed of the role the NSC can play in implementing and executing a President's integrated defense and foreign policy.

At times, the NSC has most ardently pursued the policy implementation and execution roles, and at other times these roles have been eclipsed by the ever-important function of coordination throughout the Executive Branch. The seemingly never-ending tension in the NSC system, between the functions of coordination and policy planning, must be emphasized. The two processes seem irrevocably to produce a tendency either toward efficient coordination or an involved, charismatic national security adviser. Why has this historically been the case? Why have some come to argue that the coordinating function, the attempt to counter organizational and administrative disarray . . . resulted in an excessive and dangerous centralization of power?[20] Indeed, some argue that "By the late 1960s, the NSC and especially the Security Adviser had become a powerful locus of national security advice and formulation."[21] Moreover, such claims are accompanied by the contention that rather than coordinate foreign policy across the disparate departments and agencies of the executive, "The Special Assistant and the NSC staff had become the center of an inordinate and dangerous concentration of policymaking power within the White House."[22]

While attempting a brief review of the NSC's involvement in the coordination and planning roles, one should keep in mind the interesting thesis advanced by James Oliver and James Nathan that planning in the American political environment must take into consideration the complex Madisonian system that intentionally fragments authority and was designed as "a political and institutional environment initially contrived and subsequently evolved in a manner to frustrate the planner's efforts."[23]

This holds true especially when it comes to anything approaching what, at best, could be termed long-range planning. With one very important part of the Congress, the House of Representatives, constantly concerned with reelection, is it not likely that allowing short-term interests to predominate must be an outcome of our fragmented system?[24]

In order to facilitate this examination, the historical record should be surveyed.

The Truman NSC

Approaching the newly mandated National Security Council with the obstinacy of a Missouri mule, Harry S. Truman was slow to take advantage of the NSC, possibly fearing that the purpose of the body was to " . . . constrain the President, to bind him more closely to his senior cabinet advisers."[25] Whatever his actual thoughts on the Council, during the Truman Administration the body itself began to prove its value in the coordination and policy planning functions. Interdepartmental reviews and policy papers reflecting a strong State Department role were produced early in the period. In fact, by April 1950, approximately twenty months after the Council was organized, NSC-68 was published. This number, in itself, reveals a dynamic level of activity that has come to be associated with the birth of new Administrations.

After some initial differences over the nature of the Council's authority—operational or advisory—it was decided clearly that the advisory mission was primary.[26] The chair of the Council, after the initial NSC meeting in September 1947, when Harry S. Truman presided, fell to the Secretary of State in recognition of the major role to be played by that department.[27]

The supporting personnel structure of the Council during this early phase consisted of three principal elements: the Executive Secretary, the secretariat, and the staff. This latter element produced the studies and policy recommendations that were forwarded to the Council for its consideration.[28]

Headed by a seconded senior Foreign Service official from State, called the "Coordinator of the Staff," this group consisted of personnel detailed from the Departments of State, Army, Navy, Air Force, and the Central Intelligence Agency and became the principal interdepartmental component of the NSC.

In November 1947 a fourth element was added to the overall NSC structure in the form of "consultants" to the Executive Secretary. These consultants consisted of the chiefs of plans and operations for the Army, Navy, and Air Force; the Chief of the Policy Planning Staff, State Department; and the Director of Central Intelligence. Seven months later, the NSRB also appointed a consultant. Eventually, in 1949, the Director of the Joint Chiefs of Staff, JCS, was also designated as an NSC Consultant.[29] Thus, the basic two-level interagency staff organization that has functioned in the NSC to the present was created.

Four general categories of policy papers were produced during this period for Council consideration: wide-ranging, overall policy papers dealing with national security strategy issues having political, economic, and military implications; regional or country specific studies; functional policies related to such subjects as arms control, proliferation and East-West trade; and organizational policies relating to the NSC itself and its coordination in certain intelligence areas.[30]

After several years of experience, the Executive Secretary of the NSC requested the Coordinator to have the staff accomplish the following tasks:

> a. conduct a periodical review of all current national security policies in order to determine what revisions were necessary; and
> b. undertake a program of studies on major policy problems and analyze alternative courses of action open to the United States, *without, however, making policy recommendations.*[31] (Emphasis added)

Recommendations for studies came from a variety of sources during those early years. Most requests, by far, for agenda items came from the State Department, with the combined topics of the Secretary of Defense, and Departments of the Army and Air Force coming a close second. Other sources of projects were the NSC Staff itself, the State-Army-Navy–Air Force Coordinating Committee (terminated in June 1949), the CIA, and the Department of Commerce.[32]

Of special interest to an observer, some thirty-five years later, is the fact that staff members, although located in the Old Executive Office Bulding, also had offices in and maintained contact with their parent organizations. This, in theory, made it easy for staff members to obtain their parent organization's input on issues as they were processed.

Reports emanating from this initial staff were drafted by one of the members—usually from the State Department—and then forwarded, after several meetings, to the Consultants for their views. If the paper was judged adequate—not necessarily perfect—it would be forwarded to the Council itself for consideration. In the event of differences among the Consultants, the Executive Secretary might convene a meeting of that body of individuals. Opinions still "outside" the paper were recorded and the entire paper was submitted to the NSC. Involvement of the JCS was ensured through the Secretary of Defense, who would obtain its views on military issues and circulate them to the NSC members. Papers were brief; they outlined the problem, provided an analysis, and proffered conclusions. Normally, it was only on the conclusions that the Council acted.[33]

Occasionally papers were submitted directly to the NSC for consideration from one of the statutory members—at this time principally the Secretary of State; as the international environment more clearly divided along East-West lines, ad hoc committees of more senior membership than the NSC staff gradually came to play a greater role as sources of policies.

Once the NSC met, the Executive Secretary would forward to the President a record of the Council's recommendations, and the President would act, resolving any differences and establishing the national policy.[34] His decisions were then distributed to NSC members and implemented by the appropriate government departments and agencies. Overall coordinative oversight responsibility was established in a memo from the Executive Secretary, with the State Department being the most frequent agent. That agent was expected to implement the recommendations, disseminate the particulars of the policy throughout the government, and submit progress reports to the Council for review as agenda items. These reports were submitted, on the average, every six months, allowing for continuing oversight and resolution of differences over implementation, should any arise.[35]

As this embryonic structure was placed under the pressure of war in Korea, the overwhelming influence of the State Department was somewhat reduced and a senior staff was created from the agencies represented on the NSC, replacing the role the Consultants had played, and being brought into NSC work to a much greater degree than their predecessors.[36] Attempts were made to reduce the distance that had developed between members of the staff and their parent agencies, incorporating measures to work at the home agency more often than before.

A rather important change was made also during this period as the Executive Secretary became Chairman of the Senior Staff. This introduced greater independence and was followed by a parallel appointment of a member of the permanent Council staff as the Chairman of the second, more junior-level, interdepartmental group composed of the staff assistants.[37]

Following the outbreak of war in Korea, President Truman regularly attended the NSC meetings. This resulted in more focused debate and policy recommendations during the Council meetings.

By the end of the Truman Administration, the basic coordinative and policy planning structure of the NSC had evolved, with the formal NSC at the top, supported by a senior staff and a junior staff. A "neutral" Executive Secretary, heading the supporting staff structure to interact directly, on a daily basis, with the President, was to provide intelligence updates, prebriefs for NSC meetings, and to serve as a general conduit between the President and the supporting structure. In addition, a coordinator was also designated as the chairman for the staff assistants or junior-level groups. Off-line, but increasingly important to policy formulation, were steering committees consisting of selected representatives of the two staffs. This method of advice facilitated a candid exchange among representatives of affected agencies, prior to submission of the policy papers to the full membership of the two interdepartmental groups.

The relationship between the senior- and junior-level staffs had been reversed since the first days, with the senior level becoming more closely involved and the junior level being expected to be present at their home agencies on a more frequent basis, to prevent the "semi-estrangement" that had occurred earlier. They continued to do the "pick and shovel" work with regard to draft policy papers, but their location in their home agencies allowed for greater identification with vital agency desires.

This system permitted a high degree of formal coordination, alerting departments early when an issue of interest was developing. The State Department remained the originator of most policy papers at this stage of the NSC's development; it appears that the papers not actually drafted by the NSC staff were introduced either at the senior staff or "membership" level and were then distributed to the junior staff for first review, coordinative comments, and "scrubbing," prior to review by the senior staff and consideration by the Council itself.

Prior to consideration by the Council, distribution of the draft paper was made to the membership; JCS comments were also solicited. The responsible senior staff representative prebriefed his "member" or principal before an NSC meeting, and the Executive Secretary briefed the President.[38]

President Truman, during the latter stage, used the NSC meeting as an opportunity to hear the exchange of views on policy matters, but rarely used the forum as a place actually to make his policy decision. Taking the policy recommendations as agreed upon (or not agreed on) during the meeting of principals, he would later make his decisions. At that time, decisions about departmental responsibility for policy implementation were made, with progress reports expected approximately six months from the decision date.

The system seemed to ensure sufficient coordination among the main national security bureaucracies, even when the principals were at loggerheads. During this period, even though Secretary of State Dean Acheson was not on speaking terms with Defense Secretary Louis Johnson,[39] who had strong reservations, the most famous product of this new structure, NSC-68, was completed. Interestingly, President Truman never "explicitly approved" the recommendations of this significant policy paper, only asking the NSC for "further information on the implications of the conclusions. . . ."[40]

Besides successfully coordinating policy papers, the Truman NSC also provided a formalized system of implementation review. In speaking of the NSC, Dean Acheson noted that President Truman introduced to Executive administration two important elements, the concept of law that " . . . all parties in interest . . . be present before the court at the same time with the right to be heard and to hear one another," and a practice of law that "the decision . . . [be] immediately reduced to writing."[41]

Acheson stated:

It [the NSC] was kept small; aides and brief-carriers were excluded, a practice . . . that made free and frank debate possible. Those present came prepared to present their views themselves, and had previously filed memoranda. Matters brought before the council were of importance worthy of the personal attention of the highest officers and decisions by the President."[42]

His highest compliment to the system was paid when he, in speaking about Presidential responsibility, noted that it was the President's duty to perform the "anguish of decision, and to decide one must know the real issues." He thus strongly implied that it was the Truman NSC system that provided the President with the necessary adversary process to produce the "real issues."[43]

Decades of Reform, Reappraisal, and Revival

During the Administrations of Eisenhower, Kennedy, Johnson, Nixon, and Ford, the NSC structure—indeed, some argue, the entire high-level foreign-policy-making system—was adjusted to fit the personal style of the incumbent. While it is not the purpose of this study to examine each administration in detail, a few brief comments on coordination and policy formulation within the NSC are appropriate.

President Eisenhower, at the beginning of his Administration, turned to Mr. Robert Cutler to review the existing NSC system and report on any needed reforms. His report, issued in March 1953, recommended several significant changes: the recognition of the NSC and its supporting staffs as advisers to the President in their own right, not as mere agency representatives; the renaming of the Senior Staff (Assistant Secretary level) as the "Planning Board" to continue as the principal source of policy initiatives; the creation of the post of Special Assistant to the President for National Security Affairs as the Chairman of the Planning Board and principal executive officer of the NSC; the limitation of the duties of the Executive Secretary to those of head of the career staff of the NSC; and the establishment of a clear tenure distinction between the politically appointed NSC, Planning Board, and the Special Assistant, on the one hand, and the career NSC staff on the other.

Some six months later, the system was changed still further to enhance the ability of the White House to coordinate the implementation of policy decisions.[44] An Operations Coordinating Board was created, with representatives at the Undersecretary level to coordinate and develop detailed operations plans to "achieve better integrated direction of the program of the United States in the world struggle and to fill the gap which has existed in the past between the formulation of general objectives and the detailed actions needed to give effect to them."[45]

This general structure proved highly successful in meeting the challenges of government raised during the two heart attacks of President Eisenhower. With Vice-President Nixon as a participant, the NSC was used to ensure continuity of government. Eisenhower's own concept of the NSC was that it was a:

... corporate body composed of individuals advising the President in their own right, rather than as representatives of their respective departments and agencies. Their function should be to seek, with their background of experience, the most statesmanlike solution to the problems of national security.[46]

Though the above may sound too idealistic, it can be said that Eisenhower's system featured "advocacy and disagreement" at the lower levels of the policy formulation system, with policy agreements rising to the senior level on occasion, according to Alexander George. The "conventional depiction of Eisenhower's NSC system as an unimaginative, bureaucratic body laden with the preparation of presentation of cautiously formulated positions, . . . is not justified."[47] George points out also that "genuine policy debate" occurred in camera between the impacted parties, often just before the larger NSC meetings themselves.[48] However, at the time there was a perception that the formal NSC system had become "irrelevant to most of Eisenhower's actual policy decisions,"[49] and that, while coordination and policy planning had reached their formalistic heights under Eisenhower, the charge was heard that it had become a "cumbersome peppermill."[50] All this was to change under President Kennedy.

The NSC structure that had evolved since 1947 underwent fundamental dismantling with Kennedy's election. The Planning Board and the Operations Coordinating Board were abolished.[51] The NSC staff came to serve the President rather than the NSC. The position of Special Assistant for National Security Affairs went to McGeorge Bundy, but its duties were changed to focus on the management of the President's daily national security affairs. In quick order the distinction that had been carefully nurtured between planning and operations was eliminated.[52]

Others joined the NSC staff, but were soon working for Kennedy—almost directly. Robert Komer captures the new dynamism that spread to the Old Executive Building:

[The NSC label] was merely a budgetary device. Since NSC already had its own budget, it was sacrosanct. So instead of adding people to the White House staff, Bundy carried them all over here. But, in fact, Kennedy made very clear we were his men, we operated for him, we had direct contact with him. This gave us the power to command the kind of results that he wanted—a fascinating exercise in a presidential staff technique, which insofar as I know, has been unique in the history of the presidency.[53]

The staff acted as the eyes and ears of the President. The NSC continued to meet as a sounding board, but not as the decision-making locus. Coordination and policy planning were accomplished by the President's men attending interagency meetings, through interdepartmental task forces created to address key regional issues, and by the spin-off, direct and indirect, of the "collegial model" of Presidential management.[54]

Most characteristic of his method of planning was JFK's use of the Executive Committee (ExCom) mechanism during the Cuban missile crisis. President Kennedy assembled these members of the NSC and told them to "set aside all other tasks to make a prompt and intense survey of the dangers and all possible courses of action."[55]

Power in this kind of environment naturally devolves to the traditional bureaucracy for all but the items of interest to the President. The fast-moving White House staff can outdistance the slower traditional organizations, but they—of necessity—must focus only on selected issues. Coordination, planning, and follow-through were to be the product of "day-to-day decisions and actions."[56]

This apparent disdain for formal structures to facilitate coordination and policy making was continued during the years of the Johnson Administration. It might be said that informal mechanisms took on a formal hue. The Tuesday lunches became the institution of State, DoD, Presidential coordination and planning. However, the State Department took on a renewed importance, and in 1967 a newly created Senior Interdepartmental Group (SIG) process was formed.

This interdepartmental group made up of the Undersecretaries of State, Defense, and Treasury, the Deputy Director of CIA, and the Chairman of the JCS, was chaired by the Undersecretary of State. On paper it revitalized the dormant process of reviewing options before they were placed before the NSC and once again elevated oversight and policy follow-through to a collective review. Underneath the SIG was a network of regional interagency groups, all chaired by representatives from the Department of State.

However, since the NSC did not meet frequently, the SIG, created to review input to the NSC, also met infrequently. The process, according to Kissinger, was unpopular with all but the Department of State and had little but cosmetic value.[57] Of interest to our review, however, was the fact that the need for such bodies for planning and oversight was recognized. Decisions continued to be made at the Tuesday lunches.

The NSC continued to meet infrequently and was used to put the seal of legitimacy on policy decisions made in other forums. Attempts to use the system to coordinate views, plan in any rational matter, or to examine the implementation of policy apparently were so weak or haphazard that the role of the NSC in national security policy became an issue in the 1968 Presidential campaign.

In his critique of the decision-making system of the Kennedy-Johnson era, Henry Kissinger opined: "If key decisions are made informally at unprepared meetings, the tendency to be obliging to the President and cooperative with one's colleagues may vitiate the articulation of real choices."[58] To avoid such a situation, Kissinger, the newly appointed Assistant to the President for National Security Affairs, intended to utilize the "regularity and efficiency of the National Security Council" but to couple it with procedures that would ensure that the President and the remaining advisers would be exposed to all the "realistic alternatives."[59] In addition to these lofty normative goals, President Nixon added one very specific instruction: "Influence of State Department establishment must be reduced."[60]

While Nixon was convinced of the "Foreign Service's ineradicable hostility to him," and thus desired a White House focus for policy initiatives, Kissinger placed the need for a revised coordinative and policy planning structure on the more scholarly basis that a President should not be captive to the "presentation of his options" by any one department or agency.[61]

Accordingly, an intricate NSC structure that once again placed the NSC and its supporting structure at the center of the policy process was created. In essence, coordinative and policy planning was exercised by the Presidential Assistant, who ended up chairing a number of sub-Cabinet committees with participation by senior-level officials of the sub-Cabinet rank.[62]

Functions of the previous Planning Board were accomplished by several committees, all chaired by Henry Kissinger: The Senior Review Group ensured that studies from the Interdepartmental Groups were of high quality and omitted "strawman" options to meet agency policy desires; other committees, the Washington Special Actions Group (WSAG), the Intelligence Committee, the International Energy Review Group, and the Verification Panel all dealt with the short-term and long-term aspects of integrating and coordinating government planning efforts for U.S. foreign policy. Two other committees ensured that the policy decisions recommended to and taken by the President would be reflected in policy execution. These two committees were the Undersecretaries Committee and the Defense Program Review Committee—together they accomplished the functions of the former Operations Coordinating Board.

The Undersecretaries Committee was chaired by the Deputy Secretary of State and was, therefore, the only senior NSC body not headed by Henry Kissinger. Its task was overseeing the execution of foreign policy throughout the Executive Department. While the second committee, the Defense Program Review Committee, did not receive the press that the Undersecretaries Committee did, its charter to coordinate budgetary issues between contending national priorities was significant. In a sense, this committee chaired by the Assistant for National Security Affairs was in a position to influence one of the most important phases of policy—the allocation of funds.[63]

During the second Nixon Administration, the White House, emasculated by Watergate, did not continue as the locus of decision making. The role of President Nixon's key lieutenants, Secretary of State Kissinger and Secretary of Defense James R. Schlesinger, became key to the decision-making process. Severe critics of that period characterized the process as a repeat of President Johnson's Tuesday lunches, without the President and not on Tuesdays.[64]

During the Ford Administration, the NSC received new emphasis, at least in the number of meetings held by the NSC and its subgroups; however, at least two committees from the Nixon period had atrophied and continued in that condition. The two were the Defense Program Review Committee and the International Energy Review Group.[65] Considerable reorganization took place in the intelligence area, but, since many of these coordinative roles remain classified, I have not attempted to survey them in this chapter. The NSC and its Assistant for National Security, Brent Scowcroft, continued to feel the influence of a strong Secretary of State as coordination and planning seemed to come increasingly under State's influence.

The election of November 1976 brought another thoughtful academician to the post of Presidential Assistant for National Security Affairs. Zbigniew Brzezinski, in his initial talks with President-elect Jimmy Carter, learned that the new President had certain goals for his NSC. One of those goals was to have an assertive NSC that would more adequately integrate the DoD into the decision-making process.[66] Brzezinski himself saw his role as "a protagonist as well as a coordinator of policy. . . ."[67]

This concern with coordination was evinced in Brzezinski's private journal some ten days before he took up his official duties. On 11 January he wrote:

> It is . . . increasingly evident that the coordination of foreign policy and the infusion of it with strategic content will have to come from this office [the NSC]. The way the Executive Branch has been set up, and particularly the staffing of the State Department, seems to indicate that operational decisions, negotiations, and so forth may well be handled from the State Department, Defense Department, and other agencies, but that there is no single source of larger strategic thinking and innovation in the government.[68]

Brzezinski's first attempt at an appropriate NSC structure with seven committees, much like that of the previous administration, was rejected "out of hand" by President-elect Carter.[69] In its place a two-committee system was recommended to ensure coordination.

The Policy Review Committee (PRC) was to handle foreign policy, defense policy, and international economic issues and set broad and long-term policy; it would be chaired by the appropriate Secretary, i.e., the one responsible for requesting change or submitting an initiative. (Most often, during the four years, it was chaired by the Secretary of State, occasionally the Secretary of Defense, and several times by the Treasury Secretary.)[70]

The Special Coordination Committee was organized to deal with decisions relating to sensitive intelligence, U.S. arms control policy, and crisis management. In order to ensure that the President's political interests be protected and the chair be as impartial (i.e., nondepartmental) as possible, it was decided that it would be chaired by the Assistant for National Security Affairs.[71]

To help ensure that coordination actually occurred in a realistic environment, the Assistant to the President for National Security Affairs was given Cabinet rank.[72]

Brzezinski, in his memoirs, reveals how he personally looked at coordination. "Coordination is predominance. . . . And the key to asserting effective coordination was the right of direct access to the President. . . . [73]

The decision-making process in the Carter NSC theoretically had a distinct flow. First, a request for policy review would be executed either by a formal Presidential Review Memorandum (PRM) or a request for an options paper. Papers would be prepared by the chairing department for a PRC issue or by the NSC staff for an SCC meeting. Second, as a result of a meeting to review the paper or memorandum, the PRC or SCC would make its recommendations; these would be prepared by the NSC staff and forwarded to the Assistant for National Security Affairs for submission to the President. Note that the flow did not return to the Secretary who chaired the meeting, but involved the Presidential Assistant.[74] Third, the Presidential decisions were published as Presidential Directives for important matters or as decision memos for more routine items, and sent to the appropriate Secretaries for action.[75]

In assessing the success of his own coordination and policy-making system, the former Special Assistant for National Security Affairs (Brzezinski) lamented the fact that the Carter Administration in starting major initiatives on human rights, nonproliferation, Panama, southern Africa, and conventional arms sales had " . . . attempted to do too much all at once. This reduced our effectiveness."[76] One could question whether this failure was systemic or due to powerful incumbents not fully appreciating the limitation on the President's authority by a recalcitrant bureaucracy.

Perhaps the problem was systemic, since, organizationally, oversight responsibility for review of the progress of PD implementation could have been more clearly addressed. Was the creation of a Global Issues Cluster of two individuals within the NSC staff adequate to deal with such items as "human rights and the range of problems that cut across traditional foreign policy areas," as envisaged in "Zbig's" goal?[77]

In any event, the appearance of the Administration was one of too many initiatives not well coordinated and even more poorly executed. Of special note during this period was the proposal to withdraw U.S. forces from Korea. Its handling and subsequent reversal did much to create an atmosphere of the hapless giant. The impact of the Iranian hostage crisis and the failed U.S. rescue mission in large measure contributed to the election outcome that brought candidate Ronald Reagan to office.

The formal structure for coordination and policy planning did not evolve until February 1981, a good month after the Administration of President Reagan took office. In fact, this was the first of two NSC systems for Reagan's initial period.

The first system was influenced overwhelmingly by a strong Secretary of State, and the second reflected a system and structure viewed increasingly as closer to the norm. Reports indicated that the initial NSC structure was resolved " . . . after considerable discussion and some discord. . . . "[78] The system had all the hallmarks of a reaction to "activist" Assistants to the President, such as Bundy, Kissinger, and Brzezinski. The position of Assistant for National Security Affairs was retained, but it no longer had Cabinet status. Indeed, the post significantly did not report directly to the President, but to a White House chief, Presidential Counselor Edwin Meese III. Richard V. Allen, the person chosen to head the NSC, willingly accepted a "low profile" in a system that was designed to give leading roles in national security policy once again to the Secretaries of State and Defense and the Director of the CIA.[79] To an Administration that had talked of using Cabinet councils as a modern means for government, this enhancement of the role of the State and Defense Departments seemed natural.[80]

Early indications of the NSC policy coordination framework included the creation of three senior interdepartmental groups: one dealing with foreign policy issues, chaired by the Secretary of State; one focusing on military or defense measures, chaired by the Secretary of Defense; and one concerned with intelligence matters and headed by the Director of the CIA.[81] Determination as to which committee would consider what issues was to be left to Allen, but subsequent events revealed that power had, in truth, flowed to the energetic Secretary of State, Alexander M. Haig, Jr. Haig demonstrated his belief that the State Department should have the central role regarding national security policy formulation on inaugural day, when he submitted a fifteen-page memorandum arguing this point.[82] Haig's attempt was initially thwarted, but, due to his personality, his expertise in foreign policy, and the disruption caused by the attempted assassination of the President, the center of gravity for national security policy gradually shifted to the State Department.

In theory it appeared that the three NSC SIGs were to replace the Carter Policy Review Committee as the center for security policy formulation and coordination; in fact, the foreign policy SIG (SIG-FP) chaired by the Deputy Secretary of State became the principal functioning committee. Its charter was to supervise the work of the interdepartmental groups (IGs), chaired by the various Assistant Secretaries of State in the regional bureaus, such as the African, Asian, European, and Latin American Affairs Bureaus.

A decision concerning the NSC senior committee to replace the Carter

SCC was announced in March 1981.[83] The "crisis management" team was formed with the chair held by Vice-President Bush. Its responsibilties were outlined as coordinating and controlling "all appropriate federal resources in responding to emergency situations both foreign and domestic."[84] Of special significance were forward planning aspects of the charter, as well as provisions for review of implementation.

In July 1981 a further sign in the deemphasis of the role of the Assistant to the President for National Security Affairs was observed. The "long-standing" morning briefing to the President by the Security Adviser, which had started with McGeorge Bundy during the Kennedy Administration, were discontinued. In place of the briefing, two measures were taken to keep the President informed and to dampen the "personal infighting and private consternation" that was reported "within Reagan's national security inner circle."[85] Basically, the President opened his schedule to meet approximately three times a week with a body of advisers. This advisory group, seen as the core element for national security policy in the Reagan Administration, consisted of the Vice-President, Secretaries of State and Defense, the DCI, White House aides Meese, Baker, and Michael Deaver, and the APNSA. The second measure taken to keep the President informed was a continuation of the morning briefing in written form. Allen came in, waited for questions regarding the material, and left the discussion between President Reagan and his principal aides if there were no questions.[86]

This system functioned, admittedly with a high degree of friction, until Richard Allen resigned from the NSC in January 1982. While his decision to step down from his national security post was prompted by alleged improprieties, his position in the Administration had been weakened by an almost constant divisive interaction between members of the NSC staff and the State Department. His departure was followed by three events that led to the formulation of the current NSC system: the appointment of Judge William P. Clark as the Assistant to the President for National Security Affairs in January 1982; the departure in June of the same year of Secretary Haig; and the replacement of Haig with a new Secretary of State, George P. Shultz, who took office on 1 July 1982.

These personnel changes ended the period of incessant competition and confrontation among members of the national security bureaucracy and replaced it with a term of renewed vigor in the formulation and coordination of policy.

Shortly after the appointment of Judge Clark, the formal structure of the NSC was released to the press.[87] Roles of the Secretaries of State, Defense, and the DCI, were mentioned as well as those of the Interagency Group for Foreign Policy (SIG-FP); Defense Policy (SIG-DP); and Intelligence (SIG-I). Of interest was the requirement that besides policy formulation these senior groups were to monitor the execution of decisions and evaluate the adequacy and effectiveness of the line operations.

The supporting Interagency Groups (IGs) were also established by this same directive. The Department of State was given the task of establishing IGs in each of its geographic bureaus, and in the bureaus of Political-Military Affairs and International Economic Affairs.[88] The respective Chairmen of these IGs were made responsible for assuring "the adequacy of United States policy . . . and of the plans, programs, resources, and performance for implementing that policy." Regional IGs were also given the task of preparing any contingency plans "pertaining to potential crises in their respective areas."[89] Once specific contingencies occurred, IGs "will establish full time working groups" to support the crisis management team. Similar tasks were given to the IGs associated with the SIG-DP and the SIG-I. This new organizational structure for policy formulation soon began to be augmented with other bodies created for specific purposes.

In May of 1982, a planning group on potential crises was created. Chaired by the Deputy Assistant to the President for National Security Affairs, Robert C. (Bud) McFarlane, this group plays a major role in the oversight of interagency attention to possible crisis areas or situations.

Shortly after the June '82 economic summit at Versailles and the arrival of Secretary of State Shultz, a Senior Interdepartmental Group for International Economic Policy (SIG-IEP) was formed. Its charter is to be the senior coordinating mechanism for international economic policy, and it is chaired by the Secretary of the Treasury, Donald T. Regan. The Vice-Chairman is the Secretary of State. Also during the spring of 1982, the Senior Interdepartmental Group on Space (SIG-Space) was organized to coordinate policy toward the U.S. role in space. It is chaired by the Assistant to the President for National Security Affairs, and it is reported that the supporting IGs from this SIG are relatively active.

Several independent commissions also have been established or reactivated to examine questions outside the SIG network. These include the National Security Telecommunications Advisory Commission, the President's Commission on Strategic Forces (to handle the MX), the Commission on Foreign Assistance, and the General Advisory Commission on Arms Control (the latter body also changed membership). Several intelligence boards responsible for policy oversight and to check possible intelligence abuses also have been formed.

Thus, from a period of almost no activity in the NSC system, when only seven or eight Presidential security directives were issued in an entire year, during Judge Clark's tenure the number increased dramatically. The Reagan Administration has entered a period of intense systematic activity, reversing the period when practically the entire disciplined decision-making system was ignored. While this activity halfway into the first term reverses the trend of recent administrations, it has in essence—more by accident than original design—executed a midcourse NSC correction as advocated by I. M. Destler in one of his excellent reviews of the NSC system. Destler makes the point that "the advisory system that a President finds two or three years into his term is not precisely what he or anyone else intended."[90] In the case of President Reagan, he suffered through a year of confrontation and "turf battles," but by the middle of 1982 had shifted back to an NSC model more suitable to his own management style.

The staff is still moderate in size—fewer than fifty professionals, with one-third being military; one-third civilian government professionals from such agencies as State, CIA, Commerce, and Treasury; plus one-third academic or other professional advisers.

The proliferation of interdepartmental groups and the increase in activity during this later phase of President Reagan's first term required, for instance, that Judge Clark and his then deputy "Bud" McFarlane act as efficient facilitators and honest brokers in order to keep a rather complex and obviously overlapping system on track.

The willingness, even enthusiasm, of President Reagan for the new structure lends some credence to the idea that he is not at all uncomfortable with certain aspects of the competitive model of Presidential advice, as discussed by Alexander L. George. On the other hand, when such competition becomes disruptive and dysfunctional, he prefers a more formalistic model, using an efficient manager to minimize personal confrontation.

Has the current system achieved the level of coordination and policy planning potential desired by the President? Not having direct access to the President himself, this author is not in a position to be definitive; however, based on an informed assessment, it appears that the current NSC system meets extremely well the needs of President Reagan's management style. Reviewing the major roles played by the NSC leads to the following assessment:

POLICY COORDINATION

In this area of primary NSC responsibility—"to integrate all aspects of national policy relating to security affairs"[91]—the Reagan NSC can be given good to improving marks. Some technical problems have occurred. For example, on the eve of Secretary of State Shultz's visit to China, the United States government announced the imposition of textile import quotas on the Chinese texile industry. In the words of Henry Kissinger, this "makes one wonder about the coordinating mechanism in our government."[92] Coordinating the MX decision also continues to cause problems. However, these difficulties of execution do not have the same overall policy ramifications as the situation that existed during the Carter Administration, when the NSC pursued mutually exclusive policy objectives that had a very unsettling impact on our alliances and our perceived position of leadership in the world. A basic strategy has been articulated that is internally consistent, and the NSC is coordinating the development of subsequent policy.[93] In this arena, the role of the (then) Assistant to the President for National Security Affairs,

Judge William Clark, must be mentioned. It is quite evident that Judge Clark was directing the system as an equal to other White House aides and as an "honest broker." He reversed the trend, as evident in the Nixon and Carter NSCs, for the Assistant to the President to become an advocate of certain policy options. This development, of course, was directly related to the character of the Assistant and the President himself. Judge Clark enjoyed the confidence of the President and saw himself more as a coordinator than as a protagonist.

Given these basic ingredients—an overall strategy, an existing NSC framework, and an integrative management—the function of policy coordination will continue to be accomplished by the current system in an increasingly able manner.

POLICY PLANNING

The system appears to be functioning again after a very slow start. While fewer than two dozen of so National Security Study Directives requiring the completion of an interagency study, have been formally initiated by the President, the system has generated considerably more National Security Decision Directives resulting from the consideration of options by the President. Most of these have been promulgated since the arrival of Clark and McFarlane.[94]

A recent request for an NSC study was announced on national TV and called for an examination of defensive systems to guard against ICBM attack. It is apparent that the planning system is being utilized, but from appearances the initiating sources are at a sub-Presidential level, coming either from the NSC staff or the agencies themselves.

While the exact nature of current planning is not a subject for general public review, the present system is structured to engage in the broad spectrum of policy formulation. The basic assumptions necessary to produce long-term plans and strategies have been articulated, as was evident in the security review accomplished in the April–May period of 1982. The current NSC has also structured itself to carry out integrative planning for geographical area policies. This can be observed in the Caribbean Basin initiative and in measures to create an integrated arms control proposal that looks at the implications of intermediate-range missile deployments not only for Europe but also for East Asia. Finally, a third kind of activity that is generic to the NSC has been contingency planning. The current structure seems to address this area adequately, not only in the formal SIG structure, but in the unique oversight body responsible for crisis planning. This group will have the capacity to focus on areas of potential conflict, benefiting from its position at the apex of the national security structure.

In its coordinative and planning functions, the current NSC appears to be assuming the role of "honest broker," as opposed to more direct participator in the advancement of unique NSC concepts or propositions. In returning to a more neutral role in the national security decision-making arena, the Reagan NSC has taken its cue from a tradition just as successful, if not more so, than the more charismatic models for the nation.

Conclusions

As can be seen from this cursory review of the history of the NSC's development and the Council's attempt to accomplish its primary mission to ensure that U.S. national security policy is coordinated and thus, one hopes, effective, there have been many approaches to "truth."

No one system in itself can ensure that the "right" option is, in fact, delivered to the President for his review. Indeed, no system will ensure that the President, even if presented with the "right" option, will ultimately choose it. However, over time, it appears that a formalized method of coordination and policy planning is absolutely necessary to meet and overcome the challenges presented by the nuclear era. The time is now long gone when such matters could be accomplished at a leisurely pace or even after critical events begin to unfold. The NSC, its supporting staff, and the entire interagency network responsive to its calls for updated policy in the face of continuous and complex challenges, are an absolutely essential element in today's international environment. The NSC must be able to accomplish these two vital functions "but its nature, as pointed out previously, is very much dependent on the personal style and wishes of the President whom it serves. In retrospect, it has fulfilled the original charter of 1947 and continues to be adaptive to changing requirements as a coordinator of activities and interests in the formulation and execution of various aspects of national security policy."[95]

NOTES

1. Senate Subcommittee on National Policy Machinery, Senator Henry M. Jackson, Chairman, *Organizing for National Security*, vol. 2, 417. Hereafter referred to as the *Jackson Report*.
2. Gordon W. Keiser, *The U.S. Marine Corps and Defense Unification, 1944–47: The Politics of Survival* (Washington, D.C.: National Defense University Press, 1982), 17.
3. Ibid., 18.
4. Ibid.
5. Ibid., 140.
6. Ibid., 141.
7. Ibid., 9.
8. Ibid., 25.
9. Ibid., 53–54.
10. Ibid., 61.
11. Ibid., 82.
12. Ibid., 107.
13. Jackson Report, 418.
14. Keiser, 42.

15. Ibid., 120.

16. Stanley L. Falk, *The National Security Structure* (Washington, D.C.: Industrial College of the Armed Forces, 1967), 35.

17. Ibid., 35–36.

18. Jackson Report, 161.

19. Falk, 34.

20. James K. Oliver and James A. Nathan, "The American Environment for Security Planning," in *Planning U.S. Security*, Philip S. Kronenberg, ed. (Washington, D.C.: National Defense University, 1981), 42.

21. Ibid.

22. Ibid.

23. Ibid., 50.

24. Lawrence J. Korb, "On Making the System Work," in Kronenberg, 139.

25. I. M. Destler, "National Security Advice to U.S. Presidents," *World Politics*, January 1977, 146.

26. Jackson Report, 419–20.

27. Ibid., 21.

28. Ibid., 424.

29. Ibid., 425.

30. Ibid., 426.

31. Ibid.

32. Ibid., 27.

33. Ibid., 427.

34. Ibid., 29.

35. Ibid., 30.

36. Ibid., 34.

37. Ibid., 435.

38. Ibid., 438.

39. Destler, "National Security Advice," 52.

40. *Naval War College Review*, May–June 1975, 52.

41. Dean Acheson, *Present at the Creation* (New York: Norton, 1969), 733.

42. Ibid.

43. Ibid.

44. Jackson Report, 445–59.

45. Ibid., 454.

46. Ibid., 447–48.

47. Alexander George, *Presidential Decisionmaking in Foreign Policy* (Boulder, Colo.: Westview Press, 1980), 153.

48. Ibid., 152–53.

49. I. M. Destler, "National Security Management: What Presidents Have Wrought," *Political Science Quarterly*, Winter 1980–81, 578.

50. Ibid.

51. Destler, "National Security Advice," 53.

52. Destler, "What Presidents Have Wrought," 578.

53. Ibid., 579.

54. George, 57.

55. Graham T. Allison, "Conceptual Models and the Cuban Missile Crisis," in *American Defense Policy*, Head and Rokke, eds., 3d ed. (Baltimore: Johns Hopkins University Press, 1973), 277.

56. Destler, "National Security Advice," 153.

57. Henry Kissinger, *The White House Years* (Boston: Little, Brown, 1979), 42.

58. Ibid., 40.

59. Ibid., 41–42.

60. Ibid., 43.

61. Ibid.

62. Zbigniew Brzezinski, *Power and Principle* (New York: Farrar, Straus & Giroux, 1983), 58.

63. John E. Endicott, "The NSC: Formulating National Security Policy . . . ," in *American Defense Policy*, Endicott and Stafford, eds., 4th ed. (Baltimore: Johns Hopkins University Press, 1977), 317–18.

64. Leslie Gelb, "Nixon Role in Foreign Policy is Altered . . . ," *New York Times*, 24 December 1973.
65. Endicott, 319.
66. Brzezinski, 2.
67. Ibid., 29.
68. Ibid., 48.
69. Ibid., 59.
70. Ibid.
71. Ibid.
72. Ibid., 60.
73. Ibid., 63.
74. Ibid., 30.
75. Ibid., 1.
76. Ibid., 145.
77. Ibid., 125.
78. *Washington Post*, 26 February 1981.
79. Ibid.
80. Ibid.
81. Ibid.
82. Ibid.
83. White House Press Release, 24 March 1981.
84. Ibid.
85. *Washington Post*, 12 July 1981.
86. Ibid.
87. White House Press Release, 12 June 1982.
88. Ibid.
89. Ibid.
90. Destler, "National Security Advice," 174.
91. Robert H. Johnson, "The National Security Council: The Relevance of its Past to its Future," *Orbis*, Fall 1969, 720–29.
92. *Washington Post*, 30 January 1983.
93. White House Press Release, 21 May 1982; remarks by Judge William Clark, National Security Adviser to the President.
94. William P. Clark, "National Security Strategy," a speech delivered at Georgetown University, 21 May 1982.
95. Endicott, 319.

8

Policy Planning and Resource Allocations In the U.S. Department of Defense: An Outsider's View

Michael Hobkirk

"Strategy, program and budget are all aspects of the same basic decision." Has anyone ever set the context of defense resource allocation more
concisely and precisely than President Truman, in this excerpt from his
message to Congress on 19 December 1945, asking for unification of the
defense structure? However, despite this acute analysis not all the President's
aims for the new Department of Defense had been achieved by 1983, judging
by criticism, notably from General David Jones, who retired in 1982 as
Chairman of the Joint Chiefs of Staff.

Before considering the Planning, Programming, and Budgeting System, which should be the principal tool for resource allocation within
defense, it is important to see how far the Department of Defense has
progressed toward unification since 1945.

The Evolution of a Unified Department of Defense

Before 1942, the Armed Forces of the United States had no equivalent to
the British Chiefs of Staff, and any coordination of strategic plans had to be
undertaken by the President himself—often, no doubt, as in President
Roosevelt's time, with the assistance of an informal committee consisting of
the Secretaries of State, for War, and of the Navy, and their Chiefs of Staff.
The decision taken after Pearl Harbor to set up a supreme Anglo-American
military staff for the strategic direction of the war led inevitably to the
creation of the American Joint Chiefs of Staff (JCS). The British and
American Chiefs of Staff worked closely together until the end of hostilities,
but the JCS had to wait until 1947 for its status to be established formally in
the National Security Act.

Congress required two years of debate and negotiation before accepting
President Truman's view that there was enough evidence to justify the need
for a unified Defense Department. Instead of one unified department, the

1947 National Security Act created a Secretary of Defense exercising general authority and control over three separate Service Departments. Congress also retained the right to question each Service separately about its expenditures. Inevitably, the defects in these arrangements began to appear when it became necessary to suballocate defense funds among the three Services. Mr. Forrestal, the former Secretary of the Navy and an opponent of the concept of a wholly unified Department, became the first Secretary of Defense. He saw himself as the coordinator rather than the controller of defense policy and resource allocation, but he found it difficult to sustain this role when preparing defense budgets in 1948 and 1949. He could obtain no help from the JCS in putting forward realistic proposals to the President, and, when the inevitable cuts were imposed, Mr. Forrestal had to allocate these to the Services as he thought best, without help from his military advisers.

By 1949, however, Mr. Forrestal, once a strong opponent of unification, had had second thoughts. Just before his death in 1949, he told the Senate Armed Services Committee that "after having viewed the problem at close range for the past 18 months, I must admit to you quite frankly that my position on the question has changed. I am now convinced that there are adequate checks and balances inherent in our governmental structure to prevent misuse of the broad authority which I feel must be vested in the Secretary of Defence."[1] The 1949 Amendments to the National Security Act accorded with Mr. Forrestal's views. The Service Departments were abolished as separate entities and merged into an enlarged Department of Defense. The Secretary of Defense was given full control over the whole Department, and the office of the Secretary of Defense (OSD) was enlarged to assist him. In addition, a new post, Chairman of the Joint Chiefs of Staff, was created to preside over JCS meetings. Sweeping as these changes were, Congress set two important limits on the extent of unification. The Services were to be separately administered still, and the Chairman of the JCS was not required to give independent advice to the Secretary of Defense, but had to act essentially as the spokesman of the JCS.

In 1953 President Eisenhower further increased the powers of the Secretary of Defense and the Chairman of the JCS; but he found it necessary in 1958, to invite Congress to agree to additional steps toward a completely unified Department. With such changes, he predicted, "the tendency toward service rivalry and controversy which has so deeply troubled the American people will be sharply reduced."[2] Congress accepted the President's proposals, which gave the Secretary of Defense greater flexibility in the management of defense funds and enhanced control over research and development.

In the eleven years following the creation of the Department of Defense, no fewer than four major reorganizations had taken place. The result was a unified, if not a truly united, Department. The authority of the Secretary of Defense over policy and allocation of defense funds was confirmed and a separate department (OSD) was created to support him. Nevertheless, President Truman's aim of one unified strategy, supported by a single, coherent program of weapons development, funded from one defense budget, had not been achieved. The three Service Departments, responsible for raising and equipping the forces, still controlled their own shares of the defense budget. Unless firmly directed otherwise, they tended to allocate funds to the weapons programs that they deemed important, rather than to those with a higher defense priority. When President Kennedy appointed Mr. McNamara Secretary of Defense, just after the 1960 elections, inter-Service rivalry over resource allocation was still a problem.

Mr. McNamara was predisposed to be an active manager of his department, probing for facts and suggesting alternatives to prevailing strategies and weapons programs, as well as more cost-effective methods of achieving agreed defense objectives. Consequently, he felt, the Services' practice of controlling their own shares of the defense budget should be challenged, and it seemed likely even that funds for new weapons might be transferred from one Service to another. If past experience was any guide, such "crosscutting" decisions would be bitterly resented by the Services. Instead of reorganizing the Department once more, McNamara decided to introduce new management systems and techniques, of which the Planning, Programming, and Budgeting Systems (PPBS) is the best known, to deal with the problem of inter-Service rivalry. As a result, his supporters claimed that he was the first Secretary of Defense to manage his department effectively. Some background is necessary to evaluate this assertion.

Although for some time the JCS had been producing five-year plans for forces and weapons on a single-Service basis, these had not been coordinated or matched with the funds available. Before PPBS, the main method of bridging the gap between plans and resources available was to "divide the total defense budget ceiling among the three military departments, leaving to each department, by and large, the allocation of its ceiling among its own functions and activities."[3] The new procedures were designed to change this practice. Mr. McNamara directed that the JCS should submit their strategic plans to him each spring so that he could furnish preliminary guidance for the five-year force structure and financial program on which the annual defense budget would be based. This guidance and the discussions that it entailed normally would be based on the PPBS programs, which identified a common defense mission or set of purposes without regard to the Service that funded them.

If PPBS was to be effective, it was essential that the programs should be used for the all-important task of reconciling plans and budgets. In effect, this denied each Service exclusive control over its "share" of the defense budget.

This style of active management, together with the introduction of PPBS and the wider use of systems analysis and cost-effectiveness studies, gave rise to a situation that James Roherty has described as follows: "A policy framework is set by the Secretary, much of the data base is provided by the Secretary, judgments are invited by the Secretary and decisions are made by the Secretary."[4] Since ideas and initiatives tended to come from the Secretary, the style of debate that followed had important consequences for the management of the Department of Defense. The Services were encouraged to put forward alternative methods of achieving defense objectives by the prospect of receiving extra funds if their solution was accepted. They tended, therefore, to regard each other as adversaries. As the Chairman of a Blue Ribbon Defense Panel noted: "The Panel found many things which it believes should be corrected, but it believes and I agree, that many of the difficulties result from the structure of the Department itself, which almost inevitably leads people into adversary relationships rather than cooperation in the interest of the Department—and the nation as a whole."[5]

When Mr. Laird was appointed Secretary of Defense by President Nixon after the 1968 elections, he wrote that he "inherited a system designed for highly centralized decisionmaking. Overcentralization in so large an organization leads to a kind of paralysis. Many decisions are not made at all, or if they are made, lack full coordination and commitment by those who must implement the decision."[6] Laird decided to remedy this situation by introducing what was known as participatory management. As a reuslt, "the JCS had to develop force structures within stated money ceilings provided early in the planning and budgeting process. The Services could then plan, knowing how much money they could count on and could make internal decisions about how to allocate resources aginst overall priorities."[7] The initiative in the planning process had been passed back to the Services, and, more important, they could generally rely on being able to suballocate their shares as they themselves thought fit.

It would be wrong, however, to give the impression that, either in Mr. Laird's time or subsequently, the methods and style of the resource allocation process reverted to what they had been before Mr. McNamara's arrival. PPBS has been retained, together with the apparatus and techniques that enable a Secretary of Defense to control resource allocation decisions from the center, if he wishes, instead of delegating them to the Services. However, most subsequent Secretaries of Defense have preferred Laird's to McNamara's approach, and the history of defense organization since 1969 can be reviewed quite briefly.

President Nixon's most significant change in the resource allocation process was the enlargement of the National Security Council (NSC) staff and the creation, under the NSC, of a defense Program Review Committee so that "decisions not only on the total size of the defense budget but also on major programs will be made outside the Pentagon in an interagency forum where White House influence is dominant."[8] The close involvement of the NSC in defense resource allocation has continued. Thus, if they wish, Presidents can extract from the defense apparatus those issues that they prefer to review in depth, rather than awaiting DoD submissions with prepackaged options for their decision. Notable examples of Presidential interventions (although not necessarily as a result of NSC briefings) were President

Carter's decision to cancel the B-1 bomber program and President Reagan's decision to reinstate it.

Presidents Nixon and Carter both commissioned studies of defense organization, which pointed to the harmful effects of inter-Service rivalry,[9] but the cures proposed were never fully implemented. The current position is well summarized in comments made by General David C. Jones, Chairman of the JCS, shortly before his retirement in 1982. He criticized the organization of the JCS on the grounds of (1) diffused responsibility and authority, (2) inadequate corporate advice on major issues, (3) domination of the JCS by individual Services, and (4) basic contradictions in the role of Service Chiefs as JCS members and as Heads of Services respectively. He proposed that the Chairman of the JCS should be made wholly responsible for the work of the Joint Staffs so that their advice could be defense motivated, rather than single-Service oriented. In an article published early in 1982, General Jones[10] did not deal with resource allocation specifically, but it is clear from his subsequent comments that he considers this to be one of the major issues on which the JCS fails to offer adequate advice.

Despite the substantial improvements in defense organization since 1945, the effectiveness of the resource allocation process depends very much on the President and his Secretary of Defense. If the latter has the backing of his President, then major decisions on resource allocation can be implemented by the Executive, despite the misgivings of one or more of the Services. However, in the absence of a President like Eisenhower—able to impose strategic doctrine and the consequent budget cuts on one or another of the Services, sometimes against its will—or lacking a Secretary of Defense like McNamara—able, with Presidential backing, to decide how the defense budget should be apportioned—resource allocation decisions are likely to be delegated to the Services themselves, with the attendant risk that defense policy will rest on a series of compromises among them. Before reaching an overall assessment of defense policy planning and resource allocation, it is necessary to consider in some detail the allocation process itself.

Planning, Programming and Budgeting System (PPBS)

PPBS is at the heart of the resource allocation process but clearly has not fulfilled the expectations of those who designed it. Alain Enthoven has written: "The fundamental idea behind PPBS was decision-making based on explicit criteria of the national interest in defense programs, as opposed to decision-making by compromise among various institutional, parochial or other vested interests in the Defense Department."[11] Furthermore, Enthoven suggests that such criteria must relate to the coordination of military needs and costs, furnishing the bases for choices at the highest level.

Clearly, therefore, PPBS was seen, quite rightly, as being more than an information system or a method for the organization of data that analysts could use as a base. Nevertheless, the essence of the system is the display of information describing programs that supposedly represent a coherent defense mission. This is described sometimes as output budgeting, a subject that must be described in greater detail.

When the program analysis approach was first introduced in 1963, the U.S. defense budget contained some ten programs. They included, for example, Strategic Retaliatory Forces and General Purpose Forces. Since 1963, there have been some changes within these programs, although the basic approach and the main programs remain intact. From the start, the data were laid out without regard to the Service that provided them; this furnishes the clue to the main purpose behind the system.

Before his inauguration, President Kennedy had appointed a committee, headed by Senator Stuart Symington, former Secretary of the Air Force, to study the organization of the Defense Department. The Symington Report, published late in 1960, criticized defense planning as representing at best "a series of compromise positions among the military services," as a result of the fact that the JCS had to act both as defense planners and as representatives of their Services. The Symington Committee recommended far-reaching changes in defense organization in order to insulate planners from the parochial thinking of the Service Departments.

Despite the recommendations of the Committee, McNamara decided to use PPBS to overcome the organizational defects that had been pointed out. "I am here," he said, "to originate and stimulate new ideas and programs, not just to referee arguments and harmonize interests. Using deliberate analysis to force alternative programs to the surface is fundamental."[12] Output budgeting (and hence PPBS) is a method of displaying data, not a means of creating new ideas. But PPBS ensured that those ideas that the Kennedy Administration had developed before assuming office could be considered and discussed in a context that gave new proposals the best chance of success. Thus, proposals for Polaris improvements were judged against Air Force strategic missiles and did not compete for funds with the surface fleet."

"PPBS and departmental reorganization," Allen Schick wrote, "can be regarded as partial substitutes for one another. When PPB was flourishing in the Defense Department, it was utilized to accomplish many of the objectives that had been sought in earlier reorganization attempts. Even though each of the Military Services retained its separate organizational identity, it was possible for the Secretary of Defense to make cross-cutting decisions by means of the mission oriented program budget. The Air Force had charge over Minuteman and the Navy over Polaris, but both were lodged in the strategic forces program. In this way, it was possible to overcome internal organizational constraints within DoD without having to engage in what would probably have been a futile battle to abolish the tri-Service structure."[13] The most notable success for PPBS in the McNamara era (or since) has been in the field of strategic weapons. The system was able to obtain comparisons of like with like, instead of requiring each Service to balance the cost of strategic nuclear weapons with those for conventional war. Moreover, it was possible to analyze, in very broad terms, the cost-effectiveness of the components of the strategic weapons program, because there was a generally agreed scenario of a hypothetical superpower nuclear exchange.

The lack of comparable PPBS success elsewhere in defense can be ascribed, in part at least, to the original choice of programs in the budget. Any system of output budgeting (and hence PPBS) is only as good as the programs displayed. If they are relevant to the decisions to be taken, then all is well and good. If they are not, they are liable to be just so much useless information. By separating the cost of the strategic deterrent from the rest of the defense budget, PPBS enabled sensible choices to be made between competing strategic systems, but it did little to improve the analytical tools for decision making in other aspects of defense.

One program, "General Purpose Forces," covers both those likely to be engaged in a land/air battle in a hypothetical future war and those destined for combat at sea. No useful decisions about the balance of expenditure between these two distinct areas of military operations can be made on the basis of the existing programs. No doubt, Pentagon analysts can recombine the elements of the PPBS programs in order to determine the costs. If such an effort has been made, the results have not been published or made available to Congress, so that they could serve as the basis for joint decisions by the Executive and the Legislature.

There is, of course, no one perfect set of PPBS programs that would be appropriate for all time. As the problems facing defense planners change, so should the programs or outputs displayed in the budget. There are now strong arguments for revising PPBS programs so that better decisions can be made about conventional weapons. The changes should build on the success achieved in the relatively self-contained area of strategic nuclear weapons. Two other such contingencies might be a possible land/air battle on the central front in Europe between NATO and the Warsaw Pact, together with maritime operations in a general war. Such scenarios could be the subject of two new PPBS programs, within which useful cost-effectiveness analysis would be possible. Moreover, these two, together with the existing "Strategic Forces" program, would contain most of the expensive and complex weapons systems that absorb a large proportion of the defense budget.

This brief survey of output budgeting has emphasized the success that it achieved and the esteem that it generated when first introduced in the Department of Defense. At that time, the necessary budget and other financial data were displayed in a way that helped to secure general agreement for certain solutions to pressing problems in the development of the strategic-nuclear forces, based upon an understanding of hypothetical outcomes of a strategic-nuclear exchange. If it is to regain its former usefulness and prestige, as a tool for long-term planning and defense resource allocation across the board, new and more meaningful force and weapons categories will have to be devised, even if this entails a divorce between costings as a tool for the long-term planner and a budget layout that will help the financial controller and auditor of day-to-day operations.

Comments and Suggestions

Any outsider, even an ex-bureaucrat, must be cautious about probing too deeply into another organization. Only the insider can know what changes may be made without disturbing the bureaucratic balance of power. Prescribing changes from the outside is like trying to effect an organ transplant: the bureaucratic body may well reject it. With this proviso, three comments are offered on the Defense Department's methods of resource allocation.

The first has already been mentioned. It would surely be helpful for the PPBS process if its major military programs were altered so as to highlight the problems and choices involved in preparing for conventional war. This would build on the success achieved by the PPBS program for "Strategic Forces," which isolated the costs of the nuclear deterrent previously distributed among numerous Service programs. New program categories could be:

1. Land/Air Forces for the European theater
2. Maritime (including land-based Air Forces) assigned to the North Atlantic
3. Rapid Deployment Forces, with associated sea- and airlift and stockpiles
4. Continental defense of the United States

This list is by no means comprehensive. Nevertheless, the total number of major programs, including "Strategic Forces," need not exceed twelve. The new categories would enable policy makers to see the full cost of major commitments and to ascertain if any of the tasks could be carried out more effectively by another Service.

The second comment echoes a criticism that has been made by insiders, notably General Jones. The Defense Guidance given to the Services at the start of the PPBS process is so all-embracing and imprecise that they cannot (or need not) submit spending proposals within likely budget ceilings. "The military strategy contained in the defense guidance," to quote General Jones, "always demands greater force capabilities than the budget constraints will allow. Current guidance is so demanding that developing truly coherent programs to carry it out is impossible, even under the most optimistic budget assumptions."[14] He goes on to point out that the Joint Chiefs of Staff play no useful part in cutting the defense coat to fit the defense cloth available in the final budget allocation. This lack of coordinated military advice at the final and vital stage of the resource allocation process stands in sharp contrast to the arrangements in the United Kingdom, where both the Chiefs of Staff collectively and the Chief of Defense Staff individually are closely connected both with the initial guidance and budget ceilings and with the final decisions on the spending plans submitted by the Services.

Finally, the gap between the planning and the budgeting process within DoD strikes an outsider as odd. Even within the Office of the Secretary of Defense, these two parts of the resource allocation process are carried out by different groups of civilians. The scrutiny of force levels, long-term budget plans, and weapons programs is the responsibility of the Director, Program Analysis and Evaluation, whereas everything to do with the budget is the responsibility of the Comptroller. To quote a former member of PA&E, "The real crunch is the budget and the real king is Comptroller. You can write all the DPMs [Draft Presidential Memorandums] and five-year plans, but what really counts is who gets the money. In the budget crunch, Systems Analysis fights like hell with the Comptroller. After fighting the Services in the programming stage, they have to fight on behalf of the Services for funds for the approved program. The Comptroller still makes the hard decisions."[15] This statement refers to an earlier period, before Systems Analysis became program Analysis and Evaluation; however, in one form or another, the lack of coordination, or even conflict of interest, between the budgeteers in the Comptroller's Department and those in PA&E concerned with the analysis of longer-term force structures and weapon projects has persisted. There is no precise equivalent of PA&E in the British system of resource allocation, and here, as elsewhere, the outsider finds it hard to do more than simply state the difference between the two approaches. Possibly the best solution would be to create an Undersecretary post to which the Comptroller and the Director of PA&E would report—although it should be noted that such a proposal, made some years ago, was not accepted.

Relatively modest reforms such as those suggested here should enable the Department of Defense to conduct the resource allocation process more effectively and to diminish the problem of inter-Service rivalry that has been highlighted by so many critics. However, final decisions about defense resource allocation are not made within the Department of Defense or even within the Executive. The outsider from overseas must accustom himself to an extra dimension: Congress, with which the Executive shares financial control of the Armed Services, has a decisive voice both in defense resource allocation and in the organization of the Department of Defense itself. It is very unlikely that problems of inter-Service rivalry can be solved without the active and continuing support of Congress.

NOTES

1. Senate Armed Services Committee, *National Security Act Amendments 1949*, 81st Cong. 1st sess., 9.

2. President Eisenhower's message to Congress on 3 April 1958 is reproduced on p. 175 et seq. of U.S. Department of Defense, *Documents on Establishment and Organization 1944–1978* (Washington, D.C.: Department of Defense, 1978).

3. C. J. Hitch, *Decisionmaking for Defense* (Berkeley and Los Angeles: University of California Press, 1965), 18.

4. J. M. Roherty, *Decisions of Robert S. McNamara* (Coral Gables, Fla.: University of Miami Press, 1970), 70.

5. U.S. Department of Defense, *Report of the Blue Ribbon Defense Panel* (Washington, D.C.: Department of Defense, 1970), ii.

6. Secretary of Defense Laird, *Military Posture Statement for Financial Year 1971* (Washington, D.C.: Department of Defense, 1970), 8.

7. *The Politics of Defense Analysis* (New York: Dunellen, 1973), 97.

8. Morton Halperin, "The President and the Military," *Foreign Affairs*, January 1972.

9. These were the Blue Ribbon Defense Panel, 1970, and the Defense Organization Study of 1977.

10. General D. C. Jones, USAF, "Why the Joint Chiefs of Staff Must Change," *Directors and Boards*, February 1982.

11. A. Enthoven and W. Smith, *How Much Is Enough?* (New York: Harper & Row, 1971), 33.

12. Joseph Kraft, "McNamara and His Enemies," *Harper's*, August, 1961, vol. 223, pp. 41–48.

13. Allen Schick, "A Death in the Bureaucracy," *Public Administration Review*, March 1973.

14. General D. C. Jones, "What Is Wrong with our Defense Establishment," *New York Times Magazine*, 7 November 1982.

15. Murdock Clark,*Defense Policy Making* (Albany: State University of New York Press, 1974), 101.

9

National Security Decision Making: The State Department's Role in Developing Arms Control Policy

Christopher M. Lehman

Some forty years ago, President Franklin D. Roosevelt remarked to a friend that so far, during the course of World War II, the State Department had remained neutral, and he hoped that the Department would at least remain that way.[1] On another occasion, Roosevelt complained bitterly to his adviser Pat Hurley that he could not " . . . get a damn thing done through the State Department."[2]

President Truman shared similar views and agreed fully with his Treasury Secretary Morganthau's suggestion that "what we want to do is break this little State Department clique."[3] President Kennedy spared no venom when he remarked in frustration that "the State Department is a bowl full of jelly."[4]

Many of these same epithets are hurled at the State Department today despite the advent of a solid conservative Administration under President Reagan. Disagreements over policy toward China, alleged Soviet treaty violations of arms control agreements, the Soviet pipeline, and other foreign policy issues have generated a good deal of controversy over the past two years, and it is likely that controversy over State Department positions on important issues will continue in the years ahead.

Nonetheless, the State Department as an institution has an important role to play in the formulation of national security policy and will surely continue to play the dominant role in the development of and execution of America's foreign policy. President Reagan, in fact, made clear statements at the beginning of his administration to the effect that he wanted to move basic decision-making authority back to the Cabinet-level agencies of the government. The State Department was to be no exception.

When he was Governor of California, Ronald Reagan administered the state government on a pattern that stressed the responsibility of individual Cabinet officers, and shortly after his election to the Presidency, he made clear that this would be the pattern for his new Administration. He described how his "Cabinet government" approach would differ from the approach of previous Administrations:

> The main difference is the fact that I think a lot of Presidents delegated to a "second cabinet." By that, I mean that they appointed a cabinet and then found that they had to have staff members around them in the White House. And then, of course, you had turf battles or friction. You had situations where cabinet officials had no communication with the President.[5]

Needless to say, President Reagan's nominee for the position of Secretary of State was fully supportive of the "Cabinet government" approach. General Alexander Haig had served on the staff of Henry Kissinger when Kissinger was the President's National Security Adviser during the Nixon Administration, and he had seen firsthand the uses and abuses of a national security decision-making apparatus where the National Security Council was dominant and the Cabinet agencies were little more than research and analyisis resources for decision making in the White House.

As the new Secretary of State and the most senior member of President Reagan's Cabinet, Alexander Haig made it clear that he was determined to make foreign policy in the State Department. In fact, in a speech to State Department employees on the first day of his stewardship, Secretary Haig drew an unfortunate analogy by claiming that he would be the "Vicar" of foreign policy—a term that generated a number of political cartoons and became a symbol of enduring conflict between the White House staff and Secretary Haig.

President Reagan, however, did support the concept of Cabinet government and acted accordingly. When the President chose Richard Allen to be his National Security Adviser, he made it clear to Allen that the National Security Council's role would be downplayed in the Reagan Administration.

When Alexander Haig's nomination was announced to the press, Richard Allen said publicly: "Take a good look at me, because I am about to submerge."[6]

In fact, that is what happened. Secretary Haig was highly visible in the first few months of the Administration, assuming the role of chief spokesman on foreign policy matters, and Richard Allen and the NSC staff assumed the role of coordinator rather than the role of policy maker.

Upon taking office, Secretary Haig moved vigorously to establish State Department control over the policy-making process. Realizing that policy coordination was the key to policy control, Secretary Haig persuaded President Reagan to give the Department of State—not the NSC—the authority to chair Interdepartmental Groups (IGs). These groups were set up to coordinate foreign policy planning and the operations of the many government agencies involved in one way or another in foreign policy matters. Of the more than thirty Interdepartmental Groups chartered by Presidential Directive since the beginning of the Reagan Administration, the Department of State has chaired or cochaired all but six of those groups.

In this way, the State Department gained a significant amount of control over the development of policy and policy issues in the first years of the Reagan Administration. In the months since then, there has been a gradual adjustment, with the White House, and particularly the NSC, reasserting some of its influence of earlier days and the Department of State losing a little of its prominence, but still retaining an important institutional role in the formulation and conduct of foreign policy.

To illustrate the actual functioning of the policy-making and policy coordination process within the State Department, it would be useful to look at the example of the development of arms control policy, and particularly the development of the U.S. negotiating position for the START negotiations in the early months of the Reagan Administration.

These policy issues have received repeated high-level attention within the government and prominent attention in the media throughout the first two years of the Reagan Administration; thus, they can serve as an excellent illustration of the current decision-making process regarding a national security issue that cuts across both defense and foreign policy.[7]

State and the Arms Control Process

Upon taking office, the Reagan Administration, like those before it, ordered a review of nuclear weapons issues and arms control policy in order to determine what policy course should be taken in the months ahead. In the case of arms control, this study was to be undertaken by an Interagency Group chaired by the Department of State. This group came to be known as the START IG because of the emphasis on strategic arms *reductions*; it has been and remains the primary policy-making body of the United States Government on strategic arms control matters.[8]

Within the State Department, the locus of decision making on arms control matters resides within the Bureau of Politico-Military Affairs—one of more than twenty bureaus and independent offices that make up the bulk of the Department (see table 9.1). To the extent that these matters affect individual Allies, the appropriate regional bureau would be involved. In the case of nuclear arms control, the Bureau of European Affairs, which has primary responsibility for relations with the Soviet Union, is an active participant in the policy process.

Thus, as the policy-making process began in early 1981 on the important issue of strategic arms control, the principal actors within the State Department consisted of a small group of individuals from the Bureau of Politico-Military Affairs and a smaller circle from the Bureau of European Affairs, the Bureau of Intelligence and Research, and the Policy Planning Staff. Of course, the Undersecretary for Political Affairs and the Secretary of State

DEPARTMENT OF STATE

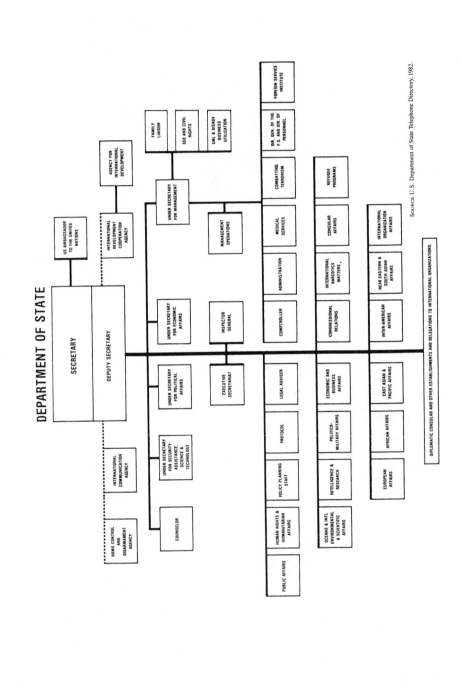

SOURCE: U.S. Department of State Telephone Directory, 1982.

were kept fully informed of important events and issues as they unfolded, and they frequently provided guidance to State's representatives in the IG and Working Group.

Principal actors from other departments or agencies of the government included senior personnel from the office of the Assistant Secretary of Defense for International Security Policy, the Office of the Director of the Arms Control and Disarmament Agency, the Joint Chiefs of Staff, the Arms Control Intelligence Staff of the Central Intelligence Agency, and the National Security Council.

The IG Process at Work

The very first step of the review of arms control policy was to establish where arms control should fit within the overall fabric of national security policy. At times in the past, it seemed that arms control was considered a goal in and of itself, which should be pursued vigorously under all circumstances. This view was rejected. Instead, it was agreed that arms control was a *means*—one of several means—to achieve the goal of national security.

Once that very basic understanding was achieved, the next step was to arrive at objectives or criteria for meaningful arms control. This was done quickly, and four criteria were agreed upon: militarily significant reductions, equality, stability, and effective verification.[9] After determining these objectives, the IG turned its attention to the problem of developing a U.S. position for negotiations with the Soviet Union. The issues were legion: How should a new agreement relate to the unratified SALT II Treaty? How long should its duration be? Should Backfire be limited in START or INF? Should we seek a strict limit upon modernization programs, or try only to direct them toward more stabilizing directions?

The most important issue, however, and the most difficult to resolve, was the so-called "unit of account" problem. What should we actually limit directly in START? The framework of SALT I and SALT II was based on limits on *launchers of nuclear weapons* or *strategic nuclear delivery vehicles*, rather than the nuclear weapons themselves, and all IG participants considered this an inadequate approach by itself. The search for an alternative framework began.

Study of these many issues and development of policy options was the task of the Working Group. This entity, chaired by the State Department, was a subgroup of the IG and included representatives of each of the interested agencies at a level one or two steps below the IG principal (Assistant Secretary level). The Working Group set about its task vigorously and on a nearly full-time basis. Meetings were held two or three times per week to review and revise analytical papers prepared by different agencies. The Working Group produced dozens of drafts and redrafts of papers analyzing different aspects of the problem. After a few weeks, the leading candidates for "units of account" were narrowed to four: strategic nuclear delivery vehicles (as in SALT II), ballistic missile warheads, ballistic missile throw-weight, and warhead weight. Because most agencies agreed that no one of these "units of account" was adequate by itself, two or more of these units were usually combined in "packages." In all, more than thirty different variants of these packages were analyzed and subjected to preliminary analysis.

The division of labor in this analysis was basically predictable. OSD and JCS would analyze the impact of a proposed limitation on U.S. forces. The Intelligence Community would provide data on Soviet forces, analyze the implications for the Soviet Union, and also provide judgment on how well the United States could monitor Soviet compliance with the proposed limits. ACDA added its own technical expertise and also combed the nego-tiating record of previous agreements for indications of how related issues had fared in the past. State, in addition to managing the process and trying to enforce deadlines, was a vigorous advocate for a particular approach to the "unit of account" issue. State also provided political judgments on antici-pated Soviet reactions and to the effect of various limitations on Alliance relations.

The IG process then took a short pause for agencies to review the alternatives and develop preliminary agency positions. Within State, PM worked closely with the Bureau of European Affairs' Soviet Desk, the Bureau of Intelligence and Research, and the Policy Planning Staff to determine which option the State Department should support. Detailed memorandums were written to the Secretary and other Department prin-cipals describing the various arguments, their pros and cons, and the Bureau views. A number of meetings were held with the Secretary and other principals to discuss the issues, and subsequently the Secretary made his decision. A State Department position was taken in support of a "short list" of favorites. Unquestionably, the same process was duplicated in ACDA, OSD, and JCS.

The Working Group then resumed its analysis, having narrowed the thirty or more options to ten that enjoyed some degree of support from one agency or another. The IG chartered a Technical Analysis Sub-Group (TASG) to perform a rigorous quantitative analysis of the favored options. CIA built an anticipated Soviet force structure, and JCS did the same for the United States. The Pentagon's computers then were enlisted in what is called "exchange analysis"—war-gaming to determine whether any of the limita-tions would lead to force structures that would be more or less likely to provide an incentive for preemptive attack during times of crisis. This would be a key factor in determining whether a package of limitations would meet the important criterion of enhancing crisis stability.

As a result of the TASG's work, more options were discarded, and agency positions began to harden around the shrinking number of surviving options. The analytical work of the Working Group on this issue was drawing to a close.

Simultaneous with the "unit of account" work, the Working Group prepared options and recommendations for the IG on additional issues such as telemetry encryption, Backfire, limits on air defenses, and ASW capability. Some options were approved by consensus, some were sent back to the Working Group for further analysis, and some were sent to the White House for decision.

The IG discussed the various options regarding the unit of account. Unresolved differences were expressed in agency views and sent to the NSC under a covering memorandum from State.

At this point, the NSC staff reviewed the papers and prepared the President for a meeting of the National Security Council. Each agency's principal (i.e., Secretary of State, Secretary of Defense) is a statutory member of the NSC, with the exception of the Director of ACDA and the Chairman of the Joint Chiefs of Staff (who is considered an "adviser" to the NSC). These principals met with the President in a full NSC meeting to decide what the U.S. position should be for negotiations with the Soviets.

The unit of account issue, along with several of the other major issues, was discussed. The President's decisions on these matters were recorded in a National Security Decision Directive (NSDD) and promulgated to the involved agencies. These decisions formed the basis for developing a detailed approach for a sound arms control agreement, and, based on the President's decisions, specific instructions were drafted for the U.S. negotiating team.

The decision of how and when to approach the Soviet Union about opening negotiations was complicated greatly by the strain in U.S.-Soviet relations caused by the Soviet pressures on Poland, but President Reagan did announce the basic U.S. position in a speech to the graduating class of his alma mater, Eureka College, on 9 May 1982.

The START negotiations began in June 1982 and will soon begin their fourth round. Since the main Presidential decisions were made in early 1982, a large number of additional decisions have been required. Many of the decisions were made at the IG level (based on Working Group recommendations) and the National Security Council and the President were kept informed. On fundamental issues or issues where major agency differences existed, however, decision papers were prepared and sent to the White House for decision. These decisions were recorded in National Security Decision Directives, which then provided policy guidance to the agencies involved.

Arms Control IGs

This basic model of the decision-making process has been repeated on a number of arms control issues and, in many cases, has involved the same persons, particularly at the IG or Assistant Secretary level. In addition to the START IG, in the early months of the Reagan Administration, IGs were established on INF, Nuclear Testing Limitations, MBFR (Mutual and Balanced Force Reduction negotiations), CBW (Chemical and Biological Weapons), and Outer Space Arms Control. All of these IGs have been chaired or cochaired by the Department of State and have pursued the basic decision process described above. The IGs and their Working Groups have developed detailed policies in each of these complex areas. In three of those areas, negotiations are now ongoing (START, INF, and MBFR); in two, the United States has proposed negotiations (Nuclear Testing and Chemical and Biological Weapons); and in the Outer Space area, the United States has studied the subject in great detail, but, because of existing arms control limitations (i.e., Outer Space Treaty and the ABM Treaty), and because of seemingly insurmountable verification tasks, the United States has not proposed space arms control negotiations.

Conclusion

The IG process, like any other system of policy coordination, has its strengths and weaknesses compared to the NSC-centered process that it superseded. More than the NSC format, the IG process operates on the basis of consensus; the chairing agency, usually State, is only *primus inter pares*, and lacks the authority to force decisions and overrule agency positions. As a result, without consensus, many more decisions must be "kicked upstairs" to the White House and the President. In addition, the process moves more slowly than in a more centralized system where the chairing agency would have sufficient authority to break deadlocks and insist on deadlines being met. On the other hand, important considerations—and dissenting views— are less likely to be left out than under a more centralized system.

There has been a good deal of criticism of the decentralized decision-making system that has evolved under the Reagan Administration, and, in fact, that system itself is developing in the direction of increased NSC authority. However, its fundamental character has remained. The Department of State still chairs the majority of IGs, and the NSC staff pursues primarily a coordinating function.

The State Department has thus been a principal actor in the arms control decision-making process, working closely with the other national security agencies, and the process seems to be functioning well. Issues have been crystalized and policies formulated.

Although the process varies by degree, this same basic interagency procedure applies to a whole range of issues for which the State Department has day-to-day responsibility. Almost invariably, more than one department of the Executive Branch has jurisdiction over an issue, and agencies, therefore, must coordinate their work and policies. In the area of trade, State must coordinate with the Department of Commerce; in the area of technology transfer, with Commerce and the CIA, and so on. For each topic, some bureau or office in State has prime responsibility and must work with counterparts in other agencies to develop policies. These decisions are communicated to the senior levels at State for approval or for information, and thus policy is made.

The memoirs have not yet been written for the Reagan Administration; therefore, we do not yet have a Reagan quotation similar to those that opened this chapter. However, undoubtedly, at some point, the policy views of the Department will be significantly at variance with those of the President, and an anguished exclamation will ensue.

NOTES

1. Martin Weil, *A Pretty Good Club: The Founding Fathers of the U.S. Foreign Service* (New York: Norton, 1978), 104.

2. Ibid., 105.

3. Ibid., 222–23.

4. Graham T. Allison, "The Cuban Missile Crisis: A Case Study of Crisis and Decision-Making," reprinted in *American Defense Policy*, 5th ed., ed. John F. Reichart and Steven R. Sturm (Baltimore: Johns Hopkins University Press, 1982), 596.

5. "Interview with the President-Elect," *U.S. News and World Report*, 19 January 1981, 26.

6. Edwin Warner, "Picking and Choosing," *Time*, 5 January 1981, 56.

7. Because of the requirements of classification and the confidentiality of Executive Branch proceedings, the discussion of this case study will necessarily lack details.

8. A parallel Interdepartmental Group was established early in 1981 to develop policy on theater nuclear issues and came to be known as the INF IG, which stood for intermediate-range nuclear forces. This IG developed policy and negotiating positions for the INF negotiations that began in Geneva, Switzerland, on 30 November 1981.

9. These criteria were first publicly announced in President Reagan's speech to the National Press Club on 18 November 1981.

10

The Specified and Unified Commands
C³—Problems of Centralization

John H. Cushman

The "unified and specified commands" are U.S.-only operational commands, organized under the provisions of the National Security Act of 1947, as amended. The following exist today:

- U.S. Aerospace Defense Command (Headquarters at Peterson Air Force Base, Colorado)
- U.S. Atlantic Command (Norfolk, Virginia)
- U.S. Central Command (MacDill AFB, Florida), into which the Rapid Deployment Joint Task Force has just evolved
- U.S. European Command (Stuttgart, Germany)
- U.S. Military Airlift Command (Scott AFB, Illinois)
- U.S. Pacific Command (Camp H. M. Smith, Hawaii)
- U.S. Readiness Command (MacDill AFB, Florida)
- U.S. Southern Command (Quarry Heights, Panama)
- U.S. Strategic Air Command (Offutt AFB, Nebraska)

There are no Allied forces in these U.S.-only major commands. Each has its designated Commander in Chief, or "CINC," so these commands are often miscalled "the CINCs." The CINC is not the command, but the commander.

The Aerospace Defense Command, the Military Airlift Command, and the Strategic Air Command are "specified commands," made up of forces of only one U.S. Military Service, the U.S. Air Force. The other six are "unified commands," made up of forces of two or more Services (although, day in and day out, only naval forces are assigned to the U.S. Atlantic Command).

However, in addition to these commands of U.S. forces only, one must discuss those multinational commands under which U.S. forces will fight if war should come.

Multinational operational commands, some of which are commanded by the same officer who commands one of the U.S.-only commands are:

- Allied Command, Europe (headquarters at Mons, Belgium), is commanded by General Bernard W. Rogers, U.S. Army, whose title is Supreme Allied Commander, Europe, or SACEUR. General Rogers, as USCINCEUR, also commands the U.S. European Command. Allied Command, Europe, has its own chain of command; officers in command represent different NATO member nations, and staffs frequently consist of more than one nationality.
- Allied Command, Atlantic (headquarters in Norfolk, Virginia), is commanded by Admiral Wesley McDonald, U.S. Navy, whose title in that position is SACLANT. Admiral McDonald as CINCLANT also commands the U.S. Atlantic Command and, as CINCLANTFLT, its U.S. Navy Component, the Atlantic Fleet. (He is also commander of WESTLANT, a NATO command, of its subordinate command OCEANLANT, and of several U.S.-only standing Task Force headquarters, which would be assigned forces when activated.)
- North American Aerospace Defense Command (headquarters at Peterson AFB, Colorado), with its United States and Canadian air forces, is commanded by the CINCNORAD, General James V. Hartinger, USAF, who as CINCADCOM also commands the US. Aerospace Defense Command.
- The ROK/US Combined Forces Command (CFC), in Korea (headquarters in Seoul, Korea), is commanded by General Robert W. Sennewald, U.S. Army, as CINC, CFC. General Sennewald is also Commander U.S. Forces Korea (USFK), a subordinate U.S.-only unified command that is part of U.S. Pacific Command. General Sennewald also commands USFK's U.S. Army component, Eighth U.S. Army, and as CINCUNC commands the United Nations Command.

The responsibility for the mission of the U.S. forces committed to the Allied commands in Europe and Korea is exercised through their Allied command structure. Thus, the defense of Europe will be conducted not by the U.S. European Command, but by Allied Command, Europe, and the defense of Korea will be conducted by the ROK/US Combined Forces Command, not by U.S. Forces in Korea.

There is a rich diversity in these commands. Each has evolved to meet its particular necessity and its own conditions of geography, purpose, composition, and threat. Each has its own unique internal command structure and makeup.

Whether the forces are U.S.-only or multinational, the problem is one of "command and control," that is exercised through "command and control systems." These "C^2" systems consist of personnel—commanders, staffs, and others—of the doctrines, procedures, and working relationships, both formal and informal; and of the computers, radars, communications links, command centers, and other facilities at the disposal of that personnel.

Through the linked webs of these "command and control systems," thus broadly defined, the various authorities, at all the levels of the operational forces, often facing other forces similarly commanded and controlled, seek to work in harmony under their responsible officers, and to accomplish the force's mission in peace and war, responsive to the political authority.

(The term "command and control," or C^2, encompasses C^3, which adds "communications." C^2 also encompasses C^3I, which adds "intelligence," and C^4, which adds "computers," and so on.)

Command and control system problems broader in range than merely "centralization" must be addressed, however.

The issue, moreover, is not simply the decision-*making*, but the decision-*executing* process. It is not only that making decisions is rather easy compared to executing them, but that decisions at the seat of government should be made in light of the real situation existing at the location where they must be executed, as visualized by the decision makers.

There are all kinds of "decisions" in the national security field. It is hard to think of any that do not involve issues of command and control, as broadly defined here.

To mention an example of a NSC or Presidential decision on a policy issue: guidance on the use of "theater" nuclear weapons in the defense of Central Europe. Command and control obviously is central to this issue.

Another example: the rules of engagement (i.e., what kind of fire can be returned and on whose authority) for the U.S. Marine Corps units deployed in Lebanon. Again, command and control is central.

This illustrates the wide spectrum of decision making. The first example applies to conditions of war, a big war. The second refers to conditions unlikely to lead directly to war, but concerns a very sensitive situation, capable of generating a "crisis." There must be hundreds of such "decisions" on the books.

With regard to decision making in a "crisis" that can lead to war:

I was involved in one of these, out at the end of the line, about seven years ago. In August of 1976, a party of North Koreans entered the site an Panmunjom, jointly patrolled by both sides, where the Military Armistice Commission has been meeting since the 1953 truce that ended the fighting of the Korean War (but did not, in fact, end the war). The North Koreans murdered with axes two American officers who were supervising a party of South Korean laborers engaged in trimming a tree.

At that time, I commanded I Corps (ROK/US) Group, a force of three ROK Army corps, with eleven ROK divisions, and the Second U.S. Infantry Division, responsible for the defense of the Western Sector of Korea's DMZ.

Suffice it to say that, in my opinion, the United Nations Command (at that time commanded by General Richard G. Stilwell) performed very well, as did the national security decision-making apparatus. The result was a measured and unmistakable demonstration of U.S. (and South Korean) resolve, through a very well performed and well-supported military operation in the DMZ through which the tree in question was cut down and the North Koreans were forced to back down.

This operation illustrates several points:

First, it was a multinational (actually binational) action, in a Korean-American, not U.S.-only command.

General Stilwell then, like General Robert Sennewald, his successor, was not a CINC of a specified or unified command. The U.S. CINC was CINCPAC, in Hawaii. General Stilwell's U.S.-only command was the forty thousand or so U.S. Forces Korea, a command subordinate to the U.S. Pacific Command. However, the command in question then (and now, too, under a different name) was not USFK but the ROK/US United Nations Command.

Second, "centralization" was only one consideration; the issue involved decision making at the U.S. seat of government, decision making in Seoul, with the President of the Republic of Korea and the U.S. Ambassador to Korea deeply involved, and the preparation and Korean-American approval of a ROK/US plan of action (including some centralization, some decentralization, and provision, above all, for detailed and effective command and control.

Third, "decision making" took place in a framework of "execution." Execution, which was of course decentralized, had to be responsive to policy direction and virtually flawless to succeed.

For the past eighteen months, working under Harvard University's Program for Information Resources Policy, I have been involved in the preparation of a study, "Command and Control of Theater Forces—Adequacy, Options, and Implications."

The study concludes that the command and control systems of these forces are by no means adequate.

By "theater forces" we mean those multi-Service, usually multinational, forces of the United States and its Allies, either deployed or in preparation for deployment in largely landmass areas of operation. They join strategic and maritime forces in a global fabric aimed at deterrence, crisis control, and, if necessary, the effective waging of war. Today these theater forces focus on Europe, Korea, and the Middle East/Southwest Asia.

Our study says that the overriding dilemma facing the United States and its friends and Allies around the world today is this: How to conduct affairs in a way that avoids all war, above all nuclear war, and at the same time permits freedom to flourish and peoples to prosper.

Because the theater forces of the United States and its friends and Allies have nuclear arms with them, or in support, and because their command and control systems are their brains and their nerves, these systems are a matter of transcendent importance to coalition statesmen.

Specifically, deterrence of war requires command and control systems that, above all, do not invite a crippling strike because of their vulnerability.

Further, superior command and control systems make possible the warning and intelligence essential for success in times of crisis and war, as well as the skillful and timely control of forces in such periods, in order to attain the objectives of policy.

Command and control thus constitutes the essential apparatus for using military means effectively.

It is in the highest interest of the elected leaders of the American people, therefore, and a policy objective of the greatest urgency and importance, that the command and control systems of theater forces be of the highest quality that technology, military foresight, and human ingenuity can provide.

Although much good work has been done and the situation is better today than it used to be, and recognizing that an authentic assessment must be made by more knowledgeable persons and would be classified, our assessment is that:

- Our performance in providing the full range of means necessary for command and control systems for theater forces has been, and all too likely continues to be, gravely deficient. Although the means of command and control in the hands of U.S. and Allied field forces may possibly be adequate for conditions short of war, they are seriously inadequate for war and hence for war's deterrence.

- Theater forces' command and control systems are not well tied together, top to bottom. They are not being exercised adequately under the expected conditions of war. Great sections of them will probably not survive the attack against them that is sure to come in war. For the typical senior commander, Allied or U.S., whose forces must use these systems, they represent the largely unplanned splicing together of ill-fitting components that have been delivered to his forces by relatively independent parties far away, who have coordinated adequately neither with him and his staff nor with each other. And they do not exploit the present capabilities of technology, nor does the system for their development adequately provide that future systems will.

This alarming condition urgently requires that its causes be understood—and that timely, measured correction be undertaken.

The basic cause of the above inadequacies is that:

Responsible senior officers who are in the operational chain of command below the President and the Secretary of Defense, and who will surely be held accountable in the event of command and control failure, have not been given the means necessary to meet their responsibility and accountability.

Technical and conceptual failings are contributory:

We have not understood and appreciated the meaning of theater forces' command and control systems as living webs of systems, each web consisting of a full spectrum of individual components, each different, and each undergoing a process of development in its particular arena.

We have not appreciated, nor taken full advantage of, nor reinforced, the mission-oriented field commander's commitment to the timely evolutionary improvement of the specific web of systems that make up his means of command and control.

For those line item components that can be called "mind extenders" (or "aids for decision" to the commanders and staffs that use them), we have failed to use an evolutionary acquisitions approach deeply involving the real user.

We have made insufficient use of readily available and adaptable commercial gear that can be brought swiftly "off the shelf" into the webs of systems serving commanders in the field.

And we have done poorly in working out an approach to systems architecture and nodal points that can accommodate the needs for evolutionary change and for interoperability of forces.

Bureaucratic/institutional causes are more fundamental:

First is the failure of the Service provider to view in an integrative fashion the operational commander's entire web of command and control. This stems from the narrowly based, Service-oriented outlook that comes naturally and institutionally to the individual Services and is most difficult to eradicate.

Next is the failure to give sufficient influence on the process of developing and operating systems to the only authorities that are driven by their overriding mission responsibilities to look at the problem holistically, namely, the multi-Service and multinational major operational commanders of theater forces.

Then there has been the failure to date of the Joint Chiefs of Staff to make the Services meet the genuine needs of field commanders, allowing the Services to acquire command and control systems that do not look at the operational user's web of systems in a fully integrated way.

Finally, there is the general failure to evaluate command and control systems against operational mission performance under conditions of stark reality.

For some reason, if one were to be with the theater forces in NATO and Korea, if one observed the plans and exercises of the RDJTF, or if one saw the training of the theater forces held in readiness for deployment with these three commands, one would find that, all too often:

- They train and practice with command and control systems unlikely to work under enemy attack in war.
- They have not designed their operating methods for training in peacetime to accomplish the essential needs that must be performed while using those limited means that can be made to survive in war.
- And, they do not practice under the conditions that these forces are likely to encounter should war come.

It is unclear why senior commanders with important mission responsibility, upon taking over their commands and observing this state of affairs, eventually came to accept it, to serve their time, and to leave their commands to their successors in essentially the same condition.

Part of the reason may be that, day in and day out, they do not fight, but only prepare to fight. They are not given the means to meet their C^2 system responsibilities. Month by month, the possibility of a tragedy seems more remote, and they learn to live with it.

Our problem is that we tend to build our systems to function very well in peacetime.

However, many peacetime systems will collapse in war. *They have not been tested against the conditions of war.*

The realistic commander, therefore, desires developers to *build systems for war*, test them against realistic battle conditions of war, and train his units accordingly.

Based on the kinds of systems that have been deployed, their complexity and their vulnerability, the evidence suggests that the effects of enemy action and the consequent disruption of command and control are undervalued. In the first days of a war in Europe, we stand to lose too much of the elaborate command and control resources that we have placed there at great cost.

It is hard to be realistic in peacetime. I found in Korea that realistic, two-sided battle simulation, in which my subordinate commanders and staffs participated, was invaluable in vividly demonstrating our vulnerabilities, and in motivating us to take corrective action that we would otherwise have omitted.

The ultimate test of the command and control system, or of its components, constituting the full web of means through which the commander accomplishes his tasks is "mission accomplishment in war."

In sum, responsibility and capacity are out of balance:

Operational commanders charged with mission performance responsibility, down to the corps and tactical air force level, seriously lack the means either to influence the command and control resources they receive or to make the best use of the resources provided.

Their authority and capacity, as well as that of the Joint Chiefs of Staff and its Chairman, are very much out of balance with their responsibility and accountability.

These conditions stem in large part from the fact that the Department of Defense is required by statute to be organized into provider and operational user establishments. Corrections have to be implemented within that framework.

The Secretary of Defense is responsible for such corrections, since, by statute, only he is in charge both of the operational chain of command and of the provider establishment.

IV

U.S. Decision Making on Defense
The Congress

11

The U.S. Senate and the Presidency

William S. Cohen

It has been asserted that Congress should keep its nose out of foreign and military policy; admittedly, most of us in Congress tend to apply the technique of the plumber when, actually, that of the surgeon is required in dealing with international affairs. I believe, however, that it is unrealistic, in a society such as ours, to expect that we will rush to change the Constitution—because our Constitution, in fact, does establish that it is not Presidents who declare war, but the Congress. We are not about to place ourselves in a position allowing a President to commit us to a course of action—call it a "conflict" or a "skirmish"—that might lead to a war ultimately without Congress's being informed in advance and, at least, having an opportunity to decide whether to express some degree of concurrence.

Even though Congress may have stubbed its toe and interfered, perhaps, in the diplomatic process and in foreign policy decision making in the past, nevertheless, that same Congress does play a very important role (which has been acknowledged many times by the Armed Services, however belatedly). For example, the formation of the Scowcroft Commission, to study basing modes for the MX, resulted from a Congressional—not a Presidential—initiative. It rose from the ashes of a Congressional rejection of the funding of the so-called "Densepack" basing mode for the MX missile.

A second example concerns the creation of a separate unified command for the Southwest Asian region, specifically the Persian Gulf. Again, this was not a Presidential or Pentagon initiative; it originated in our Subcommittee on Sea Power and Force Projection. Two years later, after the formation of this separate unified command, we heard testimony from generals thanking the Subcommittee for its initiative and for forcing the issue.

On the other hand, the Senate's work in dealing with national security issues reminds one of the British diplomat who wired back to the Foreign Office, during the Second World War, stating, "It is impossible for me to exaggerate the gravity of the situation, but I'll try." This has to be my guideline in attempting to describe the Senate process of addressing security matters. Actually, it is not a process—it is more of a happening, an event, taking the form or shape of a casserole.

The way in which legislation ultimately is made does not follow, precisely, along the formal path of calm deliberation by an authorizing committee, the Budget Committee, the Appropriations Committee, with members reasoning together on the question of how to put in shape a particular appropriations package. Those who have ever seen the Congress in action, especially about two or three in the morning, when major decisions are being made by individuals who can barely stay awake, and who are angry and contentious and fractious, will understand that this really does not fit the concept of a "process." Senator Sam Nunn recently used an appropriate metaphor when he said that "Military Strategy is the art of looking for danger, finding it everywhere, diagnosing it inaccurately, and prescribing the wrong remedy." Perhaps this was pronounced tongue in cheek, and it amounts to a paraphrase of Murphy's Law, but it contains elements of truth with regard to the legislative "process," which, as I indicated, is molecular in nature, perpetually in motion, and not necessarily coherent.

Very few of us, myself included, can claim the title of "expert." Some of us are, perhaps, more knowledgeable than other colleagues, but not much more. Moreover, to view this aspect in proper perspective, one must keep in mind that membership on the Senate Armed Services Committee, or the parallel Committee of the House, is not an exclusive task; it is just one of a number of assignments. I am also on the Intelligence Committee and I used to be the Chairman of the Indian Affairs Committee. I am, moreover, on the Governmental Affairs Committee; I am on nine subcommittees, all of which tend to meet at the same time. Consequently, I am required, like other members, to come in for one hearing, stay for half an hour, or perhaps a little longer, before leaving to go on to another hearing. Between all of these activities, we have our constitutents coming to Washington, especially during the months of March through June, who insist on seeing us and are very upset if we do not take the time away from these careful deliberations on military strategy, to go out and shake their hands and be photographed, as well as having our pictures taken with the students from one of our local high schools, who want to have us on the Capitol steps to pose with them.

All of these activities are likely to take place in the course of a single day, in addition to the other responsibilities that we shoulder. Obviously, therefore, we cannot claim title to being experts, in the sense that defense affairs constitute the total, single focus of our work or that we fully anticipate or comprehend the consequences of everything that we are doing. Having offered this caveat, let me attempt to discuss our responsibilities within the national security framework:

First, there has been a fundamental consensus between the Presidency and the Congress, at least since World War II. We possess shared national objectives that include protecting the American homeland, preventing Soviet domination of the Eurasian landmass, and ensuring our access to foreign and overseas markets.

During the 1950s and 1960s, of course, we enjoyed a marked superiority in nuclear capablities. Consequently, we were able to translate this factor into considerable leverage, leading to the belief that we could implement a so-called "2½-war" strategy, meaning that we had the capability of fighting, if necessary, both in Europe and Asia and still have enough left over as a contingent reserve to deal effectively with a minor conflict in some other area. During the 1970s, three major changes occurred, namely, the Soviet Union acquired nuclear parity—if, indeed, it did not overtake us; American dependence on foreign trade and markets increased; and the Soviet Union vastly enhanced its conventional military capability.

In the latter part of the 1970s, President Carter issued his declaration proclaiming our vital interest in the Persian Gulf, virtually drawing a line across the deserts of Saudi Arabia and challenging the Soviet Union that, if it impinged upon this American sphere, it was inviting a U.S. response. I am not at all sure what the JCS reaction may have been, at the time, to this proclamation, but Senator Jackson and others sounded a warning note to the effect that, before one drew lines in the sand around the Persian Gulf, one had better be careful to ensure there was a capability to match that commitment.

Essentially, this is the problem confronting us today, namely, our commitments have been expanded to what may be described as a "3½-war" strategy. We have added the Persian Gulf to Europe and East Asia as a specific area to defend. The difficulty is that our forces have remained relatively static; testimony has been presented to the Senate Armed Services Committee to the effect that our resources do not match either the rhetoric or the established strategy of the United States. We do not have the capability of carrying out the commitments that we have made.

This raises another issue, namely, whether the Congress, or the Senate, is receiving the kind of objective, candid military advice that is required to formulate some sort of viable strategy or, at least, to comply with an established policy. We have heard testimony indicating that we may be at least $750 billion short, if we take into account President Reagan's $1.6 trillion five-year defense plan, and if we are going to provide the means to implement the articulated strategy of today. It is clear that we have a problem: We can reduce our global national security objectives, we can increase the share of resources devoted to defense, or we can revise our military strategy. Essentially, these remain our three options.

From time to time, fairly strong sentiment emerges that we ought to pull out some or all of our troops from Europe, either immediately or in the near future. Others propose to forget about the Persian Gulf and simply to engage in more conservation efforts here, so as to reduce dependence upon oil from that area. These are not yet majority opinions, nor are they likely to attract a majority unless certain adverse trends prevail within the Atlantic Alliance itself.

Failing such developments, we could resort to the second option, that is to vote an increase in the size of the defense budget: however, in 1983 the House severely cut back the President's proposed 10 percent real-growth increase in the defense budget; the Senate Budget Committee voted to cut real-growth in half, to 5 percent; when the House and Senate went to conference, they agreed on 7.0 percent.

Consequently, we are left with the third option, i.e., to consider ways of revising our military strategy. There may be another, partial, option, namely, a new look at domestic procurement practices. In assessing military strategy, obviously one has to consider nuclear and theater forces, as well as strategic doctrine. As far as the nuclear aspect is concerned, I personally am committed to modernizing our strategic forces, believing such a move to be essential.

A "Nuclear Freeze," as I understand it, would mean that we will have no MX, no B-1, no ATB or Stealth Bomber; there will be no advanced Trident, no Pershing II or any of the cruise missiles. Ultimately, of course, that would cut down the budget. However, I would not regard it as a particularly wise decision. To quote the *New York Times*, the "Freeze Movement" is engaged in "simplistic sloganeering." The *New Republic*, not a publication enamored of Reagan programs either, has said that, as a goal, the "Nuclear Freeze" is wonderful; as a policy, it would be a disaster. The *Washington Post*, also not known for its strong support of the President's policies, has criticized the "Freeze Movement" as being unrealistic and, indeed, possibly dangerous, in terms of its consequences for America's strategic posture.

The Freeze Movement calls for a mutually verifiable treaty on a mutual "Freeze." How do you verify that? Declaring it to be verifiable does not make it so. Without on-site inspection, it would be virtually impossible to verify the cessation of research, development, and production of nuclear weapons. We have wonderful satellites, but they cannot see through the roof of a building. That is one of the major problems with the "Nuclear Freeze." Moreover, it is not mutual; it is unilateral as it applies to our Allies. We have the Soviet Union in Geneva talking about an SS-20 trade-off for the Pershing II and the cruise missile. Why in the world would we want a "Freeze" now, so that the Soviet Union could stand up and say it does not have to talk about a trade-off any longer? As a result, we would have frozen the 351 SS-20 launchers in place, and we would have zero comparable systems in the European theater. This is why I say that a "Freeze" would be unilateral in its application to our European Allies. Finally, it would lock us into systems that we have determined to be either destabilizing, namely, a potentially vulnerable Minuteman land-based missile force, or obsolete, such as our B-52s and the Poseidon missile, systems that are due to be retired by 1990. For all of these reasons, the "Freeze" does not make a great deal of sense.

Nevertheless, a "Freeze" resolution passed in the House of Representatives because members wanted to "signal" to the Administration that we have to stop the way in which we are doing business. "It is not binding," they say; "after all, it is only a statement, and we really do not want to stop the Pershing or the GLCM." "We just wanted to pass this statement so that we can go back to our constitutents and say, 'You see, we are for peace.'" The way in which the argument has been presented, if you are for a "Freeze," you are for peace; and if you oppose a "Freeze," you are for war!

Together with my colleague, Senator Nunn, I have attempted to formulate another strategy, and that is to point out the practical deficiencies of the "Freeze Movement." I must point out that, by building more modern and, one hopes, more stabilizing systems, one can actually be raising, rather than lowering, the nuclear threshold. By deploying more systems that are mobile, that are difficult to target, one does not increase the risk of war, one reduces it.

I have attempted to get this message across in the proposal for a "Guaranteed Builddown." Essentially, it recognizes that we have to modernize while acknowledging also that supporters of the "Freeze" have a legitimate complaint, namely, that nuclear weapons are being piled upon nuclear weapons, wiithout an end in sight. Consequently, I propose that we have a Guaranteed Builddown, so that, for every nuclear warhead (not launcher) deployed we would retire two others. Thus, if we decide to go forward with the MX, we would have to take out twenty warheads for each ten-warhead MX. If we deploy the planned one hundred MX, this would mean the retirement of two thousand warheads. Under this particular Guaranteed Builddown, to be mutually agreed upon with the Soviet Union, the inventories of both sides would be reduced by nearly five thousand warheads in a short period of time, if we implemented our modernization program. This appears to me to be a rational and sensible approach to take.

We are trying to persuade the Administration that, both politically and militarily, this is necessary if we are to have a modernization program. Without it, in my judgment, they will pass a "Freeze" resolution in the House, the supporters of which will vote then to kill the MX, the B-1, the Trident, every single system, because the "Freeze" means no new nuclear weapons. I am trying to formulate a mechanism whereby we can achieve modernization at the price of reduction, which is, after all, close to what the President wants. His START proposal calls for a reduction in warheads to five thousand. Thus, we are both aiming at the same goal, and the question is how to achieve it.

The Scowcroft Commission report is a positive step, stressing arms control, an indispensable companion to any weapons modernization program. The report suggests that the President should revise START proposals, which address MIRV systems, while the Commission recommends moving toward single Reentry Vehicle missiles, viewing MX, ultimately, more as a political factor than a military item. This is so since, for a decade, we have spoken of a window of vulnerability, referring to Minuteman deployed in fixed silos, vulnerable to preemptive attack. Obviously, such vulnerability is not diminished by replacing Minuteman with MX—unless you adopt a "Launch on Warning" posture. In this sense, MX could be destabilizing, since it would be an even more valuable target, and just as open to elimination. This view is shared by such military authorities as the former Chairman of the Joint Chiefs of Staff, General David Jones, who stated that, from a purely military point of view, there were better ways of utilizing $16 billion than placing an MX in a fixed silo. For these reasons, I view MX essentially as a political signal.

It raises the question of whether we have the national will, or can formulate a national consensus, to go forward with the production of a system that has been on the drawing board for a decade. In the meantime, we have been arguing about basing modes, from a vertical MPS, via a horizontal racecourse, to a "Densepack." To go ahead, therefore, becomes a test of national will—a factor that is as important to our Allies as it is to us. It would be much more difficult to have the Federal Republic of Germany continue to support deployment of Pershing II, should we abandon the MX. This is an important consideration in itself, but one has to add to it the arms control component. Without that aspect of the Scowcroft Commission Report, placing MX in Minuteman silos, or deploying single RV "Midgetman" missiles would not make much sense, unless one could diminish the number of SS-18s deployed by the Soviet Union. The proliferation of the latter enables the Soviet Union to annihilate any fixed system.

That is why arms control is a twin companion, in the Commission's Report, to the MX itself. While the Administration, understandably, has stressed the latter, the Congress will insist on emphasizing the former, particularly a revision of START proposals to count RVs, rather than launchers. The strategy proposed by Senator Nunn and myself, the "Build-down," constitutes one way of achieving this aim.

However, even if we succeed in dealing satisfactorily with the issues relating to strategic nuclear forces, we still have to address nonnuclear theater forces. Here the question is how to persuade our Allies to more equitable burden-sharing. I share the view that it is preposterous for the United States, with less than 28 percent of the population of the OECD countries and less than 35 percent of their GNP, to be providing as much as 40 percent of their active military manpower and almost 70 percent of their defense expenditures. This reflects a growing sentiment within the Congress. In 1978 NATO committed itself to a 3 percent real growth in military expenditures; most members of the Alliance, including the German Federal Republic have not met their commitment. Former Chancellor Schmidt claimed that 3 percent was a purely arbitrary amount, without relevance to real capabilities, and that, moreover, the Europeans, unlike the United States, had national service. The implication was that their Armed Services were qualitatively superior to ours, so that monetary levels provided no real indicator. However, how does one measure contributions without any quantitative criteria?

Another issue relates to NATO's inability or unwillingness to deploy its forces beyond its geographical confines. It is not self-evident why the United States, which is far less dependent upon Persian Gulf oil than Japan or the NATO countries, should be required to shoulder alone the commitment to defend that part of the world. This troubles our constituents, who see us voting to cut back on food stamp and other social programs in order to devote greater resources to defense. NATO members will have to assume a larger burden, either in defense expenditures or in the form of a greater commitment to forward defense. They will have to substitute some of their manpower for ours, if we are to be solely responsible for defending the Persian Gulf. The same military manpower that was intended to constitute reinforcements for NATO is being designated now to form part of the Rapid Deployment Force. The same individuals cannot be simultaneously in Europe and in Southwest Asia.

There are some problems, also, with the concept of a Rapid Deployment Force. Originally, the JCS had in mind an expeditionary force to be flown from the United States to the Persian Gulf. However, as the mystical seagull said to Jonathan in *Jonathan Livingston Seagull*, when he was attempting to fly faster and faster, "Jonathan, you don't understand. Speed is not a matter of going faster and faster, it is a matter of being there." The real problem we confront in the Persian Gulf is that we have to be there. However, there is no friendly Arab government that is willing to permit a significant land-based U.S. presence in any portion of its country. Arab officials have told me that they want "to feel us being there without seeing us." In other words, they want us "over the horizon."

That implies a naval presence, having our aircraft carriers at sea to rescue these governments in case of a local insurgency. The problem is that one cannot bring the RDF quickly enough to the confrontation area. Some prepositioning is required, and some type of forward base. It seems to me that the RDF should consist primarily of Navy and Marine units, reinforced by the Army and Air Force. It has been evolving along such lines for the past few years. However, we are novices and we have been improvising.

Mindful of the failed hostage rescue operation in Iran mounted by the United States in April 1980, caused to a considerable extent by the absence of clear command lines, I called for an open hearing with the JCS to testify as to what type of command and control structure they envisaged for the Rapid Deployment Force. We did not want to see a repetition of competing and overlapping command entities attempting to determine just who will organize and run the unit in question. The JCS was notably reluctant, indicating that it was the business of Congress to authorize and appropriate money, but not to become involved in command and control issues. However, I felt that the latter were highly relevant for the shape of the budget. The number of aircraft, as opposed to the number of ships, is a direct function of a decision to place the command entity in Europe, as opposed to Florida. Incidentally, because of political considerations, there was a desire to place the command in Europe, in the hope that this would impart greater awareness to the Europeans of their own concern for the safety of the Persian Gulf. In fact, however, because of European politics, this decision would be more likely to impede than to assist command and control.

In any case, command and control is highly relevant to appropriations because of such questions as whether a C-17 transport plane is required, or more aircraft carriers, or smaller vessels that can carry air-cushion landing craft. After our open session discussing command and control, two years later, we finally have a separate unified command for the Rapid Deployment Force, and we were thanked by the military officials in question for having held the hearings. In this case, also, therefore, Congress stumbled, as it were, into an important role helping to shape strategy as well as budgets.

Another Congressional development that has proved to be very useful is the Military Reform Caucus of essentially pro-defense-minded Senators and Congressmen. Despite our favorable attitude, our very name tends to set off all kinds of mistaken reactions. Those in the media are under the impression that we are negative in our view of defense needs. In fact, we are not intent simply upon reducing the defense budget. Instead, we are concerned with matters such as the reform of the procurement system, increasing competition, and reducing sole-source contracts. Regrettably, some of the Armed Services misunderstood our role and believed that we have to be combatted.

The fact is that the Services do exert pressure on the political process. Two years ago, I voted to delete funding for the C-17 transport plane, not because I opposed it as such, but because no one seemed able to describe its precise functions. Consequently, I maintained that $200 million for research and development should await the submission of the appropriate plans. The Air Force perceived that I was "killing" the transport plane as such, and a large number of reserve officers in Maine called me to express their disappointment in my action.

Unfortunately, the Department of Defense and the Congress keep treating one another as adversaries, when, in reality, they are allies. More dialogue is required between the politicians and the professional officers. We want to have strong military forces, but our manner of arriving at this role may require changes of approach. We may need a "maneuver strategy," instead of attempting simply to match the Soviet Union. We may have to refrain from going for the most exotic weapons systems feasible, and try to spend money more economically. While we pride ourselves justly upon our technological lead, the consequence seems to be that we are obtaining fewer and fewer weapons at a higher and higher cost. One author, extrapolating from current trends, stated that at this rate, by the year 2050 the entire defense budget would be able to purchase one airplane. The projected cost of the F-18 program has tripled to the point where the price tag for each aircraft may be as high as $30 million. It should be recalled, however, that the F-18 was designed as a low-cost alternative to the F-14!

It is important to emphasize the role of the procurement process, especially because it sounds dull. I have been supporting the Competition-in-Contracting Act, but even an audience of businessmen does not find this very exciting, despite the fact that its purpose is to achieve more competition, so as to obtain a better product at a lower price. That is the reason why we have had hearings for a full day on the Office of Federal Procurement Policy. The commission to reform the procurement system began its work in 1969, but the results were not scheduled to take effect until April 1984. Yet this issue is at the core of the economic problems of defense. We are spending as much as we do because contractors deliberately underestimate the cost of their product in order to prevail in bidding; the Department of Defense, even under the direction of the Office of Management and Budget, deliberately underestimates inflation for the project years, and the Congress goes ahead, because individual members cannot withstand the temptation of supporting any system that happens to be produced in their particular constituencies. Thus, we deceive ourselves and each other by deliberately underestimating costs in order to make contract bids, defense procurement plans, and employment opportunities in various parts of the country look more attractive.

Once the costs inevitably start to escalate, we find that we have a huge deficit, and the Congress starts to cut down requests from the Department of Defense rather arbitrarily in order to deal with the economic problems. However, at that stage one cannot attempt to ask which system is more useful militarily, because a major constituency has been built up, with voters whose jobs are at stake, whether we are talking about the B-1, or the F-18, or aircraft carriers. For the Congress to do its work efficiently, it has to know at the very outset what the real costs are likely to be of any particular system, so that it can make rational choices between feasible options in a manner that is not likely to hurt the defense effort of this country. This is the only sensible way to avoid the ongoing seesaw between the Executive attempting to maintain its planned defense expenditure levels and members of Congress trying to slash the defense budget.

In sum, the Congressional and Executive Branches of government, respectively, have constitutional responsibilities that are complementary. The tension that is built into the American political system, with the separation of powers, ensures that the Congress will exercise a form of oversight in the national security decision-making process. Nevertheless, the Congress cannot provide leadership; only the President can articulate the goals and propose the necessary means. The Congress can then play a significant role as a critic, or in support of the Administration's chosen course of action. The history of American national security decision making in this century contains numerous examples of the contribution made by the Congress to foreign policy and defense.

Inevitably, Executive-Congressional relations will mirror the differences of perspective on national security policy that exist in our society, although the contentious issues will be the types and levels of armaments, rather than the need for adequate capabilites for the common defense—upon which the Congress and the President, of whatever political party, are basically in agreement. The issue is how, rather than whether, we shall be defended.

12

Congressional Limitations and Oversight of Executive Decision-making Power: The Influence of the Members and of the Staff

Richard C. White

Are there adequate "Congressional limitations and oversight of Executive decision-making power? What is the influence of the members and of the staff?"

Since the very nature of this work is to establish identifiable patterns for future applications and understanding, principles should be defined as precisely as possible. In view of reality, however, I must present a kaleidoscope of maneuverings directed by 535 independent-minded legislators, hundreds of staffers, many self-interested contractors, thousands of demanding constitutents, the political or policy requirements of the President and the Pentagon, and, sometimes, the conflicting wishes of persons within the Pentagon. All of these elements are telescoped into one legislative year, principally to produce one authorizing bill and one appropriations bill for defense.

Normally, the way the system is structured, the President consults with the Secretary of Defense, who has consulted closely with the Chiefs of each Service on determining what the defense needs of this nation are. The product is somewhat altered by the all-pervasive and growing power of the Office of Management and Budget. Then, at some early point in the session, the President may outline to Congress broad parameters of defense costs, usually by way of a message to Congress.

Then Congressional hearings begin in the respective Armed Services and Appropriations Committees, where the Secretary of Defense gives general appraisal of international challenges in the global situations, and the needs and general requests of the Services, backed up by his aides and project managers. The Chiefs of each Service then make their broad presentations, having already had their requests coordinated and approved. They elaborate on the particular weapons systems, with informed projects managers present to field specific questions. Then the various project managers and divisions of each Service develop the particulars. In most areas, these presentations are partially a formality, because the staff of the various subcommittees in the Armed Services Committee and Subcommittee on Defense Appropriations have already reviewed the various items in depth.

To demonstrate the magnitude of the legislative chore, before the Research and Development Subcommittee of the Armed Services Committee there are approximately four thousand items to consider, and on the Procurement Subcommittee there are also about four thousand items. Thus, the members must rely on the staffs for guidance.

The staffs are very competent, but they normally number only two or three science-engineering-trained members of the Research and Development Subcommittee and no more, at any time, each on the Procurement and Seapower Subcommittees. Fortunately for their responsibilities, analysis and review is really a year-round process. One cannot praise the professional staffs enough. They are not only extremely competent in their fields, and have accommodated to the imprecise legislative process, at salaries far less than they could command in private industry, but they are arrayed against hundreds of also highly competent and well-paid scientists in industry and the large numbers of scientists and engineers in the Department of Defense.

The scientists and engineers of the contractors and Defense Department tend to concentrate on a few weapons systems, but the House and Senate staffs must become experts on all the weapons systems. They have to winnow through a maze of contentions and give the members of their committees their best recommendations. They also have the advantage of a memory spanning several Administrations. Reliance on the expertise of the professional staff and the usual acceptance of their recommendations constitutes the normal legislative oversight and decision exercised over Executive proposals—i.e., staff recommendation, and approval by the committee membership.

On less-publicized weapons systems or equipment, it is unusual that the committee would reject a staff recommendation. Any rejection of a recommendation usually stems from the constituent interest of some member, or special knowledge or expertise of a persuasive member of the subcommittee. Representatives bring with them a broad spectrum of skills and experiences that often find application in their committee work.

Why would members of a committee place such reliance on committee staff? First, there is the appreciation of the expertise and integrity of committee staff members. Second, their reliance is a matter of practicality. The representatives are running for office every other year; they are constantly attentive to their political position back home, on a myriad of national and local issues. They address one thousand to two thousand letters per week with the aid of a small personal staff, plus mass mailings, plus serving on two full committees and five subcommittees. If the member of the majority party has been in Congress into his third term, there is a fair likelihood that he is a chairman of a subcommittee, if, for example, he is on the Armed Service Committee. If he is in the minority party, he would be a ranking member of a subcommittee.

The member tries to study floor issues, may testify before other committees, takes part in floor debates, attends sessions, and votes; he meets with visiting constituents virtually every day, answers telephone calls, puts out political brush fires and press releases, conducts political campaigns, participates in television and radio programs, usually has two or three subcommittee meetings simultaneously each day; attends luncheons, receptions, and banquets. He leaves after the week's session for his district, usually late on Thursday afternoon, and returns Sunday or Monday morning. During all this time, he is preparing the next series of speeches to be given in his district or before various associations. When does he have time for deliberative study of any less prominent weapon system, unless it is called to his attention by his staff or by an industry in his district? He may be contacted by that industry, or a consultant for that industry, or that particular branch of the Service. Naturally, in view of the many other responsibilities, he relies on his staff and on the committee staff.

The exception occurs when the member has constituent interest either in the system itself or in a component of the system manufactured in his district or nearby. These systems translate into jobs for constituents. Often these conditions make a representative an advocate, despite the recommendation of the staff or virtually any other factor. At the top, our American government system is very "political."

Probably 95 percent of the items on the defense agenda are not truly controversial, or the committee accepts the recommendation of the staff. However, the remaining 5 percent can become very prominent and are the topic of major articles in the newsmagazines and newspapers. These are usually the "big ticket" items: aircraft, aircraft carriers, cruise missiles, MX missile, M-1 battle tank, and a number of other familiar systems.

The staff focuses on issues by tentatively recommending certain programs, or cuts in certain programs, or termination or postponement of certain projects or programs.

When controversial issues are identified, these usually surface early with the staff and Pentagon personnel, or in the course of hearings when the members and/or the staff target in on certain Executive recommendations.

After the hearings, the subcommittee will vote, and whether the item is accepted or rejected, it can come again before the full committee, although the latter usually is inclined to accept the subcommittee's recommendation.

Again, once a project is accepted or rejected by the full committee, the full House is inclined to approve the committee recommendation, but with some notable exceptions. There is a tendency to defer to the expertise and deliberations of a full committee. The House will overturn such full-committee decisions only if the specific question has worked prominently into the realm of national issues and is surrounded by constituent emotions. Everyone knows that the legislative process is two-tiered, the first being authorization from the authorizing legislative committee and the second consisting of a separate bill from the appropriations committee, funding at or below the figures set by the authorization bill. In fact, the appropriations bill does not have to fund a provision set forth in the authorization bill. Both bills must pass both houses, and, if different, each respective bill must have an approved conference report in agreement, before each can go to the President for approval and therefore become law.

The procedure described for the authorization bill is followed simultaneously in the Defense Appropriations Subcommittee and in the Senate Appropriations Committee, with approximately the same psychological attitudes at work.

The House usually does not overturn the decisions of the House Armed Services Committee, but on notable and exceptional occasions has rejected the position of the majority of the House Appropriations Subcommittee, such as with MX missile basing in 1982, when the House supported the Subcommittee Chairman, Joe Addabbo, over the Committee's majority position.

One of the Executive proposals that ended in the controversial 5 percent category was the titanic struggle between the Executive and Legislative branches (with internal warfare, in Congress), over the air carriers of outsized cargo—which involved the Lockheed C-5B, the McDonnell Douglas C-17, and the Boeing 747. This issue eventually tested many aspects of Executive decision and Legislative oversight.

Studies of the military airlift capabilities of the United States concluded that serious airlift replacement shortfalls are documented in seventeen major studies since 1974. The outsized problems of transportation will become even more acute as ground force firepower/equipment is modernized during the 1980s.

In arriving at a decision and making a recommendation to Congress, the Executive Department (through the Secretary of Defense's Office, together with the various Services) concluded that the Civilian Reserve Air Fleet Program was inadequate to meet the future needs of airlift, and that it would soon be necessary to begin phasing out, by retiring from service the aging C-130s and C-141s, beginning in the 1990s. CRAF was rejected as the near-term bulk/oversize choice. CRAF is principally composed of contracted-for commercial aircraft that can be converted into troop and cargo carriers in times of emergency.

The Services recommended the KC-10 for its bulk/oversize capability, because of an existing contract at favorable prices, its peacetime contribution to force readiness refueling training, and its war flexibility as a refueler or cargo carrier.

Defense planners realized long before the buildup of tensions in Southwest Asia that the U.S. strategic mobility requirements exceeded our capabilities. NATO coped with this evident problem by pre-positioning equipment and supplies at key points in Europe. However, the increasing threat in the Persian Gulf area and the Indian Ocean, and the U.S. response of developing the Rapid Deployment Force made the problem stand out in bold relief. As Marine Commandant Burrow stated, "We have more fight than ferry." The airlift shortfall alone is 25 million ton-miles for the 1983–87 period.

In 1981 the Pentagon recommended the C-17 to address the outsize intertheater airlift shortages. The air-refuelable smaller C-17 would carry all types of air cargo over intercontinental distances directly into small airfields, and could carry outsized cargos such as the M-1 battle tank, self-propelled artillery, attack helicopters, fighting vehicles, large trucks, vans, etc., into intratheater fields closer to the point of use. Within five years, 40 percent of the Army cargo would be outsized.

At the time of presentation, the C-17 was still in experimental development, untested, while the C-5 production line had been discontinued. The C-5s had been tested and in service for years and could do the job. The wings were modernized and the metal-fatigued wings replaced.

The House Armed Services Committee came down hard, demanding to know why the C-5 line could not be reopened and production commenced on a known quantity, rather than putting our chips on a plane not yet in being.

The Air Force resisted the thrust of the Committee and the House Armed Services Committee rejected all but the continued research and development on the C-17.

Then, in 1982, the Pentagon altered its position and came to the Congress urging authorization and funding for fifty C-5bs and forty-four KC-10s on the premise that, with increased near-term funding, the Secretary of Defense could address the airlift problem immediately, and C-5 production could be accelerated more readily than C-17 development. There was a fixed-price, low-risk contract offer by Lockheed, the manufacturer of the C-5b. The C-5b could be delivered to the airlift nineteen months sooner. Thus, based on earlier availability and lower risk, the C-5b was recommended by the Air Force just as vehemently as, the year before, it was rejected and the C-17 was urged. The remaining shortfall in airlift would be met in the long term with the CRAF for the oversize/bulk cargo, and with the C-17 type aircraft, for outsized cargo. The C-5b would provide twice as much airlift capability as the C-17 would provide from 1985 through 1990. The C-17 would be phased in later.

It was then that the Boeing Company, the manufacturer of the 747, submitted an unsolicited proposal offering four different freighter alternatives. This was after Braniff had gone into receivership, and many Boeing

747s languished at airfields around the country. As long as these were available, it was unlikely any orders would be placed for new 747s.

So the debate continued in Congress on what is the best near-term solution for airlift: that is, the C-5b/KC-10 versus the Boeing 747 proposal versus the C-17.

In April 1982 the Senate Armed Services Committee authorized the C-5b/KC-10 alternative, and it appeared that this would be the recommendation of the Senate when the bill hit the Senate floor. Then the issue became derailed. At midpoint in the budgeting process, Boeing decided to challenge the Department of Defense executive decision, contending that, in fact, the Boeing 747 was a superior choice because it is available now, that there was used surplus available at bargain prices since Braniff went into receivership, and the Boeing 747 could carry most of the equipment needed by the Rapid Deployment Force.

An able advocate, Senator Scoop Jackson of the State of Washington, wiith an interest in his constituent manufacturer, Boeing, amended the Senate Armed Services bill to substitute the 747 for the C-5b, with strong Senate support. The members were convinced that the surplus caused by the recession could satisfy the military airlift requirements at a lower cost than the C-5b, and much sooner, with modifications to the aircraft.

The switch caught the Pentagon totally off guard, and an intense lobbying effort was commenced by it to reverse the Senate floor action. General Hecker of the Air Force was given the duty of orchestrating a broad effort to convince the members of the House to endorse the original Pentagon proposal of fifty C-5bs and forty-four KC-10s. Members of the Air Force personally visited members of the House Armed Services Committee to ensure their espousal of the Executive's proposals. Lockheed in Georgia, the builder of the C-5bs, enlisted the enthusiastic advocacy of the members of the Georgia delegation, who fanned out among their friends in the House, especially among members of the Armed Services Committee.

General Hecker held almost daily strategy sessions to which he invited high-ranking officials of Lockheed. It was at this point that the battle became particularly acrimonious and led to future Armed Services Committee investigations of the lobbying effort by the Pentagon.

One of the officials of Lockheed who had the primary responsibility for coordinating and spearheading the Lockheed effort, began to record the results of the strategy sessions on a computer and sought to distribute these results to those attending the strategy sessions. He was advised against this procedure by the Air Force personnel, but persisted. At some later date before a resolution of the airlift issue, the press came into possession of one of these computer printouts, and a great cry of improper lobbying was raised by the 747 advocates. The controversy of alleged illegal lobbying became entwined in the debate of the issue. But, on 21 July, the House by a vote of

127 to 289 rejected an amendment identical to the Senate action that would have killed the C-5 plan.

So the House and Senate defense authorization bills, being diametrically opposed on this airlift issue, raised a major conflict for the conferees to resolve. On 13 August 1982 the House and Senate conferees agreed to restore funds to go ahead with the C-5b purchases, authorizing $697.5 million for one C-5b in fiscal year 1983 and $102.5 million in advance procurement funds. The conferees also authorized $144.8 million to purchase three used 747 widebody aircraft.

On 23 September 1982 the Senate Appropriations Committee approved $750 million for C-5bs, overturning the decision of its Defense Subcommittee to cut C-5b money to $600 million. In the end, all three major airlift contractors obtained something: $750 million for the Lockheed C-5b, $200 million for the C-17, and a total of $144 million for surplus Boeing 747s.

The reason that the C-5b was finally favored over a substitute is that, while the initial purchase of the 747 was much cheaper, its military utility was lower than the other choices, and it could not carry outsized cargo without time-consuming disassembly, and without violating Air Force criteria for minimum clearance between cargo and fuselage. To load a 747, a special structure would be needed to lift the cargo from the ground, and carrying of this superstructure and lift created special problems of space and supply. Outsized cargo of large quantity could be driven into the hold of the C-5b in a matter of minutes without disassembly, and off-loaded quickly at its point of delivery, merely by driving or pulling it out of the hold.

The matter did not rest there on Legislative oversight, for by the later weeks of the maneuvering, intense feelings were surfacing. After the publication of the computer printout and revelation of the strategy sessions, an irate House member from the State of Washington, a strong advocate for Boeing, and an influential member of the Defense Appropriations Subcommittee, introduced an unusual privileged resolution, calling for the immediate investigation of the Department of Defense for alleged illegal lobbying on a number of grounds, principally contending illegal use of appropriated funds for grassroots, extra-Congressional lobbying activities to influence members of Congress improperly. The resolution was rejected by the House Armed Services Committee and successfully argued against on the floor, on the premise that timely investigation could commence without the mandate of the resolution to determine if illegal lobbying was involved. On 14 September 1982 these investigations were commenced by the Investigations Subcommittee of the House Armed Services Committee, which I chaired. Hearings were held on 14, 15, 16, and 30 September and on 30 November 1982, and thirty-four witnesses were called and sworn in for an exhaustive inquiry into the allegations raised by the Washington State Congressman.

Before the investigation hearings commenced, the Washington State Representative also went to the Chairman of the Government Operations Committee to request an investigation of his allegations by the General Accounting Office, an investigative arm of the Congress. Thus, two Congressional investigations were under way simultaneously on the same allegations.

Our Investigations Subcommittee called those identified with the strategy meeting process or the Executive decision process affecting the Legislative effort, as suggested by the complainant, as well as others alleged to have knowledge of or implication in any activites under question. In time, the GAO Director and investigators were also exhaustively interrogated. A published report of 434 pages contains the verbatim text of the investigation.

The findings of the Investigations Subcommittee were that the lobbying effort was not in violation of existing law. It also found "that the complaining member of Congress presented insufficient evidence to support his charges. Those charges against the Department of Defense arose from an erroneous perception of the multiple meetings between the DoD and the contractor to plan strategy to influence members of Congress. This procedure is frequently followed in varying degrees. This procedure, while not presently a violation, should be reviewed for future guidance of all agencies."

The recommendations of the subcommittee were:

(1) The appropriate committees of Congress should review existing laws prohibiting the expenditures of appropriate funds for lobbying as they pertain to any agency, determine what ambiguities, omissions or impracticalities exist, if any, in such existing laws, and make recommendations by legislation to correct any such defects and clarify the responsibilities of executive branch agencies in lobbying the Congress.

(2) The Secretary of Defense should provide guidance to all personnel of the Department concerning permissible lobbying activities. Such guidance should establish clear standards so that Department of Defense personnel can avoid even the appearance of involvement in improper lobbying activities.

(3) In examining future allegations of possible violations by an executive branch agency, the rules of evidence should be adhered to as much as possible in testing the validity of the allegations.

(4) Request for future hearings should be accompanied by a bill of particulars and sufficient evidence to justify the time and money required to conduct the hearings.

Thus, each authorizing committee, appropriations subcommittee, and the conference committees exercised considerable oversight over this celebrated issue through normal channels. In addition, the Investigations Subcommittee, the GAO, and possibly the Government Operations Committee

exercised extraordinary oversight over the decisions and procedures supporting the decisions by the Executive branch, and the Department of Defense.

After an authorizing bill becomes law and has been funded by appropriations, there are constant revised decisions by the Pentagon.

Normally, it is expected that the Pentagon provides sufficient hidden
padding so that these changed positions can be funded, through a process
known as reprogramming.

The Pentagon will decide that more money or some money needs to be
expended on some program, and will so advise Congress. If Congress has
approved a weapons system or item, and the cost is less than $25 million,
then Congress need not be consulted.

But if the matter is over the $25 million threshold or Congress has not
previously approved the item, then the DoD will advise Congress of the
requested diversion of money from one program to support the new request.
Both the authorizing Armed Services Committee and the Defense Appropriation Subcommittee must approve, but Congress as a whole does not need to
approve such reprogramming.

Any authorization and subsequent appropriation that has been successfully seen through all the pitfalls of Legislative oversight is a true child of
evolution, or stamina. I have never seen rubber-stamp legislation as such.
Some programs are more popular or persuasive than others, but all have been
scrutinized and manhandled in their elements and have stood the test. Nor
does it mean that any weapons system or device approved and funded one
year won't find itself terminated in some future year as Congress, aware of
the need for new economies, will try to cut the losses on ineffective or too-
costly programs, regardless of how many years they may have been funded.

While there are obvious built-in defects and inefficiencies, somehow
the system does work. In a democracy, the process is much slower and often
frustrating. It is amazing that our national defense has been of such high
quality over the years, considering the stop-and-start pattern we have often
followed. It would be easy to attribute much of the erratic course to Congress. Yet, whether from a taxpayer's viewpoint or the viewpoint of the
general citizen concerned with defense, it would not serve the best interests
of this nation to reduce or eliminate Legislative oversight.

13

Congress and Defense Policy Making: Toward Realistic Expectations in a System of Countervailing Parochialisms

Stanley J. Heginbotham

Considerable confusion and frustration surround the role of Congress in the making of U.S. defense policy. Jack Maury, a former Assistant Secretary of Defense for Congressional Relations and head of CIA Congressional liaison, in a recent article, "Can Congress Run the Defense Department?" answered the question posed in his title as any informed observer would—in the negative.[1] Faced with this reality, many who inquire further into the appropriate role of Congress in security affairs conclude that it should be as limited as possible.

Maury is not atypical. He sees dealing with Congress as "one of the burdens of those who toil in the vineyards of bureaucracy." Again, like many, he recognizes, reluctantly, that Congress does have a constitutionally mandated role to raise and maintain armies. He pleads, however, for Congress to "show responsibility and restraint in exercising its pervasive powers over the national defense," and to realize that "in the nuclear age it is unwise to have too many fingers pressing too many defense buttons." Others who look at the Congressional role conclude that the system would work more effectively if Congress simply closed its eyes when faced with a defense budget and voted "yes."

I would argue that Congress plays a significant role in American defense decision making, but that it is of a peculiar and limited sort. It must be understood as part of a broader system in which Congress does not replicate or substitute for the policy-making and management abilities of the Executive. Rather, as befits a deliberative body, it constrains, vetoes, modifies, and refines policy and legislative proposals that come before it. It can also counteract the sometimes parochial concerns of Executive branch agencies. That is not to suggest that Congress has no parochial concerns of its own. Rather, its constituency, state, and regional orientations are often counteracted by pressures from the Executive branch. Thus, the system is one of countervailing parochialisms in which the charateristics of Congress as a deliberative body need to be seen as a source of strength rather than weakness.

The first part of the chapter suggests some of the more important differences between the defense policy bureaucracy of the Executive branch and the deliberative bodies that make up the U.S. Congress. The second part identifies—as a corrective to a common assumption that bureaucracy produces rational defense policy—some of the patterns of parochialism and irrationality that characterize defense bureaucracies. The third part spells out some of the constructive—if quite limited—roles Congress can reasonably be expected to play in defense policy making.

CONGRESS IS NOT A BUREAUCRACY

Perhaps the most common and most serious mistake observers make in defining a Congressional role in defense policy is to think of Congress as a bureaucracy. To do so leads to notions of Congress "running" the Defense Department, or making general policy while the Executive branch implements it, or second-guessing the Pentagon. Congress invariably appears inept and irresponsible from the perspective of anyone who thinks of it as a bureaucracy that can formulate policies, manage operations, or even systematically assess and review programs. Congress does not have the structure of a bureaucracy, it is institutionally incapable of doing what bureaucracies do, and it is unrealistic to expect otherwise. Because this point is so important and so commonly neglected, it is worth elaborating.

Congress is made up of two largely autonomous legislative bodies, a fact that makes the idea that it should produce coherent, single-minded leadership implausible from the outset. Each member has equal formal power within his or her respective house, deriving from electoral success in an individual state or constituency. Sustaining that electoral base must be the primary imperative of members. They have limited time and staff left over to meet their responsibilities for legislating on the full range of domestic and foreign policy issues facing the federal government. A measure of specialization is possible because members of both houses belong to committees.

Those committees, however, are organized around principles that produce high redundancy rather than mutual exclusivity of jurisdictions. Authorizing, appropriating, and budget committees all have responsibilities for defense policy. Moreover, foreign affairs, energy, and maritime committees have jurisdictions that overlap with those of the armed services committees. Membership on selected committees provides some grounds for specialization, but members must divide their time among competing assignments. Senators generally belong to three or four committees, and members of the House to between one and three committees. Finally, the legislative process itself is designed to prevent hasty decisions and to ensure that the interests of many competing perspectives are reflected in its eventual determinations. This reminder of the essential characteristics of Congress should be sufficient to stimulate awareness of the difference between Congress and a bureaucracy such as the one that manages U.S. defense policy. The five types of differences in organizational characteristics spelled out below give greater specificity and detail to the distinctions that need to be made.

Authority Structure

A BUREAUCRACY HAS A CLEAR HIERARCHY.   Its pyramidal chain of command provides a structure through which instructions can be passed in order to assign authority and tasks to its members and ensure flows of information to appropriate parts of the organization.

CONGRESS IS NEARLY DEVOID OF HIERARCHY.   It consists of two coequal bodies, each of which jealously guards its autonomy. Even within each house, the fundamental voting equality of all members remains the critical structural element. "Leadership" positions are primarily concerned with institutional and party management. Committee Chairmen often cooperate with, but do not take direction from, "the leadership," and, though they have considerable control over resources, few are able to impose their wills systematically on members of their committees.

Many casual observers of Congress believe that its committee staffs, at least, and to a lesser extent its member office staffs, constitute something of a hierarchy. In fact, however, those staffs are very much the products of the personal authority of members. Though patterns differ, individual committee staff members have direct responsibility to members. The staff directors have substantial powers, but often more as coordinators of diverse entrepreneurs than as superiors who systematically assign work and manage operations within a hierarchy.

Some observers bemoan the lack of hierarchical structure in today's Congress, looking nostalgically back to the 1950s, when Senators Vandenberg and Russell were able to command far greater compliance from their colleagues than are their counterparts of today. In an important sense, however, the strong "leadership" of that period reflected the abdication of authority by many "followers." Behavior in Congress then was closer to notions of bureaucratic norms, but that is hardly an appropriate criterion for assessing the performance of a legislative body.

Character of Subunits

A BUREAUCRACY HAS CLEAR FUNCTIONAL DIFFERENTIATION.   Its primary subunits are traditionally designed to provide comprehensive but mutually exclusive responsibility. Staff units help the organization's leadership coordinate activities of the primary subunits.

CONGRESS HAS OVERLAPPING AND REDUNDANT JURISDICTIONS. The basis of committee organization is not to separate functions for maximum efficiency, but rather to build in redundancy and cross-checks for maximum protection from the tyranny of any one faction. Because its committees so reflect the styles and concerns of their leaders and members, they invariably assume distinctive approaches. Defense is dealt with in the armed services committees, but it is also the province of the defense appropriations subcommittees and the budget committees of both houses. Thus, though these six subdivisions of Congress have overlapping and duplicative responsibilities for defense issues, each approaches its tasks from a different perspective, and resulting legislation reflects compromises among them. For anyone who approaches the system with the expectation that the purpose of committee jurisdictions is to establish functional differentiation comparable to that of a bureaucracy, however, the system itself often seems to be an exquisite tyranny, worse than any it might hve been devised to protect against.

Observers who expect that committee, let alone member, staffs will follow proper bureaucratic principles of differentiation and specialization are also generally disappointed. Because there is so much substantive redundancy in the committee structure, there is limited scope for specialization, even with the several thousand staffers who serve in Congress. Moreover, even committee staffers, in the final analysis, are responsible to individual members and not to an element of institutional structure. Consequently, groups of committee staffers who owe allegiance to the Chairman, the ranking minority member, and often to their counterparts at the subcommittee level, will have duplicative functional assignments. Moreover, such assignments are flexible and shifting. It is not at all unusual for staffers to spend extended periods working on issues that are at best marginally related to their presumed responsibility and expertise.

In member offices especially, the organizing principle of bureaucracy is stood on its head. It is not the function of the member as leader to organize work so that the product of a group of subordinates is maximized; rather, it is the function of the group to maximize the personal and political effectiveness of the member-leader. Principles of differentiation and specialization are routinely sacrificed to the idiosyncratic requirements of a member's personal, political, and legislative agenda.

Responsibility for Operations

BUREAUCRACIES ROUTINELY PROVIDE CONTINUOUS OPERATIONAL MANAGEMENT. The primary subunits of a bureaucracy generally have continuous responsibility for some aspect of operations. Military commanders, for example, have continuous responsibility for aspects of the national defense. Their structures provide and maintain institutional expertise and memory on detailed aspects of their areas of responsibility.

CONGRESS INTERVENES EPISODICALLY IN OPERATIONAL ACTIVITIES.
Even staff personnel with reasonably narrowly defined substantive responsibilities frequently shift their attention from issue to issue and problem to
problem. Budget cycles require building to peaks of attention on certain
issues and then permit turning to other concerns. In few Hill offices is there
the continuous monitoring of a given area of operations that one finds in
many places within the national security bureaucracy.

Members themselves are even more episodic in their attention to
defense issues. Though some specialize in national security matters, they all
must vote on the full range of issues facing the Congress. That requires at
least a basic familiarity with an extraordinarily diverse range of technical
issues and commitments of time that drain attention away from the subject
matters in which one would like to become expert. The demands of the
legislative and political calendars are such that only occasionally can most
members focus attention on national security decisions. The budgetary focus
of most action on national security affairs produces amendments that must be
drafted and votes that must be cast during a brief period of time, but that will
have relatively long-term consequences. The key members and staff in this
process may be extremely industrious and competent, but (from the perspective of anyone who applies the standards of a bureaucracy to Congress) they
will almost invariably seem to be responsible for an impossibly broad range
of issues and unable to give critical and highly technical issues the sustained
and expert attention they need.

Selection and Advancement

A BUREAUCRACY HAS A SYSTEM OF MERIT SELECTION AND PROMOTION.
Formal job-related knowledge and skills are identified as criteria for selection
and promotion. Experience and training in specific fields influence promotions through defined job levels. Other personal characteristics play a role in
the process, and, at senior levels of the civilian federal bureaucracy, the merit
system is displaced by one of political appointments. Nevertheless, merit
system criteria strongly influence bureaucratic selection and promotion
processes.

THE CRITERION FOR SELECTION OF MEMBERS OF CONGRESS IS THE SATISFAC-
TION OF THE VOTERS.   Substantive expertise and detailed familiarity with
issues may not be required. Rather, the ability to convey dedication to a
constituency, an understanding of its basic concerns and attitudes, and
shrewd common sense often outweigh in the voters' minds the characteristics
of education, training, and job experience that qualify one for positions of
responsibility in a contemporary bureaucracy.

Members achieve greater power within the Congressional system
through two mechanisms, seniority and mobilizing support of their colleagues in elections to a wide range of leadership roles. The former reflects

the continuing confidence of a voting constituency and an expanding body of experience in the institution. The latter generally seems to reflect an ability to work problems through a cumbersome system, generally through a combination of procedural and interpersonal skills. Again, substantive expertise, though often present, is not necessarily a primary criterion for upward mobility.

The criterion for staff selection and promotion is the satisfaction of the employer-legislator. Again, substantive expertise often plays a significant role, but sensitivity to a member's instincts and predispositions, loyalty, political acumen, and dedication are often more critical determinants of staff success.

Relation of Individual to Organization

A BUREAUCRACY CLEARLY SEPARATES THE POSITION FROM THE INDIVIDUAL. Loyalty, commitment, and responsibility are presumed to be to the position rather than to the incumbent. When the head of an office is reassigned, the subordinates are expected to accept the authority of his or her replacement, and the head is expected to assume the competence and institutional loyalty of the staff.

THE ROLE AND THE PERSONA OF A MEMBER OF CONGRESS ARE INSEPARABLE. It is the individual who is elected; no deputy can vote in his or her place in committee or on the floor. A staffer works not for a state, constituency, or committee, but for an individual. The defeat or death of a member or a change in committee chairmanship has enormous implications in Congress because it can result in wholesale replacement of staffs. Whereas the personal, political, and professional lives of an official in a bureaucracy are supposed to be kept clearly separated, they often become indistinguishable in the activities of a member of Congress. One's legislative duties, constituency-servicing responsibilities, reelection efforts, and personal life simply do not fit into neat compartments, but rather are often conducted simultaneously. Style, personality, ideology, political party, constituency political base, and substantive expertise all come into play when a member acts in Congress. To expect otherwise would be to deny a fundamental characteristic of a legislature.

CONGRESSIONAL ROLE

In Theory

Reminded of these congressional realities, many who are concerned with the development of a rational national security policy are likely to ask, "What conceivable positive role could an institution that operates under such principles possibly play?" The response is frequently an embarrassed recourse to the Constitution: the founding fathers, in their presumed wisdom, gave Congress the power of the purse, and the responsibility for raising armies.

The question, however, often is grounded on an assumption that, because bureaucracies have such rational features as clear authority structures, coherent systems of functional differentiation, operational continuity, merit personnel systems, and separation of person from role, they necessarily produce rational policy. There is an extensive body of literature that demonstrates quite persuasively that this is not the case, whether in national security or any other field of policy making and implementaton.

The following review of some of the forms of bureaucratic perversity and parochialism is not intended to denigrate or diminish bureaucratic institutions. They are, after all, remarkable in, and extremely valuable for, what they are able to produce. Just as it is dangerous and demoralizing to establish inappropriate and unrealistic goals for Congress, it does little good to ignore the less positive predispositions of bureaucracies.

SUBUNIT AUTONOMY.   Though it is widely recognized that the country needs an integrated national security strategy and organization, it is also clear that leadership in the individual Armed Services—indeed, in components of those Services—pursues parochial interests that sometimes weaken the effectiveness of the overall force.

DISPLACEMENT OF ENDS ONTO MEANS.   Technology is a means of achieving the ends of a force that can protect the national interest. There is a strong tendency, however, for the development of new technologies to take on lives of their own, so that the technologies available begin to determine elements of force structure rather than the needs of force structure development determining the direction of technological innovation.

CO-OPTATION.   Every bureaucracy operates in an institutional environment and tends to serve the interests of those on whom it depends. We know that the corporations that produce hardware and other products for our national security structure are nominally providing contractual services to our public bureaucracies. We recognize, however, that the institutional interests and needs of those corporations can easily come to dominate in the making of bureaucratic decisions.

BUDGETARY INCREMENTALISM.   Though principles of zero-based budgeting are accorded great rhetorical respect, they are virtually ignored in practice because every manager has a valuable institutional structure and capability to build and protect. Those structures and capabilities are the real budget base, and every organization tends to work back from them to create or redefine rationales for their continued existence and growth. Requirements, capabilities, and costs are almost invariably misrepresented to some extent in efforts to make them fit the institutional imperatives of continuity and expansion.

MALINTEGRATON.   Large institutions must separate critical functions for purposes of efficiency. They often find it difficult, however, to ensure the effective integration of the activities of their separate parts. Planners, budgeteers, developers, producers, and operators carry out their activities in relative isolation from each other. They are being forced continually to adapt to new situations, however, and communications often fail to reach, or penetrate, other parts of the organization that need to adapt as a consequence. Weapons systems may meet threats that no longer exist, organizational structures may be inappropriate for new strategies, and cost estimates may become totally unrealistic.

DISASSOCIATION FROM CONSTITUENCY.   Every bureaucracy is dependent on external constituencies. American national security bureaucracies, for example, serve the perceived national security needs of their citizenry. The leadership of those institutions, however, develops its own very clear notions of what those needs are and is predisposed to pursue them even in the face of opposition from its constituencies. Thus, the defense specialist who loses sight of broader budgetary perspectives is often inclined to define requirements and pursue goals that are well outside the bounds of what is politically feasible.

The Practice

Given these forms of bureaucratic parochialism, and the pathologies they can produce, what kind of roles can Congress reasonably be expected to play that might mitigate resulting irrationalities in national security policies and programs?

Four distinctive roles that are consistent with Congressional capabilites can frequently strengthen U.S. defense policy making. To identify these roles is not, of course, to suggest that Congress always recognizes irrationalities or that it operates in a coherent and consistent way to combat the ones its members do recognize. As was pointed out earlier, Congress is a body of highly personalized subunits that compete and overlap. Their activities will almost necessarily be disjointed and will often be internally inconsistent.

CONGRESS CAN FORCE REASSESSMENTS OF THE SCALE OF DEFENSE EXPENDITURES.   The dynamics of defense bureaucracy create continuing pressures for great growth in defense budgets. Congress frequently forces restraints on these dynamics. Often this process is nearly invisible. Politically sensitive officials in the Executive develop reasonably accurate estimates of what Congress will tolerate, based on prior actions and current mood. Thus, the consequences of one year's Congressional budget cycle feed in to requests for the following year. The Executive Branch usually asks

Congress for more money than it may wish to appropriate, but the differences are marginal if the range of Congressional flexibility has been reasonably anticipated in advance.

Two recent cases suggest interesting departures from this pattern. The first occurred in 1979, when a number of key members felt that the Carter Administration was not asking for sufficient money to meet minimal U.S. defense needs. The budget debate was not a particularly useful setting for pressing their case because it would have been difficult if not impossible for Congress to formulate and build a consensus around specific ways to spend additional funds. Instead, these members raised the issue as a part of the debate over ratification of SALT II. Arguing that the treaty would be consistent with U.S. national interest only if general defense capabilities were strengthened, they extracted from President Carter a commitment to increase the real growth rate of defense expenditures to 5 percent from the 3 percent previously envisaged.

The FY '84 budget presented the reverse pattern. Having supported major defense increases asked by President Reagan in the two preceding budgets, many members were unwilling to support the 10 percent real growth in defense spending requested by the Pentagon. Though it is difficult to distinguish between bargaining strategy and real expectations in this case, the Pentagon may well have lost track of citizen sentiment on this issue. Its strategy during the budget debate was to refuse to indicate where cuts could be made so as to force Congress to choose between acceptance of its program and making its own cuts.

This case illustrates an interesting pattern of Congressional-Executive interaction. The Administration, by refusing to suggest where cuts should be made, challenged Congress to act like a bureaucracy: to devise an alternate plan for spending a lesser sum of money. Congress, on the other hand, recognized that it is ill-equipped to play such a role and pressured the Defense Department to generate bureaucratic solutions. Clearly, compromise is likely to produce the best public policy result, and the playing out of competing bargaining strategies could well lead to less-productive outcomes. In this case, compromise came from the House Armed Services Committee. Though strongly supportive of high levels of defense spending, the Committee reported an authorization bill that contained specific cuts designed to preserve a coherent defense program. This action provided guidance for the final appropriation.

Many observers believe that the Congressional budget process should produce a full-blown debate on whether U.S. defense policy is appropriate. This seems unlikely, however, because the budget process is at best highly contentious. Allen Schick, an astute Congressional analyst, points out that debates over fundamental policy issues intensify conflict and that the kind of incremental bargaining over relative budget shares that characterizes the budget cycle may well be the only way in which Congress can cope with the political pressures it faces.

CONGRESS CAN CHALLENGE THE RATIONALE FOR MAJOR ADMINISTRATION
PROGRAMS.   Serious challenges come from Congress relatively infrequently. One of the most memorable was the 1969 debates over the development of ABM and MIRVs. Of more current interest was the 1982 rejection of
MX in a closely spaced basing mode, and the challenge to the Administration to reassess its options and to come up with a new basing mode for MX
that could command a majority of both houses of Congress. The Scowcroft
Commission report, and the President's endorsement of it, clearly represented a compromise proposal vis-à-vis Congress, designed to draw the
support of moderates in the House through its endorsement of a single-
warhead, small ICBM (Midgetman), and its linkage between deployments
and a new approach to arms control. This agreement generated an extended
process of Congressional-Executive bargaining over numbers of MX, frac-
tionation plans, a schedule for Midgetman development, and arms control
approaches. Many analysts see such a process as an irrational approach to the
making of U.S. strategic policy. It does, however, provide a mechanism
whereby Congress injects specific public concerns into the defense debate,
while allowing both defense production and arms control activities to proceed.

CONGRESS CAN CHALLENGE THE COST-EFFECTIVENESS OF WEAPONS SYSTEMS.
The planning, design, development, testing, and production of major weapons systems is an inordinately complex and difficult task for the most
sophisticated of bureaucracies. Under the best of circumstances, much will
almost certainly go wrong. The realities of bureaucratic pathologies simply
add to the list of problems.

Consequently, Congress is faced with difficult and painful choices.
Problems usually do not become apparent until huge sums of money have
been spent. Reliable data that reflect current realities are difficult to come by.
Promises of contractors and project officers are suspect. Cancellation robs
money spent of any measurable return. The stretching out of schedules
generates additional cost inefficiencies. To condition funding on specific
achievements (such as successful completion of testing) is difficult to do
wisely and invariably produces cries of Congressional "micromanagement." Simple faith in the bureaucracy to correct its own inadequacies seems
to many in Congress to be an abdication of responsibility and unlikely to be
very productive.

It is the efforts made by competent and diligent staff of the authorizing
and appropriations committees that make it possible for Congress to examine
at least some of the more serious weapons systems in detail. Challenges,
threats, and budgetary cuts are sometimes effective. The hand of Congress
has also been strengthened in recent years with the development, in the

Congressional Budget Office, of a capability to identify and cost out alternative programs to meet specific mission requirements.

CONGRESS CAN CHALLENGE LINE ITEM REQUESTS AND ADEQUACY OF PROJECT FUNDING.   In a budget as large and complex as the one required to support the U.S. defense effort, there is great opportunity and incentive for including unnecessary and marginally unproductive items. Though reasonable attempts to delete such items are made, presumably within the budget formulation process, many clearly survive.

Moreover, economic projections must be made early in that process and need to be reassessed by the time the proposal is being considered in Congress. Finally, it is widely believed that the long-term costs of many procurement items are significantly understated in DoD budgets. Managers of new projects being considered for production funding keep cost estimates low to make the project seem highly cost-effective. Also, new and unanticipated changes are frequently made in systems during development.

A key function of the Appropriations Committee staffs is to analyze DoD budget submissions in considerable detail to detect, challenge, and correct for inaccurate costing and projections. Though the costs of individual items can be small relative to the total defense budget, the aggregate consequences of this process often are measured in the billions of dollars.

CONCLUSIONS

These illustrations of the types of functions Congress can and does usefully perform suggest several conclusions:

THE CONGRESSIONAL ROLE IS USUALLY ONE OF CHALLENGE AND DENIAL. It has extremely limited capacity to develop coherent proposals of its own and less ability to provide continuous support for operational activities. These limitations are inherent in the character of the institution, and it is unrealistic to suggest that changes in structure, norms, or personnel will change its capabilities significantly.

THE CONGRESSIONAL-EXECUTIVE RELATIONSHIP ON DEFENSE IS MOST EFFECTIVE WHEN IT IS NEARLY INVISIBLE.   Indeed, its most visible "achievements" often can represent failures of the system to function effectively. The main role of Congress is to stimulate greater efficiency and effectiveness in our national security bureaucracies. Often this can be done relatively quietly, as a result of hearings, informal staff interactions, or private interventions by members. Failure to achieve bureaucratic response often produces closer Congressional oversight, increased bureaucratic subterfuges, and eventually the cancellation of programs, usually at considerable cost to the taxpayer and our defense capabilities. The debate over strategic programs and arms control is an important case in point. Failure to reach an accommodation would certainly be costly in terms of international perceptions of our ability to develop a coherent strategic policy, arms control prospects, and the integrity of our strategic force structure.

THE DYNAMICS OF CONGRESSIONAL-EXECUTIVE RELATIONS ARE PAR-TICULARLY TROUBLESOME WHEN THEY PRODUCE REINFORCING, RATHER THAN COUNTERVAILING, PAROCHIALISMS.   The danger that a major corporation will co-opt both a key part of a bureaucracy and a key unit of Congress is ever-present.

THE DEVELOPMENT AND PROJECTION OF PROGRAMS AND SPENDING LEVELS THAT ARE SUSTAINABLE OVER THE LIFE CYCLE OF RESEARCH, DEVELOP-MENT, PRODUCTION, AND DEPLOYMENT CONSTITUTE CRITICAL CHALLENGES TO DEFENSE POLICY MAKERS.   Since the generation of these data is subject to great political pressure within defense bureaucracies, it is especially important that Congress have a strong capability for generating independent projections.

IMPROVED RELATIONS BETWEEN CONGRESS AND THE EXECUTIVE ON DEFENSE DEPEND ON REASONABLE MUTUAL EXPECTATIONS.   rstanding the imperatives of those in the other branch can help to define appropriate working relationships. Tension and conflict cannot be eliminated. Indeed, at their best they produce improved policy. Patterns of distrust between Congressional and Executive officials need to be diminished, however, because they produce vicious cycles of bureaucratic obfuscation and Congressional micromanagement that are almost invariably counterproductive.

NOTES

1. John M. Maury, "Can Congress Run the Defense Department?" *Armed Forces Journal International*, November 1976, 30–32.

V

U.S. Decision Making on Defense

Nongovernmental Factors

14

The Media and National Defense

S. Robert Lichter and Stanley Rothman

Introduction

On 23 January 1982 CBS News broadcast a documentary under the title of "The Uncounted Enemy: A Vietnam Deception." For ninety minutes, correspondent Mike Wallace sought to prove that General William Westmoreland and high-ranking military intelligence officers conspired to deceive the President and the American public about the size and strength of enemy forces during the Vietnam War. The broadcast charged, among other things, that the scope of the Communists' crucial Tet offensive in early 1968 shocked and surprised American political leaders because military intelligence had deliberately understated North Vietnamese infiltration figures during 1967.

Four months later, *TV Guide* published an investigative report charging that the CBS documentary was a seriously flawed "smear" that was "often arbitrary and unfair . . . misshapen by personal bias and poor supervision."[1] In response to the ensuing controversy, CBS conducted an internal investigation. It released a summary version of the resulting report, which admitted to some inappropriate journalistic practices but stood by the substance of the program. A more pungent conclusion was delivered by Hodding Carter on the PBS press criticism series "Inside Story," broadcast on 21 April 1983. After reviewing both sides of the case, Carter concluded that CBS's prosecutorial approach in the program was more like that of "a lynch mob" than a fair trial.

Meanwhile, General Westmoreland filed suit against CBS for libel. His case in now in the courts. A definitive study of the whole affair must await disposition of this case. It will come as no surprise to most military officers, however, that television news, in its never-ending search for entertaining morality plays, would cast the military in the villain's role.

There has been no love lost between the Armed Services and the national media, at least since the Vietnam War cast the two as adversaries. Indeed "The Uncounted Enemy" can be seen as the latest round in a decade-long struggle over television's role in reporting the Vietnam conflict. At least since the Tet offensive, many in the media have remained suspicious toward a military establishment that, they believe, sought to use them to delude the public with false or misleading reports about the War. By the same token, many military leaders are convinced that the media, especially television, undermined public support for the war by transmitting "dovish" reports.

It is our thesis that the national media and the Armed Services today are natural adversaries because the media increasingly represent one of the most liberal cosmopolitan leadership groups in American society. Thus, their skeptical antiestablishment perspective is antithetical to that of a more traditional leadership group like the military. After presenting profiles of the backgrounds and attitudes of today's leading journalists, we will consider, as a case study of their military coverage, the role of television in reporting the Vietnam War. For this was the watershed event that created a lasting rupture between the journalistic and military communities and solidified the media's current self-image as the public's tribune against the "military-industrial complex."

The Media Elite: A Profile

As part of a larger study on elites, we surveyed members of the national media during 1979 and 1980.[2] We wanted to discover their backgrounds, attitudes, and outlooks toward American society and their own profession. We conducted hour-long interviews with 240 journalists and broadcasters at the most influential media outlets, including the *New York Times*, the *Washington Post*, the *Wall Street Journal*, *Time*, *Newsweek*, *U.S. News and World Report*, and the news departments at CBS, NBC, ABC, and PBS, along with major Public Broadcasting Stations.

Within each organization, we selected individuals randomly from among those responsible for news content. In the print medium we interviewed reporters, columnists, department heads, bureau chiefs, editors, and executives responsible for news content. In the broadcast medium we selected correspondents, anchormen, producers, film editors, and news executives. A very high proportion of those contacted, 76 percent, completed the interview.

The media elite is composed mainly of white males in their thirties and forties. Only one in twenty is nonwhite; one in five is female. They are highly educated, well-paid professionals. Ninety-three percent have college degrees, and a majority (55 percent) attended graduate school as well. These figures reveal that they constitute one of the best-educated groups in America. They are also one of the better-paid groups, despite journalism's reputation as a low-paying profession. In 1978, 78 percent earned at least $30,000, and one in three had salaries that exceeded $50,000. Moreover, nearly half (46 percent) reported family incomes above $50,000.

Geographically, they are drawn primarily from northern industrial states, especially from the northeast corridor. Two-fifths come from three states, New York, New Jersey, and Pennsylvania. Another 10 percent hail from New England, and almost one in five was raised in the big industrial states just to the west—Illinois, Indiana, Michigan, and Ohio. Thus, over two-thirds of the media elite come from these three clusters of states.

Many among the media elite enjoyed socially privileged upbringing. Most were raised in upper-middle-class homes. Almost 50 percent of their fathers were college graduates, and one in four held a graduate degree. Two in five are the children of professionals—doctors, lawyers, teachers, and so on. In fact, one in twelve is following in his father's footsteps as a second-generation journalist. Another 40 percent describe their fathers as businessmen. That leaves only one in five whose father was employed in a low-status blue- or white-collar job.

In sum, substantial numbers of the media elite grew up at some distance from the social and cultural traditions of smalltown "Middle America." Instead, they were drawn from big cities in the northeast and north central states. Their parents tended to be well-off, highly educated members of the upper middle class, especially the educated professions.

All these characteristics might be expected to predispose individuals toward the "new liberalism" that emerged during the 1960s. The new liberal rejects traditional bourgeois values, cultural norms, and older codes of behavior. He supports a "new morality" and endorses alternate life-styles. He seeks government action in the service of social change. He is critical of the United States and its international role. In sum, he is alienated from the traditional social and political order. Every element of this description fits substantial numbers of the media elite.

A predominant characteristic of this group is its secular outlook. Exactly 50 percent eschew any religious affiliation. Very few are regular churchgoers. Only 8 percent attend religious services at least once a month.

Ideologically, a majority of leading journalists describe themselves as liberals. Fifty-four percent place themselves to the left of center, compared to only 19 percent who choose the right side of the spectrum. These subjective ratings are borne out by their voting records in Presidential elections since 1964. (The interviews were conducted before the 1980 elections, so that our most recent data are for 1976.) Of those who say they voted, the proportion of leading journalists who supported the Democratic Presidential candidate never dropped below 80 percent. In 1972, when 62 percent of the electorate chose Nixon, 81 percent of the media elite voted for McGovern. This does not appear to reflect any particular personal aversion to Nixon, despite the well-publicized tensions between the press and his Administration. Four years later, leading journalists preferred Carter over Ford by exactly the same margin. In fact, in the Democratic landslide of 1964, media leaders picked Johnson over Goldwater by the staggering margin of 16 to 1, 94 to 6 percent.

These Presidential choices are consistent with the media elite's liberal views on a wide range of social and political issues. They show a strong preference for welfare capitalism, pressing for assistance to the poor in the form of income redistribution and a guaranteed employment. Sixty-eight percent agree that the government should substantially reduce the income gap between the rich and the poor. They are almost evenly divided over the issue of guaranteed employment. Forty-eight percent believe the government should guarantee a job to anyone who wants one, while a slight majority of 52 percent oppose this principle of entitlement.

Many leading journalists voice a general discontent with the social system. Virtually half, 49 percent, agree with the statement, "the very structure of our society causes people to feel alienated." A substantial minority would like to overhaul the entire system. Twenty-eight percent agree that America needs a "complete restructuring of its basic institutions."

In their attitudes toward sex and sex roles, members of the media elite are virtually unanimous in opposing the constraints of both government and tradition. Large majorities oppose government regulation of sexual activities, uphold a pro-choice position on abortion, and reject the notion that homosexuality is wrong. In fact, a majority would not characterize adultery as wrong.

When asked whether the government should regulate sexual practices, only 4 percent agree, and 84 percent strongly oppose state control over sexual activities. Ninety percent agree that a woman has the right to decide for herself whether to have an abortion; 79 percent agree strongly with this pro-choice position. Three-quarters disagree that homosexuality is wrong, and an even larger proportion, 85 percent, uphold the right of homosexuals to teach in the public schools. (A mere 9 percent feel strongly that homosexuality is wrong.) Finally, 54 percent do not regard adultery as wrong, and only 15 percent strongly agree that extramarital affairs are immoral. Thus, members of the media elite emerge as strong supporters of sexual freedom or permissiveness, and as natural opponents of groups like the Moral Majority, who seek to enlist the state in restricting sexual freedom.

In addition to these social and cultural issues, we inquired about international affairs, focusing on America's relations with Third World countries. Fifty-six percent agree that American economic exploitation has contributed to Third World poverty. About the same proportion, 57 percent, also find America's heavy use of natural resources to be "immoral." By a 3-to-1 margin, leading journalists soundly reject the counterargument that Third World countries would be even worse off without the assistance that they have received from Western states. Indeed, precisely half agree with the claim that the main goal of our foreign policy has been to protect American business interests.

Two issues dealing more directly with American foreign policy elicit a similar division of opinions. A majority of 55 percent would prohibit the CIA from ever undermining hostile governments to protect U.S. interests. The question of arms shipments produces an even split of opinion. Forty-eight percent would ban foreign arms sales altogether or restrict them to democratic countries. Forty-seven percent would supply arms to any "friendly" country, regardless of the regime. Only 4 percent would be willing to sell arms to all comers. We noted earlier that many leading journalists criticize the American system from within, as "alienating" and in need of an overhaul. It appears that even larger numbers extend their criticisms to the internatoinal arena. About half charge America with economic exploitation, and seek to limit CIA activity and arms sales as instruments of our foreign policy.

If these questions on international relations bear indirectly on the media elite's attitudes toward national defense, one question in the survey addresses this topic directly. We asked our respondents about the goals America should pursue during the next decade. From a list of eight choices, we asked them to select the most important and least important goals. The choices included:
1. Maintaining a high rate of economic growth
2. Making sure that this country has strong defense forces
3. Seeing that the people have more say in how things get decided at work and in their communities
4. Trying to make our cities and countryside more beautiful
5. Maintaining a stable economy
6. Progressing toward a less impersonal, more humane society
7. The fight against crime
8. Progressing toward a society where ideas are more important than money
Only 6 percent, about one in sixteen, picked national defense as our most important social goal. Precisely double that proportion, 12 percent, selected national defense as the least important goal listed. (By way of comparison, we showed the same list to a sample of high-level business executives in major corporations. Their responses were almost exactly the converse of the media elite's. Thirteen percent picked national defense as our most important goal, and just over half that number, 7 percent, selected it as least important.)

These results suggest that the media elite could be expected to take a critical posture toward the American military as part of a much broader social and cultural orientation. They are cosmopolitan in their backgrounds, liberal in their politics, and alienated from traditional values and institutions. In short, they emerge as natural opponents of both the "military-industrial complex" and Middle America. Moreover, the mind-set of leading journalists is unlikely to change significantly in the near future. In 1982 we gave the same survey to a random sample of students at Columbia University's prestigious Graduate School of Journalism, a primary source of tomorrow's media elite. When asked to select from our list of social goals, none of the students chose national defense as most important, and a staggering 41 percent, over two out of five, picked strong defense forces as least important.

These survey findings are quite suggestive in pointing to an adversarial relationship between the media and the military. Yet these data are also strictly limited in their implications for media coverage. The question remains whether the values and attitudes of journalists influence their coverage and transmission of the news. This is by no means a foregone conclusion, since journalists pay very serious heed to the norms of objectivity and professionalism. That is, they claim either to have no subjective viewpoint at all on their subject matter or, at worst, to be able to divorce their personal biases from their professional activities.

Of course, the matter is considerably more complex, for a great middle ground lies betwen Agnewesque conspiracy theories and ritualized claims of objectivity. Social scientists are well aware that "reality" is not simply a given, and that all persons, including social scientists and journalists, tend to view reality selectively. The selective perception of reality is influenced by many factors, one of which may be social ideology.

Thus, it is necessary to proceed on a case-by-case basis and analyze systematically whether actual news coverage presents the perspective that would be predicted on the basis of journalists' attitudes. In the area of national defense issues, the largest body of available evidence concerns television's coverage of the Vietnam War. Therefore, we shall examine this topic as a case study in media coverage of national defense.

Television and Vietnam: A Case Study

As we noted at the outset, the recent CBS documentary "The Uncounted Enemy" and General Westmoreland's subsequent lawsuit represents the latest skirmish in a long-running and rancorous dispute over television's Vietnam War coverage. The first volley was fired in 1965, when CBS correspondent Morley Safer reported that U.S. Marines had burned the village of Cam Ne in retaliation for Vietcong sniper fire. Tensions between the press and the military reached a crescendo during and after the 1968 Tet offensive, when journalistic criticism of Vietnam policy was capped by Walter Cronkite's on-air call for a negotiated withdrawal of American forces. Press critics, most prominently former Saigon correspondent Peter Braestrup, later charged that the media had misrepresented the outcome and significance of Tet.

After our troop withdrawal in 1973 and the collapse of Saigon in 1975, the controversy simmered as most Americans tried to forget about the unsuccessful and profoundly unsettling episode in our history. Then Asian correspondent Robert Elegant published an article excoriating the media for "losing" Vietnam, and the debate was renewed, with the next phase to be determined by the courts.

In this section we shall examine television's coverage of the Vietnam War, first focusing on the substantive nature of coverage, then reviewing the scholarly literature dealing with alleged TV bias, examining the effects of TV coverage on public opinon, and finally assessing the implications of Vietnam as a case study in television's news treatment of the military.

In Vietnam the media followed the flag—press coverage expanded in response to the growing presence of American troops. Thus, CBS established its Saigon bureau in 1965, the year that American advisers were supplanted by regular troops. That summer correspondent Morley Safer accompanied a Marine unit on a search-and-destroy mission in the village of Cam Ne. Safer sent back a critical report, aired 5 August, showing the Marines using their cigarette lighters to ignite the huts of the villagers. His story stressed the futility of the operation and did not try to rationalize the Marines' apparent casual cruelty. In his "closer," he asserted that "today's operation is the frustration of Vietnam in miniature," and concluded, "to a Vietnamese peasant whose home means a lifetime of back-breaking labor, it will take more than Presidential promises to convince him that we are on his side."

Safer's piece produced a rapid and widespread response, beginning with an angry late-night phone call from Lyndon Johnson to CBS executive Frank Stanton, and extending through a myriad of newspaper columns and letters to the editor. In fact, the public response provided a good early indication of the selective perception that would meet later war coverage on all sides of the ideological spectrum. Hawks used the Cam Ne incident to argue for battlefield censorship of the media, arguing that it showed antiwar bias. Doves viewed the story as evidence of the war's futility and the moral degradation it occasioned. Indeed, the *Saturday Review* started a subscription campaign to rebuild the village.

The story even affected military tactics. The next time the Marines went into Cam Ne, the mission was preceeded by briefings to officers and enlisted men about proper conduct, a leaflet airdrop explaining the mission to the villagers, and similar messages broadcast by bullhorn in Vietnamese. Safer's report on this foray was much more positive, to the effect that it was a much better way to win hearts and minds. There was no mention as to how many suspected Vietcong remained in the village to be questioned following the leaflet and loudspeaker barrages.

The story's most important impact, however, was on the media. Safer survived a police investigation and loyalty check ordered by Lyndon Johnson, and went on to win many of his profession's prestigious awards for his story, including the Sigma Delta Chi, Peabody, and Overseas Press Club awards. CBS made sure that the key footage was shown repeatedly on documentaries and wrap-ups, and the evening news ran follow-up stories to update the progress (or lack of it) in winning hearts and minds in Cam Ne. Moreover, Safer's original piece was shown to young reporters and correspondents about to leave on Vietnam tours as an example of a well-done battle story.

The Cam Ne story thus became the prototype for the battlefield vignette, a genre of reportage that presaged a new style of television coverage. For it was not simply Safer's criticism of American policy that distinguished his report. It was the entire style of the story, which was far more emotional, analytical, and interpretive than traditional television journalism. The use of *cinèma vèritè* techniques were employed to pull the viewer into the action. Instead of using a stand-up or voice-over, Safer was seen walking, crouching down to avoid fire, talking to his cameraman. He became part of the action, a guide inviting the viewer to join him. His vocal tone was at once world-weary, suggesting the war's futility, and occasionally biting in its criticism of American tactics. Finally, his closer, with its reference to the emptiness of "Presidential promises," conveyed editorial judgment both in its sarcastic intonation and its critical substance.

Safer's report thus paved the way for a drastic shift away from the partisan pro-American war coverage of World War II or even the more objective or nonpartisan tone that had dominated the national media since the advent of the wire services. If the reporter saw the story in terms of right versus wrong, and the American forces were in the wrong in his opinion, then he was under no compunction to refrain from saying so. As sociologist Herbert Gans put it,

> The unwritten rule is that conclusions or opinions which are deemed to be ideological can survive if they are supported by evidence. During the Vietnam War, television reporters on the scene of a fruitless battle or a search-and-destroy mission resulting in large numbers of civilian casualties could end their stories with critical comments about the war without anyone questioning them.[3]

Beyond its role in legitimizing greater interpretive and editorial leeway, Safer's story had a more immediate substantive impact on the way television would portray the war. As a sympathetic David Halberstam wrote,

> Safer's film not only helped legitimze reporting by all other television correspondents (they all resolved that if they witnessed a comparable episode they would film it), it prepared the way for a different perception of the war among Americans at large. There was simply, from that moment on, a greater receptivity to darker news about Vietnam, to accepting the fact that despite all the fine words of all the expensive public relations men the Defense Department and the President employed, and all the fine postures of high administration officials on "Meet the Press," there was something terribly wrong going on out there. Overnight one correspondent with one cameraman could become as important as ten or fifteen or twenty senators.[4]

So the Cam Ne story was part of a historic shift in both the form and substance of television news coverage. But it must be remembered that such reports were the exception rather than the rule. Safer's report caused such a furor precisely because it was the first major Vietnam story to portray American soldiers as villains on the nightly news. And even though similar critical reports from one battlefield followed in its wake, they represented only one facet of Vietnam coverage. For years, these battlefield vignettes were more than balanced by straightforward coverage of Johnson Administration spokesmen defending their policies, as well as spot reports and other "tell stories" that basically recounted the day's wire-service reports.

Moreover, for all the increasing cynicism of reporters in the field, the final decisions on what stories would run rested with senior producers and executives in New York and Washington. And these senior staffers, who often had their own contacts with Administration officials, often killed or substantially watered down the antiwar stories sent from Saigon. Of course, there was substantial disagreement on how to "play" the war among New York staffers as well. But the decisive turning point in media coverage did not come until much later. The watershed was the Tet offensive in February 1968. As Gans noted,

> Conscious opinions generally change only in the wake of highly visible and traumatic events, for positions can then be altered without loss of credibility. Even so, these events are often the culmination of a series of less visible events which had led journalists to doubt their earlier stands. Perhaps the most significant example in recent times is the change of stands toward the Vietnam War, taken by almost all major news media after the Tet offensive of 1968. Many Saigon reporters had long expressed their doubts that the war could be won, and some news organizations were embroiled in internal conflict over whether to listen to them or to their more senior—and more optimistic—reporters in Washington. The Tet offensive was thus the last straw in a lengthy process of increasing uncertainty, not only about the war, but about the government's honesty in informing journalists about it.[5]

The irony, of course, is that Tet is now widely regarded by historians as a major military defeat for the Communists, just as American military spokesmen claimed. Yet the American press presented the battle primarily as a psychological victory for the Communist forces, hence a political setback for the Americans, whatever their advantage in purely military terms. Television and other media coverage of Tet have been exhaustively examined by former Saigon correspondent Peter Braestrup in his book *Big Story*. Braestrup argued that several years of overly optimistic assessments had created a credibility gap between the American military and the Saigon press corps. Reporters' growing suspiciousness and cynicism led them to mistrust anything they were told by American authorities. By 1968, they were more or less automatically prepared to discount the official "line." As journalist

Robert Elegant later recalled,

> The reaction against official mendacity was initially healthy but
> later became distorted, self-serving, and self-perpetuating. A
> faulty syllogism was unconsciously accepted: Washington was
> lying consistently, Hanoi contradicted Washington; therefore
> Hanoi was telling the truth.[6]

So when the Tet offensive began, Braestrup concluded, "Newsmen,
this reporter included, were willing, even eager to believe the worst."[7]
Reporters were shocked by the scope and intensity of the fighting, which for
the first time engulfed Saigon itself. For many, this was the first real exposure
to the gruesome realities of hand-to-hand combat. Braestrup suggests that
they projected their own dismay and disillusionment onto the Vietnamese
populace. For example, NBC's Douglas Kiker reported on 22 February that,

> Even before these city attacks, the South Vietnamese people were
> in retreat from this war and now they have withdrawn even more
> from it. . . . They're tired of military rule. They're weary of this
> war. They're people caught in the middle. They find it hard, almost
> impossible, to commit themselves to anything anymore. Their big
> concern now is survival.

How Kiker, a newcomer to Vietnam who spoke no Vietnamese, came to
these conclusions is not clear. Certainly the South Vietnamese people did not
react as the Vietcong hoped. The government did not collapse and the army
(ARVN) fought well. There was no popular uprising in support of the
invaders, and the populace did not substantially assist their effort to gain
military footholds in urban areas.

Yet the correspondents often suggested that the Vietcong's very ability
to launch such an offensive constituted a kind of triumph, regardless of its
outcome. Thus CBS's Jeff Gralnick reported from Hue on 2 February that,
"the Vietcong proved they could take and hold almost any area they
chose . . . to take it and hold it for even six to twelve hours would be a
tremendous triumph. And this they have done." And ABC commentator
Joseph Harsch charged one night earlier that,

> The enemy has not yet, and probably never will, run out of enough
> manpower to keep his effort going. What this city yearns for is
> someone like a Winston Churchill, who would frankly admit the
> fact that after two years of massive military intervention in Viet-
> nam, the enemy has been able to mount and to launch by far the
> biggest and boldest and most sophisticated offensive of the whole
> war.

Later reports often took note of assertions that the Vietcong were
suffering a military defeat, but they tended to discount this aspect of the

struggle. NBC's Howard Tuckner concluded during a special aired on 10 March: "Militarily the allies won. They held (Saigon). Psychologically, the Vietcong won. They got into the capital in force." In the same broadcast, Frank McGee put the case even more starkly:

> The cities are no longer secure; perhaps they never were. . . . The government is weaker than ever, though it still exists. . . . The grand objective, the building of a free nation, is not nearer, but further from realization. In short, the war, as the administration has defined it, is being lost.

The most important television commentary was delivered by Walter Cronkite on a 27 February CBS special. He suggested that the South Vietnamese government might yet "salvage a measure of victory from defeat," then concluded,

> It seems now more certain than ever that the bloody experience of Vietnam is to end in a stalemate. . . . On the off chance that military and political analysts are right, in the next few months we must test the enemy's intentions, in case this is indeed his last big gasp before negotiations. But it is increasingly clear to this reporter that the only rational way out then will be to negotiate, not as victors, but as an honorable people who lived up to their pledge to defend democracy, and did the best they could.

It is hard to fault CBS producer Gary Paul Gates's assessment that "Cronkite's antiwar stand had plenty of impact and was a definite milestone."[8] Rarely has there been a more clear-cut case of a news broadcast directly influencing military policy. For when President Johnson heard Cronkite's broadcast, he turned to an aide and confided that, if he had lost Walter Cronkite's support, then he'd lost the country as well. As David Halberstam later wrote, "It was the first time in American history that a war had been declared over by a correspondent."[9]

For all the controversy over television coverage of Tet in particular and Vietnam in general, surprisingly few scholarly studies have assessed that coverage in a systematic and reliable fashion. Moreover, some of the few studies that exist are remarkable in their failure to address the most interesting and obvious questions that one would expect about fairness or bias. For example, one study analyzed interpretive reporting of Vietnam by anchormen between 1965 and 1970. Unfortunately, the study concluded only that "roughly 35 percent of anchormen stories were interpretive,"[10] without concern for the nature or direction of interpretation. The author's perspective is perhaps revealed by his complaint that anchormen referred to the combatants as "the Americans and the South Vietnamese against the Communist enemy or the Vietcong, a most simplisitc and overgeneralized shorthand. . . ."[11]

Another study analyzed CBS Vietnam news specials and documentaries from 1965 to 1969. In this case the author examined only the broad topics covered (e.g., American policy, North Vietnamese, South Vietnamese), rather than the way they were covered. He did report one suggestive finding regarding the sources of assertions made in those newscasts. In 1965 Administration spokesmen made a plurality of all assertions heard in these newscasts. In 1966 and every succeeding year, network commentators themselves accounted for the largest number of assertions. In 1968, the year of Tet, 85 percent of all assertions were made by correspondents rather than outside sources. Unfortunately, the author failed to examine the substance of their assertions. He did single out for criticism one report as "embarrassing to CBS for its unabashed support for the role and style of American airpower in Vietnam."[12]

By far the most comprehensive and systematic study was carried out by Ernest Lefever under the auspices of the Institute for American Strategy. As part of a larger study of how TV news portrays national defense, Lefever analyzed the themes and viewpoints presented in all 1972 "CBS Evening News" segments and special programs dealing with Vietnam. Lefever found that themes critical of U.S. policy outnumbered those supportive of policy by roughly a four-to-one margin on evening newscasts, and a five-to-one margin on specials. For example, the single most frequent theme coded was, "U.S. involvement is wrong because the war is cruel, expensive, or senseless."

In addition, he carried out a viewpoint analysis that categorized viewpoints presented as (in effect) hawkish, moderate, or dovish. For example, policy viewpoints on military action were divided into advocacy of increased U.S. military efforts, gradual U.S. withdrawal and increased ARVN responsibility, and immediate U.S. withdrawal. Overall, dovish viewpoints accounted for 70 percent of those coded, moderate viewpoints 29 percent, and hawkish viewpoints just over 1 percent. Not surprisingly, Lefever concluded that "CBS Evening News employed various tehniques of selective reporting and presentation to advocate a position opposed to U.S. military involvement in Vietnam."[13]

Unfortunately, the case is not quite so conclusive as these figures suggest. Lefever is a prominent conservative, and the sponsoring organization was hardly a neutral source on defense issues. Moreover, the tone of the study is often contentious rather than analytical. For example, Lefever accused CBS News of "undesirable anti-authority, anti-establishment bias" that frequently crossed "the line (between) constructive criticism and irresponsible attack. . . ."[14]

Given the orientations of the researchers, it was crucial that they support their conclusions with a scientifically reliable and valid methodology. This they apparently failed to do, despite the considerable effort they devoted to their coding system. One of the most basic requirements of social-scientific content analysis is that results be reliable. Independent observers must be able to come to similar conclusions about the same material. In studies of television, this is normally accomplished by having two coders independently examine the same broadcast or transcript and then compare their code sheets to assure agreement. The amount of disagreement across many programs is summarized by one of several common reliability statistics.

Unfortunately, Lefever and his researchers apparently did not do this. For the thematic analysis, "three staff members . . . examined all the transcripts, attempting to note only those themes that were objectively present. Additional staff members were consulted to decide difficult cases."[15] Moreover, this process took place in-house, superseding an unsuccessful attempt to use outside analysts from the academic community. For the viewpoint analysis, two readers separately examined transcripts, and a third reader was used in cases of disagreement, but no figures are presented on the actual degree of consistency achieved.

The researchers obviously followed a careful and laborious set of procedures designed to ensure reliable coding, and they present examples to justify their decisions. But the absence of a systematic accounting of the reliability level attained precludes unqualified acceptance of their findings. These criticisms do not mean that Lefever's conclusions are necessarily wrong, only that they do not meet all the standards of a scientific content analysis.

An instructive contrast is provided by a much more limited study of television's Vietnam coverage. To assess bias, the author first selected 100 statements about the war from such sources as the *New York Times*, *New Republic*, and *National Review*. The hawkish versus dovish content of the statements was then rated on a scale of 0 to 100 by five students of diverse political persuasions. Ten statements were then selected from the original hundred on the basis of their distribution along the opinion spectrum and the judges' agreement on their placement. The statements were ranked on a scale of support for American intervention in Vietnam that ranged from $+5$ ("The U.S. should vow to stay in Vietnam until it is safe from Communist aggression") to -5 ("The U.S. should unilaterally withdraw from South Vietnam").

Next, several researchers not involved in constructing the scale coded the statements when they appeared in a magazine article and on several TV broadcasts. High intercoder reliability ratings were obtained. Only then did the actual study commence, based on a random sample of ninety-six newscasts chosen equally from NBC and CBS during 1969 and 1970. By adding up the values assigned to the statements and dividing by the number of statements, the study sought to identify the average "bias."

The overall mean values obtained were very slightly on the "dovish" side of the midpoint: -0.3 for CBS and -0.6 for NBC. The author concluded that "these results . . . provide factual evidence that there was no 'bias' against the Nixon Administration's policies in Vietnam . . . on specific aspects of the war there was bias in coverage, but this was cancelled out in the overall reporting on the war."[16] For example, the most "positive" coverage concerned the ability and will of ARVN (+ 1.5) and the POW issue (+ 1.4). The most "negative" coverage was given to civilian casualities caused by U.S. forces (− 2.4) and to the lack of South Veitnamese popular support for the government (− 2.1).

Equally important, the study noted that an average score midway between the most hawkish and dovish positions would not necessarily indicate "fair" coverage. That depends on one's own conception of what was actually happening in Vietnam; fairness is in the eye of the beholder.

Certainly this study shows that TV's Vietnam coverage was by no means pro-war, and it raises the issue of journalists' potentially conflicting roles as both citizens and nonpartisan professionals. One recalls the recent public furor in England over some BBC reporters attempting to provide "nonpartisan" coverage of the Falklands war by giving equal weight to Argentine and British viewpoints. In essence, that is what the preceding study found regarding American television in Vietnam; their coverage was slightly more favorable toward the antiwar than the pro-war arguments. Perhaps the difference between public response in the two cases was attributable to the Falklands conflict providing a quick victory, while Vietnam offered a protracted struggle with an ever-receding light at the end of a seemingly endless tunnel.

This raises a final crucial question. How clear-cut was television's alleged influence in turning public opinion against the Vietnam war? Given that leading journalists have little sympathy for the military, that their Vietnam coverage was at least somewhat more receptive to antiwar than to pro-war themes, and that the critical case of Tet was misreported, what difference did it make in public support for the war effort?

Many on both sides of the political fence take for granted that television coverage hastened our departure from Vietnam. Robert Elegant states flatly that, "For the first time in modern history, the outcome of a war was determined not on the battlefield but in the printed page and, above all, on the television screen."[17] Robert Northshield, a self-described "dove" who was executive producer of "NBC Nightly News" during most of the period in question, described television's role even more succinctly: "We ended the Vietnam war."[18]

The truth is a bit harder to come by than such bold assertions would suggest. By far the most thorough examination of this question was conducted by sociologist John Mueller in his book *War, Presidents, and Public Opinion*. Mueller disputed the conventional wisdom that years of nightly uncensored television coverage conveyed the brutality of war as never before and thus undermined public support for continued military action. His approach was to compare poll data on support for the wars in Vietnam and

Korea. He found that public support for these wars followed a very similar pattern of decline, despite the far more vocal opposition to the Vietnam War among certain subgroups of the populace. Indeed, support for the war in Vietnam dropped below the levels found during Korea only after the war had gone on considerably longer and far more casualties had been sustained. Mueller concluded,

> The poll data . . . clearly show that whatever impact television had, it was not enough to reduce support for the war below the levels attained by the Korean War, when television was in its infancy, until casualty levels had far surpassed those of the earlier war.[19]

The chief limiting factor on television's power to persuade lies in the set of psychological mechanisms by which persons selectively reinterpret new information according to their existing predispositions. For example, although television coverage of the 1968 Democratic Convention was favorable to the demonstrators, it did not increase public support for them or their cause. The reason was that the majority of the populace already had made up their minds about student demonstrators and were predisposed to react negatively toward them.

Television's potential impact, like that of other media, is greatest at the outset of an ongoing story, before viewers have developed perspectives and additional information sources that might counteract the images they see. This is one reason Presidential candidates pour so many resources into the New Hampshire primary and, more recently, the Iowa caucuses. They hope to build momentum by establishing an early image as a winner that will stick in the electorate's memory. In the case of Vietnam, though, the evidence suggests that television coverage was at its most positive in the early phases of American involvement, before reporters became disillusioned with the course the war was taking. By the time press criticism became widespread, the response of much of the audience was to charge the media with bias rather than to shift their own opinions.

On the other hand, Mueller's conclusions should not be overstated. His findings counter claims that television makes a lengthy conventional war impossible, since public support for the "living room war" continued longer than for the Korean "police action." Yet there is one striking instance of a shift in public opinion that followed the contours of media coverage. That instance was Tet. As we have seen, it was the crucial event that swung senior network staffs around to the critical views long expressed by field correspondents. Moreover, it is by far the best-documented case of a major battle whose outcome was reported in a negative fashion despite the claims of victory voiced by American military and political leaders. And in this case media coverage seems to have occasioned a drastic and lasting shift in public opinion.

A Gallup poll taken early in March 1968 found that the proportion who believed we were "losing ground" rose 15 percent over the pre-Tet figures, while the proportion believing the war would be over in less than two years dropped by 15 percent. So the media's interpretation of Tet's significance seemed to penetrate quickly into the public consciousness.

Even more striking are poll data on policy preferences reported by Mueller himself.[20] One question was asked several times during the late 1960s: "People are called 'hawks' if they want to step up our military effort in Vietnam. They are called 'doves' if they want to reduce our military effort in Vietnam. How would you describe yourself—as a 'hawk' or a 'dove'?" In the period preceding Tet, hawks invariably outnumbered doves by wide margins. In January 1968 the margin was precisely 2 to 1, or 56 to 28 percent, with the remainder undecided. Early in February, following first reports of the Tet offensive, the public's hawkishness actually rose to 61 to 23 percent. However, this initial tendency to rally round the flag quickly lapsed. By March, the doves had actually gained a plurality of 42 to 41 percent, a shift of one-sixth of the populace. Moreover, this dramatic shift resumed before the Administration announced a partial bombing halt that marked the beginning of America's de-escalation and eventual disengagement. By November of 1969, public opinion had made a complete turnabout from less than two years earlier, with doves outnumbering hawks by 55 to 31 percent.

The enormous impact of Tet has been chronicled by media researchers Robert Entman and David Paletz:

> The result was a striking change in public opinon within a few months. . . . Tet also destroyed the accord that normally pervades foreign policy leadership circles. Important senators . . . were emboldened to dissent by the news out of Saigon; criticism was increasingly and regularly voiced in official Washington. . . . It would be wrong to believe that television news alone caused these drastic shifts. Certainly the Johnson administration's moderate dovish platform of ceasing the bombing and beginning negotiations had much to do with the new public sentiment. But the administration's decision itself was, if not caused, at least encouraged by television's pictures of disaster. After all, if TV news had accepted the administration's official line that Tet was a stunning defeat for the NLF, the pressures on the administration would have been quite different.[21]

Summary

Tet provides the clearest instance of television's impact on both mass and elite opinion toward the Vietnam war. A military victory was covered as a psychological defeat, and this had major implications for American policy and public opinion alike. But television's coverage of Tet must be understood in the broader context of a growing rift between the media and both military and political authorities.

We have suggested that this schism was perhaps to be expected in view of the social and political perspectives of the national media. Even Robert Elegant, whom many journalists regard as a kind of traitor to his profession for his views on Vietnam, refers to the "quixotic American Army establishment, itself often confused . . . by their moralistic attitudes and political prejudices."[22] The major media's reaction to Vietnam was partly a function of their growing self-consciousness as a liberal elite charged with protecting the "people" from the "establishment." Braestrup concludes that,

> We saw at Tet the first show of the more volatile journalistic style . . . that has become so popular since the late 1960's. With this style came an often mindless readiness to seek out conflict, to believe the worst of the government or of authority in general, and on that basis to divide up the actors on any issue into the good and the bad.[23]

To that judgment it must be added that Vietnam, along with the vast political and cultural changes in America during the late 1960s and early 1970s, immensely strengthened these tendencies within the media. One lasting legacy of the living room war was the adversarial media of late twentieth-century America.

NOTES

1. Don Kowet and Sally Bedell, "Anatomy of a Smear," *TV Guide*, 29 May 1982, 15.

2. This study was directed by Rothman and Lichter, under the auspices of the Research Institute on International Change at Columbia University. The surveys of media leaders were supervised by Response Analysis, a survey research organization.

3. Herbert Gans, *Deciding What's News* (New York: Pantheon, 1979), 195.

4. David Halberstam, *The Powers That Be* (New York: Knopf), 491.

5. Gans, 200.

6. Robert Elegant, "How to Lose a War," *Ethics and Public Policy Reprint 35* (Washington, D.C.: Ethics and Public Policy Center, 1981), 14.

7. Peter Braestrup, *Big Story* (Boulder, Colo.: Westview Press, 1977), 86.

8. Gary Paul Gates, *Air Time* (New York: Harper & Row, 1978), 211.

9. Ibid.

10. George Bailey, "Interpretive Reporting of the Vietnam War by Anchormen," *Journalism Quarterly* 53 (Summer 1976): 321.

11. Ibid., 323.

12. Thomas McNulty, "Vietnam Specials: Policy and Content," *Journal of Communication* 25 (Autumn 1975): 178.

13. Ernest Lefever, *TV and National Defense* (Boston, Va.: Institute for American Strategy, 1974), 131.

14. Ibid., 157–58.

15. Ibid., 38.

16. Frank Russo, "A Study of Bias in TV Coverage of the Vietnam War," *Public Opinion Quarterly* 35 (Winter 1971–72), 542.

17. Elegant, 1.

18. Northshield, speech at George Washington University, 23 November 1980.

19. John Mueller, *War, Presidents, and Public Opinion* (New York: John Wiley, 1973), 67.

20. Ibid., 107.

21. Robert Entman and David Paletz, "The War in Southeast Asia: Tunnel Vision on Television," in *Television Coverage of International Affairs*, ed. William C. Adams (Norwood, N.J.: Ablex, 1982), 186–87.

22. Elegant, 3.

23. Braestrup, 726.

15

Government-Industry Relations
And Defense Decision Making

P. A. Phalon

The breadth of the topic permits the writer to wax philosophic on its vagaries and complexities, or to attack with scientific precision the errors in judgment made in the past, or to forecast doom on the horizon prophetically if his own erudite suggestions for correction of the system are not quickly adopted, or "none of the above."

At the outset, I should confess that I represent a company that was awarded quite a bit over $2 billion worth of contracts from the Department of Defense in fiscal 1982. With all of these awards, I can only say that the DoD acted most competently and with that wisdom that is born of careful study and experience. Conversely, DoD, last year, through either ignorance or carelessness, awarded to our competitors about $1 billion worth of contracts that we wanted. Obviously, these are the areas wherein the system is in great need of repair!

The point of the foregoing is simply to demonstrate that it is extremely difficult for a representative of industry to tackle the topic without a good deal of personal bias very much in evidence. However, a few fundamental premises may be in place:

First, government-industry relations are good or bad, depending upon where you stand at any given moment in time. I have experienced the comaraderie and feeling of accomplishment that exists between members of the government and industry teams when a system, long in development, finally passes its last crucial test before being declared "ready for production." At that moment in time, for all the members of both teams, government-industry relations are wonderful. Anyone who saw the NASA Control Center during lift-off of Challenger could see this in the eyes of all those present. In a moment like that, the decision-making process has been vindicated, the technical squabbles forgotten, and cost justified.

At the other end of the scale, government-industry relations are at their worst when a program is canceled. Then come the Monday morning quarterbacks in full regalia. Clothed in righteousness, they condemn the decision-making process from all sides as clumsy and inept, bogged down with technical incompetence, and with costs out of sight, caused by veritable robbers from the taxpayers' meager coffers.

Is the situation really so good or so bad? As with most issues, truth lies somewhere in between.

Second, we must recognize that the pressures on DoD decision-makers are vast and come from many directions. The defense budget, large and growing, must be the subject of great debate in these difficult economic times. We should not expect it to be otherwise. Indeed, the American system depends on just such a process of clarification and justification. However, beyond that debate over national priorities, there are the other pressures: from Congress, from the American public, and in more recent years, from our Allies. These pressures cause friction even within the DoD itself, as services battle for programs, project offices fight for dollars, production vies with research and development, operation and maintenance offices justify their funding requirements versus new program starts, and engineers and scientists argue the merits of state-of-the-art technologies. The task of decision making in the present socioeconomic international environment is indeed difficult—not to be envied in the least.

The difficulty of the task, however, is a reality that will not go away. It must be faced squarely, and the wise decision maker will use every tool available to him in accomplishing his task. It is within the context of these generalities that a few observations may be useful:

Government-industry relations are quite in line with what one might expect them to be. We, as suppliers, are viewed with a certain amount of skepticism by those who are the buyers. I do not think we are viewed by the government as the worst of used-car salesmen, but, on the other hand, it recognizes that all of us, from the American defense industry, are proponents of our own systems and products and have obligations to our stockholders, employees, and management to put our best foot forward. Its job is to assess the relative merits, in performance and cost, of our systems and product, to meet their requirements. Thus, I would not suggest that the relationship between the parties should or could be revised very much. Competition among suppliers helps to keep the game on a relatively even keel.

However, with respect to the decision-making process, I believe there is room for a great deal more involvement of industry to the betterment of all concerned. To cite some examples:

A concept was generated, during the last Administration, called the "Family of Weapons." This idea was promulgated because of the alleged need to reduce redundancy of research and development efforts undertaken by the United States and its NATO allies. What happens under this concept is the assignment, by agreement between the governments, of specific developments to one side of the Atlantic Ocean or the other. I contend that the assignment of exclusive developmental responsibility for specific weapons systems to a foreign government will seriously weaken the U.S. defense industrial base.

Although the need for conservation and prudent use of investment in technology is a worthy goal, I believe that the Family of Weapons concept, as presently formulated, would:

1. Substantially weaken U.S. research and development in specific areas
2. Jeopardize the ability of the industrial base to respond in the event that the foreign source were immobilized
3. Impose a dependency on foreign source products for critical needs in times of emergency

It is the stated policy of the U.S. government to promote a system of standardization and interoperability of arms, so as to develop a strong collaborative defense posture with our friends and Allies. I wholeheartedly agree with this policy. Yet, the United States must not depend on foreign sources for the production of systems essential to U.S. defense. Further, even though there may be areas of foreign technology that are superior to those found in the United States, we cannot afford to retreat from continued developmental effort in every area of technology critical to national defense. Consequently, decisions with respect to the allocation of responsibility under the "Family of Weapons" concept must be the subject of intense discussion between the U.S. government and U.S. industry.

In the sale of defense equipment to friendly foreign industrial countries, it is most common these days for those governments to require what is known as "offsets" or the reverse purchase of products of equivalent value from them. We must recognize that the foreign buyer, in Germany or the Netherlands, has his own set of economic problems, so that his requirement for offsets is not surprising. The policy of the United States, at the moment, is to reach a Memorandum of Understanding with the foreign government, under which the sale is permitted, but at the same time it takes a "hands off" attitude toward involvement in the offset requirements to be imposed on industry. The writing of the MOU itself is an area in which U.S. industry must become much more deeply involved and in which a much greater degree of cooperation must be generated between our industry and the government. For I believe that any defense offset dilutes the U.S. defense industrial base.

If the U.S. industrial base is to remain strong, concessions can no longer be made without proper guidance and concern for possible negative consequences of such measures. The U.S. government should promote negotiations of multinational agreements to eliminate, or set limits on, the level of offsets that are acceptable in an international procurement—with the participation and concurrence of the industries involved. Offsets should be the exception for most programs, rather than the rule.

Finally, the subject of "Technology Transfer":

A set of guidelines should be developed and carefully updated for the transfer of technology to friendly governments and Allies, similar to, but less restrictive than, the Military Critical Technologies List (MCTL), which was developed to prevent access by unfriendly countries. Well thought-out analysis must be undertaken to determine which technologies are truly critical. Technologies that were considered critical previously, but today are well-known and accepted, and technologies that are quite peripheral and therefore inconsequential to our mainstream development effort, should not be on a restrictive, critical list. Protection of critical technologies is essential to the continued health and competitiveness of U.S. industry in the international market. Further, U.S. security demands that consideration be given to the possible dissemination of this technology by a foreign government or industry to countries hostile to the United States. Since industry generally is most conversant with the status of the technology in question, it should be consulted prior to reaching firm decisions with respect to technology transfers and should likewise be consulted during any updating process.

For its part, the U.S. government through its intergovernmental MOUs and other agreements, must establish the ground rules for technology transfers within each international program. This must be done in cooperation with the U.S. industry teams concerned. The ground rules should address security, amount and time phasing of technology transfers, sales rights, recoupment of IR&D, limitations on third-party transfers, etc.

However, the MOU agreements made by governments normally are implemented by industry, usually on the basis of commercial agreements that must include terms and conditions for licensing, intellectual property rights, hardware and technical services to be provided. The industrial agreements should be consistent with the intergovernmental MOUs. Therefore, government and industry must work closely together during the formulation and negotiation of these international agreements.

Perhaps there is some office within the giant bureaucracy called the U.S. government to which these remarks might be addressed appropriately. For instance, I wish that someone could tell me where the headquarters of that great partnership called the "Military-Industrial Complex" are located. I have heard that this "Complex" is in the Pentagon, but no one there seems to know its whereabouts, let alone feels that I am its partner. In fact, the attitude in many offices there is downright hostile. I have tried also finding that "Complex" in the Capitol, but, in my search through the labyrinth of that imposing structure, I found the inhabitants to be bent on *inhibiting* foreign sales by such mechanisms as the Foreign Corrupt Practices Act, the "Specialty Metals" rider on last year's continuing defense resolution, and the prohibition against the use of Export-Import Bank financing of defense equipment.

Thus, I have concluded that no such headquarters exist, except in the mind of those who simply fail to recognize the fact that the U.S. defense industrial base is a national asset that cannot be allowed to deteriorate further than it already has.

The machine tool industry, research and development, and productivity of our manufacturing plants are among areas of deep concern for those of us who view our defense posture not only in terms of present-day stockpiles of arms and munitions, but also as far as industry's ability is concerned to achieve and maintain the defense capacity that would be required to sustain a long-term military confrontation. To achieve our national goals, U.S. defense industry must be made a more constant participant in the decision-making process.

VI

Policy Implications

16

National Security Decision Making: Policy Implications

Robert L. Pfaltzgraff, Jr.

Indispensable to the formation of national security policy is the decisional process and structure. In turn, the organizational framework within which such decisions are made reflects the basic characteristics of the society on whose behalf national security policy is formed. Ideally, the basis for national security policy rests upon the existence of a national strategy that flows from national goals and a conception of national interest. Moreover, while decisional processes and structures inevitably form the context within which national security policy is shaped, they bear resemblance not only to the society whose interests they serve, but also reflect the scope and level of effort undertaken by the state: the greater the national security interests, commitments and capabilities of a state, the greater and perhaps more complex its decisional process and structure are likely to be. So, too, the more pluralistic the society, the greater the number of constituent elements likely to be represented in its decisional process and structure.

Political pluralism, therefore, taken together with global interests, commitments, and capabilities, describes the principal setting within which the national security decision-making system of the United States has evolved in this century. Yet, it accounts as well for some of the shortcomings in American policy planning. For if political pluralism leads constitutionally, organizationally, and bureaucratically to the fragmentation of the decisional process and structure, the inevitable result is to limit severely the prospect for a coherent and cohesive national security strategy. National security policy based upon shifting coalitions of interest among such diverse forces as the Congress, the Executive, and interest groups in the private sector, not to speak of the demands of Alliance politics, is not easily compatible with, and may make impossible, the development and creative utilization of a coherent national strategy. Strategy and national security policy—and national capabilities in support of strategy and policy—all interact within the decisional process and structure.

Each of these closely related themes is present, to varying degrees, in the chapters contained in this volume. Indeed, a unifying theme among the contributions is the multidimensionality of national security policy, with its political, diplomatic, military, economic, cultural, and psychological aspects. The result of such diversity has been the extension of the decision-making network across a broad spectrum of departments and agencies within the United States government, and the need, within specific bureaucratic structures, to develop detailed procedures and criteria for the allocation of resources in support of national security policy. In its wake, this diffusion of the policy process has prompted considerable efforts at structural change, as reflected in the passage of the National Security Act of 1947 and the formation of the National Security Council (as well as other agency committees and groups), with a view toward achieving higher levels of policy coordination. In essence, it was the absence of such coordination in the early post–World War II period, as Admiral Thomas Moorer reminds the reader in the Introduction, that created the need to develop new structures for national security decision making in the United States.

Nevertheless, nagging difficulties remain in the formulation and implementation of American national security policy. In particular, there have been continuing problems and frustrations in achieving necessary levels of policy consistency, as a result of such factors as frequent changes in Administration and the lack of a broadly shared national consensus on goals and means or strategy. The abiding question, then, is the impact of institutional-jurisdictional-bureaucratic compartmentalization upon the national security policy process and, specifically, the formation of a national strategy. Are the determining factors in the shaping of national security policy in the United States the strategic circumstances of the global security environment, or the domestic structure of our society and political system? How can these two sets of fundamentally different variables be reconciled, especially in the United States, as a pluralistic superpower, to produce an adequate national security policy based upon a concept of strategy that reflects national goals, interests, and values within an appropriate decisional process and structure? It is on these and similar questions that preceding chapters are focused.

Defense Planning and the General Staff: Historical Comparisons

The relationship among doctrine, strategic circumstances, and institutional development was explored by reference to the evolution of General Staffs in Great Britain and the Soviet Union. According to Peter Nailor, the British experience, perhaps reflected in its own way by that of the United States, relied primarily upon strategic improvisations, with decisional processes and structures evolving in response to external circumstances—in the case of Britain, continental threats to her security that demanded the mobilization of Imperial resources and capabilities. Indeed, it was the need to mobilize for, and to wage and manage, modern warfare, demonstrated first in the Boer War, and then again with the outbreak of World War I, that led to the formation of more adequate structures for that purpose—namely, the Imperial General Staff.

This particular institution reflected, moreover, a conscious effort by London to bring about a reconciliation between the need for central war-planning authority and the equally pressing requirement for a more effective means of burden-sharing between Britain and a number of political entities within the Empire that were moving increasingly toward eventual self-government. As a matter of fact, in many ways, the Imperial defense structure resembled that of an alliance rather than a hierarchical system dominated by a metropolitan power. The inherent limitations of the Imperial Staff, therefore, were those of coalition partners, who maintain distinct, and at times conflicting, national perspectives, while nevertheless sharing common values and apprehensions. The Imperial Staff could not impose a strategic coherence that was not already present, nor could it address successfully problems of strategy for which Imperial resources were inadequate. Partly for these reasons, the history of Imperial Staff operations has direct relevance to the alliance diplomacy, strategy, and decision making of the United States in the late twentieth century.

The British Imperial experience, however, stands in stark contrast to the mode of operations developed by the Imperial Russian and Soviet General Staffs, especially with respect to the question of central authority. To a large extent, as John Erickson points out, the contemporary Soviet General Staff inherited its organizational structure from Tsarist defense-planning bodies. It represents, therefore, the culmination of a system that is deeply rooted in modern Russian history, the purpose of which has been to achieve efficient, centralized military leadership based upon coherent, cohesive strategic thought and military policy. In this way, the Kremlin hopes to maintain rapid command, control, and communications with the various military districts, fronts, battlefields, fleets, armies, and other units that make up the Soviet war machine. In addition, the General Staff performs an important policy-review role, particularly in the evaluation of operational lessons and experiences, and in the application of this knowledge to the design of future military forces. In essence, the Staff constitutes both the "military brain" and the "command-in-being" of the Soviet Union.

The Conduct of National Security: Soviet and American Practices

The doctrine that informs strategy and force level planning in the Soviet Union provides an additional basis for assessing the continuity of Soviet military thought over time, as well as its predilection for the Clausewitzian concept of war as a continuation of politics. As Uri Ra'anan suggests, the unity of theory and action, insofar as Soviet security policy is concerned, extends beyond the organizational structure embodied in the General Staff, to the development of an integrated, operational military doctrine that rejects policies of mere defensive reaction, and emphasizes the primacy of offensive—if sometimes indirect—strategies that take full advantage of deception and surprise. The Soviet Party leadership, which maintains ultimate control over the articulation of doctrine, does not see war and peace as necessarily antithetical to one another, nor does it draw sharp distinctions between the military and civilian components of national strategy. Theirs is a broad, classical, political view of strategy, within which ideological struggle is seen to encompass a broad spectrum of capabilities by which the global correlation of forces can be altered in support of the objectives of the Soviet state. Thus, it should come as no surprise that the ideological struggle, from Moscow's perspective, may very well include the organization, training, arming, and logistical support of surrogate forces in regions remote from the Soviet Union, in addition to the strengthening of Soviet national forces.

In contrast, there is far less unity of purpose and perspectives among U.S. defense planners. For example, the process of policy planning and resource allocation in the Department of Defense, surveyed in detail by Michael Hobkirk, has been complicated by several structural problems. These include: (1) the evolving relationship between the National Security Council and the President in defense decision making; (2) ongoing uncertainty as to whether the Secretary of Defense should serve primarily as a manager of resources or as an active participant in resource allocation, including choices of weapons; (3) disagreement over the extent to which defense decision making should be centralized, and concern over the effects that excessive centralization may have upon the efficient allocation of resources based upon agreed priorities; and (4) the substitution of explicit criteria governing choices of appropriate weapons for decision making by a process of inter-Service bargaining.

Closely related is another potential problem area that has not yet received sufficient consideration by defense policy analysts—namely, the extent to which the infusion within a large bureaucratic structure of the efficiency ethos of management science, together with the methodologies of systems analysis, has produced a military establishment less than adequately equipped for combat. Has the careerism of the defense bureaucracy contributed to the dearth of strategists? Can managers fight international wars—as contrasted with bureaucratic struggles—to a successful conclusion? Questions such as these, it was said, do little to engender faith in the efficiency of defense management within the United States.

Special attention has been focused on the role of the Joint Chiefs of Staff, and the mission to be performed by the most senior members of the professional military, within the broad organizational-bureaucratic structure of the Department of Defense. Just before his retirement as Chairman of the

Joint Chiefs of Staff in 1982, General David Jones called for the strengthening of the position of the Chairman, and criticized the present organization for its excessive diffusion of responsibility and authority, for its inability to render corporate military advice, and for the alleged failure of the Joint Chiefs of Staff adequately to transcend the particular interests of the four Services represented.

It is in this context, moreover, that the contradictions between American and Soviet national security practices emerge most clearly. Soviet decision-making authority on issues of military strategy rests in the hands of a small group within the Politburo known as the Council of Defense, an elite policy-making body that can trace its institutional roots to Lenin's Council of Labor and Defense (*STO*) and Stalin's wartime State Committee of Defense (*GKO*). It is believed, moreover, that Gosplan and the Military-Industrial Commission (*VPK*) serve under the direct guidance of the Council of Defense, in order to ensure proper resource allocation to military security programs. There is also an additional advisory group known as the Main Military Council—attached to the Ministry of Defense and chaired by the Minister of Defense—which provides policy planning guidance and strategic direction to the General Staff and the Armed Forces as a whole. But the preeminent national security organization remains to this day the Soviet Council of Defense, which is given additional extraordinary powers in time of war, and is generally chaired by the General Secretary of the Communist Party, who, increasingly, doubles as Chairman of the Presidium of the Supreme Soviet. The contemporary Soviet defense decision-making structure and process were examined by Harriet Scott.

The major strength of such centralization of power is readily apparent: once a decision is made it can be swiftly executed without the prolonged public debates that bedevil the policy process in the United States. Nevertheless, centralization can render the decision-making process vulnerable to disruption and/or arbitrary rule, because it concentrates final authority in the hands of a few, who may not always prove adequate to the task. In this context, reference may be made to the virtual mental collapse that Stalin suffered during the first weeks of Hitler's invasion of the Soviet Union in June 1941, a collapse that brought an abrupt halt to effective decision making at that time and may have led to the needless deaths of millions of Soviet citizens.

At the present moment, of course, it is difficult to weigh the precise influence of individual personalities on the Soviet national security decision-making process. Some uncertainty remains even as to the present membership of the Council of Defense, and to whether or not a Soviet Leader could become Chairman of the Council of Defense without first having been "elected" Chairman of the Presidium of the Supreme Soviet. Not only does the Soviet Union lack an institutional process for leadership succession, but even a clearly visible means of ascertaining at all times the relative power of the members of the national security decision-making elite. Far from validating any Western theory of institutional-bureaucratic politics, therefore, research on Soviet national security decision making leads one to the view that highly centralized power is sought for its own sake, rather than to promote one specific set of issues—guns versus butter, hawks versus doves—or to strengthen one part of the bureaucracy against another. To superimpose upon a closed Soviet hierarchical totalitarian structure the organizational-bureaucratic models and images drawn from our own pluralistic system is to make even more difficult the development of an adequate understanding of the national security decision-making system of the Soviet Union.

Problems of Command and Control

If the pervasive problem confronting the United States in an era of organizational-bureaucratic proliferation has been policy coordination, equally compelling is the need for the rapid communication of policy decisions within an effective system of command and control. Unfortunately, bureaucratic-institutional divisions in the decision-making system, it was noted by General John Cushman, are reflected as well in the structure that has been developed for the execution of decisions by the various military commands. So, too, this problem is compounded if the field commander of a multi-Service force must work within a divided command structure.

Numerous deficiencies are said to exist in the present command and control system. In addition to the formidable problems of ensuring survivability under attack, the basic difficulty is the building of command structures that will function in peacetime, but that are unlikely to stand the crucial test of war. Nowhere is this problem more evident than in NATO-Europe, where, it was suggested, the command structure was likely either to be disrupted in the early days of war, or to function with such complexity and inefficiency as to contribute to the vulnerability of NATO forces.

There are, moreover, numerous issues of centalization versus decentralization that affect decisions with respect to the types of weapons to be used in combat, as well as the rules of engagement of capabilities against specific types of targets, and of escalation from political crisis to actual warfare. The effect of modern technology has been to increase the capacity for rapid communications, and thus for the centralization even of the most trivial decisions of national security policy at the highest level, far from the actual scene of conflict. Such concentration of the decisional process and structure carries certain inherent disadvantages with respect to flexibility on the battlefield, and calls into question the wisdom of burdening the macro-level decisional level with micro-level decisions for which, for example, the field commander or the ambassador may be more appropriately situated, while taking from the highest authorities the time and energies needed to focus upon issues of grand strategy. In this respect, technology, no less than organizational-bureaucratic structure, becomes the enemy of strategy.

The Executive Branch

The need for policy coherence based upon coordination among the various units in the Executive Branch of government is addresed in this volume. In tracing the evolution of the National Security Council since 1947, for example, as Colonel John Endicott does, it becomes obvious that some such organization in the White House is essential if the President is to be adequately apprised of the policy options and management tasks before him. But it is suggested as well that, however indispensable may be the organizational structure for national decision making, in the final analysis that structure will reflect not only the external demands of the policy process, but also the distinctive decisional style of the incumbent President. In this respect, the personality of political leaders—the idiosyncratic variable— emerges as important in shaping the decisional context, and, especially in the case of coalitions and alliances, in providing an alternative to formal decisional structures. It is evident also that the national security advisory group within the Executive Office must be sufficiently flexible to provide timely options for Presidential decisions, both on a routine daily basis and in the extraordinary circumstances of international crisis; and whatever the organizational and personnel problems that have confronted Administrations past and present, it is suggested, the NSC structure available to American Presidents is sufficiently adaptable to perform these missions in accordance with the particular policy needs and stylistic preferences of each Chief Executive.

This is not to assert that the White House national security policy apparatus has always functioned smoothly. Indeed, as control over policy coordination often translates, in effect, into control over policy formulation, there are ongoing "turf battles" between the NSC and the various Executive Departments—State, Defense, CIA—over the management of the decision-making process. In an effort to lessen bureaucratic turmoil, President Reagan, it was said, leaned, especially during his first months in office, toward an American version of "Cabinet government," passing to the State Department, for example, the leading role in developing U.S. arms control policy. According to Christopher M. Lehman, this process has worked particularly well in the development of official negotiating positions for the START talks, which have been thrashed out in a special Interagency Group (IG) headed by State.

To be sure, problems of personnel, policy consistency and departmental jurisdiction remain, and the Reagan Administration subsequently shifted back toward a more centralized system focused on the NSC. The decentralized decision-making process associated with "Cabinet-style" government tends to move too slowly, since the chairing agencies for the various IG groups do not often have sufficient authority to break deadlocks and impose deadlines. As a result, many more decisions must be "kicked upstairs" to the White House and the President for final approval and review. However, the full range of opinions on critical issues—including dissenting views—is less likely to be overlooked than under a more centralized process.

Turning to another key issue of Executive coordination—namely, the more effective interaction of the policy planning and budgeting processes—attention also is focused on the utilization within the Department of Defense of the Planning Programming and Budget System (PPBS), perhaps the best-known management reform of the McNamara era. As Michael Hobkirk points out, over the years, PPBS, or "output budgeting" as it is often called, has emerged as a useful tool of analysis in reaching difficult decisions as to the cost-effective allocation of scarce defense resources in support of the major missions of the Armed Forces. Nevertheless, output budgeting does not necessarily help the decision maker in choosing between two or more weapon systems designed to achieve the same end and, therefore, presumably to be funded from the same development program.

There have been problems as well in designing a PPBS system that could be used both for the purposes of long-range planning and day-to-day fiscal management. If output budgeting is to be used for the analysis of future needs and the evaluation of future options, it must be flexible enough to change when defense planners perceive that those needs have changed, or when new options come to the foreground. If, however, it is to be used also as a tool for audit and a check on past expenditure, then the output categories or functions chosen must remain unchanged for several years at least, while it is assimilated throughout the central defense organization, so that costs, wherever incurred, can be ascribed with certainty to their correct program and category by every clerk in the financial machine. Needless to say, the task of combining the flexible-type output budgeting needed for planning purposes with the more rigid type needed for day-to-day management and audit has proven to be a formidable challenge.

Congress and National Security Planning

National security decision making in the United States has the unique feature of the Executive-Congressional relationship that is part of the American constitutional structure, although the proliferation of Congressional committees having a direct interest in national security policy represents only on a less grand scale the parallel development that has taken place within the Executive branch. Senator William Cohen addresses the inherent difficulties confronting the Congress in exercising oversight of the national security policies of the Executive branch. This results primarily from the inability of members of Congress to focus sufficiently, for long periods, on any one issue to develop the range and depth of expertise needed to evaluate strategies, programs, policies, and weapons choices. Without such an understanding, it becomes difficult, if not impossible, for the Congress to play fully and effectively its constitutional role in the budget process. Moreover, no easy solutions to this vexing problem seem to be available. For although members of Congress face increased demands upon their time resulting from the flow of legislation both in domestic policy and national security policy, the tendency has been for greater—some would say excessive—legislative oversight of the details of defense and foreign policy in the last generation, without necessarily having enhanced the efficiency or effectiveness either of the Congressional or Executive branches of government.

The Congress is even less fully equipped than the Executive to design strategy, or to ensure consistency within and among the diverse elements of national security policy. Can Congress, as a result of the vast number of constituencies represented by its members, be expected to review objectively the national security programs of the Executive and, where appropriate, substitute its own judgment? The effort, extending over many years, of the Congress to mandate the development of a land-based ICBM with mobile, rather than fixed, basing represents a case in point. But should the Legislative branch take upon itself the defense decision-making process in such detail? The role of the professional staffs of members of Congress has grown over the last generation. Former Congressman Richard White suggests that most of the work of staffs—which are composed of individuals of great expertise, dedication, and integrity—is focused on the vast number of national security programs and weapons systems that are not controversial.

Objectivity is often abandoned, however, it should be added, when a particular weapon system, or a major component, is produced in the district or state of a member of Congress. Is it possible to draw clear distinctions between legitimate advocacy of a program or system in support of overall national security policy and what, in effect, becomes the lobbying of constituent interests that may or may not be consistent with a broader national interest? How can the tendency be strengthened for the Congress to purchase mission capabilities, rather than simply weapons systems, within an agreed strategy?

Such a choice forms an indispensable element in any national security policy that would narrow the widely criticized mismatch between national strategy and force structures—between commitments and capabilities. Yet, Congress, as Stanley Heginbotham writes, can challenge or deny more easily than it can propose or actually develop coherent proposals of its own. Nevertheless, the legislature represents a necessary link in a pluralistic political system between the government and the constituencies that are governed. The question that remains unresolved, therefore, concerns the precise limits of the Congressional role in the national security decisional process of the late twentieth century. Here, it may be hypothesized that because the Congress reflects the diversity of domestic interests and perspectives at any time, its role is likely to be greater when the national security consensus diminshes. Conversely, the greater the level of such national consensus, the greater will be the focus upon the Executive Branch of government, as happened in World War II.

Government-Industry Relations

The development, production, and acquisition of weapons systems constitutes both an indispensable and highly controversial aspect of the national security decision-making process. It is beset with numerous critiques whose focus has been on such issues as: the lengthening of lead times between the development and deployment phases; the need for a closer nexus between strategy and force structure; the cost, and efficiency of operation, of complex high-technology weapons; the problems of cost overruns, especially in an inflationary economy; the extent to which weapons should be multipurpose in design; the degree to which emphasis should be placed upon procurement of larger numbers of less-complicated weapons, as contrasted with lesser quantities of more-sophisticated systems; and the decision to purchase for the mid-term, current state-of-the-art weapons rather than systems that lie in the more distant future, with the better, longer-term, becoming the enemy of the good that is more readily available.

Central to the issues under debate is the relationship between government and industry, for the defense mobilization infrastructure in the United States lies almost exclusively in the private sector of the huge American economy. One important dimension of government-industry relations is the need to reconcile the growing dependence of the United States upon a production base that extends beyond our shores to Allies in Europe and the Asian-Pacific area, with the requirement to retain a domestic production capacity in systems vital to our national security so as to ensure that the United States remains at the cutting edge of an advanced technology. In this context, Philip Phalon criticizes the NATO "family of weapons" concept, generated during the Carter Administration, according to which exclusive developmental authority for specific weapon systems may be assigned, by intergovernment agreement, to one side of the Atlantic or the other. This concept, it is suggested, could irreversibly weaken U.S. research and development in specific fields of military technology, rendering the Americn defense industrial base incapable of responding, if access to a key foreign source were disrupted.

Still, in view of America's interest in promoting defense collaboration and interoperability of arms among the NATO Allies, the United States cannot expect to remain entirely self-sufficient in the production of defense technologies. Friendly countries overseas can and should develop local defense industries upon which the United States may wish to draw. Another issue to which greater attention should be given than was possible in this volume is the creation of a decision-making structure, both within the United States and between this country and its Allies, for the acquisition of advanced technologies developed abroad, notably in Japan, by the United States. In summary, we face not only the problems attending the transfer of defense-related technologies directly or indirectly to an adversary such as the Soviet Union, but also the need to have access to technologies from our Allies. In meeting these challenges, there is a need for much closer policy coordination between the federal government and the private sector, most especially in setting the national security criteria for technology transfer policies.

The Role of the Media

Last, one of the most important dimensions of contemporary national security decision making is the role of the media, which, like that of the Congress, has increased greatly since the Vietnam era. On current issues such as Central America, the Vietnam legacy in the form of continuous scrutiny by the electronic and print media, as well as by direct Congressional intervention into the policy process, is abundantly evident. As S. Robert Lichter and Stanley Rothman emphasize, the impact of the media on the shaping of public attitudes and hence official policy on national security exceeds that of any individual member of Congress, and a gap has widened between the value structures of representatives of the media and the professional military. The adversarial media of the late twentieth century are said to have enhanced the difficulty of building a broadly based national consensus in favor of sustained defense capabilities and national security policies.

Policy Recommendations and Implications

From preceding chapters, several conclusions and broad policy implications emerge, although this is not to suggest that what follows represents necessarily a consensus among the various contributors to this volume:

1. Especially in the Western World, both in historic and contemporary context, the national security decision-making structures of states have evolved in accordance with the current official perception of national security interest. Decision-making structures have usually been created after, rather than in anticipation of, the problems that must be resolved.
2. Ideally, the decisional structure should be shaped by a clearly stated concept of goals. Under such circumstances, the purpose of the organization for decision making would be the development and management of the means needed for the translation of goals into policies. In the absence of such commonly accepted goals, there will remain inevitably a gap between decision-making structures and strategy. In turn, the capacity of a state or other political unit to maintain coherence and consistency in policy will be diminished.
3. The problems of formulating goals, developing strategies, providing the necessary means, and creating adequate political structures are formidable in pluralistic societies and alliance systems as a result of the diversity of constituent groups whose interests must be accommodated.

4. In sharp contrast to an Anglo-American tradition of improvisation of decisional structures, the Soviet Union, despite institutional differences, has evolved, in the General Staff, what appears to be a highly centralized structure, both for the formulation of integrated strategy based upon the politico-military doctrine articulated by the Party Leadership, and for the execution of this strategy by means of a command structure. Although the Soviet system is not without its weaknesses, the Soviet decisional structure should be studied both for its lessons relating to decision making in the United States and for its implications for our security.

5. In the United States, a sharp distinction exists between military command structures in wartime and in peacetime. The military vulnerabilities of existing command structures should be reduced. Moreover, existing commands represent all too often the unplanned joining together of components that do not fit together. The result may be the repetition of failures such as the abortive hostage rescue effort in Iran in 1980. Greater attention should be given both to the basic architecture of command structure, and to the technologies and other means available to increase communications and the interoperability of forces. At the same time, it will be necessary to reconcile the tendencies of the past generation toward command centralization, with the needs, perspectives, and inherent advantages of the operational commander in the field. Last, but not least, the command structure in peacetime should resemble more fully the system that would exist necessarily in wartime. This may be accomplished in part by the timely use of simulation exercises and by taking steps to enhance the survivability of the command structure under attack.

6. Within the United States government, the need exists for more clearly articulated and more widely understood national goals upon which national security policy can be based and in support of which more adequate decision-making structures can be created. The prerequisite to such a restatement of national goals is the strengthening of an American domestic consensus on national security policy and its sustained maintenance.

7. There exist inherent constitutional and practical limitations in the development of more efficient and effective working relationships between the Congress and the Executive branch of government. Nevertheless, the appropriate balance between Executive leadership and Congressional oversight of national security policy should be addressed. Although the perceived deficiencies in national security policy proposals emanating from the Executive branch in successive Administrations must remain the object of Congressional scrutiny, the inherent inability of Congress to lead or to maintain complete mastery of complex issues and weapons systems must also be recognized.

8. The proliferation of national security policy as a complex and heterogeneous set of issue areas has been reflected in the diffusion of the policy

process within a vast pyramidal bureaucracy. Interdepartmental and inter-agency committees and working groups, whatever their inherent defi-ciencies, will remain principal organizational devices for achieving consensus, consistency, and coordination.

9. Alliances and coalitions represent in macrocosm the problems of developing strategy, mobilizing resources, reconciling leadership, and consultation with member units in a pluralistic system, and the sharing of burdens for the common defense. Dominant partners in pluralistic group-ings confront the need to elicit from lesser partners agreed shares of the defense burden. Whatever the difficulties, the experience of pluralistic groupings, tested in two World Wars, demonstrates their ability to mobilize vast resources even without elaborate mechanisms for Alliance consultation and policy execution. It was the World War II experience, after all, that underlay the innovative experience in Alliance decisional structure later embodied in the Atlantic Alliance. Finally, it is instructive to note that the burden of NATO defense is shared more widely among its members than that between the Soviet Union and its Warsaw Pact allies.

In sum, the task confronting the United States remains the development of clearly stated goals and strategies, matched by appropriate means. Deci-sional structures in themselves are clearly no substitute for goals, strategies, and means. Without decision-making procedures, however, that reconcile our inherent diversity both within international alliances and our own politi-cal system with the exigencies imposed by a dangerous external environ-ment, the task confronting us in defending the values reflected in our pluralistic domestic and international structures will be difficult, and per-haps impossible.

Index